D1236812

PILGRIMS ON THE ICE

PILGRIMS ON THE ICE
Robert Falcon Scott's
First Antarctic Expedition

T. H. BAUGHMAN

University of Nebraska Press
Lincoln and London

© 1999 by the University of
Nebraska Press. All rights
reserved. Manufactured
in the United States of
America
∞ Library of Congress
Cataloging-in-Publication
Data. Baughman, T. H., 1947–
Pilgrims on the ice : Robert
Falcon Scott's first Antarctic
expedition / T. H. Baughman.
p.   cm. Includes bibliographical
references and index. (p.   ).
ISBN 0-8032-1289-5 (cl.:
alk. paper) 1. Discovery (Ship)
2. National Antarctic
Expedition, 1901–1904.
3. Scott, Robert Falcon, 1868–
1912. 4. Antarctica—Discovery
and exploration.
I. Title. G850 1901.D63   1999
919.8′9—dc21
99-20685
CIP

TO

Allison	Megan
Stephanie	Tessa
Ryan	Gwyneth

Contents

Illustrations

Preface

After decades of neglect interrupted only briefly by scientific curiosity or consideration of its commercial potential, international interest in the Antarctic burst onto the scene in the early twentieth century with four important endeavors designed to unlock the mysteries of the south polar regions. From Great Britain, Germany, and Sweden, national efforts were sent forth in 1901 and 1902. Of the four expeditions, the one with the greatest impact on the course of Antarctic exploration was the *Discovery* expedition (1901–4), which strongly influenced the course of British Antarctic exploration for twenty years and introduced the major British figures to the south polar regions.

Heroic Era (1901–22) expeditions are usually referred to by their principal ships. Two of the three greatest Antarctic explorers of this period sailed on the *Discovery*, Robert Falcon Scott (1868–1912) and Ernest Shackleton (1874–1922). The other member of the triumvirate, the Norwegian Roald Amundsen (1872–1928), had had his initiation to the south polar regions during the *Belgica* expedition of 1897–99. Scott and Shackleton later became rivals in their polar work, but in this first effort, Shackleton served as Scott's third officer.

The *Discovery* expedition introduced a number of other important figures to polar work, among them Edward A. Wilson (1872–1912), who later died with Scott on the South Pole attempt of 1911–12; seamen such as William Lashly (1868–1940) and Thomas Crean (1877–1938), and petty officer Edgar Evans (1876–1912), who were also on the ill-fated 1911 venture; and Frank Wild (1874–1939), who rose from able-bodied seaman on the *Discovery* to commander of the ship on Shackleton's last expedition. This account seeks to credit more than just the work of Scott — this expedition was not a one-man show. This story makes a determined effort to place the

Discovery expedition in the context both of Antarctic exploration and the larger setting in which the endeavor took place.

One problem in studying the *Discovery* expedition might easily be overlooked. Most of those familiar with the careers of Robert Falcon Scott, Edward A. Wilson, Ernest Shackleton, and the others in this account know them based on later events in their lives. Some aspects of their behavior during the *Discovery* expedition, which I describe here, will seem strange or out of character; but remember, in 1901 these men were young. Edward Wilson, who on Scott's second expedition was treated as the old man — the revered one — by the young men, in 1901 was "Billy Wilson." Similarly, Captain Scott of the Antarctic, Britain's penultimate hero, was a young and often unsure naval officer plucked from relative obscurity to a high profile position leading a major national Antarctic expedition. In the *Discovery* days these people were less certain, less confident.

Looking into the career of Great Britain's eminent polar hero, Robert Falcon Scott, can be dangerous, as I learned while lecturing in Antarctica on the expedition cruise ship M/S *Explorer*, an opportunity made possible by Victoria Underwood. I ventured to note in one of my lectures that Scott lost his temper at one point during the *Discovery* expedition. The next morning I was descended upon by an entire table of British subjects who spent an hour trying to persuade me that "surely you must be mistaken." Heroes do not cease to be heroes by having their human frailties revealed. I am reminded of what nineteenth-century historian Alexander William Kinglake (1809–91) wrote in the introduction to his monumental account of the Crimean War:

And now I have that to state which will not surprise my own countrymen, but which still, in the eyes of the foreigner, will seem to be passing strange. For some years, our statesmen, our admirals, and our generals, have known that the whole correspondence of the English Headquarters was in my hands; and very many of them have from time to time conversed and corresponded with me on the business of the war. Yet I declare I do not remember that any one of these public men has ever said to me that there was anything which, for the honour of our arms, or for the credit of the nation, it would be well to keep concealed. Every man has taken it for granted that what is best for the repute of England is, the truth.[1]

Understanding this expedition gives one an appreciation for the talent and hard work of the Royal Navy enlisted men who served aboard the *Discovery*. Turning their hand to every task, from washing and repairing clothes to sledging in temperatures thirty degrees below zero, the enlisted men suffered every hardship, shared every drudgery, for three years. To have written an account of this expedition without recognizing their efforts would be to miss part of the story of the adventure. The sense of duty, honed by living in the nineteenth century, one in which duty was the watchword of the age, strikes one in the late twentieth century as being so foreign as to be from another world. This story attempts to provide the reader with an understanding of both the officers and men of the expedition and an appreciation of the character of these pilgrims on the ice. This volume also attempts to place the *Discovery* into the context of contemporary events and expeditions.

Because of the time associated with teaching at a small liberal arts college at which scholarship is not a high priority, I have spent six years working on this volume. After fitful starts and stops, I suspect the project really began to take off in my own mind when I began lecturing aboard the M/S *Explorer* in Antarctica. My colleagues on the ship and the passengers provided an environment in which my scholarly work was encouraged.

This monograph began as the second part of a trilogy that I hoped to write on Antarctica in the late nineteenth and early twentieth centuries. *Before the Heroes Came* (Lincoln: University of Nebraska Press, 1993) surveyed the period before the Heroic Era began and "Lure of the South: Antarctica, 1901–9" was to be the sequel. When I began work on the *Discovery* expedition I became so convinced that this single voyage was so important for understanding the whole of the Heroic Era that I departed from my original plan to write about Scott's first expedition. Later, I hope to return to the original proposal and provide readers with an account of the first half of the Heroic Era (1901–9). Whether time and financial limitations will allow me to complete the third volume, tentatively entitled "The End of Heroes: Antarctica 1909–22," I have not yet determined.

Along the way a scholar accumulates many debts, and a scant mention here cannot convey the degree of appreciation one feels for those who give their time and expertise to make a book such as this possible. I want to thank Robert K. Headland, archivist at Scott Polar Research Institute (SPRI), for all his help. The Royal Geographical Society (RGS) lost a brilliant archivist when Paula Lucas left that organization. Regrettably, the RGS appears unable to fund a full-time archivist to safeguard its wonderful and important collection. Philippa Smith, at Scott Polar, was consistently helpful and kind, a model for all who work in archives. I also want to mention the assistance I received at Scott Polar from William Mills and Shirley Sawtell in the library and A. W. Billinghurst and Mandy Dunn in the archives.

Dr. Beau Riffenburgh and Dr. Liz Cruwys have been wonderfully helpful, friendly, and considerate. When I have dinner with them I leave the meeting inspired by their example of diligent, consistent publication efforts. Maria Pia Casarini and Peter Wadhams not only provided me with access to the Heald diary but also extended me every possible kindness, consideration, and help throughout this research process. I want to thank the Heald family for allowing me to use William L. Heald's diary, a wonderfully insightful volume.

In an earlier book I noted that the RGS library felt like home, and it still does, now under the able stewardship of Rachel Rowe.

Among my academic colleagues, I wish to thank Scott Baird, William P. Hyland, George Nicholas, and Rupert Pate for their encouragement. My student worker of four years, Stacey Petesch, did a great deal of the detailed work of organizing research notes. No academic accomplishment I achieve could have occurred without the support and kindness of Judith and Richard L. Greaves.

Among polar enthusiasts, I wish to acknowledge the help and encouragement of Matt Drennan and Megan McOsker, Kim Robertson, Larry Hobbs, Kim Crosbie, Victoria Underwood, Peter Graham, and Michael and Maxine Rosove. I want to thank A. G. E. Jones for both the example of his scholarship and his kindness to me in providing me with insight based on his considerable research in polar history. Anyone who has followed Antarctic affairs for the past thirty years has at one time or another met John Splettstoesser, a doyen of Antarcticans and a person deserving the title, "Mr. Antarctica." John has been both extremely kind and wonderfully helpful in every aspect of my Antarctic career.

No mention of great late twentieth-century Antarcticans would be complete without the name of Colin Bull, a wonderful fellow, the consummate Ph.D. adviser, and the premier glaciologist of his day — a mantle now worn by his former graduate students. And two lifelong friends, Russell P. Buchan and Barbara Knox, have been consistently supportive of this project.

Katherine Immel, John Splettstoesser, and Colin Bull read this work in manuscript, which was especially helpful, as the latter two know far more Antarctic history than I do. Kim Crosbie provided many of the illustrations in this volume.

I would be remiss to omit Charlene and Bob Wilkinson. Bob originally suggested to me that I go to the Antarctic, and Ian Whillans made that first trip possible.

Press policy forbids me from praising my editor and the staff at the University of Nebraska Press, but I would have thanked them had it been allowed.

Finally, let me comment on the dedication. Having had no children of my own, I am grateful beyond words for the blessing of six godchildren, to whom this volume is dedicated.

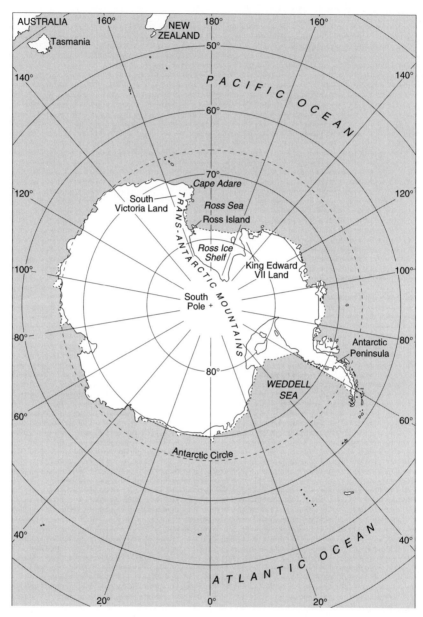

1. Antarctica including Ross Sea.

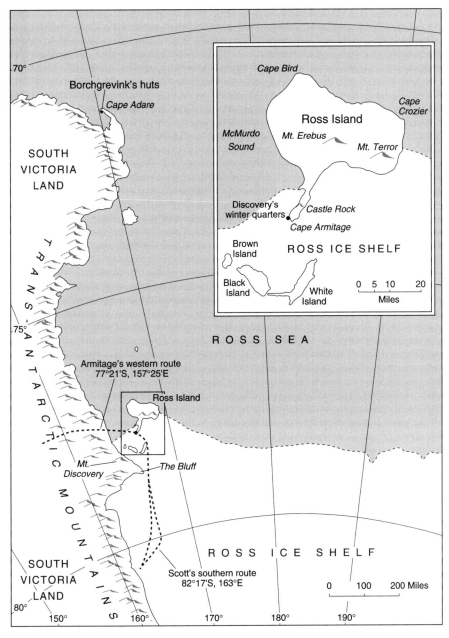

Cape Bird

Ross Island

Cape
Crozier

McMurdo
Sound

Mt. Erebus

Mt. Terror

Discovery's
winter quarters

Castle Rock

Cape Armitage

Brown
Island

R O S S   I C E   S H E L F

Black
Island

White
Island

0   5 10   20
Miles

2. Ross Island area, including main physical features and routes of Armitage's western party and Scott's southern party.

1

To the Land of Unsurpassed Desolation

The south polar regions have captured human imagination since ancient times. The Greeks postulated the existence of such land, and although the European medieval world lacked the desire to explore the area, interest renewed with the modern era. In the eighteenth century fantastic ideas were promoted: that a great new world, lush in vegetation and populated with a new race of people, would be found at the bottom of the earth.

Captain James Cook (1728–79) was the first to intentionally approach Antarctica for noncommercial reasons. He was the first to cross the Antarctic Circle and observe the pack ice that guarded the continent. His response was negative: "Should anyone possess the resolution and the fortitude to elucidate this point by pushing yet further south than I have done, I shall not envy him the fame of his discovery, but I make bold that the world will derive no benefit from it."[1] Cook's assessment has not been borne out by later generations, but after Cook's report no hope existed of finding the temperate continent so long speculated.

The early nineteenth century saw three waves of exploration in the South. Three explorers—Nathaniel Palmer (1799–1877), William Bransfield (1795–1852), and Thaddeus von Bellingshausen (1778–1852)—have each been declared the discoverer of the continent in the period 1819–21.[2] Bellingshausen's claim is the strongest, but given the international nature of contemporary Antarctica, credit may be shared among three nations: the United States, Great Britain, and Russia.[3] Curiously, two of the explorers encountered one another in the vast region of Antarctic waters. When Bellingshausen arrived in the South Shetland Islands he encountered Palmer's vessel and invited the American aboard for a visit.[4]

Discovery led to the economic exploitation of the continent by seal hunters determined to plunder the newly available lands for short-term gain. These men met with great success: temporary riches spelled the virtual extinction of the hunted animals. Not all the hunters who pushed southward were devoid of scientific interest. James Weddell (1787–1834), taking advantage of what were later to be determined as extraordinarily fine ice-free conditions in 1823, was able to push farther south than any previous effort. Weddell established a new farthest south point, reaching 74°15′ S, 34°16′ W, and eclipsing Cook's record by more than 214 miles (345 kilometers). Similarly, the Enderby Brothers, a sealing and whaling firm whose ships plied the Antarctic waters for forty years, encouraged its captains, including John Biscoe (1794–1843) and John Balleny, to explore. Although this secondary activity rarely added to the profit of the voyage, much new territory was investigated.[5]

In the 1830s and 1840s three great expeditions explored the South. The motivation for Antarctic exploration was, as it remained throughout the century, a combination of commercial and scientific reasons. The continuing demand for whale and seal products encouraged sailors to push ever farther south, beyond the known areas. Sailing beyond the charted world in search of new quarry, the ships often wrecked. Early nineteenth-century scientists clamored for information about this unknown segment of the world, as part of an overall growth in scientific study in the nineteenth century.

Jules-Sébastien-César Dumont d'Urville (1790–1842) led a French expedition (1837–41) during which he discovered a part of the Antarctic continent and a new species of penguin, both of which he named after his wife, Adélie. Before sailing to Antarctica, d'Urville had achieved fame in the world of art by discovering and bringing to France the *Venus de Milo*.

Contemporaneously, Lieutenant Charles Wilkes (1798–1877) was directed by the U.S. government to investigate the regions around Antarctica. The Wilkes expedition (1838–42) was plagued by faulty and inadequate equipment and problems of leadership.[6] Moreover, authorities questioned the mapping of his discoveries, including Wilkes Land, which figured in the story of Scott's first expedition.

In what was the second strange encounter in the century, Wilkes and d'Urville met one another in the Antarctic, but this time the results were not as cordial as had been the earlier meeting.

The third of these great endeavors was that of Great Britain, under the command of James Clark Ross (1800–1862). Having previously located the North Magnetic Pole while sailing in the Arctic with his uncle, Sir John Ross (1777–1856), James Clark Ross hoped to add to his reputation as an explorer by determining the location of the South Magnetic Pole. In 1840 Ross sailed into what is now known as the Ross Sea and began Britain's involvement with that sector of Antarctica. In addition to Victoria Land, Ross discovered what he called the Great Ice Barrier, now known as the Ross Ice Shelf.[7]

Following these significant efforts, in the 1870s only two small expeditions added to knowledge about Antarctica. The HMS *Challenger* (1872– 76) was an oceanographic expedition charged with investigating the waters surrounding the continent.[8] The German ship *Grönland* (1873–74) was dispatched by the German Polar Navigation Company to search for Southern Right whales. Right whales were literally the right kind for the baleen needed for a strong, flexible substance used in items such as women's corsets. The *Grönland* found no whales.

Little occurred for twenty years until the early 1890s when a series of expeditions formed a transitional period to the Heroic Era.[9] Scottish whalers were dispatched to Antarctica to find Southern Right whales, as the stocks of Right whales in the Arctic were being depleted due to excessive hunting.[10] The Dundee whaling expedition (1892–93) failed to find the elusive whale sought but did accomplish some scientific work, because the surgeons acted as scientific observers. The captains gave no specific time or effort to science, and what little was done was due to the observers' steadfast efforts. Perhaps the most important result of this endeavor was to introduce to Antarctic exploration the person who could well be considered the finest British scientist-explorer of his day, William S. Bruce (1876–1921).

The Scots were not the only ones in Southern waters in these years. A Norwegian, C. A. Larsen (1860–1924), was a key figure in early Antarctica, and although his initial effort did not meet with great commercial success, Larsen showed a keen interest in scientific work when time permitted. His accomplishments in this latter area were praised by contemporaries, including John Murray (1844–1914), the leading British academic polar authority at the turn of the century, who called Larsen's achievements "the most important made in the Antarctic regions since the time of Ross."[11]

The third chance meeting of the century occurred 26 December 1892 when Larsen encountered the Scottish whalers, and an exchange of visits was made. Subsequent meetings took place over the next six weeks.[12]

A second Norwegian effort was headed by H. J. Bull (1844–1930), a man of uncertain reputation, who was able to convince Sven Foyn (1809– 94) to allow him to take a whaler south to investigate the possibilities of commercial whaling. Foyn — entrepreneur, inventor, whaler — agreed to underwrite the venture, so Bull left Norway for Australia, en route south. William S. Bruce applied to go with Bull on the *Antarctic* but was unable to make the rendezvous at Melbourne.[13]

Bull's *Antarctic* was unsuccessful in its search for commercial gain. Seals, but no Southern Right whales, were taken while in southern waters, but the expedition did achieve an important milestone in Antarctic history. On 23 January 1895 a small boat approached the shore to make the first undis-

1. Sir Clements Markham. Drawing by Kim Crosbie.

puted landing on the Antarctic continent. Earlier ones may have taken place — no doubt sealers put ashore on islands — but this landing was the first on the mainland itself. As the boat approached shore, one of the men leaped from the back of the boat and waded ashore and helped beach the craft. Thus, Carsten E. Borchgrevink (1864–1934) became the first human on the last continent. Dubious though this feat was, Borchgrevink subsequently parlayed the incident into the command of his own expedition.[14]

The Scots and the Norwegians did a great deal to stimulate interest in Antarctica in the 1890s, but the most important incident in this regard during the decade was the passage of a resolution. In 1895 the International

Geographical Congress, which met in London under the watchful eye of Sir Clements R. Markham (1830–1916), addressed the question of the south polar regions and called for its exploration as the last major area for geographical discovery.

Markham had become the president of the Royal Geographical Society (RGS) two years before the congress met and immediately had set about achieving an important goal—to launch a national Antarctic expedition staffed by naval personnel. In November 1893 he invited John Murray to speak at the RGS on the need for Antarctic exploration. The speech was the clarion call for British scientific societies to send south an expedition to solve the many problems still plaguing those studying terrestrial magnetism, meteorology, and geology.[15] The speech was well received and, along with Markham's election to the presidency of the RGS, can be seen as the beginning of efforts that ended in the launching of the *Discovery* expedition.[16]

Borchgrevink, ever eager to capitalize on his achievements, wrote the RGS, offering to speak at the conference. Although financial support was not given, Borchgrevink did appear at the meeting in London where, on 1 August 1895, he both amazed and annoyed his audience. His brashness offended some, but those gathered were thrilled to have firsthand information about the south polar regions. Borchgrevink urged that exploration be continued and asserted that he was prepared to lead such an effort. He also stated that Cape Adare would be an ideal location for a base, and John Murray concurred.[17] Before it disbanded, the geographical congress passed a resolution declaring "that the Congress record its opinion that the exploration of the Antarctic Regions is the greatest piece of geographical exploration still to be undertaken. That in view of the additions to knowledge in almost every branch of science which would result from such a scientific exploration the Congress recommends that the scientific societies throughout the world should urge in whatever way seems to them most effective, that this work should be undertaken before the close of the century."[18]

Both Borchgrevink and Bruce joined a list of people who attempted to launch expeditions in the mid-1890s. Bruce proposed that he be taken south by Norwegian whalers who would retrieve him the following season. This idea was too risky for the staid men of scientific societies.[19] In 1896 Borchgrevink nearly had the financial arrangements in order when the source of the money and the terms of the agreements caused him embarrassment that resulted in the loss of key support and an RGS endorsement.[20]

Among the others who tried and failed in their attempts to lead the first scientific endeavor of the period were Frederick A. Cook (1865–1940), who announced his intention of capitalizing on his experience as companion to Captain Robert E. Peary (1856–1920) during the latter's attempts to reach the North Pole and started his own Antarctic expedition.[21] Similarly, efforts involving a variety of supporters in Australia came to naught, despite their attempts to enlist some prominent figures from Arctic exploration, including N. A. E. Nordenskiöld (1832–1901), uncle of Otto Nordenskjöld (1864–1928), who later led an expedition south in 1902.

In the end the first major scientific effort at the turn of the century came not from Norway, or Britain, or the United States, but from a rather unlikely candidate — Belgium. The *Belgica* voyage was the quintessential privately funded small Antarctic endeavor in its promotion and management. Adrien de Gerlache (1866–1934) wanted to go to Antarctica and had applied to go with a Swedish effort that was subsequently abandoned. Instead, de Gerlache began his own campaign, a grassroots one, in which money was obtained from dozens of small contributors. Eventually, the Belgian government made a major contribution, and with roughly 300,000 Belgian francs, de Gerlache bought an old whaler, the *Patria*, rechristened her the *Belgica*, and began to gather men and material for the voyage.[22]

A polyglot crew was assembled from across Europe. A young Norwegian applied for a post and was accepted. Thus, Roald Amundsen, conqueror of the South Pole and the first person to see both Poles, was introduced to the south polar regions. Scientists came from Poland, Romania, and Russia. When the ship's doctor backed out at the last minute a telegram arrived from a young American physician who had read of the vacancy in a New York newspaper. Sight unseen, de Gerlache offered him the post, and Frederick A. Cook, later of some fame over claims to have been the first to reach the North Pole, became a member of the company.[23]

The *Belgica* sailed on 16 August 1897 from Antwerp and arrived in Punta Arenas on 1 December 1897. Rather than sailing south immediately, the *Belgica* lingered in the region of Tierra del Fuego while its crew did research, before it finally headed south at the end of January 1898, late in the season.

Critics have charged that de Gerlache wanted to get caught in the ice and stay the winter, but no proof of this charge has been found. Hints such as the commander's father noting that the ship contained food for three years and the desertion of some members of the crew in Punta Arenas, while intriguing, are not conclusive.

The ship had not sailed long when disaster struck. One of the seamen, Carl Wiencke, fell overboard while trying to open the scuppers (the holes in the bulwarks of the ship that allow water to pass off the deck).[24] Wiencke was unable to pull himself back aboard, and Lieutenant Georges Lecointe volunteered to go into the water to try to rescue him. Despite a valiant attempt on the part of Lecointe, the sailor was lost.

At Grahamland, the coast of the Antarctic Peninsula, the vessel entered a passageway that the captain named the Belgica Strait, though its name was subsequently changed to honor de Gerlache. Moving slowly along the coastline, the ship encountered the ice pack in late February, at a time when most ships would be fleeing northward, and became beset in the ice on 2 March 1898. The ship got caught and drifted with the ice pack for the next thirteen months, until 14 March 1899. The crew aboard were prisoners of the ice in the Bellingshausen Sea.

The tale of the harrowing winter was one of misery, gloom, and madness. By mid-May the sun had disappeared, and the long Antarctic night was upon them. The men fared badly, suffering from depression and lethargy. Food — always a critical item on any expedition — was unsatisfactory. The tinned food brought from Belgium was soft and tasteless. Soon crew members began to show signs of physical and mental deterioration.

The reputation of Frederick A. Cook has suffered because of several of his later exploits, but in 1898 he was the hero who saved the men of the expedition. Along with the clear thinking of Amundsen, the doctor was able to persuade de Gerlache to institute a reform in both diet and behavior in the men. From his Arctic experience Cook knew the value of fresh meat as an antiscorbutic and believed the change of diet would improve the overall physical and mental state of the company. The captain had previously rejected eating seals and penguins, dismissing both as unpalatable. Now Cook insisted, so the crew was put on a diet of fresh meat and a regime that included Cook's light therapy, wherein the men were exposed regularly to bright fires for a certain amount of time. Together, these reforms worked, and the health of the crew improved. In March 1899 the ship was freed from the grip of the ice and returned to Belgium.

The last expedition before the Heroic Era was that of Carsten E. Borchgrevink, who had returned from Antarctica in 1895 possessing more determination and ambition than talent. For three years he sought patronage for such an effort, and in the end he was able to persuade a popular press publisher, George Newnes (1851–1910), whose magazine empire, which included *The Strand*, had made him rich. Impressed with the brash young Anglo-Norwegian Borchgrevink, Newnes offered £40,000 to launch what became the *Southern Cross* voyage (1898–1900).[25]

Sir Clements R. Markham had been trying for five years to raise money for his great national expedition, and when Borchgrevink persuaded Newnes to underwrite the *Southern Cross*, Markham was livid. In his attacks on the Anglo-Norwegian, Markham accused Borchgrevink of buying a leaking boat and of cheating his sponsor on the ship's purchase. The RGS president derided the "British" expedition as a misnomer, claiming everything but the money was Norwegian. For the rest of his life, Markham never passed an opportunity to attack the leader of the *Southern Cross*. This hostility meant that virtually everyone in official geographical circles was urged to shun Borchgrevink, and the valuable experience gained by this voyage went unheeded by the British. This refusal only increased the tendency to ignore the realities of modern polar travel (the suitability of dogs, the value of taking native Arctic people to the Antarctic for their experience, the necessity for skis) and to rely on outmoded mid-nineteenth-century British Arctic experience. Markham's dealings with the leader of the *Southern Cross* do not offer a flattering picture of certain aspects of his character.

Despite the criticism, the expedition was a success. Although Borchgrevink was incompetent as a scientist, and to a large degree deficient as a leader, he chose superb officers and a good crew for his endeavor. Louis Bernacchi (1876–1942) and William Colbeck (1871–1930) not only were responsible for much of the scientific results of the voyage but subsequently distinguished themselves in other Antarctic expeditions. Nicholai Hanson (1870–99) was an accomplished biologist, and his contributions would have been far greater had he lived to supervise the working up of the results of his research.

Borchgrevink deserved more recognition than he received. He introduced dogs and kayaks to south polar exploration and proved that dog-sleds were a superior mode of travel. His scientists produced excellent results. His design of the hut, which followed the model of a whaling vessel and gave each man a compartment that could be closed off for privacy, was an excellent one. Although his choice of Cape Adare was unfortunate because its isolation limited the amount of travel from base, this decision had been endorsed by John Murray and other leading experts. The *Southern*

Cross did important pioneering oceanographic and biological work, which the British were unable to capitalize on owing to Markham's stubbornness and his ability to isolate and discredit Borchgrevink.

Thus the 1890s provided important exploratory information about the Antarctic and on how to conduct expeditions in the region. Yet the four expeditions, from 1901–4, were much less affected by these earlier efforts than they should have been, given the valuable information presented. Lessons were lost in the rush to launch the four great national Antarctic expeditions. Although the Swedes, Scots, and Germans turned to scientist-explorers to lead their endeavors, in Great Britain one kind of amateur was to be replaced by another.

2

The Determined Old Man

Sir Clements R. Markham enjoys a respected position in the history of Antarctica.[1] Born in the year of the founding of the Royal Geographical Society, Sir Clements served in the Royal Navy from 1844 to 1852, which included a stint of Arctic exploring as a midshipman aboard HMS *Assistance*, then he engaged in the search for Sir John Franklin (1786–1847), the British explorer who had disappeared in the Arctic. Leaving the navy, Markham entered the Civil Service in 1853 and served in various posts in the East India Company and the India Office until his retirement in 1877, during which time he introduced the cinchona tree to India. The quinine derived from this tree brought relief from malaria, an accomplishment that might well have been the crowning achievement of any scientist's life work. After his retirement he devoted himself to writing and traveling. Markham had a long association with Peru and the history of the Americas.

Markham served the Royal Geographical Society as secretary from 1863 to 1888, editing the *Geographical Magazine* from 1872 until it was merged into the *Proceedings of the Royal Geographical Society* in 1878. He was also secretary to the Hakluyt Society (1858–87) and became its president in 1890. Elected a Fellow of the Royal Society in 1873, Markham was created a Companion of the Bath in 1871 and Knight Commander of the Bath in 1896. Elected vice president of the Royal Geographical Society in 1891, he became president in 1893. Markham authored eighteen biographies and numerous historical works among his fifty volumes. Kindly put, occasionally the quality of his writing suffered, for he "was in all things an enthusiast rather than a scholar."[2] Less generously, Markham was capable of intentional mis-translation or omission of inconvenient facts.[3]

An Antarctic expedition allowed Markham to combine his two great passions — polar exploration and the Royal Navy. Building on his personal experiences with both, and his knowledge as an historian, Markham was determined to crown his life's work by creating, controlling, and seeing through to completion a great national Antarctic expedition. His vision of a south polar expedition was molded by British Arctic exploration in the nineteenth century.

Markham's term as president of the RGS was a turning point in British Antarctic developments in the 1890s. From the time of his election to the end of the period under consideration (1891–1901), the shadow of Sir Clements fell over all British activity regarding the south polar regions.[4] Markham's perspective in polar matters spanned seventy-five years of exploring: he knew many of the veterans of Ross's Antarctic expedition, he was involved personally with Arctic affairs in midcentury, and he dealt with most of the polar explorers of the first two decades of the twentieth century. His cousin, Albert H. Markham (1841–1918), was also a noted Arctic explorer and in 1876 set the then-existing record for the farthest north. An inveterate scribbler and a committee man par excellence, Sir Clements was an ideal schemer to launch a great national Antarctic expedition.

British Antarctic efforts in the 1890s were launched by John Murray's 27 November 1893 address. His speech, which demanded the launching of a great Antarctic expedition, was the clarion call to the British scientific community and laid the foundation on which Markham built. In his presidential remarks to the RGS, Markham had touted Murray's upcoming address as one that would "stir up our enthusiasm as geographers and our patriotism as Britons."[5]

Murray began by reminding his audience that nearly all the geographical advances had come from commercially minded maritime peoples. He asked his audience: "Is the last great piece of maritime exploration on the surface of our earth to be undertaken by Britons, or is it to be left to those who may be destined to succeed or supplant us on the ocean? That is a questions that this generation must answer."[6] This appeal to nationalism was a theme often repeated in the promotion of early twentieth-century polar exploration, both North and South.

While reviewing the history of Antarctic exploration from ancient times, Murray reminded his audience that only three explorers — Cook, Weddell, and Ross — had been south of 66° S. Beyond, almost certainly, lay a great continent that had barely been explored. Murray noted that wintering as far south as possible was critical to gathering an entire year's meteorological records and to investigating the atmospheric pressure of the area, which was an issue of great interest to scientists of the day. He discussed the importance of the work, saying, "indeed it is impossible to overestimate the value of Antarctic observations for the right understanding of the general meteorology of the globe."[7]

Murray then explained the program of a proposed expedition:

To determine the nature and extent of the Antarctic continent; to penetrate into the interior; to ascertain the depth and nature of the ice-cap; to observe the character of the underlying rocks and their fossils; to take magnetic and meteorological observations both at sea and on land; to observe the temperature of the ocean at all depths and seasons of the year; to take pendulum observations on land, and possibly also to make gravity observations at great depths in the ocean to bore through the deposits on the floor of the ocean at certain points to ascertain the condition of the deeper layers; to sound, trawl, and dredge, and study the character and distribution of marine organisms.[8]

This ambitious undertaking was to be accomplished by a two-ship expedition under the direction of the Royal Navy.

After Murray spoke, the Duke of Argyll, president of the Royal Scottish Geographical Society, voiced his enthusiasm for the project, noting that the Antarctic was far more likely to yield new insights than the Arctic. He urged his countrymen to take up the challenge: "I always feel a little shame that civilized man, living on his little planet — a very small globe — should, in this nineteenth century of the Christian era, not yet have explored the whole of this little area; it seems a reproach upon the enterprise, civilisation, and condition of knowledge of the human race."[9]

Others joined the chorus citing a variety of reasons for the renewal of Antarctic exploration, including the glory of Great Britain and of science. An expedition to open this vast unknown area for pure science would bring great benefit. Old naval hands insisted that the navy would provide men and equipment for the endeavor, an appeal that was echoed by Admiral Robert E. Peary in the United States in his promotion of North Polar exploration. Advances since the days of the Ross expedition of the 1840s, most notably the wider use of steam-powered vessels, would allow far more work to be done in a single season.[10]

Following Murray's address the council of the RGS appointed an Antarctic committee to report on the best means to achieve Murray's objectives. From the outset the strong naval influence in the committee was evident, but in the long run this led to problems. Despite the possible difficulties, for now, Markham believed that "if men of science are unanimous, both as to the importance of the work and the best method of executing it, and if they are backed by enlightened public opinion, the Admiralty will be only too glad to take the subject into favorable consideration."[11]

When the committee — the composition of which made it likely to respond favorably on Markham's proposal — reported its findings on 7 December 1893, it listed magnetic work as the most pressing need, citing Dr. Georg Balthasar Neumayer's (1826–1909) comment that "the next important step in the study of terrestrial magnetism cannot be taken until further observations have been obtained from the Antarctic regions." Beyond that, marine biology, deep sea dredging, and studies in sea temperature were paramount, and the committee noted the opportunities for geographical discovery in a vast, unexplored land. The report called for the dispatch of two ships and estimated three years would be required in the south polar regions. Finally, the committee reminded the council of the benefits to the navy and to national pride that would accrue from this effort.[12]

Markham's attempt to launch a national Antarctic expedition was made in the context of earlier trials. Thrice previously in the nineteenth century, scientific agencies had successfully lobbied the government to back an expedition. The Ross expedition (1839–43) was prompted by the work of the British Association for the Advancement of Science. The RGS and the Royal Society had collaborated to prompt the government to send Captain George Nares (1831–1915) to the Arctic in 1875–76, and the Royal Society had taken the lead in supporting the *Challenger* expedition of 1872–76.[13]

Aware of these previous efforts, Markham attempted to enlist the support of the Royal Society for his new Antarctic effort. On behalf of the RGS, he wrote to the Royal Society on 20 February 1894, enclosing copies of the report of the Royal Geographical Society's Special Committee on Antarctic Exploration and the paper from November 1893 by Murray. Markham appealed to the Royal Society to assist in taking "the lead in approaching the Government in this subject."[14] The Council of the Royal Society appointed a committee comprising Sir J. D. Hooker, Sir J. Kirk, Sir J. Lubbock, and Captain W. J. L. Wharton to look into the matter. Nearly a year passed before Michael Foster (1836–1907), secretary of the Royal Society, responded to Markham on behalf of the council.

In November 1894 Foster informed Markham that although the council believed "forcible reasons for the immediate undertaking of such an expedition existed," the time was not appropriate to approach the government. During that intervening year the Royal Society had asked officials about support and found little. In July 1894 Foster queried the Lords of the Admiralty to receive a deputation from the Royal Society on this matter, but that meeting failed to elicit government support for Antarctic research. Markham bemoaned the lost year and complained about the Fellows of the Royal Society approaching Treasury officials on their own. Although this first attempt to enlist the Royal Society in the cause failed, Markham resolved to appeal to other learned societies to build a case for a national Antarctic expedition. When the plans were developed, Markham argued, money would be forthcoming. Throughout the remainder of the decade he spoke whenever possible to organizations throughout Britain to promote Antarctic exploration.[15]

In December 1894 Markham launched a correspondence campaign to various scientific and geographical societies. Markham argued that money was irrelevant at this early juncture; besides, the initial projections may have been unduly high. Better that such estimates would come later, after the united scientific bodies could present more accurate figures. Agreement among the scientific organizations that the renewal of Antarctic research was of vital importance was now needed. Markham called on all agencies to turn their attention to the issue of exploring the south polar regions and to unite to launch such an expedition.[16]

Markham began receiving replies in early January 1895. Most were favorable, agreeing with his ideas and often enclosing a supporting resolution — but little money was forthcoming.[17]

Undaunted, Markham used the Sixth International Geographical Congress to further his cause. The RGS hosted the event, which met in London from 26 July through 3 August 1895 and brought together geographers from around the world. Two incidents at the congress dealt with the Antarctic — Borchgrevink's speech and H. R. Mill's resolution on Markham's behest. Thus the most important international geographical organization had called for the renewal of Antarctic research.

Having prepared the way with endorsements from scientific agencies throughout Britain and with the approval of the International Geographical Congress, Markham thought it a suitable time to approach the government. He wrote to the first lord of the Admiralty, G. J. Goschen (1831–1907), requesting that a deputation be allowed to meet with government representatives to present arguments for a Treasury-sponsored Antarctic expedition. Goschen refused to meet with the group because official support for such a venture was out of the question.[18]

Thus far no one had succeeded in arranging the funding necessary to launch a new Antarctic venture. Markham's cause appeared doomed in November 1895 with the government's refusal to provide financial support. With the conclusion of the Expeditions Committee of the RGS, in January 1896, that the time was not right to attempt an Antarctic campaign, Markham's fortunes were at a low ebb.

Meanwhile, in 1896 it appeared that Borchgrevink might successfully launch an expedition to Antarctica. During much of that time Sir Clements R. Markham and the Royal Geographical Society declined to pursue their own project. After Borchgrevink's plans fell through, Markham renewed his attempts to encourage the Society to promote an Antarctic enterprise.

In November 1896 Markham met with First Lord of the Admiralty G. J. Goschen, who occupied the same office he had held twenty years earlier, when he had assisted in the launch of the *Challenger*. Sir Clements followed that conference with a letter reviewing the need for such an undertaking and appealing for Treasury support. He stressed the benefits that polar experience gave naval personnel and reminded people: "Alike in the days of Cook, as it was in the days of Ross, Antarctic work has always been undertaken by the Government, and is strictly naval work."[19]

This appeal was rebuffed, as was the first one. Not only did the Admiralty deny funds, but it also turned down Markham's request for the loan of naval officers. Faced with a second refusal from the government, the Expeditions Committee of the RGS called for the Society to take the lead in Antarctic exploration. Any expedition without Treasury backing would be "deprived of numerous advantages," but an independent undertaking was the best alternative. In April 1897 the council resolved to begin such an effort and, to show its determination and good faith, subscribed £5,000 to the Antarctic Fund, a major contribution considering the Society's limited resources.[20]

Markham persisted in his attempts to gain a government grant, writing in October 1897 to the prime minister, Lord Salisbury (1830–1903), to argue his case. Markham listed several examples of previous grants-in-aid and expressed hope for similar backing. He reminded Salisbury that the prime minister had been president of the British Association for the Advancement of Science in December 1894 when that body recommended the dispatch of an expedition to the South Pole. Now other nations were stealing Britain's lead. Appealing to nationalism, Markham noted that Germany was gathering funds for an expedition and that Belgium already had a ship fitted out and ready to sail. Markham argued that it was not the time for "our country, so long the mother of discovery and of maritime enterprise, to abdicate her leading position." If the government would supply the money, the effort could be guided by a special committee and staffed with capable individuals who were ready to depart.[21]

Yet again Markham's appeal was refused. Salisbury regretted his inability to grant the request, adding that he was "unable to hold out any hope of Her Majesty's Government embarking upon an undertaking of such magnitude."[22]

Late in 1897, with progress agonizingly slow, Markham again turned to the Royal Society for assistance. Having received the Society's support, Markham continued to speak and write on behalf of his project. Throughout 1897 few offers of assistance were received, and at year's end only £12,000 had been raised. Most of that amount came from the RGS and from a gift of £5,000 from Alfred C. Harmsworth (1865–1922), a publisher who had previously underwritten the cost of the Jackson-Harmsworth Arctic expedition to Franz Josef Land.[23]

Despite the increased attention to Antarctic science, the proposed expedition lacked a research plan. Therefore, even as Markham was attempting to raise funds, he suggested a scientific program for the various proposed expeditions being discussed throughout Europe. Speaking at the Seventh International Geographical Congress in Berlin in 1899, he reminded his audience that the opportunities for Antarctic exploration were vast, suggesting that only one fully equipped expedition, that of James Clark Ross, had ventured south. In doing so Markham overlooked the significant efforts by d'Urville, Wilkes, and Bellingshausen. Sir Clements proposed to divide the Antarctic into four quadrants. Not surprisingly, these were named for Queen Victoria and three British explorers — Ross, Enderby, and Weddell. Markham outlined the work that needed to be undertaken in each section.[24]

Since Antarctic exploration would include an assault on the South Magnetic Pole, Sir Clements used this occasion to present his ideas about Antarctic land journeys. He deplored employing dogs in polar travel, arguing that this cruel practice had been proven unworkable. The one successful use of dogs for transport, Markham argued, was in Peary's expeditions in Greenland, an accomplishment achieved only at the expense of the lives of all the animals. Markham added that dogs were useless on ice or broken ground. As neither of these statements was true, Markham reached the incorrect conclusion that men were the only reliable form of polar transport. Citing statistics based on two Arctic man-hauling sledging parties, Markham attempted to show that a group could travel from McMurdo Sound to the South Magnetic Pole and back in three months "without the cruelty of killing a team of dogs by overwork and starvation."[25]

Markham implicitly espoused polar work as a test of manliness. Noted polar historian Roland Huntford perceived this equation of suffering with achievement as an aspect of the English Romantic movement. The subsequent disaster at the Pole in 1911–12, when Robert Falcon Scott and his party died in their attempt to return from 90° S, can be traced to Markham's ideas and his refusal to recognize the benefits of dog transport in polar regions. At the same time that Markham was denigrating the use of dogs, other explorers were convinced of their value. Frederick A. Cook planned on taking dogs for land transport on his proposed turn-of-the-century Antarctic expedition had he succeeded in launching it. Norwegians Fridtjof Nansen (1861–1930) and Roald Amundsen were early converts to the use of dogs for polar travel. Huntford has cited some of the reasons why dogs are well suited for polar transport: they are efficient in conserving body heat, are sure-footed in snow and ice, eat meat readily available in the Antarctic, and can move heavy loads long distances at far greater speeds over the ice than can other animals. Eventually, British explorers became convinced of the value of dogs but not until Scott's death in 1912.[26]

Markham explained the broad scientific goals of the proposed expedition and how they related to society. In addition to the work done aboard ship during the anticipated three summer seasons, a landing party, consisting of an executive officer and a geologist supported by ten men, would conduct sledging activities. As originally proposed, the expedition's ship would take only three civilian scientists, including the surgeon, fewer than the *Southern Cross* carried when it sailed in 1898.[27]

Meanwhile, the efforts of the Royal Geographical Society and the Royal Society to launch a British National Antarctic expedition proved disappointing. By early 1899 less than £8,000 had been added to the £5,000 the RGS had originally subscribed. The money came in very slowly; small donations of £200 were more common than large grants, such as Harmsworth's £5,000. Still, Markham remained optimistic. In his address to the Royal Geographical Society in 1899, he reminded his listeners that he and Sherard Osborn (1822–75) had worked twelve years before the 1875 Arctic expedition came to fruition. With this campaign, though, time was more pressing, as other nations threatened to steal Britain's lead. The Belgians were already in the South, and the Germans were dispatching an expedition the following year. "The Antarctic agitation has spread over Europe," and Britain needed to respond.[28]

In March 1899 prospects for the whole project turned around when L. W. Longstaff, a businessman and long-time fellow of the Royal Geographical Society, asked Markham if £25,000 would launch the project. The president responded enthusiastically. Longstaff, who by his own admission had been "all my life much interested in scientific matters," offered funds for "the advancement of our knowledge of the planet on which we live."[29]

Having made some progress in raising funds Markham began construction on the *Discovery*, the research vessel of the expedition, but he still lacked much of the £100,000 he believed he needed. Despite Longstaff's munificence additional large donations were not forthcoming. Hopes were dashed that this contribution would open the purses of other wealthy Britons. The subscription campaign, excepting Longstaff's kindness, stalled. Because the government remained the one great resource, Markham began in early 1899 to maneuver behind the scenes to tap it.

In April he drafted a letter to the Treasury that contained the signatures of the presidents of the Royal Society and the Royal Geographical Society. The letter outlined the reasons for an Antarctic expedition and requested that a deputation be allowed to call on the government. The Joint Antarctic Committee of the Royal Society and the RGS decided that it would be best to delay official contact until the opinion of A. J. Balfour (1848–1930), first lord of the Treasury, could be determined. F. Sidney Parry, private secretary in the Treasury, was asked to ascertain Balfour's mood and to help devise a plan for approaching the government.[30] Parry proved to be a key figure in gaining government support.

Parry advised Sir Clements that the Joint Committee delay contacting the government until the position of Sir Michael Hicks Beach (1837–1916), chancellor of the Exchequer, could be ascertained. Parry strongly urged Markham to defer writing, adding that he would notify Markham when "a fresh step can be taken."[31]

A month passed before Parry gave Markham a favorable report. Knowing that the plea would meet with a positive response, the Royal Society and the Royal Geographical Society then requested that the government receive their deputation.[32]

In June a letter was sent to the prime minister and the first lord of the Treasury seeking a meeting to request public funds for an Antarctic project. The message stated that this cooperation of the Royal Society and the Royal Geographical Society, in combination with other leading British scientific bodies, was unprecedented and that, although more than £40,000 had been subscribed, state support was needed to enable a modest expedition to leave Britain in 1901. Because the Germans had asked the British to cooperate with the *Gauss* venture, an Imperial Treasury contribution of £60,000 was most urgently needed. A £60,000 grant would at least allow a limited British effort.[33]

After the way had been prepared by behind-the-scenes activity, a formal deputation waited on A. J. Balfour on 22 June 1899. In a private note to Markham, Parry had urged that the group be as strong and as large as possible and that the press be notified. Noting that "the bigger the splash made, the greater the hope of success," Parry also urged that the practical aspects of exploration be emphasized, especially the role of magnetism in navigation, and that scientific details be kept to a minimum.[34]

Markham followed Parry's advice and led a delegation that met with the chancellor of the Exchequer wherein he presented plans for the expedition in the broadest possible manner. Nationalism played a major part. Markham noted that the German government contributed to the contemporaneous *Gauss* expedition and made an appeal to patriotism by telling the chancellor that "The honor of our country and the cause of science demand that we be able to cooperate with the Germans in these endeavors."[35]

Although Balfour did not claim to understand the details of the scientific questions this expedition hoped to answer, he agreed that the government needed to consider this proposition seriously. He was not dissuaded by the emphasis on pure science as opposed to commercial possibilities:

I take a different view — a view based upon the scientific experience of the past. If our predecessors in the last two centuries had taken any narrow utilitarian view of their work, it is manifest that our ignorance of the planet on which we live would be much more profound than it is at present; and it would not be creditable to an age which, above all other ages, flatters itself that it is scientific, if we were without reluctance to acquiesce in the total ignorance which now envelops us with regard to so enormous a portion of the southern hemisphere of our planet.[36]

Moreover, he was particularly pleased to hear of the proposed cooperation with the German scientific community, seeing a coordinated effort as another opportunity to promote the international character of pure science. Regarding conflict in the Antarctic, Balfour added, "There cannot be any territorial rivalry between any of the countries engaged in Antarctic exploration; and that such rivalry as there may be, must be of a purely scientific character." [37]

Success was soon in Markham's grasp. The years of petitioning came to an end on 3 July 1899 when the government offered the Royal Society and the Royal Geographical Society £45,000 for the Antarctic expedition on the condition that the money be matched by private subscriptions. [38] Even though only £3,000 of the £45,000 of matching monies was lacking, that amount was not easily found, and eventually Markham cajoled the Royal Geographical Society into donating the money. Thus the RGS contributed £8,000, an extraordinarily large amount given its limited resources.

F. Sidney Parry, who had helped prepare the way for Balfour's deputation, also assisted Markham to secure the services of naval officers that Goschen had previously denied. Parry suggested that Markham ask the Sea Lords for their support as their advice would be more influential. In the end this strategy worked. [39]

Markham had gambled all along that government support would be forthcoming; he was correct. His years of toiling had resulted in the funding of a great national Antarctic expedition. Thus Markham's dream was realized. The *Discovery* sailed in August 1901 and was one of the four great national expeditions that opened the Heroic Era. Although his obstinacy regarding the use of dogs as transport, his irascibility toward others, and his jingoist patriotism caused problems in the years to come, Markham rightly can be seen as the father of British Antarctic exploration in the Heroic Era. His single-minded resolve, his willingness to convince himself of the rightness of his cause, and his steadfast determination to succeed proved the difference between failure of others and his own success.

From the announcement of the receipt of a government grant in July 1899 to the dispatch of the *Discovery*, controversy engulfed the national Antarctic expedition. The years 1899–1901 forewarned difficulties that would hamper British Antarctic exploration in the first two decades of the twentieth century. Indeed, the problems that led to the tragedy of Scott's *Terra Nova* (1910–12) endeavor can be traced back to the decisions made in the twenty months before the *Discovery* sailed.

Markham had used the Royal Geographical Society as an instrument to achieve his dream of geographical discoveries in the south polar regions. [40] In his quest for financing for a naval expedition, he had turned to other British scientific organizations, principally the Royal Society. In doing so, Markham successfully campaigned for Treasury support to supplement the funds raised through private subscription. The Royal Society's intervention had been crucial in persuading Balfour's cabinet to underwrite the venture. The government recognized the Royal Society and the Royal Geographical Society as the guardians of the finances for the endeavor. Once funds were assured, Markham and the RGS were left in a partnership with the Royal Society that nearly wrecked the enterprise before the first sail was rigged on the *Discovery*.

Markham, the inveterate committeeman, decided that a Joint Committee of the two societies was the ideal way to supervise the myriad of details that would transform his ideas into reality. This body superseded a similar previous board used by the two societies to persuade the government to fund the campaign.

As proposed by Markham, the expanded commission was not to replace the councils of the two societies but merely to act as an advisory board for the venture. The councils remained the final authority.[41] Ten subcommittees were appointed to handle details: Ship Equipment, Landing Parties, Hygiene, Provisions, Outfits, Magnetism, Meteorology, Physical Geography, Oceanography, and Biology. These organizations were to prepare a list of scientific goals for the voyage.[42]

Each society nominated to the Joint Committee thirteen members who were tapped for their skills and experiences. Those chosen by the Royal Society were among the most prominent figures in British Antarctic circles, including Sir John Murray; J. Y. Buchanan, leading authority on botany; Sir Joseph Hooker; and E. W. Creak, one of the leaders in magnetic research. The RGS delegation was dominated by old Arctic hands: A. H. Markham; Vice Admiral Sir George Nares (1831–1915), Arctic explorer; Sir Leopold McClintock (1819–1907); and Sir R. Vesey Hamilton (1829–1912), veteran of several Arctic campaigns.[43] From the outset these two factions were at odds over the goals and plans of the expedition. The Royal Society appointees were men drawn to Antarctic exploration by the opportunity for scientific research. Those named by the RGS believed geographical discovery was the main purpose. Moreover, the RGS contingent agreed with Markham that a strong naval influence was essential for the success of an Antarctic mission.[44]

The limitations imposed on the Joint Committee — its size and the great variety of problems brought before it — led to difficulties. Because all important decisions had to be referred to the two societies, the advisers had no real authority.[45]

For four months the committee grappled with the details of the expedition, but it was soon apparent that the organization was too unwieldy. In November 1899 the councils of the Royal Society and the Royal Geographical Society appointed a four-member Executive Committee, two persons named by each body. The four members — Captain T. H. Tizard; Edward B. Poulton (1856–1943), professor of zoology at Oxford University; Sir Clements Markham; and Sir R. Vesey Hamilton — guided affairs until November 1900. After the creation of the Executive Committee the Joint Committee continued to approve the actions taken by the smaller body and remained influential in the preparations.

Unlike contemporaneous expeditions of Germany, Sweden, and Scotland, the two societies used a labyrinth of committees to provide day-to-day direction to the enterprise. As originally conceived, the Executive Committee was to work in consultation with the subcommittees, directing activities, including hiring staff and allocating funds subject to the approval of the Joint Committee. The Executive Committee was charged with providing a general plan of operations and with producing a set of instructions for the leader and for the director of the scientific staff. By giving the small board authority to supervise details and sign contracts, the two councils erroneously hoped to streamline preparations. Quickly problems developed. A dispute as to whether the new board should be entitled to spend money split the two societies. The RGS favored such an allowance, but the Royal Society's opposition prevailed. That power was deleted in the final version of the resolution creating the committee. Both councils hoped that the Executive Committee would give the undertaking needed guidance. For nearly a year this organization worked haltingly.[46]

Bureaucracy proliferated. The new agency had limited success with the subcommittees, although several produced good results, issuing guidelines for research in the scientific fields in their charge. For the most part, though, the smaller bodies became mired, producing far less than expected and exacerbating the troubles inherent in launching the venture. The geology subcommittee delayed its work pending input from the director of the civilian staff. The oceanography subcommittee met once and produced nothing.[47]

Among the most important actions taken were the appointments of a commander of the expedition and a director of the scientific staff. Yet these selections, and the relative powers assigned to each, created a crisis for the Joint Committee and for the expedition itself.

Markham envisioned a small scientific team headed by a civilian under the overall command of the ship's captain, as Wyville Thomson (1830–82) had worked under Captain George Nares on the *Challenger*. In Markham's view the civilian staff director advised, the captain commanded. Others on the Joint Committee, especially those representing the Royal Society, believed the director should be the leader of the enterprise. That faction could point to the splendid results achieved by the *Valdivia* under Professor Carl Chun, chosen to command the mission because he was a leading authority in deep-sea research. The captain of the *Valdivia*, Adalbert Krech, took his orders from Chun. When Edward Poulton first raised this issue in a Joint Committee meeting, the navy men had insisted that under English law such an arrangement was impossible as the captain's authority could not be prescribed.[48]

The other contemporaneous expeditions pointed in a different direction. The German *Gauss* effort was lead by Erich von Drygalski (1865–1949), a professor of geology at the University of Berlin. Georg Balthasar von Neumayer would have been an obvious choice, but he declined because of his advanced age. Even before the *Gauss* endeavor, Drygalski was an accomplished leader of scientific forays, having directed expeditions to India to pursue geodetic science, and to Greenland to investigate glaciers.[49] Chosen to command at the very outset of the effort, Drygalski devoted five years to planning the campaign, in consultation with leading German researchers. Unlike arrangements on the *Discovery*, a single person directed the *Gauss*, thus avoiding the divisiveness of group supervision. Drygalski's scholarly accomplishments were considerable; his bibliography listed more than a dozen books and articles on polar matters. In Drygalski the Germans had a proven leader, one who already had an international reputation as a scientist and whose experience gave him an intimate knowledge of the task before him.[50]

Similarly, the Swedish *Antarctic* enterprise was led by Otto Nordenskjöld, a scientist whose research in Patagonia had made a significant contribution to the study of glacial geology. Nordenskjöld headed the Swedish endeavor by virtue of his stature as a scholar. C. A. Larsen, who had commanded the *Jason* on its Antarctic voyages in the early 1890s, was the captain of the *Antarctic*.[51]

The third of the four major endeavors of the period 1901 to 1904 was also led by a scientist, arguably the most qualified Briton in the period to embark on polar work. William S. Bruce, who was described by a biographer as "the first of the scientist-explorers," and whose accomplishments in polar expeditionary work were unequaled by any another Briton, led the Scottish National Antarctic expedition from 1902 to 1904. Although not chosen for his scholarly achievements — Bruce organized his own campaign — his ability to attract financial support was based largely on his reputation as a scientist, and, therefore, he was seen as a logical person to command a scientific expedition. Bruce chose an Antarctic veteran, Thomas Robertson, to command the ship, the *Scotia*.[52]

Thus the four great national enterprises, except for the *Discovery*, were organized with a scientist in control and with a competent sea master to direct the sailing aspects of the voyage. The results of each expedition were to some degree presaged by the choice of command.

The British may have seemed to be following the model of the other three expeditions when J. W. Gregory (1864–1932) was appointed director of the scientific staff in February 1900. Then, in May 1900, the Executive Committee named Robert Falcon Scott commander. The two appointments were made before the instructions for either position were written and without settling questions regarding the relative roles of the two offices.

Gregory was a scientist and explorer of considerable accomplishment. He was educated at the University of London and later worked at the British Museum's Geology Department. In 1892 he participated in an exploration of British East Africa. He subsequently reorganized that group and led it to the region of Mount Kenya, where important studies were carried out. In this adventure he demonstrated substantial ability in leading men in difficult circumstances. He followed this triumph with a campaign near Spitsbergen. His expertise in geology was expected to be especially useful for Antarctic work. Shortly after his appointment to the *Discovery* Gregory was named professor of geology at Melbourne. Gregory was eminently qualified to guide the scientific program of the venture.[53]

Robert Falcon Scott lacked a background in either science or polar matters. A naval officer, he first came to Markham's attention in March 1887 when the latter had observed the young eighteen-year-old midshipman in a cutter race. Markham later claimed to have decided on Scott at that moment as the commander of the future Antarctic expedition. By Markham's account, he next met Scott in 1897 and again in 1899.[54] At this point the story becomes somewhat muddled. Markham noted that Scott volunteered to command the Antarctic expedition at this 1899 encounter, and Markham immediately saw him as "the best man for so great a trust, either in the navy, or out of it."[55]

Scott's version differed. Writing in his account of the *Discovery*, he noted that one day in early June 1899 walking down Buckingham Palace Road, he chanced to encounter Sir Clements and followed him to the latter's house in Eccleston Square. There, Scott wrote, he first learned of the proposed Antarctic expedition. Scott contended that he wrote Markham two days after this meeting, applying to command the expedition and "a year after that I was officially appointed."[56]

Roland Huntford, a leading polar authority—though not without a strong prejudice against Scott in general—described a different scenario. Painstakingly tracing the background to the Scott selection, Huntford

2. Robert Falcon Scott. Drawing by Kim Crosbie.

asserted that Scott was only one of Markham's several possible choices, and by no means the most likely or desirable. Determining that Scott felt pressured to advance his career in the navy, Huntford argued that Scott saw Antarctic exploration as a career-enhancing opportunity and finagled the older man to choose him as commander. Though not Markham's first choice, Huntford noted that Scott could be very charming, and that Markham's choices may in any event have been limited, because the Royal Navy in 1899–1901 was not inclined to spare gifted officers.[57]

Each version no doubt contributes to the whole truth. In any event

Markham, having decided on Scott, made a case for his young officer. Scott was a torpedo officer in the Royal Navy, had a scientific proclivity (although this was little known at the time of his appointment), and was eager to lead the enterprise, although he later admitted that at the time of his appointment, he was largely ignorant of polar matters. Years before, Markham detailed the qualifications he sought in a commander: "He must be a naval officer, he must be in the regular line and not in the surveying branch, and he must be young. These are essentials. Such a Commander should be a good sailor with some experience of ships under sail, a navigator with a knowledge of surveying, and he should be of a scientific turn of mind. He must have imagination and be capable of enthusiasm. His temperament must be cool, he must be calm yet quick and decisive in action, a man of resource, tactful and sympathetic."[58]

Sir Clements did not require the appointee to be a scientist. Yet two years earlier in 1896, one of the reasons given by the Markham's council of the RGS for not supporting Carsten E. Borchgrevink's Antarctic venture was that the leader of such an effort ought to be a scientist.[59]

At the time that Scott applied to Markham, the Admiralty had shown no interest in releasing men for the expedition. Markham wrote directly to the Admiralty petitioning for two officers. When Markham's appeal came to the attention of the Joint Committee several members objected to the unilateral action. Moreover, the same faction that objected to Markham's methods also had misgivings about his choice of Scott. The Royal Society members believed that someone from the surveying department would make a more appropriate selection, given the training such officers received.[60] Markham, having decided on Scott, objected to the suggestion of someone from another section of the navy, but Sir Clements did not have a majority to support his position in the Joint Committee.[61]

Markham used a ploy to gain his goal. A special board of naval officers was named to study Scott's appointment. When it met two factions emerged, one of which backed Markham and Scott; the other fiercely opposed Scott and offered several other nominees.[62] None of the alternatives satisfied the first group, and the men appeared deadlocked. Wharton and Tizard were among Scott's most vociferous opponents and showed no sign of compromise.[63] When the panel met a second time on 24 May 1899, Markham's fortunes improved. Two of Scott's detractors were absent, and two others were persuaded to vote for the RGS president's candidate. At the Joint Committee meeting on 25 May 1900 Scott's nomination as commander was moved by Markham, was seconded by Lister, and was carried unanimously. Scott was appointed, but the controversy over command within the expedition was to surface again.[64]

Regardless of the other possible reasons, Scott met Markham's over-arching criterion as a commander — he was a naval officer. That he was young and willing to take direction from the old Arctic hands that populated British exploring circles was no disadvantage.[65] Moreover, having made the decision in Scott's favor, Markham soon adopted the stance that Scott was the best candidate possible.

Throughout 1900 the Executive Committee struggled to oversee the details of the adventure. Among its primary tasks was the supervision of the construction and equipping of the *Discovery*. The Executive Committee dealt with provisions, scientific instruments, and even the purchase of suitable dogs. Contracts provided the enterprise with equipment and food. Whenever possible, manufacturers were persuaded to donate to the expedition. Cadbury, Coulman, and Lipton's offered their products, publishers gave books for the library, and clothing makers, such as Jaeger, contributed woolen goods. Tinned meat was to be a staple of the crew, although plans included a concerted effort to supplement tinned food by providing the men with fresh meat from New Zealand livestock, before departing for the ice. Regrettably, the planners failed to provide consistently excellent foodstuffs, and a large amount was condemned as unfit while the ship was at McMurdo Sound. Spoilage was later cited as a reason for sending a vessel to relieve the *Discovery*. Similarly, the *Discovery* planners failed to capitalize on the evidence from the *Southern Cross* expedition that Antarctica could supply much needed fresh food.[66]

The Executive Committee commissioned an *Antarctic Manual* for the venture, an idea that hearkened back to the British Arctic expedition of 1875. The *Discovery* edition contained chapters written by experts in the fields of science the staff was to investigate. Although Markham hoped that the government would cover the cost of publication, the RGS eventually agreed to underwrite the project. The volume, admirably edited by George Murray (1858–1911), was well received.[67] One reviewer noted: "No future explorer is likely to go to the Far South without familiarizing himself with its contents, and the book is bound to remain a standard work on the Antarctic."[68] Fridtjof Nansen, the greatest explorer of his day and the beau ideal of the scientific explorer — thought enough of it to ask for a copy.

The Executive Committee was charged with naming the ship's officers

and the scientists. First, an explanation is needed as to why the best qualified British polar explorer was omitted from the *Discovery*.

William S. Bruce was an obvious choice, if not to command, then to be
the director of the scientific staff. Bruce's work on the *Balaena* (1892–93),
along with his work in Franz Joseph Land on the Jackson-Harmsworth expedition (1894–97), gave him as wide a range of experience as any candidate. Between voyages he had worked at the Ben Nevis Observatory, gathering data under extremely harsh climatic conditions. His interest in the
Antarctic was well known — he had applied for a position on H. J. Bull's
Antarctic expedition (1894–95). He was prevented from joining it by his
inability to reconnoiter with the ship in Melbourne. This failure had given
Borchgrevink his opportunity. Subsequently, Bruce had petitioned for
money for a small foray to South Georgia Island but had failed to persuade
the RGS to fund his program.[69] Bruce also tried to join a Norwegian whaling expedition in 1896, but nothing came of it. Instead, when no good opportunity to go south presented itself, he had gone to the Arctic noting
that although he preferred Antarctic work, he could not refuse a good offer. Borchgrevink recognized Bruce's ability and requested H. R. Mill, an
important figure at the RGS and a friend to generations of Antarctic heroes, to ask the Scot to accompany the *Southern Cross*. At one point Borchgrevink and Bruce talked of cooperating when the Anglo-Norwegian
nearly got his 1896 Antarctic expedition off the ground, but at the time
Borchgrevink opted not to join with Bruce. That Bruce chose to go to the
Arctic is more a reflection on Borchgrevink than it is an indication of a diminished interest in the Antarctic on Bruce's part.[70]

When Bruce heard of the forthcoming national Antarctic expedition,
he wrote Markham offering his services. According to his old associate,
Reginald Koettlitz, Bruce was eager to join.[71] In his letter of application
Bruce demonstrated that he had spent the previous seven years preparing
for just such an opportunity. He referred to his exploration experience and
his scholarly work, both of which would be valuable to Markham's venture. In a subsequent note Bruce added a list of his references that included
some of the most important contemporary figures in polar exploration:
the Prince of Monaco, Sir John Murray, Dr. Alexander Buchan, J. Y. Buchanan, Fridtjof Nansen, Andrew Coats, and Alfred Harmsworth. This list
includes seven of the eight men most qualified to recommend a leader. The
eighth man was Bruce himself.[72]

Markham replied in April 1899 that he would be glad to meet with the
Scot when he came to London. Markham added that no steps had been

taken about personnel for the venture. Markham demonstrated an easy virtue with the truth, and it would not be the last time.[73]

For eleven months Bruce's place on the staff remained undecided. Bruce feared that Markham was prejudiced against him because Bruce was a Scot. Certainly, Bruce had not always curried favor with the president of the RGS. When Bruce returned from the Arctic he had presented the first results of his Jackson-Harmsworth adventure to the Royal Scottish Geographical Society instead of the RGS, a slight Markham noticed. As Mill cautioned Bruce,

You are too unworldly, and have too high an idea of the unselfishness of the scientific societies. The RGS quite naturally wished to have the first news of your Arctic work and as you went in my place I had expected you would have given the paper to the society that would not let me go! However I know you did not mean to slight the RGS and I still take pleasure in seeing the Scottish Society getting a good thing. But you don't realize how necessary it is to keep on cordial terms with such powerful corporations as the RGS if you hope to enlist their aid in helping you to subsequent expeditions.[74]

Markham also may have had reservations about such a strong, superbly trained, well-connected person becoming a rival to Scott. Clearly, Bruce's veiled threat, that he might launch his own expedition, discouraged Markham from promoting Bruce's candidacy. Markham dawdled with Bruce's application.[75]

The matter was resolved in the spring of 1900 with Bruce's announcement that he was leading his own enterprise, scheduled to depart for the Antarctic in 1902. Mill was surprised, as were Markham and others, by the sudden declaration that Bruce had secured the financial backing for his adventure. Mill wrote to congratulate Bruce. Markham took the news as yet another threat to his endeavor and wrote Bruce,

I am sorry to hear that an attempt is to be made at Edinburgh to divert funds from the Antarctic expedition in order to get up a rival enterprise. Such a course will be most prejudicial to the expedition which is much in need of more funds. A second ship is not the least required. It is not true that the whole area is not provided for. If the Germans do not undertake the Weddell Quadrant, it will be undertaken by our expedition as a first object. I do not understand why this mischievous rivalry should have been started, but I trust that you will not connect yourself with it.[76]

Bruce had cut himself adrift from the events unfolding at the RGS, and the eventual successful work of his Scottish National Antarctic expedition indicated that Bruce might have served well as director of the scientific staff of the larger enterprise that Markham controlled. Without question, given the resources available to the enterprise, the results of the expedition would have been far greater had Bruce been in charge of the scientific staff.[77]

The Executive Committee's appointments to the *Discovery* continued in May 1900 with Albert B. Armitage (1864–1943) as second-in-command. Armitage had been second in command of the Jackson-Harmsworth expedition to Spitsbergen. In recognition of this, he received the Murchison award from the RGS. Armitage was the oldest man in the expedition, and his years of Arctic service gave him more such experience than anyone else on the *Discovery* except Koettlitz. Armitage's four years on sailing ships proved to be a considerable advantage to the venture. Armitage was employed by the P. & O. Line at the time of his appointment to Scott's expedition and came highly recommended by his employer who agreed to give him leave for the expedition. Armitage was expected to serve as the ice master for the voyage. Harmsworth, one of the principal benefactors of the *Discovery*, recommended Armitage, but he was also known to Markham through friends. Armitage in his autobiography claimed that Harmsworth gave £5,000 on the condition that Armitage and Koettlitz be appointed to the *Discovery*. Armitage further stated that he had been chosen second-in-command to be Scott's "advisor, a sort of wet-nurse" to overcome Scott's lack of experience. Armitage wrote that at the time of his appointment it was understood that he was to be independent of Scott and that he was to be given command of a landing party charged with encamping for two years. Armitage's claim almost certainly overstated his proposed role and may as much reflect the considerable dissatisfaction he felt during and after the *Discovery* voyage. Markham petitioned the Admiralty to have Armitage made a lieutenant in the Royal Naval Reserve, and that was granted in February 1901.[78]

Charles Royds (1876–1931), the nephew of Wyatt Rawson, an old messmate that Sir Clements regarded as the ideal polar explorer, first came to Markham's attention in the 1890s. Unlike Armitage, Royds was in the Royal Navy, a young lieutenant, but without polar experience. He had attributes that commended him to Markham, however. Royds was well connected in naval circles and came with strong references. Markham liked Royds and his family connections and pushed for his selection. Typical of his approach, Markham in a memorandum on Royds's qualifications listed all the first lieutenants on nineteenth-century Arctic expeditions with their ages to put Royds's appointment into the context of polar work. Royds had volunteered to serve on the expedition as early as 3 April 1899, and Markham requested his services for the expedition in June 1900. The Admiralty appointment followed within a few days. Typically, Markham wrote Royds telling him of his appointment before receiving the official written reply. Royds was thus one of the two officers that the Admiralty released for *Discovery* service at the outset. His appointment was confirmed by the Joint Committee 6 June 1900. His responsibilities on the voyage included the normal running of the ship. As such he served as an intermediary between Scott and the rest of the crew. In this work Royds performed well. He also was in charge of meteorological observations and assisted in magnetic observations. To prepare for the latter work he took a brief course with Captain Creak. Royds proved an able officer, was very popular, and after the *Discovery* rose to be a rear admiral in the Royal Navy before retiring in 1926.[79]

Three other appointments deserve note. Michael Barne (1877–1961) had been a shipmate of Scott on the *Majestic*, and Markham secured Admiralty permission for him to join within a week of the request. Barne was appointed second officer by the committee in June 1900. His duties included assisting Armitage with magnetic studies and taking charge of deep-sea temperature research. Reginald Skelton (1872–1952), who had also sailed with Scott, was named engineer of the *Discovery* and was soon appointed to oversee the building of the ship and engines at Dundee. Scott was eager to have this officer and the committee complied. On the expedition Skelton's additional duties included photographic work and assisting with the preservation of bird specimens. After the expedition, Skelton resumed his naval career, retiring in 1932 as vice admiral.[80]

The third nominee became, after Scott, the most famous British Antarctic explorer of the Heroic Era and was considered by many to be the greatest leader of the period. Ernest Shackleton, born in Ireland on the day that the *Challenger* crossed the Antarctic Circle, grew up in England and attended school at Dulwich College. He did not distinguish himself academically. Later in life Shackleton returned as a polar hero to his old school to distribute end-of-year prizes, noting that this was "as close as he had ever gotten to one of these prizes."[81] Still, before he left school, he had shown in childhood two aspects of his later character: adventure — he dug a hole in his backyard in an attempt to reach China; and blarney — he persuaded his sister that the London Monument had been erected in his honor.[82]

Shackleton had entered the merchant service, where he made steady progress through the ranks, acquiring his master's certificate in 1898. In these years he acquired extensive experience with sailing ships.[83]

While Shackleton later claimed to have a long-standing interest in polar matters, that statement was true in the sense that his biographer, H. R. Mill (1861–1950), suggested that Shackleton "liked to tell stories that were true in the larger sense."[84] To this point, Shackleton probably had not

3. Ernest Shackleton.
Drawing by Kim Crosbie.

given any real thought to the Poles — what he had thought of was his desire to marry Emily Dorman, whom he had met in 1897, and his desire to make a name for himself. A shipmate listening to Shackleton at that time noted Shackleton's ambition to do something worthy, not only for himself but for Miss Dorman.[85] Fame could have come in Africa, Whitehall, or literature — it was all the same to Shackleton, as long as fortune came with it.

In March 1900 Shackleton found himself aboard a ship loaded with troops bound for the South African War. As with his later experiences on the *Discovery*, Shackleton established himself as the life of the ship, organizing activities for the soldiers and writing a book about the voyage.[86] Never shy, Shackleton wrote Rudyard Kipling (1865–1936) — then at the height of his fame — and asked him to write an introductory poem for the book. The two met, and Kipling agreed. After a leave of absence from the sea, Shackleton presented the completed book to Queen Victoria.[87]

Also, during his voyages to South Africa, Shackleton met Cedric Longstaff, a young officer bound for the Boer War. When Shackleton learned of the *Discovery* expedition he was eager to join it, and young Longstaff provided his entree. The principal benefactor of the *Discovery*, whose £25,000 gift made possible the launch of the expedition, was Llewellyn Longstaff, young Longstaff's father. Although Albert B. Armitage, second-in-command on the *Discovery*, claimed to have played a key role in Shackleton's appointment, the Longstaff connection was probably paramount. Shackleton was appointed 17 February 1901.[88]

Markham was eager to find officers with skills that would supplement those of his commander, in this case Shackleton's experience under sail. Shackleton demonstrated considerable ability when placed in charge of the ship's holds, provisions, and stores. His scientific assignment was deep-sea water analysis, for which he received training from H. R. Mill.[89] Markham worked behind the scenes to secure for Shackleton an appointment as a sublieutenant in the Royal Naval Reserve and as such Lieutenant Shackleton took his position as third officer.[90]

The Executive Committee also chose the scientists. The second-in-command on the scientific staff, similar to his counterpart on the ship, was a veteran Arctic explorer, another member of the Jackson-Harmsworth expedition, Reginald Koettlitz (1861–1916), who was appointed in May 1900. Koettlitz had been educated at Dover College and did medical training at George's Hospital before joining the Jackson-Harmsworth expedition. Markham was aware of Koettlitz and early in 1900 approached him regarding a position as scientist and medical officer. Koettlitz indicated that he was eager to go and that his references — including Harmsworth, Sir Archibald Geikie (1835–1924), and Sir Vesey Hamilton, an old Arctic veteran with whom Markham was closely associated — would speak well of his work.

Once again Harmsworth used his leverage as an important financial contributor to the expedition to promote his former colleague. Although Markham regarded Koettlitz as competent, citing his success in keeping the members of the Jackson-Harmsworth crew healthy for three years, Sir Clements thought Koettlitz "exceedingly short of common sense." As medical officer Koettlitz immediately began supervising the selection of tinned foods. Koettlitz deemed this extremely important, because he believed, as others at the time continued to assert, that scurvy was caused by improperly preserved food. Koettlitz's activities in the Arctic made him, along with Armitage, one of the two most experienced explorers on the *Discovery*.[91]

The last appointment, that of Edward A. Wilson, opened a chapter in Antarctic history that was finally closed in the spring of 1912 when Wilson and Scott perished together returning from the South Pole. Wilson, a deeply spiritual person with fragile health, was trained in medicine at Caius College, Cambridge. Following a period of recuperation from tuberculosis in Switzerland in 1898 and 1899, he assisted the British Museum in analyzing the samples brought back by the *Southern Cross*. Wilson's uncle, Sir Charles Wilson, and Philip Sclater, president of the Zoological Society, recommended the young physician to Markham. When first directed to take the medical examination, Wilson was permitted a delay to allow a severe wound in his armpit to heal. After failing the exam because of a diseased right lung, Wilson went to the expedition headquarters and told Scott that he would go on his own responsibility. Despite these difficulties, according to Markham, Scott insisted on taking Wilson. Markham's influence prevailed, and the Executive Committee endorsed the choice of Wilson subject to the approval of Gregory.[92]

Thus the principal figures of the *Discovery* expedition had been assembled. Problems of organization and international cooperation remained. In the coming months Markham and the others associated with the *Discovery* found themselves at loggerheads about the purpose and goals of the expedition. For the time being the dangers that faced the ship in south polar waters would have to wait until the problems facing it in central London had been solved.

3

Old Men Bicker

Even before the funds for the expedition had been secured, the Royal Society and the Royal Geographical Society indicated their desire to work with agencies from other nations to assure a coordinated effort in the Antarctic. Considerable support existed for what Mill described as "the value of simultaneous expeditions working in friendly rivalry [producing] far greater results than . . . consecutive or isolated work."[1] In 1898 representatives from the Royal Society attended a meeting of the German Academies to discuss a possible concerted project. Markham used his influence at the International Geographical Congress in Berlin in 1899 to promote his plan for a four-quadrant geographical division of the Antarctic that Drygalski and Baron Ferdinand von Richthofen (1833–1905), president of the Berlin Geographical Society, accepted. Beyond that, Drygalski and Markham compared notes on the construction of the *Gauss* and the *Discovery*, and developed a common plan of record keeping for meteorology and magnetism.[2]

International cooperation had supporters outside Germany and Great Britain. Henryk Arctowski, veteran of the *Belgica* expedition, was a consistent advocate of such systematic coordination. He reiterated his call for a series of stations located around Antarctica to gather simultaneous observations. A very limited version of such a program was put together for the period 1901 to 1904. The Argentine government offered to assist the German and British effort by maintaining an observatory on Staten Island (Isla de los Estados), the easternmost island of Tierra del Fuego. With the proposed posts at Melbourne, Cape Town, Kerguelen Islands, and a second observatory in the South Shetlands, a set of stations on the circumference of Antarctica appeared to have been a possibility. This early precedent established a pattern of international cooperation that continues today.[3]

Thus the leadership of the *Discovery* was settled, and preliminary plans for international cooperation were put in place. Yet behind the scenes, problems and controversies were developing that threatened to sink the enterprise before the launch of the *Discovery*.

As 1900 proceeded, the day-to-day operations of the expeditions clearly required a better means of executive authority. For Markham, an executive signified constant supervision, not the monthly meetings that occasionally brought members in from the country. Correspondence was increasing, and in the absence of other assistants, the majority of the work fell to Sir Clements. In a memorandum to the RGS council he noted: "The executive work from the beginning in 1894 has been done by your president, including the whole of the work for raising funds. He has had no help whatever. He has had to conduct the whole of a rapidly increasing correspondence, to decide many questions in connection with the ship building and engine building people and their payments and to pass on the equipment for the various departments. The Committees have been a great and serious hindrance."[4] Markham, chafing at the hesitancy and laggard progress of the Executive Committee, urged all decisions be turned over to Scott.[5]

Markham noted that had the Joint Committee been abolished when the Executive Committee had been created, the situation might have improved. Instead, another body merely created more problems. The Germans, Sir Clements noted, were unhampered by committees; Drygalski had directed the *Gauss* expedition from its first day. Markham now wanted the same powers for Scott. The Joint Committee concurred, and the councils of both the Royal Society and the Royal Geographical Society voted to turn over all authority to Scott, with only a small board to assist with financial matters.[6]

By November 1900 Scott was in effective control of the entire enterprise, which included the details of assembling tons of supplies, a ship, scientific equipment, and two score men who were to represent Great Britain in the Antarctic expeditions being sent out in August 1901. Much remained to be done in the last months before departure.

Before Markham could be satisfied with the transfer of power to the commander, he wanted to ensure that the Joint Committee, which he described as "a scene of obstruction and friction," would not hinder Scott as it had himself. In December 1900 Sir Clements wrote to Michael Foster, secretary of the Royal Society, noting that the role assigned to the Executive Committee had now been transferred to Scott. Furthermore, ten of the eleven functions of the Joint Committee had likewise been given over to the commander. That one remaining responsibility was to write the instructions to the commander and the director of the scientific staff, work only the councils could assume. The instructions were, in Markham's words, "too grave a matter to be decided by a chance show of hands at a committee" meeting. Therefore, Sir Clements presumed that the two committees were abolished. Foster replied two days later, categorically refuting Markham's conclusion. Quoting from the original resolutions creating the two committees, Foster insisted that the plan for the voyage and the instructions be approved by those bodies. No other existing agency could perform this role, and therefore the Joint Committee and the Executive Committee were to remain in existence until those documents were prepared. Markham was defeated in his plan to abolish the committees. That single remaining task created a major conflict within the Joint Committee and between the two societies that nearly led to a rupture of relations between the Royal Society and the Royal Geographical Society that would have threatened the future of the entire endeavor.[7]

In December 1900 the Joint Committee debated a general program of operation for the expedition. Not only Markham but Nares, Wharton, and Buchanan contributed plans. Which one of these programs was chosen would determine much of the outcome and scientific results of the voyage. Nares described a two-year, possibly a three-year, voyage. If a landing party was to be part of the operation, it must be put ashore either in the first season in a fairly well-known area, or during the second summer of a three-year voyage in a less familiar region. If a base camp were established, the focus of the vessel's actions would be shifted to delivering the shore party and then moving safely out of harm from the ice to assure the steamer of being able to reembark the explorers the following summer. Nares had reservations about wintering the ship — having the entire party confined to a single area for such a length of time. He favored exploration in the Weddell Sea, especially as exploration in South Victoria Land "would do little more than repeat Borchgrevink's voyage."[8]

Admiral Wharton's suggestions also stressed complications that would arise if an encampment were part of the program. He agreed with Nares that if a base were to be established in the first season, its location must be known in advance. Otherwise, in the event of the loss of the *Discovery*, rescue would be far more difficult. Delaying the placing of a shore party until the second summer required a third year, although funds for such an extension were not then available. In addition Wharton questioned the benefits of a station when overland travel would be far more difficult than in the Arctic. The responsibility for a land party would greatly limit the vessel's movement and activities, and the omission of such a station would save the expedition £2,500, enough money to allow a third season of sailing. Wharton suggested that the best plan would be to go to the Weddell Sea and explore the coast between there and Graham Land, avoiding the better-known South Victoria Land.[9]

Buchanan took a different approach. The main emphasis of the voyage should be exploration of the continent; therefore a station on the mainland was essential. The entire focus of preparations, of expenditures on supplies, and of use of the steamer should be to assure that the land party successfully complete its mission. The first summer would be devoted to delivering men to the base camp. The *Discovery* would then return to safe waters, where sounding and dredging research could be conducted. Buchanan reminded the committee that "whether we like it or not, we are, in this matter, in competition with the Germans, and the success of the one expedition will be judged largely by comparison with the other."[10]

Markham's plan was the most detailed and was essentially the same program he had drawn up in 1897. He dismissed devoting the ship's cruise to sounding and dredging work that could be performed "at any time by any vessel."[11] His plan called for the barque to sail south, winter, and continue its scientific work the second summer. He rejected the idea of a small landing station, arguing that a limited group could not perform the tasks that the entire company could undertake. Moreover, splitting the crew would weaken both parties, particularly the ship's contingent, making navigation more dangerous. Sir Clements outlined a program that included meteorology and magnetic work in addition to zoology, geology, and glaciology. Returning to his thesis of the four quadrants, he urged that the *Discovery* explore the Victoria Land area to enlarge upon Ross's discoveries. Markham noted that McMurdo Bay (as he called it then) was the best place to winter and that the area would afford an excellent locale for forays inland.[12]

Thus three of the four plans called for the *Discovery* to sail south, land a party to remain for the winter, and then the ship would be free to conduct a scientific program in high latitudes. Only Markham called for the ship to winter. In Markham's plan lay the potential for the very problems that hampered the expedition's affairs for the next few weeks and which led eventually to the removal of the two societies from effective control of the voyage.

The Executive Committee met on 31 January 1901 and approved Markham's plan of operations. Poulton was absent, and Gregory stated his opposition to the program but he did not list specific objections.[13]

Although the program had been approved previously, members of the Joint Committee who disagreed with the thrust of Sir Clements' proposals decided to use the draft of the instructions to the commander and to the director of the scientific staff to change how the voyage would be conducted and thereby alter the program of the endeavor.

In February 1901 the Joint Committee turned its attention to the two sets of instructions. As drafted and amended, the two documents brought into focus the fundamental conflicts between the two factions. Four main points of contention existed: the goals of the campaign, whether to have a landing party, the wintering of the ship, and the powers of the commander and of the director of the scientific staff. All four points were intertwined, and any change to the orders to either person altered the responsibilities and powers of the other. The whole imbroglio came to a crisis in February 1901. The outcome shaped British Antarctic work for twenty years.

Two divergent goals for the enterprise developed. One part of the Joint Committee, generally the Royal Society members, wanted to focus on scientific study. Those men saw the expedition as a great opportunity for science and had less interest in adventure. For Markham and the RGS, geographical discovery was the cynosure of the project; everything else, including magnetic studies and meteorology, was secondary. Markham's faction included a strong element of Royal Navy enthusiasts who saw this endeavor as a chance to replicate the glories of Arctic exploration of a half century earlier.[14] Markham was the most outspoken of this company, and in his private reminiscences of the expedition he blatantly set out his purpose for it:

Its main object would be the encouragement of maritime enterprise, and to afford opportunities for young naval officers to acquire valuable experiences and to perform deeds of derring-do. The same object would lead to geographical exploration and discovery. Other collateral objects would be the advancement of the sciences of magnetism, oceanography, meteorology, biology, geology; but these are springes to catch woodcocks. The real objects are geographical discovery, and the opportunities for young naval officers to win distinction in time of peace.[15]

The issue was science versus adventure, and both sides were adamant about the rightness of their cause.

Closely associated with these goals was the role of a landing party. If scientific inquiry were to be paramount, establishing an encampment on the continent that could be used as a station for forays inland was essential. Adventure required that the vessel be free to maneuver and explore unimpeded by the necessity of providing shuttle service for the landing party to the continent.

Having the *Discovery* winter would permit further research over the dark months and allow for a larger company to perform experiments and record data. However, keeping the ship for the winter meant that the captain of the vessel would command at the base camp. This created a situation that the scientific contingent, especially Gregory, vigorously opposed.

The entire controversy rested on the relative powers of the commander and the director and what roles each would play. Obviously the navy veterans considered any impediment to the captain's authority an anathema. The opposing camp feared that with the director subservient to a naval officer, science would always be second to adventure. The instructions to the commander and to the chief science officer became the battleground between the two factions.

At the end of January the draft of the commander's instructions outlined Scott's authority and responsibilities. The original version was Markham's work and reflected his approach of listing the goals, leaving the execution to the commander. The guidelines stated that the main purpose was geographical discovery and the gathering of magnetic survey data. The documents made clear that the director was to be under the commander in all respects, although the latter was to observe the scientist's wishes and suggestions. By these terms the relationship of Scott to Gregory was patterned on the roles played by Nares and Thomson aboard the *Challenger* (1872–76). Scott was directed to proceed to the Antarctic coast where he was to use his own discretion whether to spend time seeking a place to encamp or to explore along the Barrier. The commander was left to follow his own judgment regarding wintering ship or landing a party, although Markham's original draft contains a reminder that better work would be accomplished if the ship wintered. While his contemporaries, lacking access to Markham's private thoughts, may have failed to see that Markham intended the ship to winter, without doubt that was his intention.

Markham also wrote the original draft of the instructions to the director of the scientific staff, modeling it after Thomson's directives on the *Challenger*. The document indicated that the scientific director was under the control of the commander who was obliged only to consider the suggestions of the director. One section declared that all journals, logs, and collections remained the property of the two societies and limited the right of the staff to publish its results until six months after the appearance of the official narrative of the voyage. The final paragraph reminded the scientists that they were "cabin passengers joining the expedition at their own risk" and required from each a statement acknowledging that fact.[16]

Gregory returned to England on 5 December 1900 and expressed his reservations about the proposed instructions. He met with Markham to discuss the issue. Gregory reminded Markham that he had written a letter on 19 January 1900 outlining his thoughts about the voyage. Gregory's missive indicated that he favored, among other things, a landing party under the science director's command. Gregory's note was circulated among the members of the Executive Committee. After the missive was read, the committee had cabled Gregory stating, "your letter of 19 January 1900 has been received and approved." Gregory understood this as an acceptance of proposals for a base camp under his control which represented a considerably broader role for him than Markham planned. For his part, Sir Clements later stated that by "accepted" he meant he concurred with those elements in the letter that dealt with matters that were the concern of the director. Markham claimed he did not bind himself on the issue of the landing party as that was out of Gregory's ken, making his opinion of no matter.[17] Markham's disingenuous interpretation stemmed from the old man's ability to reshape his perception of the past.

In January 1901 Gregory submitted to Scott his own version of guidelines for the director. Scott and Markham replied, rejecting the alternate program because the expedition could have only one leader — Scott. Markham wrote Gregory reiterating that he had all along planned a naval expedition and, failing that, opted for an endeavor with personnel and a commander from the Royal Navy. Markham also expressed surprise that Gregory would not accept the same position as that of Thomson on the *Challenger*.[18] The lines now were clearly drawn, with Gregory, backed by Poulton, Geikie, and others in the Royal Society, opposing Markham and his supporters.[19]

Prior to the meeting of 8 February 1901 the Royal Society's representatives to the Joint Committee met to discuss amending the two sets of instructions with the intent of strengthening the civilian director's position. This action was taken in response to Gregory's threats of resignation if changes were not forthcoming. Gregory rallied his associates to the cause of science. The Royal Society contingent, joined by two RGS representatives, met and determined to reconsider two points: wintering the ship and putting the shore party under the command of the science director. A series of amendments was prepared for introduction at the next Joint Committee meeting.[20]

Markham had again presented his view of the situation to the Joint Committee, arguing that Gregory's desire to have control of the routes was impossible. Scott had been appointed to command, and "it would be a breach of faith" to take away that control. Finally, Markham noted, "a divided command is but another name for failure and disaster."[21] At the meeting on 8 February 1901 the Royal Society contingent put its plan into operation when Markham moved to accept instructions to the commander and the director, as approved by the Executive Committee. Geikie declared that he wanted clearer guidelines and moved the adoption of a pre-arranged series of amendments that radically altered the document. The commander was directed to proceed to Antarctica and immediately begin an examination of the coast, from Wood Bay to McMurdo Bay, to find a suitable location for the shore base that would be under the command of Gregory. The members assigned to the encampment were listed. Once the primary objective had been met, Scott was allowed to "turn his attention to exploration," if time permitted, but he was to take care not to risk allowing his vessel to be hindered in its return to warm waters. The guidelines stated emphatically, "in no case is the ship to winter." Alterations to Gregory's orders supported these changes, strengthening his position and noting that the commander was charged with landing Gregory and his staff.[22]

The RGS members fervently objected to the series of amendments, arguing correctly that they represented a complete reversal of policy, and so requested a delay. After a heated debate, the committee agreed to postpone a vote on the changes for four days.[23]

On 12 February 1901, the Royal Society's protagonists renewed their drive to revise both the civilian director's orders and the instructions to the commander. The mood of the 8 February meeting had been boisterous; this subsequent session was rancorous and characterized by personal attacks and rudeness. Geikie again proposed his changes, now supported by Wharton, who originally had opposed a shore party. Representing the RGS, R. Vesey Hamilton riposted by moving an amendment to the amendment that called for a postponement until a study could be made of the impact that a shore base would have on the entire enterprise. Markham's cousin, A. H. Markham, seconded Hamilton's motion, but it failed to muster sufficient support in the ensuing debate, and the proposal failed by a vote of sixteen to six. Resuming the discussion on Geikie's amendments, Hamilton asked Geikie how long it would take to unload the supplies and equipment for an encampment. Geikie did not respond. Sir Clements railed at his colleagues that these alterations would force the ship "to waste all the navigable season in landing Gregory," and then lose a sizable portion of the following summer picking him up again. Markham believed all these measures were being taken, "to give more importance to what [the Royal Society members] called science." [24] Markham may or may not have realized that landing Gregory's party would not severely limit time for exploring, but in the heated argument, Sir Clements cared more for winning the point than accuracy of the details.

Poulton and Markham became involved in an angry debate over the reading to those present of a private letter from Sir Clements. Markham protested and announced that he would leave the room unless Poulton desisted. At that point Geikie shouted, "Then go!" Markham left. Once he was out of the room, the RGS contingent made a feeble effort to delay, but, in the end, Geikie's amendments were carried. Several RGS members joined the Royal Society group to provide a large majority for the proposal. Poulton and Geikie went to meet with Gregory, who had been waiting upstairs. They informed him of the changes made, and Gregory agreed to them. Within two days, he sailed back to Melbourne. The committee at the 12 February meeting had appointed a deputy director, George Murray, to act in Gregory's absence. [25]

In the five days before the next meeting, the Royal Geographical Society's representatives reacted. Markham fumed about the RGS members who had voted for Geikie's amendments, calling them "deserters." Hoskins registered his strong dissent to the actions of the previous meeting by resigning from the Joint Committee. He protested that the Royal Society representatives had met privately and drafted changes that were sprung on the RGS members unexpectedly. Hoskins also expressed grave reservations about Gregory's ability to lead such a party, noting that at the time of the geologist's appointment, no mention had been made of Gregory directing a base camp. Markham vowed not to attend another Joint Committee meeting and informed the RGS of his intent. Markham persuaded the RGS council to pass a resolution stating that any instructions passed at the 12 February gathering would be considered provisional, ostensibly to give the council an opportunity to determine how the subscribers to the fund would react to any changes. By the time the committee met five days later, Gregory had sailed for Australia. At the 19 February meeting the RGS request that any changes be accepted as provisional was approved. Further debate took place on the question of the vessel wintering. Major Leonard Darwin proposed alterations designed to bring about a compromise. These would have given the commander greater opportunity for exploration. Moreover, they granted Gregory responsibility for his own party, which was an attempt to separate the authority of the two leaders. Finally, the language addressing the *Discovery* wintering was to be altered to read, "the ship is not to winter in the Antarctic regions, unless it is unavoidable." Because Poulton, Geikie, and others interpreted this wording as an attempt to undermine Gregory's position, they opposed the plan. The amendments failed.[26]

Another meeting changed the situation again. Behind-the-scenes maneuvering continued. Hamilton followed Hoskins in resigning. Hamilton strongly protested both the changes that had taken place and the way they were instituted. He objected to the procedures that he termed unprecedented. Furthermore, at no point had he been given "any information as to any service Gregory has ever performed to prove his capacity for [leading the shore party]." Hamilton's resignation was prompted by a desire to clear "myself of all responsibility for the appointment of Dr. Gregory."[27] Markham replaced Hamilton and Hoskins with men he could count on to support his viewpoint. Before the next meeting, Geikie was persuaded to support Darwin's proposals "in the interests of peace." When the group met again the debate once more focused on the question of the *Discovery* wintering. One group believed that the safety of the vessel required that it not be allowed to winter. A second faction maintained that unless the ship remained and set up a station, Scott risked losing the chance to accomplish anything significant. The remaining members believed that because Gregory had left England with an understanding of how the voyage would be conducted, those plans should not be reversed. When Darwin proposed his alterations on 5 March 1901 Geikie and several others supported them. Darwin's motions were carried by a large majority. Poulton, Tizard, and Buchanan entered their protest in the minutes. A "final" set of instructions to the commander and to the director of the scientific staff, still allowing Gregory to be leader of the landing party, was approved by the committee.[28]

By March 1901 the situation was rapidly deteriorating. Less than five months before the scheduled departure, the internal division brought on by the bickering of old men threatened to cripple the enterprise. The council of the Royal Society accepted the instructions passed at the 5 March meeting and wrote the RGS council that it "cordially approved" the guidelines, trusting that its counterpart would do the same. Instead, Markham went on the offensive, attacking the instructions in general and Gregory in particular.[29]

In a set of letters to Sir William Huggins (1824–1910), who had replaced Lister as the president of the Royal Society, Markham criticized the instructions approved by the committee. He dismissed the idea that great danger might result from having the vessel establish quarters in Antarctic waters, citing at least nine instances of single ships wintering in the Arctic. He pointed to historical precedent — that the Arctic voyages had wintered and that Ross had intended to do so in the Antarctic in the 1840s had he found a safe harbor. Markham noted that the *Gauss* planned to winter. Citing McClintock, whom he described as "our highest polar authority," Markham erroneously argued that the danger was in traversing the ice pack, not in being beset in the ice. Besides, to Sir Clements, detailed guidelines carried with them potential disaster for the expedition. The "wise custom of the Admiralty in the days of the early Arctic voyages" was to keep instructions general and leave virtually all decisions to the discretion of the captain. Markham reminded Huggins that the Admiralty orders for nineteenth-century Arctic expeditions included the statement: "with the very imperfect knowledge we have, the manner of proceeding to fulfill the object, your destination must be entirely left to your discretion, in the exercise of which we rely on your zeal and skill for the accomplishment, as far as it can be accomplished, of the service on which you are employed."[30]

Tied to this issue was the question of having a separate land-based party. Markham repeated his belief that a limited group could accomplish only a fraction of what the entire ship's company could. A smaller party would be more affected by the loss of men due to ill health and would be hard pressed to gather data when members were exploring inland. Markham avowed that those forays required the presence of a larger group, as the idea of smaller parties using dogs was invalid. Markham again repeated the folly of advocating manhauling over using dogs.[31]

Markham rejected absolutely the idea of using the *Discovery* merely to ferry a group of scientists to the ice and pick them up again the following season. That would severely restrict the opportunities for geographical discovery. He argued that he had raised the money on the basis of exploration and that changing the program now was wrong.[32]

Markham then launched a searing attack on Gregory. A separate base camp meant a divided command, an idea that was almost unprecedented.[33]

Markham suggested that Gregory's purpose was self-aggrandizement. Although Markham had nominated Gregory as director, he had at no point envisioned Gregory being in charge of a separate party. Gregory's scientific achievements notwithstanding, they did not qualify him to lead. Markham even went so far as to suggest that the professor's experiences were limited, noting that he had never had command of "white men." [34] Finally, Markham summed up by writing:

My impression is that Dr. Gregory is very reckless and impulsive, and of an exceedingly nervous temperament. His health has been impaired by tropical fevers. I do not wish to dwell further on this point, but my conclusion is that these are the very worst qualities for the leader of a Polar wintering party; where solid judgment, sound sense, and, above all, a perfectly sound constitution are essentials. I consider Dr. Gregory to be unfit to have charge of the lives and safety of men for a long period of time under exceptionally difficult and trying circumstances of which he has had no previous experience. I, therefore, cannot take any share of responsibility for placing him in command of a landing party. [35]

The councils were deadlocked. The RGS refused to allow Markham to sign the two sets of instructions on the grounds that the money had been raised for other purposes than those stated therein. Furthermore, the current orders prevented significant geographical exploration. The council repeated its opposition to a small, independent shore station. [36]

An informal meeting between representatives of the two societies paved the way for a compromise. The RGS visitors were Markham, McClintock, and Sir George Goldie (1846–1925), the man most responsible for solving the problem. [37] The two groups decided the instructions should be reconsidered. To avoid returning the issue to the Joint Committee, the councils decided to create a Select Committee comprising three members nominated by each society. The Royal Society nominees were Lord Lister, Lord Lindley, and A. B. Kempe, the treasurer of the Royal Society; all were non-experts and were expected to review the evidence without bias. The Royal Geographical Society nominated Goldie, McClintock, and G. Sutherland Mackenzie.

The Select Committee first met on 26 April 1901. It soon became apparent that everything hinged on the question of the wintering of the ship and, in particular, how this decision would affect the safety of the crew. According to Markham, Goldie, whom Markham called "the pilot who weathered the storm," [38] intended all along to steer the conference in this direction. At the 30 April meeting the six men concluded: "owing to our very imperfect knowledge of the conditions which prevail in the Antarctic seas, we cannot pronounce definitely whether it will be necessary for the ship to winter or not."[39] Prevented by insufficient evidence from making a final decision, the committee declared that it would have to be the commander's judgment once he was in the Antarctic. The six men believed that the need for a single authority on the expedition was paramount. Once that was settled the question of selecting a landing site was entirely dependent on whether the vessel wintered. The issue of possible dual leadership evaporated. With the ship as a winter station, clearly there could be no higher authority than the captain.

As soon as these decisions were reached, the Select Committee directed George Murray to cable Gregory to inform him of these changes in the commander's orders and ascertain the director's reactions. Murray's cable contained the gist of the changes, and he added at the end a personal note, "strongly advise acceptance." Murray's effort was to no avail. Gregory's reply stated, "No decline accepting responsibility for scientific work of expedition under altered instructions."[40] The committee was uncertain what Gregory meant, so Murray sent another message asking for clarification.[41] Gregory's second response left no doubt, "Cable meant committee having altered conditions my provisional acceptance lapses and connection with the expedition ends."[42]

With Gregory removed from the scene, the Select Committee found it easier to agree on the two sets of instructions. Essentially, the six men restored the original guidelines that were written by Markham in 1897 and approved by the Executive Committee in January 1901.

Gregory's resignation caused an outcry from his supporters and those who backed his version of the endeavor. Poulton wrote a lengthy letter that was printed in the 23 May 1901 issue of *Nature*. In it he emphasized the fears he and others had that, with Gregory's resignation, science would give way to adventure.[43] Poulton was right. If one looks at the British involvement in Antarctica in the Heroic Era and concludes that it twice took a wrong turn, this episode was one of those two false steps. Markham had had his way.[44]

The old navy hands had triumphed — the *Discovery* was to be an imitation of their visions of the mid-nineteenth-century Arctic expeditions. That victory assured survival of the old naval thinking, planning, and practices. One effective result was the ascendancy of manhauling, a decision that led to the tragic death of Scott and his companions in a bitter cold March twelve years hence.

The major hurdles crossed, Markham was able to carry other decisions in committee. George Murray, Gregory's replacement as director of the scientific staff, was in Markham's mind, "our good man."[45] Scott's authority was left unchallenged. Indeed, Murray only journeyed part way out with the *Discovery* and never approached the ice.

The British contribution to the great Antarctic expeditions from 1901 to 1904 was made ready. The *Discovery* was launched at Dundee on 21 March 1901 and prepared to sail in August. After ten years of planning and scheming, Markham stood on the deck of the *Discovery* as it steamed into its berth at the East India Docks in June 1901. He had triumphed after all.

4

From the East India Docks

Robert Falcon Scott paced the decks of the *Discovery* on 31 July 1901, waiting to give the order to cast off lines and begin his voyage to the south
polar regions.[1] Surveying the scene at the East India Docks that summer,
Scott might well have reflected on the events of the past few months — of
the issues and solutions that had brought him to this point. Before the *Discovery* departed, important problems had to be solved. In the weeks before
sailing, Scott had had to answer questions related to the ship itself, supplies, equipment, and staffing.

The ship that Scott paced, first a concept and now a reality, began, like
the voyage itself, in the mind of Sir Clements Markham, who was determined from the beginning to have a purpose-built vessel. As the expedition was taking shape at the end of the nineteenth century, Markham had
decided to construct the first ship specially built in Great Britain for research. He surveyed ports in Britain and Norway looking for whaling ve-
hicles but found none to his liking, despite the existence of some potential
craft.[2] Privately, Markham conceded that one could buy a suitable vessel
merely to make the round-trip to the Antarctic, but that was not Markham's wish or goal.

Markham began preparations for the construction of a vessel specifically
designed for polar work before the Joint Committee assumed responsibility for the expedition. The committee endorsed Markham's opinion that
no suitable craft existed and that one would have to be built, a questionable decision as whaling vessels, capable of undertaking the voyage, existed
and could have been purchased.[3] Markham was determined to have a new
ship, purpose-built, and his view prevailed. Markham gathered his Arctic
cronies to discuss the design of the *Discovery*. Not surprisingly, the barque
bore more resemblance to the mid-nineteenth-century British vessels that

had plied Arctic waters, than it did to the designs of Colin Archer, whose creations such as the *Fram* incorporated the more modern features of polar ships.[4]

As Markham believed, incorrectly, that the dangers of being crushed by the ice were less severe in the Antarctic than in the Arctic, the design did not incorporate the more rounded hull of the *Fram*.[5] This decision contributed to the eventual besetting of the *Discovery* for two winters. Bruce, who observed both the *Gauss* and the *Discovery* during and after their construction, commented that though both were similar in outward appearance, inside, the German ship much more resembled the *Fram*. Bruce suggested that the British vessel seemed the more seaworthy of the two, but the *Gauss* appeared to be more iceworthy.[6] The plans for the *Discovery* were approved in June 1899, and the contract was awarded to the Dundee Shipbuilding Company on 26 January 1900.[7]

During the fourteen months of construction a few minor difficulties arose, but the real problems with the steamer appeared only after launching. That more difficulties did not occur was due in part to Scott's decision to send Reginald Skelton, the ship's engineer, to Dundee to oversee the building. Moreover, at various times both Armitage and George Murray, who had been appointed deputy to Gregory in February 1901, went to Dundee to lend a hand, coordinating aspects of construction related to the scientific program.[8] Scott's steady correspondence to Skelton showed both concern and good insight into the potential problems with the vessel. Together, Skelton and Scott mediated the design flaws.[9]

From its trial run the ship proved to be a poor sailor. Coal consumption was greater than anticipated, and the *Discovery* had difficulty in beating to windward. Moreover, it leaked badly, forcing substantial repairs. In July 1901, before leaving Dundee for England, the vessel was put into dry dock for alterations, which were unsuccessful. Later, en route to Antarctica, water in the hold irreparably damaged a significant percentage of the provisions, necessitating costly replacement. During the New Zealand stop, the barque was again repaired not once, but twice, and at that time investigation uncovered a number of flaws not corrected during production at Dundee.[10]

The *Discovery* was rigged as a barque and painted black with yellow masts and funnel with white boats emblazoned with a single "D" in black and gold, highlighting the profile of the ship. The 1,620-ton *Discovery* was 198 feet long (172 at the waterline) and 34 feet abeam.[11] The engines, with 570 indicated horsepower, were coal fired, and planners expected the vessel to sail much of the time to save fuel. All the water could be drained easily from the engines to prevent freezing.[12] Solidly built to withstand the pressures of the ice, the ribs were of English oak (grown in Scotland) and placed very closely together to provide maximum strength. Two outer layers approximately twenty-six inches thick covered the sides of the barque, one of oak, the other of greenheart, a wood so tough that it withstood the glancing blows of the ice.[13] The main yard had a strong block for dredging work. The stern incorporated a new feature to protect a portion of the ship — both rudder and screw could be detached from place and brought up into the vessel.[14] The bow was particularly strong, essentially eleven feet of slow-grown, carefully chosen Scottish oak and ironwood, which allowed the ship to act as an icebreaker.[15] Similar to whalers of the day, the *Discovery* had no portholes.[16] To guard against the cold, a sheet of asbestos was placed between two layers of wood, and the underside of the deck was similarly sheathed in asbestos.[17]

Because terrestrial magnetism was to be an important part of the scientific investigations undertaken, Markham consulted Captain E. W. Creak, a leading authority on terrestrial magnetism, regarding the demands that such research imposed on the design. Creak suggested several improvements to facilitate magnetic observations.

Special care was taken to ensure that no iron was used within thirty feet of the observatory on deck. The builders used rolled naval brass where metal was needed within the protected area. The iron-free area encompassed part of the officers' wardroom, which explained why some cabin beds had metal springs while others did not. Care was taken to prevent even a steel key in the pockets of the scientists. All these precautions were to safeguard the magnetic studies. As one journalist suggested, "It is a coy love this magnetic pole in whose quest the knights of ocean are to sail. She must be wooed in a wooden ship."[18] Despite these precautions, some observations were tainted, as the scientists later realized that the bird cage in the part of the wardroom that was within the metal-free zone was iron.[19]

The ship was registered under the Merchant Shipping Act of 1894.[20] The vessel cost £51,000 (including the engines), a staggering figure representing more than half the money raised by the time the *Discovery* departed.[21] Considering what Scott might have accomplished had he had more time to sail and explore, the expense might have been justified. As events developed, the ship did little exploration, and the steep price was questionable. Several contemporaneous expeditions achieved significant results using old whaling vessels. Because the *Discovery* on this inaugural voyage did little more than ferry the staff down and back to Antarctica, the *Discovery* was an expensive fop to Sir Clements's desire to construct anew the nineteenth-century experiences of the Royal Navy.

Early in the discussion of a national Antarctic expedition, two ships were considered essential, not only to carry out the work of the endeavor but for safety. Had Markham purchased two whalers (for far less than the *Discovery* cost) he could have used the second as a relief vessel, within the budget of the expedition. In the long run the failure of the *Discovery* expedition to live within its means brought drastically different and most unpleasant results than Markham anticipated. Building an expensive ship had long-term effects both on the expedition and on future polar exploration.

Moreover, the decisions made regarding the vessel evidently played a vital role in answering the question central to the planning of the expedition — what was to be the relationship of science and adventure. The *Discovery* did more than house the men; its eventual fate in the ice did more than merely confine the ship's company to a narrow field of research. In the end the decision to build the *Discovery* defined not only the physical space in which the men labored; it defined the expedition itself, an endeavor in which, at a critical moment in the planning — in this case the decision to build the *Discovery* — adventure triumphed over science.

The *Discovery* had been brought down to London after trial runs supervised by Royds and arrived at the East India Dock on 6 June 1901.[22]

If the ship represented Markham's idealized vision of the past, the commander, Robert Falcon Scott, embodied Sir Clements's hopes for the future. The president of the RGS had wanted a naval officer to direct the largely naval expedition, and Scott was Markham's choice to lead.

As the ship prepared to sail, Scott was thirty-three years old and had been a naval lieutenant at the time he was chosen to lead the endeavor. He was a career naval officer by training and was promoted to commander on 30 June 1900.[23] To what degree his naval career had languished and how that affected his desire to seek the appointment to the *Discovery* are questions worth investigating. Both Huntford and A. G. E. Jones believe that Scott's career was not advancing well and that Scott believed the proposed expedition would help his progress.[24]

Scott was a handsome man, about five feet nine inches tall, who could be extremely charming when the need arose. Scott charmed his second-in-command, Armitage, when they met,[25] and Scott easily succeeded in persuading Markham to choose him as the leader and as the single man who would shoulder Markham's polar ambitions. At the same time, Scott's training as a naval officer developed in him a tendency to make decisions autonomously, and to place less value on the opinion of non-Royal Navy personnel. He could be quick-tempered and was not above holding a grudge.[26] Scott allowed no one to challenge openly his authority, and some have argued that he had no desire to have anyone on his expedition who dared rival him or who could make a claim to authority by virtue of the strength of his personality.[27]

Also busy on the docks was the second-in-command, Albert Armitage. The contrasts between Armitage and Scott were noteworthy. Armitage had a good deal of experience with ships under sail; Scott did not. Armitage had had three years of polar work; Scott had none.[28]

When Armitage returned from the Jackson-Harmsworth expedition he was awarded the Murchison medal for his efforts on that voyage. After this endeavor Armitage stayed in touch with Markham, and they appear to have been on friendly terms, because Armitage asked Markham to be the godfather of his child.[29]

As Armitage strode on the deck of the *Discovery* in August 1901, he may well have considered his appointment to be independent from Scott's and that a shore party would be under his command. Given the decision that had already formed in Markham's mind regarding the wintering of the ship, Armitage's assumptions in 1901 seemed unreal. Although questions about his role in the venture lay in the future, for the present Armitage was enormously helpful in preparing the *Discovery* for departure. Markham and Scott depended heavily on Armitage in the last months before sailing, relying on the experiences the second-in-command gained in the Arctic on the Jackson-Harmsworth expedition. Armitage's suggestions were wide ranging — how to package provisions, what types of tents and sledges to use, even the amount of sugar to budget — because he noted that men in the Arctic used more than expected.[30] On all matters, including tobacco consumption (figured at a pound and a half per man per month), underwear (Jaeger), or choosing buttons for trousers, Armitage's recent practical experience brought polar insights to the expedition.[31]

Armitage was correct in his expectations that Fridtjof Nansen, the greatest polar explorer of his day, would lend his expertise to the venture. The Norwegian gave assistance to his fellow explorers when Scott's men were in Scandinavia and advised by letter on other issues. Nansen helped with the selection of furs, skis, sledges, and cookers, the latter two of Nansen's own design.[32]

On one matter of importance for later developments in the Heroic Era,

Armitage shared Markham's dislike of using dogs for transport and agreed with Markham as to the "cruelty of their use."[33] Still, Armitage believed that some dogs should be taken.[34]

Considering the amount of work Armitage undertook to prepare the expedition to set sail in August 1901, Markham chose Scott's second-in-command well. The other polar veteran, Reginald Koettlitz, may have had similar experiences — he was with Armitage on the Jackson-Harmsworth expedition — but he possessed neither the personality nor credibility to command the degree of influence with Markham and Scott that Armitage did.[35]

However, Koettlitz, as appointed medical officer, did play an important role in getting the provisions ready. He inspected all the tinned foods and insisted that frugality regarding staples was not a wise virtue. Koettlitz's previous experience allowed him to suggest specific firms for items such as tobacco (two shillings a pound) and boots.[36]

Shortly before sailing, the expedition found itself without a physicist. Originally, the position was offered to a Professor Pollack of Sydney, but he declined the opportunity. His replacement, William Simpson, failed an Admiralty medical exam.[37]

A third choice, William Shackleton, no relation to Ernest Shackleton, was appointed in his place. William Shackleton had previous polar experience, having served as physicist on Sir George Baden-Powell's expedition to Novaya Zemlya in 1896.[38] William Shackleton began work on the expedition, helping with the preparations but then, suddenly, was dismissed. Bad teeth was the official reason given for his firing. Shackleton responded angrily, noting that his teeth were fine; moreover, he was the only officer whose teeth had been examined.[39] Additionally, the record shows that suggestions were made that he did not get along with his fellow officers. However, William Shackleton claimed that he got along well with his fellow officers, citing specifically Hodgson and Ernest Shackleton and called his dismissal "hypocritical."[40]

Although it was impossible to determine for certain, William Shackleton's dismissal may have been prompted by his support for the ideas of J. W. Gregory. Gregory had urged him to fight for science on the voyage, continuing the argument of science versus adventure. Though differences between William Shackleton and both Royds and Armitage over scientific policy existed, the official statement of the RGS cited the physicist's teeth as the only official reason for his departure. William Shackleton briefly protested his mistreatment, noting that he had been hired by the chief of the scientific staff and now had been fired by Scott, the commander. Because the post of chief of the scientific staff had been effectively eliminated, the physicist seemed unlikely to succeed in his petition to remain. Scott was adamant: "Shackleton's dismissal is final and his appointment will not be reconsidered."[41] Although Shackleton threatened to contact an attorney the matter was closed.

Lacking a physicist so close to the expedition's departure, the Executive Committee turned to a veteran of Borchgrevink's *Southern Cross*. That effort was vilified by Markham, who refused to profit from that pioneering effort, but the animosity that Markham felt toward the commander was not directed to his staff. Scott, taking a lead from his mentor, rarely referred to Borchgrevink by name. The *Southern Cross* physicist Louis Bernacchi was described by Scott as having gained experience on the Sir George Newnes expedition, referring to the voyage by the name of its patron rather than its leader. Nor was Bernacchi likely to promote Borchgrevink, as their relationship had not been good.[42]

Returning from the *Southern Cross* voyage, Bernacchi had worked at the Royal Society preparing for publication the magnetic data from Cape Adare. He kept close ties to the RGS and was the first person to speak to that society on the Great Ice Barrier, as the Ross Ice Shelf was then known.[43] His diligence impressed the Royal Society members, and he was awarded the Cuthbert Peek Grant by the RGS for his work in the south polar regions. Still, Bernacchi was the fourth choice as physicist.[44]

Shortly after receiving his appointment Bernacchi surprised his family with the news one evening at dinner. His father, a polar enthusiast, commenting on the forthcoming *Discovery* expedition, said to his son, "I bet you would like to be going with it." Bernacchi replied, "I *am* going with her."[45]

Two years earlier Bernacchi, while sitting in the *Southern Cross* hut at Cape Adare, had written in his diary: "Ah well. We are not sorry to leave this gelid, desolate spot, our place of abode for so many dreary months! May I never pass another 12 months in similar surroundings and conditions."[46] But the South continued to have a hold on Bernacchi as it has had on so many others. Thus, despite his earlier statement, he found himself preparing for a second visit.[47]

Bernacchi was not the only last-minute appointment to the *Discovery*, as H. R. Mill was invited to go as far as Madeira to help instruct members of the staff on issues related to oceanographic and meteorological data gathering. Mill never crossed the Antarctic Circle, but as a friend to generations of Antarctic heroes and as the principal historian of the south polar regions in his era, Mill was an ideal choice to be added to the *Discovery* staff.

Born in 1861, H. R. Mill earned his doctorate in science in inorganic chemistry at Edinburgh. He became librarian of the RGS in 1892 and thus found himself at the center of the planning for Markham's great national Antarctic expedition. This continued even beyond Mill's resignation from the RGS in 1900 to pursue a career with the British Rainfall Organization.[48] Before 1901 Mill had written extensively about polar history, and although Markham may have written more on that subject, Mill's accounts were devoid of the partisan politics that marred much of the RGS president's work.[49]

For the three decades after the *Discovery* expedition Mill continued to write about Antarctic affairs, most especially the history of exploration in his lifetime. His *Siege of the South Pole*, published in 1905, immediately assumed a place in polar literature from which even a century of writing has not displaced it. Mill's history remains the best account of Antarctica to 1890.

The basis of Mill's knowledge was his firsthand dealings with all the British and most of the non-British explorers of his day. The correspondence of Scott, Shackleton, Bruce, Armitage, Borchgrevink, Bernacchi, Charcot, and Nansen attest to their appreciation of his contributions and kindnesses. Scott went so far as to call him a "trump card."[50] In these early *Discovery* days, Shackleton and Mill established a friendship that lasted until the former's death. Their common love of poetry first brought them together. Later in life Shackleton thanked Mill for always being "one of my strongest supporters."[51] Shackleton often confided in the older man and frequently sought his advice and counsel. Shackleton later wrote that Mill was "my polar mentor for many years."[52]

In 1892 Mill played an important role in securing scientific equipment for the Dundee whalers and drew up a "valuable set of instructions for naturalists."[53] Mill helped secure places for the two surgeons, one of whom was William S. Bruce. Mill arranged instruments, books, and advice in an attempt to use the whaling voyage to advance the cause of science.[54]

Mill served as an intermediary in these early Heroic Era days and recommended Bruce for the Jackson-Harmsworth expedition. When C. E. Borchgrevink was readying his staff for his *Southern Cross* expedition, the Anglo-Norwegian asked Mill's help in securing scientists and particularly wished Mill would help persuade W. S. Bruce to join that endeavor. Mill suggested that Bruce write Borchgrevink regarding the appointment, and Mill worked hard to secure the Scot's potential contributions to the voyage. At one point, through Mill, Borchgrevink offered to put Bruce in charge of the proposed Cape Adare field site but then reneged on the offer.[55]

Virtually alone of the RGS circle, Mill braved Markham's animosity to be at the docks to see Borchgrevink off, offering a toast to the success of the voyage.[56] For this action Mill was severely criticized by Markham. After the *Southern Cross* returned, when Borchgrevink found himself embroiled in controversy and out of favor with Markham, Mill urged the Anglo-Norwegian to see the RGS president in an attempt to reach a compromise.[57]

Mill tried to help Bruce in the latter's attempt to join the *Discovery* expedition and offered fatherly advice to the younger, unworldly Bruce on how to handle Markham.[58] Later, Mill introduced Bruce to his principal benefactor of the Scottish National Antarctic expedition (1902–4), Andrew Coats.[59]

In the same vein Mill contributed to the preparations for the *Discovery*, helping to secure instruments from the Admiralty when Markham's efforts were stymied.[60] Mill wrote the bibliography for the *Antarctic Manual*, based on his superb bibliographical work at the RGS library.[61]

Mill never visited the polar regions except in his mind. But the memory of Mill's kindness and consideration was carried in the hearts of men who went to the farthest corners of the earth. For all this Mill was an ideal choice as a last-minute addition to the *Discovery*. No one deserved more than Mill the title, "friend to heroes."[62]

Although Mill was well thought of, Scott was not without foes, even this late into the venture. His qualifications were still being criticized in June, less than eight weeks before departure. In the 20 June 1901 issue of *Nature* the principal issues were noted. Scott had no training or experience as a naturalist, was devoid of polar experience, and gave no indication of any expertise in geology or glacial problems.[63]

In the weeks leading up to the departure of the expedition, criticism continued to mount over the failure of the *Discovery* to include in its crew an ice master, someone well experienced with the extremely dangerous task of guiding a ship among ice floes. This lack caused some of the British with the most service in ice conditions — Dundee whaling captains — to be skeptical of the success of the venture.[64] A practiced ice master could take the ship where a less experienced person would not dare to venture. One whaling master interviewed by the *Pall Mall Gazette* indicated that Armitage had gained no real familiarity with navigating a large ship such as the *Discovery* through ice fields during the Jackson-Harmsworth expedition. On that voyage Captain Brown, a whaler from Peterhead, Scotland, had taken the *Windward* to the expedition's base and then returned to guide its crew back to civilization.[65] Moreover, an experienced ice master might see conditions in the ice that could indicate the likelihood of a suitable safe harbor, one likely to be free of ice each year.

The official counter to these charges came from Markham, who explained that an ice master had been taken on the 1875 Arctic expedition and had been "practically useless."[66] Moreover, he asserted that any skill that one really needed to have could be acquired by a knowledgeable naval commander in a matter of weeks.[67] In addition, Markham noted that among the men were four Dundee whalers and that Armitage had considerable service in ice conditions.[68]

Despite Markham's refutations an appointment may have been offered, but if so it was refused, because the ice master, given the rigid class separation of the Royal Navy, would have been required to mess with the warrant officers rather than with the officers and gentlemen in the wardroom.[69]

Despite this criticism and the relative lack of experience that Armitage had commanding in ice conditions (how much value can be attached to the able-bodied seamen with experience cannot be determined), the *Discovery* sailed without an ice master. In fairness to Markham, given the small amount of actual exploring done by the ship as the expedition turned out, the lack of an ice master did not handicap the voyage unless an ice master could have foreseen difficulties in the location of the winter quarters of the *Discovery*.

On 31 July the *Discovery* pushed away from the East India Dock in London and proceeded down the Thames.[70] The vessel was still not completely shipshape. Geese and sheep were housed on deck, and some last-minute detail work on the cabins remained undone.[71] A photograph of the *Discovery* and crew on the eve of departure depicts them all in what appear to be naval uniforms. The RN personnel were indeed in uniform, special permission having been given by the Admiralty. Interestingly, non-naval men such as Wilson, Armitage, and Shackleton were in outfits that, though not regulation, were designed to imitate Markham's desire for an all-naval voyage.

Aboard were many dignitaries, including Markham, Keltie, and Goldie (who brought along his daughter).[72] From London the ship proceeded to Gravesend and Greenhithe, then to Portsmouth. Along the route, at various points, friends and relatives bade farewell to their loved ones and departed the vessel. Although the *Discovery* hoped to proceed to Cowes with little ceremony, all along the route many of the craft that plied the Thames saluted the southward-bound barque, and the blue ensign "had to be dipped unceasingly."[73] Wilson, newly married, left the ship so that the young zoologist could spend the last few days with his young bride.[74] The *Discovery* proceeded to Cowes where a special visitor was scheduled to tour the ship.

King Edward VII and Queen Alexandra and a small entourage came aboard to inspect the barque. Markham had arranged the visit to lend the royal cachet to his endeavor. Edward VII's entourage was at Cowes for the annual yachting event and on 6 August was joined by Queen Alexandra and several others to tour the ship. Markham introduced Scott and his officers, and both royal personages asked questions about the proposed voyage and the vessel. During the tour the king must have been amused to see the grog tub, which was inscribed with the words, "God Save The King."[75] During the brief stay a minor disaster was narrowly avoided when the queen's dog fell overboard but was quickly rescued by one of the sailors. On a lighter note, Alexandra was amused when one of the sailors forgot his place and addressed her as "Miss."[76] The king bestowed on Scott the Victorian Order, Fourth Class, the presentation momentarily delayed as the corpulent monarch had some difficulty recovering the award from his pocket.[77] The king addressed the officers and crew, noting that he had often visited warships setting out on important missions, but this occasion was different: "You are starting on a mission of peace and for the advancement of knowledge. The results of your labours will be valuable not only to your country but to the whole civilised world." He added that he wished them well and hoped that they would all return "safe and well."[78] The king and his party then returned to the royal yacht *Osborne*. Only then was it discovered that the cases of champagne and of whiskey brought aboard from the king's yacht had been overlooked and not opened. The *Discovery* prepared for the unknown South, with the unopened cases of spirits safely in the hold.[79]

What were the goals to which the king alluded? Clearly, terrestrial magnetism was a primary concern, to continue the work of Ross from the 1840s and to gather data that would lead to safer shipping routes in southern oceans. For commercial shipping to take advantage of more direct routes in high latitudes such information was essential.[80] Meteorological studies similarly had practical application. Lingering questions about Ross's Great Ice Barrier (Ross Ice Shelf) begged answers; to solve the mysteries of that immense block of ice as large as France was important. Other studies related to tides, investigations in geology and glaciology, formed another part of the goals of the expedition. International cooperation with other contemporaneous expeditions was a priority. However, geographical discovery was closest to Markham's heart, and great hopes were held that vast new lands in the uncharted continent would be found.

With the ship about to depart England a terribly important question remained. Were the various goals of the voyage going to be met given the limited time and opportunities? Many, such as Professor Poulton, feared that the expedition would sacrifice science to geographical exploration, yet the scientific objectives were clearly delineated. Still, three years would have to pass before the question of science versus adventure could be answered definitively.

The expedition that made its way south into the Atlantic in early August was formed in Markham's image. Sir Clements wanted the *Discovery* to be molded in the tradition of nineteenth-century British Arctic expeditions. Cynically, one might say that to be in their image was to ignore physical realities, to fail to learn the lessons of other explorers, to maneuver the expedition into a helpless situation or condition, and to bring oneself to a point where one cannot extricate oneself without the help of others. This assessment does contain an element of truth and forms part of the framework within which Scott and his companions operated.

5

From England to Cape Town

The blue ensign of the *Discovery* flapped in the breeze as the ship departed English waters on the evening of 6 August 1901 en route to Madeira and Cape Town.[1] As the lights of England faded in the distance the great national Antarctic expedition that Markham had dreamed of was steaming southward.

The proposed route of the voyage was from England to Madeira, and then on to Cape Town. From there the ship was to proceed to Melbourne to gather supplies and staff. The schedule called for the ship to arrive at Madeira by 15 August and at Cape Town by 25 September. The voyage to Melbourne would take until 14 November. Markham hoped that while in Melbourne the governments of Australia (the various regions were not yet unified into a single entity) would contribute money to the expedition. Scott expected to arrive in Lyttelton, the port of Christchurch, New Zealand, by 1 December and depart for the ice by 10 December 1901.[2]

Of the people aboard, one was scheduled to travel only as far as Melbourne. George Murray, who sailed as the director of the Civilian Staff, had been involved with the expedition since his appointment as deputy to J. W. Gregory in 12 February 1901. Murray had edited the *Antarctic Manual* and had overseen matters related to the scientific staff during Gregory's absences in Australia. When Gregory resigned, Murray assumed many of his duties.

Murray was a man of strong opinions and did not wait long after succeeding Gregory to express them most forcefully to Markham and Professor Poulton, one of the leading Royal Society figures, who had been a keen supporter of Gregory and the RS approach to the expedition emphasizing scientific inquiry. Murray soon found himself embroiled in the controversies that plagued the voyage before departure. At one point he declared that he wished he had stayed at the British Museum rather than get involved with the affair.[3] Murray complained of Markham's handling of the details of the endeavor, especially in areas in which the RGS president had little or no expertise. In time Murray foresaw the eventual outcome of the expedition, when he indicated his fear that "that ridiculous person would make a mess of the expedition."[4] On another occasion, exasperated with the old man's machinations, Murray thought that the best solution to Sir Clements's interference was to send him on the expedition.[5] Murray saw Markham's good and bad qualities and had hoped that the Royal Society would stand up to the old man,[6] but Poulton was not seen as likely to withstand the efforts of the RGS president. Moreover, the acting director believed that Poulton was "a first class ass."[7] Murray's hope of a counterbalance to Markham was tempered by a genuine, though at times begrudging, admiration for the old man. At least Markham, Murray noted, was a man — the rest on the Joint Committee were mere "invertebrates." Fighting Markham was not the answer; guiding him was.[8]

Murray had acerbic remarks for the whole idea of a committee directing the expedition. Once he joined the staff, and with Scott assigned more control of affairs, the two worked quickly to solve problems that would have taken the committee weeks of effort. Playing on words, Murray described the situation before he and Scott took things in hand as "disjointed." Nor had Gregory been immune to Murray's criticism, and even before the former resigned, Murray found Gregory's suggestions from Australia tiresome. Murray perceived many of the scientific director's suggestions as unnecessary, having often anticipated them and handled the situation better than Gregory would have done. Fortunately, Murray's initial impression of Scott was as a fine organizer and a "good chap."[9]

The *Discovery* was not Murray's first cruise. He had sailed on the *Oceana* in 1898 on a dredging voyage that gave him a little experience of the sea.[10] On the outbound voyage on Scott's ship Murray organized the routine of the scientists. Murray fulfilled the same role regarding the scientists that Lieutenant Royds did toward the officers and men — he was the one who made things run smoothly under Scott's overall command. Murray gave lectures on the voyage and encouraged the other scientists to do the same. Among the duties his status afforded him was to read the lesson at Sunday divine services.

Almost immediately after departing England the scientific work began. By the second day the tow netting equipment had been put into use, and from that point until Cape Town, trawling became a regular activity of the vessel. The *Discovery* was fitted with a large reel on which five miles of cable was wound, with a strong winch attached, to haul in the trawl and its contents.[11] These endeavors did not meet with great success. Handicapped by a lack of expertise with the apparatus, many of the early attempts resulted in the loss of the line or some other mishap. So common were the problems that when one of the exercises was completed without a hitch, the success was noted as unusual.[12] The difficulties associated with deep-sea work were caused by the inexperience of the scientific staff, even with George Murray aboard. Apart from Murray no one aboard had ever taken a deep-sea sounding. Murray had predicted problems more than a year earlier, suggesting that there would be "a pretty bill for breakages."[13]

From the outset the ship was found to be a poor sailer. Both in terms of speed and handling Markham's prize proved troublesome. The *Discovery*'s weight contributed to its sluggishness. One observer described the vessel as "a perfect dead weight" and suggested that it needed twice the spread of canvas to move at any real pace. The *Discovery* showed a lack of grace in maneuvering and would not sail close to the wind. The lack of speed meant that the expedition had trouble keeping to its schedule, which caused problems later. And the ship rolled! Aside from the problems related to seasickness — the crew adjusted, although Koettlitz continued to suffer most in this regard — most hands reported some degree of discomfort from the buffeting the ship took. The rolling of the ship meant that china, books, instruments, and people were likely to be thrown about in heavy seas. At one point in the voyage to Cape Town, Wilson noted in his diary that, despite heavy seas, nothing broke, because everything had already been broken. One advantage of the ship's stiffness was that the captain did not need to shorten the sails no matter how violent the storm.[14]

The vessel was handsomely appointed, and both officers and men enjoyed excellent quarters. The former were lodged in cabins that opened on to the wardroom, which became the center of activity for the officers and scientists, who were considered officers and gentlemen for the purposes of the expedition. Mahogany was used throughout the wardroom and cabins, each of which was furnished with a bed, chest of drawers, cupboard, writing table, and a place for books. The wardroom housed a pianola (a type of player piano), which was a gift from a Dundee lady. Included with the instrument were more than one hundred pieces of music. The wardroom was heated by a series of pipes, one of which ran up to the upper deck and drew in air from outside. The air was heated by passing it through the stove in the wardroom and then circulated into the room itself.[15]

One problem with the wardroom was its location — directly above one of the coal bunkers — which meant that coal dust constantly was wafting up through the floor, causing discomfort to the inhabitants.

In keeping with class distinctions of the late nineteenth century, warrant officers were housed separately and had fairly comfortable quarters. The men's living area, however, was not stylishly furnished, but the mess deck had the advantage of being warmer than the wardroom in the winter.[16] The men's lives were organized around their mess — the men worked and ate together. Their quarters, though small, were made more spacious by the use of hammocks for sleeping. These items could be put away during the day to allow maximum free space for the crew.

Class differences were evident in other ways as well. Though the food was the same for officers and men, the quality of the silverware was noticeably nicer in the wardroom. The officer's housing area was also equipped with cloth napkins and fine table linen. Servants waited on the officers, and the standard of living was significantly higher.

A small hospital was included but rarely used during the voyage. Class distinctions did not limit access to the library, and both officers and men took advantage of the fine selection of books aboard. The thousand volumes were stored in the wardroom, officer's cabins, and the forecastle, as no separate room for a library had been included in the ship's plans. Many volumes were donated by publishers and included treatises on polar exploration as well as a fine selection of literature. One visitor's eye noted a prominent place for Jules Verne's "An Antarctic Mystery." In this period before the First World War, one common bond that bridged the gap between the classes was poetry. The two classes, officers and men, still read the same poets and authors. The education level of the mess deck occupants was not equal to that of the wardroom residents, but some of the bluejackets showed not only considerable breadth of literary taste but also some real promise as writers, as the ship's magazine would prove.[17]

Salaries were another indication of the differences between the officers and men. Scott received an annual salary of £500, Armitage £450, Koettlitz, £400, and Wilson £200. Among the men (most of whom also drew their pay from the navy) the salaries ranged from Warrant Officer J. H. Dellbridge's £69 7 and Petty Officer Edgar Evans's £41 1 to £27 7 for the seamen.[18]

The galley, designed to provide extra heat for the interior of the ship during the winter, unintentionally also added some smoke. Behind the galley was a large tank for melting snow for the ship's water while in the polar regions. In addition, a distilling apparatus that converted salt water to fresh-water supplied the crew and laboratories when the ship was at sea.[19]

Man was not alone onboard. Scott had his terrier with him en route to New Zealand, while the crew had a small kitten as a pet. Wearing a small "Discovery" ribbon like those worn on the sailor's caps, the cat was a popular addition to the ship.[20]

A temporary wardroom guest was H. R. Mill, who was seen by all as a welcome addition to the staff.[21] Scott credited Mill and J. Scott Keltie with doing so much for the expedition before sailing,[22] and now Mill was aboard as an acknowledged authority on oceanography and meteorology. George Murray asked him to accompany the ship as far as Madeira, to organize the oceanographic and chemical work.[23] In addition, Mill was to help train Hartley Travers Ferrar (1879–1932), whose last-minute appointment as geologist was an attempt to replace the skills lost to the expedition with the departure of J. W. Gregory.[24] Ferrar had arrived at the *Discovery* on 23 July 1901.[25]

Ferrar, twenty-two at the outset of the voyage, had been born in Ireland but had spent much of his early life in South Africa. Educated first at the Arnold school in Pretoria, he returned to England to attend Oundle in Northhampshire, a popular choice for South Africans. He entered Sydney College, Cambridge, in 1896 and earned his degree in natural science in June 1901. At the university he served as captain of the football team and participated in swimming and aquatics. Given his lack of practical experience, he could hardly be seen as a replacement for the much more widely experienced J. W. Gregory. The delay in choosing a replacement geologist seemed an oversight. Ferrar's tardy appointment meant that the young and inexperienced scientist had little opportunity to prepare himself for his responsibilities. However, Mill's instruction and Ferrar's dedication to his studies en route to Antarctica helped overcome some of the lack of preparation.[26]

Mill was also a valued addition as far as the third officer was concerned. Shackleton spent a good deal of his time with the former librarian of the RGS during the early part of the voyage, enjoying their mutual love of poetry. Shackleton used his knowledge of the sea to teach the older man about life on the water.

Early on, Shackleton befriended the young zoologist, Edward A. Wilson, known to all on the expedition as "Billy."[27] Wilson, who joined the voyage not yet recovered from the wound in his armpit,[28] proved an apt companion for the outgoing Shackleton. Wilson noted that the third officer had taken him in hand and helped him in every way to adjust to the sea and to learn to enjoy their surroundings. Shackleton would call his friend when interesting specimens were sighted or opportunities for sketching appeared. Shackleton often visited Wilson in his cabin, and the two spent many hours together reading poetry, especially Robert Browning (1812–59) and Algernon Charles Swinburne (1837–1909), and on occasion Shackleton woke Wilson in the morning to see an especially beautiful sunrise.[29]

Wilson worked hard on a wide range of activities aboard ship. As the resident artist — and if a valid reason existed for appointing someone of such questionable health, the quality of Wilson's illustrations was that motivation — the young zoologist was often called on to capture an image too fleeting or too obscure for the camera.[30] In addition to sketching and painting birds related to his own responsibilities, Wilson was often sought out by the other scientists to capture the image of one of their specimens. Wilson also amused officers and men alike with his caricatures of them. Wilson's seriousness and fixity of purpose soon became apparent to all. Wilson was "precise, delicate, and deft in all he touched."[31]

Also, this first leg of the voyage saw the beginning of a lifelong friendship between Scott and Wilson. Wilson clearly impressed Scott, who noted the zoologist's efforts, not only in his zoological work but also in his willingness to lend a ready hand to whatever task appeared. As the voyage progressed the admiration each man had for the other grew. Scott, accustomed to the solitude of naval command, eventually developed a great affection for the pious, Christian gentleman.

One did not have to know Wilson long before the strength and commitment of his religious beliefs became apparent. Devout even before the period of reflection while recuperating from tuberculosis at Davos, Wilson returned from Switzerland with a profoundly deep faith in the Christian message and in the belief that God's hand could be seen in the events of one's life. Even as a young man on the *Discovery* Wilson's quiet piety impressed others. By the time of Scott's second expedition, the *Terra Nova*, the then-older Wilson had a profound impact on his companions. Two impressions from that second voyage provide insight. H. Pennell, captain of the *Terra Nova* after Scott had landed for the winter in 1911, said that until he met Wilson he did not believe the Christ-like life possible on this earth. Charles Wright, the young glaciologist in 1910, later remarked, "you must understand that for me, Bill Wilson was the personification of Christ on earth."[32] On the *Discovery* Wilson's religious faith was only beginning to be noted by his companions.

Every voyage takes a few days to establish a routine, and the *Discovery* was no exception. Soon the research aspects of the voyage were clear: Scientists were using the tow net, were doing ocean water salinity testing, and were keeping records related to cloud cover and meteorology.[33]

In those days of sails even the scientists literally had to learn the ropes. Scott gave the scientists specific duties regarding safety aboard ship, responsibilities they took most seriously. Scott put the scientists in charge of provisions for the lifeboats, and the experienced sailors, both wardroom and mess deck, were amused at the diligence of the scientists. For the most part the scientific staff were concerned with their own branches of inquiry, with Murray giving an occasional bit of direction or advice.

The officers settled into a routine, and watches were taken by Royds, Barne, and Shackleton. Royds had a particularly important role as the man who ran the ship under Scott's overall command. Royds was six feet tall, lithe, handsome, and quite strong.[34] Much of the success of the ship's operation can be attributed to Royds's deft hand in dealing with the men of the *Discovery*.

All the officers had scientific duties to perform. Royds, in charge of meteorology, maintained temperature statistics and kept barometric records. Additionally, he had undergone training in magnetism under the direction of Captain Creak and at Ben Nevis.[35]

The other officers had similar scientific duties. Michael Barne was responsible for the sounding gear, with which so many problems developed. Shackleton was trained by Mill to do seawater density and salinity studies, a task he took much to heart. Scott noted his third lieutenant's diligence, praising him in his diary. Even the engineer, Reginald Skelton, played a role in the scientific program. Early on, Scott asked him to develop an interest in photography, and throughout the expedition he served as the semi-official photographer.[36]

Monday through Friday each day was much the same as the others. On Saturday afternoons the *Discovery* was given a general cleaning. Sunday morning, following naval practice, Scott made the rounds and inspected the men and the ship. Divine service followed, at which the captain presided, while Murray read the lesson, and Royds, the only officer ever suspected of musical talent, played the piano. Hearty singing formed an important part of the service, which was generally well received by all.[37] Scott used this weekly occasion to address the ship's company on general matters or to deal with specific problems. Sunday, after church, was a day of leisure, time to write or read, or to catch up on sleep as naps were a popular pastime.

The crew adjusted to their new ship. Five members of the crew will be introduced now. Thomas Feather, the boatswain, proved throughout the voyage a valuable addition to the crew. The boatswain's duties included supervising all activities on deck. Scott had high praise for Feather, noting, perhaps with some exaggeration, that on the three-year voyage the *Discovery* never lost a rope or a sail.[38]

J. H. Dellbridge was the kind of man every exploring party needed. As Skelton's assistant engineer, Dellbridge's work primarily included maintaining the engine. In addition, the engineering department was called on to perform all repairs and to manufacture the various instruments and devices as the need arose. Skelton's praise of his assistant engineer formed a constant theme of the chief engineer's interesting seven-volume diary.

Petty Officer Edgar Evans had served with Scott on the *Majestic*. Evans was one of the two strongest, and at nearly two hundred pounds, powerfully built men on the ship; in the navy he had been a physical conditioning instructor. On this expedition he developed a loyalty to Scott that lasted until Evans's death in 1912 while returning from the South Pole with Scott.

William L. Heald joined the *Discovery* from the *Jupiter*, where he had been an expert in explosives. Heald was one of the prototype bluejackets in whom Scott and Markham had so much faith for their ability to turn their talents to whatever project was at hand. Heald's diary reveals him to be an interesting and perceptive member of the mess deck.[39]

Finally, Frank Wild may be seen as one of the most interesting of the ship's sailors. Small, wiry, and extremely bright, Wild was introduced to Antarctica by this voyage. Subsequently, he served under Shackleton and Douglas Mawson (1882–1958) on later expeditions and became the most experienced British polar explorer of the Heroic Era. Aboard the *Discovery* many times he demonstrated intelligence, quick thinking, and good sense, and he might well have acquired his master's certificate but apparently his battle with alcohol prevented it. Curiously, Wild almost did not apply for the *Discovery* as he thought only big men would be taken. Wild's Antarctic career was a great success story, rising as he did from able seaman to commander of Shackleton's last expedition.[40]

Scott had command over all the men. Even before the ship arrived at

Cape Town, Scott displayed qualities that continued to win him acclaim on this voyage and on his second Antarctic expedition. On this outward voyage an unexpected dividend became apparent early: that Scott had a scientific bent. Although such a criterion had never been a keen quality in Markham's mind, already en route to Cape Town Scott had displayed a far greater interest in scientific matters than Shackleton did on the three expeditions he led.

Scott was determined to play an important role in scientific work. He directed George Murray to have the scientists file weekly progress reports on their research programs. In this way, Scott was able to oversee the various projects and effectively serve as his own scientific director.

Scott surprised Murray by taking interest in microscope work. In response, Murray had an instrument set up to satisfy Scott's curiosity.[41] Similarly, Scott's diary betrays a keen fascination with tow netting and the entire scientific program. At first content to leave such matters to his staff as problems developed with the process of conducting the experiments, the captain became determined to take a greater responsibility in the research process. Furthermore, Scott decried the lack of concern with scientific work outside an individual investigator's own province. He resolved to urge the men toward greater cooperation. In all this, Scott, as a commander, exhibited qualities that made him popular as a scientific leader and allowed him to be credited for the scientific achievements of the voyage.

Eight days out of England, the ship approached Madeira, the first port of call, and with some difficulty arrived at Funchal on the evening of 14 August 1901. In the process of docking, the crew of the *Discovery* had a narrow escape, nearly hitting another vessel.[42]

At Madeira the ship took on coal to replace the supplies that were being depleted at a more rapid rate than anticipated. As engineer, Skelton oversaw the coaling — a dirty and backbreaking job. Preparing for coaling required the seamen to go through the entire vessel and paper over all ventilators and any cracks in walls or floors. Otherwise, the coal dust would make its way throughout the ship. Leave was granted and both officers and men took advantage of the opportunity for entertainment ashore. Hodgson went for his first horseback ride and acquired the nickname "Muggins," which stuck for the rest of the voyage. The scientists eagerly used the occasion to gather specimens. Not all such efforts were met with success; Wilson's belief that he had found a new flower was shattered when it was discovered to be nothing more than garlic.[43]

The brief Madeira stop meant the departure of H. R. Mill, of whom all in the wardroom had become quite fond. He and Murray had known one another since their days at Edinburgh University, and their conversations at dinner enlivened the meals. Mill, a man of encyclopedic knowledge and genuine kindness, took leave of the *Discovery* via the tug as it guided Scott's vessel out of the harbor at Madeira. Before he left, Mill gave each in the wardroom a little gift that he had brought from England.[44] Mill returned to London where he continued to help the expedition by providing information and by sending out needed supplies.

Meanwhile, when the *Discovery* was in Madeira, on 15 August 1901 the German exploring ship *Gauss* under Erich von Drygalski departed Elbe en route to Cape Town and the Antarctic. Scientific cooperation between the two endeavors formed part of the scientific program of each expedition, but the problems that eventually beset the *Gauss* limited the value of this cooperation.

Setting sail, the *Discovery* departed Madeira for Cape Town with a planned intermediary stop at South Trinidad Island. Four events while en route merit noting. Skelton was diagnosed by the doctor as being in need of immediate dental attention, and on 19 August he was operated on by Koettlitz and Wilson for an abscessed tooth. The operation proved troublesome and resulted in the removal of the tooth and part of Skelton's jaw.[45]

The second incident was by far the most serious of the four. The *Discovery* was found to be leaking, taking on water at a serious rate — twenty tons a day. All hands turned their attention to the crisis, and the men soon discovered that a portion of the provisions had been damaged. A faulty design meant that the foodstuffs had not been placed high enough in the hold to prevent damage from bilge water. Shackleton was put in charge of unloading the holds, and rearranging and restowing all the materials. Even the scientists were pressed into service in what was a foul and smelly business. In the course of the work the men discovered that workmen in London had opened some tins to sample the wares, and the half-consumed tins had been cast into the area where the bilge water gathered. The stench of rotting food and bilge water was overpowering. A hole was cut to ease the process of repacking and to allow for ventilation. The whole operation occupied several days, but in the end Shackleton won praise for rebuilding the storage area and for repacking everything better than the original effort. The leak continued to plague the crew throughout the voyage despite several attempts to locate and plug it.[46]

On 31 August 1901, the good ship *Discovery* had a visitor from the deep as Neptune came aboard to greet those who were crossing the line (the equator). Several of the men dressed up as Neptune and his court and those that had not passed the equator previously were initiated "in a most thorough manner." Neptune, richly adorned in seaweed and carrying a triton on to which was impaled a dried codfish, addressed the captain and bade him explain his reasons for entering Neptune's realm. The victims were inspected by the "doctor," then made to swallow a pill and to have their heads "shaved." Then the stool on which they were sitting was jerked from beneath them, and they fell backward twelve feet into a sail bath. Wilson's name was the first to be called, but he got off more easily than most because he was prematurely sent backward into the seawater bath. Ferrar made the mistake of resisting and was treated rather roughly by the men. Koettlitz was not dunked as he had little time for this kind of frivolity. Following the officers, the uninitiated men had their turn. The situation became boisterous; Neptune's queen twice lost her balance on the slippery footing and went down into the sail bath. By the end the men got "a little rough," but finally the on-deck ceremony ended, and, armed with a couple of bottles of whiskey, the men withdrew below decks to continue the celebration. Several of the men got drunk in the process of the festivities, and John Mardon, one of the merchant seamen, was logged by Scott for drunkenness.[47]

The fourth event was the landing at South Trinidad Island on 13 September 1901. The island had been visited only once before by scientists; an account of one such visit by E. F. Knight was in the ship's library and was read by several men in the days before their arrival at the island.

As they lay offshore in the light of dawn, Wilson was awakened and came on deck to sketch the outline of the island. Frigate birds sailed overhead as the whale boats were lowered, and Scott along with several of his officers and scientists made their way to shore. Bluejackets were assigned to each of the scientists to aid in the collection of specimens. The island, a volcanic rock rising in the middle of the Atlantic, roughly five hundred miles from South America, was not much to look at, but after a certain number of days at sea, one's standards of what was of interest changed. The land rose from the shore, and at roughly twelve hundred feet a fern line appeared. Only Skelton, in his search for specimens, made it all the way to the top.[48]

Limited time was allowed for the shore visit, and the goal was to gather as much as possible during the stay. Black petrels, gannets, and white terns were among the sixteen types of birds collected. The birds were very tame, and one could approach them readily. Skelton was busy shooting birds for the collection, as Wilson was ordered to devote his time to sketching as many birds as he could. Marine specimens were taken from the shore area. Two kinds of crabs were observed — a red and green type whose numbers were estimated in the millions and a larger yellow crab with claws capable of cutting through a man's finger.[49]

Landing on the rugged shore had not been easy in the heavy swell, and Scott steered for the natural jetty described by Knight in his book. The turbulence of the water prompted Scott to ask those in his boat if they could swim; all but one could. Departing was no easier, as the tide had risen, limiting the value of the boat's relatively safe landing spot.[50] Attempting to return to the ship, Scott slipped getting aboard one of the whalers and broke an oar that subsequently was lost overboard.[51]

When the officers and scientists were ashore in the interests of science, sailors on board occupied their time by dropping lines over the side in the interest of cuisine. They had no luck; sharks only came to nibble. Armitage was also gainfully employed during the day, staying aboard to take advantage of the stop to swing the ship and check the compass.[52]

In the days that followed the visit to South Trinidad Island, the scientists were kept busy examining and preserving their specimens. Skinning birds was a time-consuming job, one Wilson considered "excellent practice for temper and patience."[53] Wilson, who had received instruction in the process from the Natural History Museum staff, had help from Skelton and Hodgson, but the work went on for several days. Not all shared Wilson's enthusiasm for the task, the smell being "fairly high."[54] One of Skelton's finds was a petrel that had been previously undiscovered and was subsequently named for the young zoologist, *Oestrelata wilsoni*.

Sailing on to Cape Town the routine of the ship resumed. Undaunted by the *Rhyme of the Ancient Mariner*, catching albatross became a pastime. Skelton soon demonstrated his engineer's knack for problem solving and became adept at capturing the large birds. Several cape pigeons were also caught.[55]

The run from South Trinidad Island to South Africa was made largely under sail, as Skelton had become quite concerned about coal consumption. The speed of the *Discovery* under sail was a motivation to steam, but coal consumption drove Scott to rely on the wind. Still, several stops were made to allow tow netting. One result of the series of this work was the discovery of two new genera of algae, one of which was named for the ship and the other for Captain Scott. Skelton and Dellbridge used the interlude of sailing to turn their attention to the engine, making essential repairs.[56]

Other than scientific work, the crew busied themselves painting, readying the coal chutes, and preparing the ship for arrival. Also, as they approached the Cape, the crew thought of home and the possibility of mail. To Wilson, it seemed an age since the last mail at Madeira. What, he wondered, would two years without mail be like. Birds of several varieties became more regular visitors to the ship as it approached shore, providing Wilson more specimens to sketch and skin.[57]

On the last Sunday before arriving at Cape Town, Scott used the occasion to address the men on the proposed events at the Cape and also to review what he expected of them in terms of dress and behavior ashore. Later in the week, Scott, in his responsibility as captain, met with the sailors to help them make out their wills. The unknown South beckoned.[58]

On 3 October 1901, South Africa was sighted. The *Discovery* arrived at Cape Town nine days late, delayed by the ship's failure to sail as quickly as expected. The tardiness caused some concern in the Cape Colony and prompted several changes in the plans of the voyage. To allow adequate time to sail from New Zealand to the ice and to have some time for exploration in the first season, Scott decided that they would have to forgo the scheduled stop in Melbourne, a decision that created several problems. Much-needed supplies were awaiting the ship in Australia, and Markham had hoped that while in that colony supporters would come forth with financial aid for the expedition. By late September, though, Scott had decided that word would have to be sent to Australia that the *Discovery* would not call at Melbourne and that stores would have to be forwarded to New Zealand to meet the ship at Christchurch.[59]

Moreover, Scott decided, in consultation with Armitage and George Murray, that the latter would depart the ship at Cape Town, given the changes regarding Melbourne, and would return to Britain to oversee details related to the expedition there. Not the least of the various concerns was the need to raise additional money, if the expedition were to be able to stay longer than one winter and two summers. Just as important was Scott's desire that Murray have "a finger in the pie" regarding the relief ship. Scott hoped that Murray would prove as competent in dealing with the relief ship as he had been in getting the *Discovery* ready to sail.[60]

As the ship was being guided to its coaling berth in port, the men of the *Discovery* saw their first penguins, jackass penguins, along the shore. After docking at South Africa, Scott gave leave to the ship's company. Scott, Shackleton, and Skelton went ashore to the Mount Nelson Hotel for dinner and a game of billiards. The next day coaling began with Skelton supervising, while the rest of the officers and men turned to other pursuits. Armitage and Barne went to Simon's Town with the magnetic instruments to conduct experiments. With no observatory at the Cape, the two men established a tent camp and, working with two local professors, accomplished some good work.[61]

The scientists went off on their own to do research or to relax. Scott, however, was busy with his own onerous tasks. His naval training made him determined to maintain strict naval discipline aboard the *Discovery*. Once ashore Scott drew funds from the merchant shipping office to be able to dismiss John Mardon, whose behavior on the ship led Scott to believe Mardon was a troublemaker. Following lunch, the captain dismissed Mardon and returned to the ship. By the end of the day 230 tons of coal had been taken aboard, though not without difficulties. William Smythe and William Page, two of Skelton's men, reported for duty drunk, a problem compounded by Page's insubordination to Dellbridge. Scott moved quickly after hearing of this breech in naval discipline and punished the offenders by stopping their pay and leave.[62]

After arriving at the Cape, the ship's company numbered about fifty. The British community in South Africa graciously entertained the ship's officers and crew during their stay. Separate activities were scheduled for warrant officers (Feather, Dailey, Dellbridge, Ford, and Roper), who were feted at a dinner hosted by the chief, warrant, and dockyard officers of the port. During the remarks afterward, Ford, asked to speak on behalf of the others, suggested that although doubtless many dangers would be met in the Antarctic, he dreaded more the last half hour, knowing he was about to speak. Ford noted that all aboard were volunteers and had been motivated by "that love of adventure and carelessness of danger which was the birthright of every Englishman."[63]

From the coaling station the ship was moved to Simon's Town, a short but rough passage in which the ship rolled 37° in rough seas. The piano went sliding across the wardroom and narrowly missed destruction.[64] In a naval port the expedition could count on a very friendly welcome from the royal naval vessels and from the commanding admiral in particular. Scott had hoped that such support would be available, and his hopes were far exceeded by Admiral A. Moore, after Scott visited him. Moore offered to do whatever he could for the *Discovery*, which was considerable. Throughout this stop, thanks to Moore, Scott noted that "our every want [was] immediately taken in hand."[65]

Thus at no cost to the expedition, the *Discovery* was refitted by the Royal

Navy at the Cape. Divers scraped the ship and inspected the hull in hopes of finding the persistent leak. Other bluejackets loaned to the *Discovery* added an engine room door and helped Skelton make other repairs to the engine room.[66] Skelton noted that the fleet engineer and the constructor of the dockyard took the problems of the ship in hand. In addition to necessities, the Royal Navy provided luxuries to the *Discovery*—in short, all that was needed or wanted.[67] Hundreds of pounds worth of goods and services were accrued to the *Discovery*, without ever appearing on the ledger.

Meanwhile on deck, the ship was besieged with visitors, especially on Bank Holiday Monday. Governor Hely-Hutchinson and other visitors upset the schedule of needed repairs to the ship, but the additional manpower provided by Admiral Moore more than made up for the interruptions. Additional stevedores were put to work stowing provisions and, because the *Discovery* was a new ship, scraping the deck, which was causing the seamen fits with splinters in their feet as they worked. Four days of scraping by local workmen left the decks ready for the next part of the voyage.[68]

Ashore, the officers and men were feted by the locals and by Admiral Moore, who hosted a dinner for the officers and a garden party for the entire crew. The Philosophical Society also hosted a dinner. The governor hosted a picnic and a dinner.[69]

The scientists conducted research and used the opportunity to make last-minute purchases of equipment or to replenish supplies that had been depleted. Skelton, for example, bought a new camera for photographing birds and a new lamp to provide winter light.[70]

Scott was busy arranging a change in crew. In addition to Mardon's dismissal, John Masterton was excused at his own request. Job Clarke, a mess servant, was dismissed. Markham's evaluation of him was that he was "useless trash."[71] John W. Waterman was discharged for reasons of health.[72] To replace these men, the *Discovery* added Robert Sinclair, E. E. M. Joyce, George Vince, and Frank Plumley, who joined from HMS *Gibraltar*.

By 13 October 1901 the *Discovery* was nearly ready to head out to sea. A one-day delay in departure was caused by the need to prepare the compasses for the voyage to New Zealand. Also, Armitage requested additional time to write letters as his schedule ashore during the stay had prevented him from doing this. The stay at Cape Town had been a most profitable one for the expedition. The ship had been extensively refitted at no cost to the expedition, and the hospitality shown the officers and men was genuinely touching. Of the assistance given by the Royal Navy, Scott noted, "There ends an experience that makes me truly proud of a glorious profession — added to the practical benefits of our visit, one is deeply touched by the real kindness and sympathy shown by all; men and officers have had a glimpse of the real efficiency and meaning of our navy."[73]

6

From Cape Town to New Zealand

Slipping out of the harbor at Cape Town on 14 October 1901, the *Discovery* set a course for New Zealand. To save time, Scott opted to take a more southerly itinerary, one that would take them off the main sea routes.

The ship had not sailed far toward New Zealand when the leak that had been so troublesome en route to the Cape returned, despite the efforts of the naval workers in South Africa. Consequently, the crew was forced to spend time at the bilge pumps every day.

Fortunately, in this second leg of the voyage, the leak did not threaten the provisions — which were considerable. The *Discovery* was victualed for a two-year stay if necessary; practically speaking, this meant enormous quantities of stores. The ship departed England with the bulk of its supplies aboard, unnecessarily so, because foodstuffs were plentiful in New Zealand. In the hold of the barque were 6,000 pounds of soups, 7,000 pounds of fish, and 42,000 pounds of meat. For libations 30 gallons of brandy and 60 of port were provided. To supply the naval tradition of regular rum rations, 800 gallons were considered sufficient to serve the needs of the sailors.[1] In general, officers and men shared the same food, but in certain instances, separate items were provided — each had their own stocks of jams and marmalade. Visitors to Antarctica today find they have arrived in a smoke-free environment. The hundreds of surviving photographs of the expedition indicate that such was not the case on the *Discovery*. A significant percentage of the illustrations show officers and men, pipe in mouth, regardless of the activity or locale. To supply this want, the ship carried 1,800 pounds of tobacco — an allowance of one and a half pounds per officer and one pound per man per month. Here again class differences emerged. The men preferred stronger smokes, such as Navy leaf, than those consumed in the wardroom, and different stocks supplied the different needs. In the wardroom were four nonsmokers, but, fortunately for the smokers, they showed no objection to being with those who indulged. On other expedition ships restrictions had existed concerning smoking — on the *Fram* Nansen limited smoking to the galley, except on limited occasions. On Scott's ship no such limitations were imposed, as Scott himself was a heavy smoker.[2]

Nor were tea and coffee neglected, as separate supplies were included for the two classes aboard. Twenty-eight hundred pounds of each were carried in the hold. One hundred and fifty-six gallons of lime juice, the staple of naval vessels since the days of Captain James Cook, were brought along as an anti-scorbutic.[3]

Meals in the wardroom were served on china, with cloth napkins and table linen, and were attended by the servants. These men also took care of the housekeeping chores of the wardroom, including bringing morning tea. Fortunately, the diary of one of the attendants survives and gives interesting impressions of life during the expedition.

In the wardroom a calendar, presented by Sir Clements Markham, listed the anniversaries of the expedition, written in the tiny scrawl of the president of the RGS. No occasion for celebration was overlooked. Anniversaries of the appointments of the various officers and scientists were included along with major dates in the construction of the ship and of the expedition itself. Certain occasions called for an extra pour from the wine of the day. Special occasions were marked by champagne, even though that libation was listed under the medical supplies of the expedition.[4]

Meanwhile, life at sea continued. At the end of October a series of storms gave the *Discovery* several very good daily runs, as gale force winds pushed the barque toward New Zealand. On 27 October 1901, the average speed was nine knots, as 217 miles were covered in establishing what was then a record run. The next day the seas worsened, and at one point the waves broke over the quarterdeck. The force of the water carried the quartermaster over the wheel, and Scott, who was on deck, found himself for a moment submerged by the torrent. Two more days of blustery weather at the end of October provided a day with more than 200 miles covered, including a record 223 miles on 31 October.[5]

By 12 November the *Discovery* was in 51° S, 131° E, an area Scott described as one of particular magnetic interest. He decided to pursue this phenomenon by turning the ship to the south. In doing so he took his vessel far out of the normal shipping lanes.[6]

Mid-November brought a week of fire and ice. At sea one of the greatest dangers was — and still is — fire, especially in the case of wooden ships. At 3:00 A.M. on 14 November the fire alarm sounded, and the crew responded quickly and extinguished the blaze. The fire began in the mess deck head, and although some woodwork was scorched, no serious damage resulted.[7] The situation might have been critical as the fire occurred dangerously close to a kerosene tank,[8] and with the *Discovery* so far from the normal shipping lanes, outside help would have been unlikely. Fortunately, this was the only fire outbreak during the expedition. Perhaps Wilson was correct in his hope that it was "a scare that will be the best guarantee against fire in the future."[9] Two days following the fire, with the *Discovery* south of 60° S, the vessel had its first encounter with ice. The small piece of ice, no bigger than a soup plate, was large enough to win Michael Barne the prize for sighting the first ice, a worthy reward — a bottle of champagne. Barne shared his champagne at dinner, and the wardroom members uncorked a bottle of Madeira brought back from one of the British Arctic expeditions of the mid-nineteenth century. That evening the mess deck also celebrated — "we spliced the main brace." Within a day the bergs were large enough to give some small indication of the powerful force of the ice, as it scraped along the side of the vessel, sounding like thunder.[10]

By nightfall the ice was all around the *Discovery*, and the first sight of the splendor of it kept Wilson on deck until late in the evening. By 11:00 P.M. the *Discovery* found itself with no open water to be seen. The barque responded well, however, riding up over the edge of the ice and splitting the floes. The sojourn among the ice floes was short-lived though, for although the ship was a mere two hundred miles from Adélie Land, its coal supply was so low that to range farther south would have been dangerous. Thus the ship turned back, having reached a farthest south point of 62.50° S, 139° E.[11]

As the *Discovery* proceeded the scientists were able to conduct research. Although occasionally one could shoot a bird and be lucky enough to have it fall on to the deck, regular stops were made to kill or capture birds, with Wilson and Skelton the usual hunters. At other times, using a variety of techniques, the scientists captured specimens while the ship was moving. Skelton and Dellbridge proved to be the most adept at catching birds on the wing. The ornithological collection was growing, and Wilson began to contemplate writing a lengthy account of the birds of the expedition, including drawings of them from different angles to make further identification easier.[12]

Soundings were regularly made but regrettably with little more success than the scientists had had en route to the Cape. The tow-netting apparatus lowered the line, but the trawl or the sounder was often lost or the cable otherwise broken while hauling back aboard. Diaries report these mishaps with painful regularity, as hundreds or thousands of feet of wire were recorded as lost. Halfway to New Zealand Skelton noted that 4500 fathoms of wire were lost to that point, plus assorted equipment, "hardly very successful so far."[13] Sounding after sounding en route to New Zealand was recorded in terms of the hundreds of fathoms of line lost.[14]

4. Chinstrap penguin.
Drawing by Kim Crosbie.

The lack of success with the tow-netting equipment was repeated in scientists' attempts to use kites to gather scientific data. Problems with techniques resulted in the loss of a kite one day, then another, until eventually the scientists lost the last of the kites. The meteorological studies that were to take advantage of these experiments ended.[15]

The most significant break in the voyage to New Zealand was the stop made at Macquarie Island. The crew expected to see it at first light on 22 November 1901, but bad weather prevented them from seeing the island until 10:00 A.M. Scott approached the island cautiously, and by midafternoon the ship was close enough for the scientists to watch the penguins onshore. Wilson was desperately eager to land and told Armitage that he would give a bottle of liqueur if the Pilot (as Armitage was known) would persuade Scott to allow a landing. Back in a few minutes, Armitage reported his mission accomplished.[16]

By the time the *Discovery* was near shore and began to lower the whalers, the time was nearly 5:00 P.M. The two boats carried all the officers, except for Royds, and most of the scientists. While ashore the party seemed more like schoolboys than experienced naturalists. Scott was worried that so many firearms were in such proximity and ordered the men to spread out.[17] Spying a seal lying on the beach, a crowd of men dashed up to him, surrounding the poor beast who was in the middle of a very important nap. Awakened from his slumber, the startled animal roared and threatened and when that proved insufficient, bluffed a charge at the camera stand. The encounter was soon ended as the seal gave up its life for science.[18]

Koettlitz dashed about gathering botanical specimens, aided by one of the seamen, James Duncan, whose diary of the expedition provides a splendid impression from the mess deck perspective. Ferrar, meanwhile, busied himself gathering geological specimens.[19]

The king penguins attracted a great deal of attention. These birds have a variable breeding season and so had young in various stages of development during this visit. The kings pecked at the men who walked among them and whacked passersby with their powerful flippers. The noise was deafening, and only the stench was more annoying to the scientists and the men who were helping them. Before the *Discovery* departed two king penguins were taken aboard and spent the voyage to New Zealand in a cage on deck.[20]

Scott joined Barne and Wilson in investigating the island. Scott appreciated Wilson's keen eye for color and form and enjoyed viewing the wildlife with such a guide, noting, "he is indeed a treasure in our small company."[21] Together the men explored a hut left by sealers or whalers who had visited the place. Cautiously opening the door, Scott and his companions were astounded to find inside a superb collection of birds, all preserved and neatly labeled and carefully wrapped in paper. No sign of the collector could be found — the scientists searched the bunks for a corpse. Nor did they find any indication of an imminent return of the specimen gatherer. The birds would have been a valued addition to the collection of any fine European museum. Indeed, in the hut were several examples of a rail so rare that only one European museum had a specimen. Despite the likely deterioration of the collection if left in place — mice had been nibbling on the specimens — Wilson and Scott left the collection in the cabin, although Wilson could not help wondering if the owner might never return and the collection would be lost.[22]

The stay at Macquarie was a rushed one; the men were on the ground only about two and a half hours. However, a surprisingly large number of specimens were added to the collection, which kept the scientists busy for several days, preserving and cataloging their finds. Not only were the interests of science met by this stop, but the larder was also well served, and both penguin and penguin eggs appeared on the menu over the next few days. Scott said a weak stomach kept him from enjoying the penguin, but to his surprise the men — whose dietary range was not extensive based on the observations of others — took a liking to it, certainly a positive sign for the days ahead.[23]

Three days after the sojourn at Macquarie Island, Auckland Island was sighted at daybreak. As the ship approached the island, a small bit of new land was discovered — a submerged rock was struck but with no appreciable damage. No landing was made.[24]

Work was not the only occupation en route to New Zealand. Diversions included golf (with a ball secured to a line) and deck cricket (the details of play are somewhat obscure). A type of hockey had been attempted but was found wanting.[25]

The last run toward New Zealand proved exciting, as the barque encountered heavy seas so rough that the water surged over the deck and rushed down into the wardroom. Just before breakfast on 26 November the ship rolled fifty-six degrees, which resulted in enormous petty breakage in the wardroom. The weather calmed by late afternoon, at which time the ship was joined by two finner whales who swam along with the ship for a period of time.[26]

Approaching New Zealand on 28 November, the captain decided to try to take the ship into the harbor before nightfall. Though the maneuver was unsuccessful, by midnight the vessel was anchored just off Port Lyttelton. Despite the lateness of the hour, Shackleton was sent ashore to retrieve the mail, a job he did enthusiastically. Finding the postmaster asleep at 2:00 A.M., Shackleton roused him and returned shortly with the mail so that many of the men passed the early hours reading the news from home.[27]

The *Discovery* was anchored for the night in the northern headland, and at eight o'clock in the morning the health inspector, Dr. Upham, made a cursory inspection of the ship and passed her for entrance into the harbor. A visitor to the docked ship could hardly mistake it for anything but a working vessel. The decks were crowded with the paraphernalia of polar exploration: sledges of ash, with iron or silver runners, and kayaks (both of Nansen's design), and sixty gas cylinders for the balloon to be used for observations in the South. The two king penguins were in a pen on deck, soon to be left in New Zealand as a souvenir of the ship's visit.[28]

The *Discovery* came alongside dock number three at 12:25 P.M., and the local greeting party, led by T. C. Field, mayor of Lyttelton, came aboard. C. C. Bowen, whose enthusiasm for the project had prompted him to board the ship from a launch before it had entered the harbor, was also a prominent figure, greeting Scott's vessel. No members of the colonial government were at dockside to greet the *Discovery* because the ship was not expected yet.[29]

En route to New Zealand Scott had determined that the holds had not been stowed in the most efficient manner. The work of rearranging existing materials and logically organizing them, in preparation for receiving the 146 tons of material awaiting the ship in New Zealand, fell to Shackleton, whose experience in the merchant marine proved invaluable.

Details of the ship's leak, combined with rumors of the soundness of the vessel owing to this problem, became a matter of public concern while the ship was in New Zealand. From London, Markham assured the press that such leaking was normal in a wooden ship, and publicly Scott supported this theory. Privately, however, Scott's attitude was different. Writing to Mill, Scott discounted the leak as more of a nuisance than a serious threat to the expedition. Thus he was surprised at the concern shown by the *The Times* and was adamant in avoiding blame for any such press reactions. Still, Scott was not happy with the work of the builders, suggesting to Mill that he would like to "have the builder people at sea for a couple of days" as we have an "account to settle for their basically scraped work."[30]

Clearly, the leak presented the most pressing problem and had to be repaired before the ship could leave for the South. In dry dock for eight days, the ship was found to have a number of unplugged holes, which were caulked. Other work that had been carelessly done in Dundee was made right. Refloated after all this effort, the *Discovery* was found to be leaking more than ever, which forced a second dry docking. The supervisor of the first docking, James Miller, was so distressed that he insisted on paying for the cost of the second dry docking himself. The second series of repairs focused on the bow plates, which were removed. That effort revealed construction problems — some screw bolt holes being too large or too deep, which allowed water to seep into the hold. The second dry dock effort proved successful, and the leak was subsequently kept in check by a few minutes at the pumps each day.[31]

James Miller, interviewed by the press, supported the idea that the disturbing sight of water leaking from the ship while it was in dry dock — a condition visible to everyone who saw the ship in that condition — gave a false impression. Miller supported the view that the hardwoods used in the *Discovery* took longer to swell and that the process of caulking such a vessel is much more difficult. Miller asserted that the harder wood does not "assimilate itself" to the caulk, which resulted in some leaking.[32]

Overall, the leaking of the ship would seem to have been excessive for a new vessel but not severe enough to have prompted action against the builders.[33]

Slight alterations were also made to the barque. Pens were constructed to hold the sheep, a gift of local farmers who provided the crew with fresh meat for a period after leaving land.[34]

The welcome of the people of New Zealand was overwhelming, and the officers and men of the *Discovery* appreciated the kindness and the contributions of the Kiwis to the expedition.

Owing to the change of plans on the outward voyage that omitted the stop at Melbourne, C. Coleridge Farr, the director of the Magnetic Observatory at Christchurch, was approached by Markham and Sir William Huggins, president of the Royal Society, for assistance in coordinating observations with the ship. Again, the New Zealanders provided valuable cooperation and assistance.[35] Farr had a very fine observatory and provided valued assistance to the *Discovery*.

The scientists used the time in New Zealand to engage in scientific work. Armitage and Bernacchi were especially busy, working with Mr. Farr to coordinate magnetic observations between the land station and the vessel at sea. As it turned out the facilities at Christchurch were much better than those at Melbourne.[36]

Ferrar engaged in geology studies, while Wilson spent endless hours preparing the ornithological collection of the expedition to that point for shipment back to England. Wilson preferred this activity to some of the entertainment offered, especially that on the naval ships.[37] Wilson also spent long hours writing to the young bride he had left in England three weeks after their marriage.[38]

The citizens of New Zealand showed great concern for their exploring visitors, and a series of events was staged on their behalf. In most cases the officers and men were invited to different engagements. The warrant officers and men were invited to various suppers, including one at the Provincial Council Chambers, smoking concerts (7 December at Sydenham and Addington Working Man's Club), and a dinner at Oddfellows Hall.[39]

At these events, short speeches usually were given, and the warrant officers would be invited to make a few remarks on the expedition. Not surprisingly, these men reflected the official policies of the expedition. They spoke about their enthusiasm and fitness for the work and how they were determined to do their duty. Still, the genuine affection the men showed for the people of New Zealand and the depth of their appreciation for the hospitality they received during their stay had a positive effect on the expedition's support in the colony. In addition to speeches, light entertainment, songs, and recitations were offered. Among the men of the *Discovery* Frank Wild, Arthur Pilbeam, Arthur Quartly, George Vince, William Heald, and William Page often contributed.[40]

The officers took part in a separate series of events. They were invited to banquets by the Philosophical Institute of Christchurch and several other organizations.[41] As was typical of these events, the dinner was followed by a series of short remarks made by local notables, visiting dignitaries, and members of the expedition. Often, Scott would speak on the background of the effort and its goals. On these occasions he would note the role of the two societies that had created the voyage, usually singling out Sir Clements Markham as the one who had been the driving force in launching the endeavor.[42] Others from the ship might be asked. Koettlitz or Bernacchi often would contribute additional comments on the scientific program. Armitage tended to speak on navigational or magnetic observation issues. Locals would add their comments about the expedition and its work. C. C. Bowen answered charges about the practicality of the expedition at one such dinner by noting that those who doubted the value of the expedition's work missed an important point: "How could they expect to know anything of the mighty universe of which the world is but an atom, if they did not explore to its uttermost recesses their own little globe."[43]

One of the special events of the stay in New Zealand was a visit by some of the officers to a group of Maoris, the native people of the colony. The Maoris apparently made a considerable effort to welcome the visitors from the mother country, greeting the visitors and feeding them traditional food — with the addition of coffee and tea — and putting on a show of native dancing. Koettlitz was the senior officer and received gifts from the old chief. A visit to a nearby battlefield and a picnic followed in the afternoon. Much of the day's activities, however, were fairly typical tourist exhibitions, as those Maoris normally dressed in the English fashion and their children all spoke English. Wilson, who was one of the members of the part for the outing, thought it all a piece of "barbarous acting, such as one might see in a pantomime."[44]

Officers and men joined together for a special service the last Sunday before they departed for the Antarctic.[45]

When the ship docked, Scott had asked the public to restrict their visits until arrangements had been made to have guests aboard. Within a couple of days, people began to arrive. On the first Sunday the *Discovery* was in port, and special trains brought as many as two thousand people from Christchurch to the port of Lyttelton.[46]

One romantic story developed during the *Discovery* stay in New Zealand. From virtually the first day in the colony, Reginald Skelton, the chief engineer, had become acquainted with the Meares family, of whom Skelton noted in his journal that Mr. Meares was a good sort and Mrs. Meares was "particularly nice looking and altogether charming." Skelton became an almost daily visitor to the Meares's house, for croquet or tea, and he noted that he found Mrs. Meares "looking most charming and dressed in most perfect taste."[47]

Mrs. Meares and other members of the family came down to see the *Discovery* in port. One day while Skelton was visiting, a brother of Mr. Meares dropped by, bringing with him his two daughters. A few days later Skelton noted that while out for a drive the group had picked up Miss Sybil Meares, who had a sprained ankle. Skelton described her as "a really pretty girl, I might say almost beautiful."[48]

Skelton spent more and more of his time ashore with the Meares, staying the night if festivities ran too late to return to the ship. One evening Skelton walked Sybil Meares home after dinner, and the next day Mrs. Meares brought Sybil down to see the *Discovery* in dry dock. Skelton enjoyed a day of croquet with Sybil Meares, just before preparing to ship out. Perhaps as an expression of his hope to be welcomed back at the conclusion of the voyage, Skelton left his watch and shoes with Mrs. Meares and her family, people Skelton described as "just about the nicest people I have ever met."[49]

Although the wardroom contained a piano, and a pianette was in the mess deck, the need of an additional instrument was perceived during the ship's stay in New Zealand. A harmonium was expected to be of special help for religious services aboard the vessel. Although time was limited before departure, a rush campaign — a shilling fund — was launched to secure the instrument for the ship. The £40 cost was soon subscribed, and three days before departure the harmonium was delivered to the *Discovery*. This gesture was one indication of the generous attitude of the people of New Zealand toward the expedition. Through the press both officers and men made clear their gratitude for the thoughtful gift.[50]

The generosity of the people of Christchurch was demonstrated in other ways. The railways gave officers and men free passes between Christchurch and Lyttelton. The Lyttelton harbor forgave the expedition all fees during its stay. Finally, the colony's government gave £1000 toward the relief expedition.[51]

During the *Discovery*'s stay in New Zealand several criticisms of the ship and crew — aside from the genuine concern about the leak — appeared in the local papers. When the *Discovery* arrived at Lyttelton, one old merchant marine man told a newspaper reporter that the ship was in terrible shape and looked a mess. Another critic suggested that the problems of the ship were caused by the lack of a good old-fashioned bo'sun to keep order, while several correspondents spoke disparagingly about the "gold braid" types. No charge was left unanswered. At various public occasions each accusation was countered. Captain Rich of the *Ringarooma* used the occasion of a dinner for the officers (and staff) at the Warner's Hotel to refute the aforementioned charges, defending all the practices of the Royal Navy. For the most part surrogates defended the expedition, although on at least one occasion Scott defended his bo'sun by noting that the latter had brought the ship to New Zealand without the loss of a single rope.[52]

In addition to the criticism though, many letters to the editor attested to the concern of the people of the Christchurch-Lyttelton area for the safety and success of the expedition. Among the issues raised was the question of the dispatch of a single ship rather than two on such a dangerous mission.[53]

Beyond the outward criticism, Scott was unhappy with the behavior of some of his men while in port. He believed that most of them were good but noted that a few black sheep would color the flock. Scott determined to be rid of Harry J. Baker, who had previously returned drunk to the ship while at Cape Town. Scott saw Baker as one of the worst offenders, and only Baker's desertion prevented his dismissal. Albert Dowsett was dismissed at Lyttelton.[54]

After speaking severely to the men again during the New Zealand visit, making an example of several of the worst offenders, Scott felt content that the behavior of his men improved.[55] Scott was quick to point out that the only men who deserted in New Zealand were those that knew they were not going to be chosen to sail south with the ship.[56]

Scott was able to add several to the crew to replace the departed men. A cook named Henry R. Brett was signed on, to replace Sydney Roper, whom Scott thought was undesirable.[57] A servant, Dowsett, was replaced by a young man named Clarence Hare, who eventually had his share of adventures on the expedition. The sailmaker, Hugh Miller, was let go owing to health problems; he was not replaced. The Royal Navy provided the expedition with two fine additions — Jesse Handsley, a strong fellow who joined from the *Ringarooma*; and another sailor, Thomas Crean, who was destined to play a significant role in British Antarctic exploration in the Heroic Era. Scott's first impression of Crean was that he was a fine, strapping able-bodied seaman. Crean was that and much more, as his actions over the next two decades would prove. Thus Crean, who would play a key role on Shackleton's Imperial Trans-Antarctic expedition (1914–17), and who was awarded the Albert Medal — the highest award for bravery in a civilian situation — for saving the life of an officer on Scott's *Terra Nova* expedition, entered the world of Antarctic expedition when he boarded the *Discovery*, his sea bag carried over one shoulder.

Also joining the ship at Christchurch was the last member of the scientific staff. Bernacchi had planned to join the ship at Melbourne but had to change his plans when Scott opted to bypass Australia. Bernacchi went to Melbourne with his passage gratis courtesy of the Orient line, another of the many donations in kind to the expedition that did not appear on the balance sheet.[58]

As part of the promotion of the voyage and also as a souvenir for the officers and men, the *Discovery* carried a series of four postcards to be sent back at various stages of the expedition. The fanciful designs appear amusing to anyone familiar with life in the south polar regions. The first one depicted Captain Scott and contained a quotation from Kipling:

When Drake went down to the Horn,
   England was crowned thereby;
Twixt seas unsailed and shores unhailed,
   England was crowned thereby.[59]

The next postcard was for use at Cape Town and showed the main deck of the vessel and the proposed route of the cruise.[60] The third to be posted before departure from New Zealand showed a group of sledging explorers, and the fourth one — which was to be posted on the ship's return to civilization — showed a polar bear sauntering over the floes and looking off at a pole flag in the distance.[61] This fourth card also had a quotation from Kipling,

> What is the flag of England?
> Ye have but my bergs to dare,
> ye have but my drifts to conquer,
> Go forth for it is there.[62]

In addition to the cards, the Eastern Extension Telegraph Company arranged to send one farewell message from each member of the expedition free of charge.[63]

Before departing for the South, the *Discovery* was given a fresh coat of black paint and tar from stem to stern. The yellow funnels and the white boats stood out in stark contrast and provided an image of a well-maintained, well-ordered ship.[64]

Among the last-minute additions to the ship before departure were the dogs. They were brought onboard 21 December 1901 at 10:45 A.M. and were chained to their kennels located slightly forward of midships. Rather than being the fierce animals some had anticipated, the dogs appeared at first friendly and boisterous. Delays in departure aggravated their confinement and altered their disposition, and soon the animals were engaged in fights with their neighbors, in which the men were required to intervene. After the dogs were aboard, the ark-like menagerie grew when forty-five sheep were led onto the ship and put in their pens, which were built over bags of coal. The rest of the deck space was largely taken up with more bags of coal, compressed fodder for the sheep, kayaks, gas cylinders, and other items that together made walking on the deck a hazard.[65]

At 11:30 A.M. the ship's bell summoned the officers and men to the men's quarters. There, in the narrow and confining quarters of the mess deck, with the officers in uniform, men in their working togs, engineering staff in grease-covered coveralls, members of the clergy, and several men and women from the town, a brief service was held. At least one visitor was profoundly moved as the men sang the hymn,

> O God, our help in ages past,
> Our hope for years to come
> Our shelter from the stormy blast
> And our eternal Home —

Closed with a silent prayer and a benediction, the ceremony ended and the men resumed their last-minute efforts to ready the vessel for sea.[66]

At eleven minutes past two o'clock in the afternoon the *Discovery* slipped her moorings. The crowd cheered dockside, and only "a dull-wit-ted spectator . . . was not touched by some unwonted thrill as, amid the cheers of the crowded wharves and shipping the little vessel moved slowly away."[67] With the marine band playing "Say Au Revoir, But not Good-Bye" the *Discovery* moved out into the harbor. As the barque made its way to Port Chalmers, its last port of call, the HMS *Lizard* and the HMS *Ringa-rooma* accompanied it out of the harbor, the latter ship joining for the voyage to Port Chalmers.[68]

The original purpose of the call at Port Chalmers was to finish coaling the ship. John Mills, from Port Chalmers, had offered to provide free an additional supply of deck coal for the voyage, and Scott was eager to add this to his limited supply before sailing. At one point some speculation was made that arrangements might be made to have the *Discovery* towed the first fifty miles to conserve coal.[69]

Yet the departure from Lyttelton was not as intended. As the cheering crowd roared its approval, tragedy struck. High in the rigging of the ship, on the truck of the mainmast above the crow's nest, a young bluejacket, Charles Bonner, was seen waving a black handkerchief. Suddenly, a disas-ter occurred when the truck (a circular piece of wood less than a foot in di-ameter) on which Bonner was standing gave way, and in an instant he crashed to the deck below, striking his head on the winch house with a hor-rid smash and falling onto the deck within inches of his comrades. Imme-diately, the ship's company fell silent and tried in vain to stifle the cheers of the onlookers. Bonner was dead.[70]

The voyage to Port Chalmers took much longer than expected owing to severe winds that limited the ship's headway at times to one knot. The warm reception planned for the *Discovery* was altered after Bonner's death.[71] Instead of throngs of ardent supporters, the ship's principal visi-tor was the coroner, who came aboard to hold an inquest into Bonner's death. Publicly, the inquest held that Bonner had been aloft when he lost his footing, fell, and died shortly thereafter. In fact he died instantly, his head shattered by the force with which it struck the corner of the winch house. Scott, assisted by Captain Rich of the *Ringarooma*, was able to squash the details of the tragedy, particularly that Bonner had been drink-ing and that excessive alcohol consumption had been a precipitating cause of the events. Skelton saw Bonner's death as an object lesson for the men who had been doing too much drinking ashore.[72] Bonner may not have been drunk when he went up into the yards, but apparently another sea-man, Robert Sinclair, had handed Bonner a bottle of whiskey once Bon-ner was aloft.

The paper reported only that Bonner was "a native of London and belonged to the Navy," that his parents were both dead, and that he was survived by two brothers. Bonner's casket was accompanied by a naval honor guard to a cemetery in Port Chalmers where he was buried.[73] The whole process, including the inquest and funeral, took less than two hours.

Sinclair, apparently unnerved by his part in the tragedy, took a suit of civilian clothing from another member of the crew and stole away from the vessel in the early hours of Christmas eve.[74]

The stop at Port Chalmers was brief. The funeral and coal loading occupied much of the time during the stay there. Soon the ship was ready to depart.

As the forty-seven officers and men — one fewer due to Sinclair's last-minute desertion[75] — of the *Discovery* prepared to depart New Zealand, one newspaper recalled the days of Drake and Ross:

The world has grown smaller since then — the pathless seas first furrowed by the keels of those brave old navigators are now the highways of liners, the "shuttles of the Empire's loom," and comparatively little remains for the discoverer by sea. Yet the spirit of those days is not dead, though the twentieth century gives it scanty opportunity and encouragement, and we saw its survival on Saturday when the little *Discovery*, whose quaint build emphasized the resemblance of the expedition to those enterprises of bygone centuries, set sail for the last great sea and continent that remain unmapped.[76]

Before departing New Zealand, Scott wrote a letter of thanks to the people of the colony, expressing the appreciation of the entire company for the generous and friendly reception they had had during their stay. His remarks were heartfelt and conveyed the genuine sense of affection that Scott's men, like the generations of Antarctic explorers, British and American, felt for the people of New Zealand as they took their leave of civilization to depart for the great white South.

Privately, Scott feared that "our success may be balked by inexperience," but as the ship sailed southward the hopes of achieving great success as an exploring scientific expedition were in the hearts of all aboard the vessel. Thus the polar pilgrims moved away from the known to the unknown, "made plain sail and with a fair wind headed South."[77]

7

May You Always Sail in Open Water

When the *Discovery* bade farewell to the last of its escort ships, and the crew and menagerie of animals — forty-five sheep and twenty-four dogs on deck[1] — moved into the violent seas en route to Antarctica, the men were virtually as isolated as Columbus had been four centuries earlier when he departed for the New World. The *Discovery* carried no wireless radio, not even carrier pigeons, which its immediate predecessors had taken with no positive result. For the next two years the crew would be dependent on the timbers of their ship and their own abilities. Sir Clements already had a relief ship expedition in the planning stage, but to be of use to the men of the *Discovery* the relief ship would have to make the dangerous crossing to the continent and then find the expedition's winter quarters.

One of the key questions of the expedition centered on whether the ship would winter. Publicly, much was made of keeping the captain's hands unfettered, but in Markham's mind — where the decision was made — the wintering of the ship was a foregone conclusion. Thus the goals of the first of the projected two seasons were to explore as much of the land as possible and especially to go beyond the limits of Ross's route. In addition, Scott was to find suitable winter quarters for the ship, even though the ship, as designed, would have been best utilized exploring as much as possible. Sailing conflicted with the need to establish winter quarters where the captain would command. Thus Markham was prepared to sacrifice geographical discovery by sea to assure that Scott remained the sole commander of the expedition.

Heading south, Scott regretted the delayed departure from New Zealand, wishing he had been able to sail toward the continent earlier in the season to allow more time for seaborne exploring. The send-off from Port Chalmers had been more moderate than that at Christchurch, but the men of the HMS *Ringarooma* did their best to cheer their fellow sailors as they departed the port. The *Discovery* was towed about fifty miles out to sea by the tug from Port Chalmers.[2]

The second day at sea was Christmas Day, but Scott decided to delay the celebration until the new year, partly to continue pushing south and, to some degree, because of the depressing impact on the crew caused by Bonner's death. A Christmas service was held on 25 December, but no other celebrations took place. Although the officers noted Bonner's death as something of a reason for the postponement, the diaries of bluejackets give a stronger sense of the loss of one who had been a very popular member of the crew.[3]

The expedition was fortunate in having good weather for the first week out of New Zealand, as Scott's ship was riding low in the water, owing to holds full of provisions and coal and a deck cargo that included forty-five tons of coal, sheep, dogs, and other paraphernalia. The favorable weather also allowed Scott to sail rather than steam, conserving valuable coal.

The sheep suffered from the action of the seas, and after seven days at sea only thirty-two remained. Skelton noted in his diary that he hoped an effort would be made to keep the sheep alive until the ship reached low temperatures. The sheep could be killed and preserved by the cold, and thus the men would have mutton for a longer period of time throughout the winter.[4]

The dogs fared better, perhaps from Scott's decision to assign each dog to one man who would then look out for the health of the animal. The interaction between man and dog no doubt boosted the spirits of each. Scott was concerned, however, when he realized that the men took scraps of food to give to their dogs. The captain was concerned that his men believed themselves to be on some sort of picnic, which Scott thought was a dangerous attitude.[5]

That the expedition was not a casual outing but one that operated under naval regulations was soon made apparent by another matter: Two of the seamen were overheard complaining about food and other conditions. Scott quickly squelched their behavior by parading the offenders before the ship's company and stopping indefinitely the grog and tobacco allowance for the two offenders.[6]

As the ship pressed southward, by New Year's Eve much speculation existed about when the first real ice would be sighted. Bernacchi, the most experienced of the crew and the only one who had ever seen Antarctic ice, speculated that the first ice would be spotted before the opening day of the new year. His estimate was off by a day.

Naval regulations allowed the men an extra tot of grog for New Year's

Eve, and the mess deck rang out with singing and merry activities late into the night. Meanwhile, the officers in the wardroom also celebrated. Armitage set about making a hot whiskey punch into which he put rather more lemon essence than was required. Judging from the late hours kept that evening and the several people who the next day felt the result of excessive drinking, the punch appears to have been well received. Several of the officers stayed up until two o'clock talking and joking on the bridge.[7]

The fine weather and the novelty of again being at sea the first week out of Christchurch encouraged many to spend their waking hours on deck, especially once icebergs began to appear. On 2 January the weather turned foggy, and the long-awaited ice appeared. Royds spotted it on his watch at about 65.5° S at roughly 2:30 P.M., and everyone rushed on deck. The press to get topside was so great that in the rush, Scott, following too closely behind Skelton, was kicked in the eye and required several stitches to close the wound. Skelton felt terrible, noting in his journal, "I'd much sooner it had happened to myself."[8]

The strange appearance of the tabular iceberg of the south polar regions captured the imagination of the men of the *Discovery* as such icebergs have impressed so many other visitors. Huge blocks of ice that can extend for many miles in length fill the imagination with a sense of wonder and awe. The first icebergs seen were much smaller — most were only hundreds of yards long — but no less impressive. Armitage, the erstwhile ice master, spent much of his time in the crow's nest as he piloted the vessel through the ice, ever alert for the clouds that determine either ice blink or water sky. Ice blink is light reflected off an ice field and visible as one studies the clouds at the horizon, while a water sky is a relative darkness reflected in the clouds at a distance. By steering toward the open water of the water sky, Armitage could guide the ship through the ice pack.

On 3 January 1902 the *Discovery* crossed the Antarctic Circle and also entered the ice pack, that band of ice formed around the continent over the winter from frozen seawater and from assorted icebergs calved from ice shelves and glaciers. In the spring, as the weather warmed, currents and winds drove the pack northward. One must pass through it to reach the open water on the other side and the continent that lies beyond. On one of the voyages of James Clark Ross, his ship had taken forty-six days to pass through this ribbon of ice.

Unlike Ross, Scott had the advantage of steam, which allowed him much greater maneuverability in the ice. Steam also provided the luxury of stopping to dredge in the pack, which the scientists did for nearly eight hours on the afternoon and evening of 3 January. Scott always showed great interest in the scientific results of these efforts, another indication of that unexpected bonus — his scientific proclivity. At one point, reflecting on the catch from one of the tow-netting efforts, Scott noted how "strange to have sailed the sea for many years in entire ignorance that such things were."[9]

Again the dredging effort brought mixed results. Hodgson had not prepared the sinkers and swivels correctly, and the line subsequently kinked as it was being brought in. Skelton's engineering mentality was offended by his colleagues: "These scientific people may be all right looking through a microscope and making theories but as a rule they are devilish little good at the practical work of catching their specimens."[10]

Pushing through the ice brought a number of opportunities for gathering larger specimens. When the ship stopped, one or more of the officers would shoot a hapless seal, and then a line would be thrown over the side to haul up the catch. In this way, during their time in the ice pack the scientists were able to gather examples of crabeater and Ross seals as well as Adélie and emperor penguins. At 3:00 A.M. one morning, Shackleton went down to Wilson's cabin to alert him to the sighting of a leopard seal, an animal they had not yet taken. Wilson went immediately to Scott and woke him up to get permission to stop the vessel to shoot the sea leopard; permission was granted. Shackleton and Skelton (who was apparently one of the better shots on the expedition and one often called out in these situations) took four or five shots to kill the eleven-foot creature who weighed nearly a ton. Anyone seeing close up for the first time one of these magnificent creatures is not likely to forget the experience of staring at the huge head (which Wilson described as being larger than that of a polar bear), the mouth full of menacing teeth, and the powerful build of a creature that even the casual observer feels is that of a magnificent predator. In the sea leopard's stomach was found an emperor penguin, which the scientists surmised must have been swallowed nearly whole.[11]

Once taken aboard, the seals were examined, especially the contents of their stomachs, to determine their diet. The animals were then skinned and preserved for shipment back to England. John Walker, one of the merchant men aboard, had served in whaling ships in the Arctic and was experienced at such work. Others helped with the preparations while the rest observed at a distance, for the "smell from the seal being skinned was distinctly fresh."[12] The waters of the pack ice area were also alive with various kinds of birds — Antarctic petrels, snow petrels, and penguins. Wilson was principally in charge of preparing bird specimens, but he could count on help from one of the bluejackets or, occasionally, Skelton.

Seals and penguins were not merely of scientific interest. From the beginning of this southward journey, seal and penguin became part of the ship's larder. Immediate reactions pronounced seal better than penguin, although the mammal's strong dark meat required care in preparation to ensure that all blubber had been removed. Seal, when cooked properly, was well received. William Lashly, one of the lead stokers, pronounced it "better than beef," and seal liver soon became a favorite dish.[13] The strong fishy taste of the bird was a taste acquired only by those in the most extreme cases of short rations on sledging expeditions.

On 4 January 1902 Scott ordered the ship tied to an ice floe to take on water. Although the ship was equipped to convert seawater to fresh, the process required steam power and depleted the limited supply of coal, the conservation of which was a constant worry for both the captain and the chief engineer.

Scott decided to pause on 5 January 1902 to celebrate Christmas. Service was held and Christmas hymns sung. Following that, the *Discovery* was tied up to a large berg and made fast with ice anchors. Included among the festivities of the day was skiing, which for almost all aboard was their first attempt at that activity. The results were humorous. That no effort was taken to gain some expertise at skiing before the outset of the expedition may seem strange because the value of this form of travel had been clearly demonstrated by explorers in the Arctic in the late nineteenth century and by Borchgrevink in the Antarctic in the immediate past. Remember, though, that nothing Borchgrevink did or accomplished was seen by Sir Clements Markham as having any value; the real standard was nineteenth-century Arctic expeditions by heroes such as McClintock, who did not use skis. Thus skis were not central in the mind of the planner of the expedition. Moreover, given the value placed in the nineteenth century on amateurism, Markham and others assumed that anyone could learn to ski without instruction or prior thought.

The first efforts on skis exposed the weakness of Markham's thinking. The trial showed far less grace by the skiers than it provided amusement to the onlookers. A schoolboy outing mentality dominated a day of practicing ski running on the ice.[14] To the credit of some, much progress was made in this opening day's effort, and eventually many of the officers and men became competent skiers. Once Scott had the experience of this expedition behind him, by 1910 he realized that skiing was too serious a business to leave to chance and he took with him on his second Antarctic expedition a Norwegian ski expert, Tryggve Gran.

Back aboard, some officers and men had a few quiet moments opening presents brought from home and saved for this day.[15] Some time was also taken up shooting seals for specimens.

The *Discovery* continued to push through the ice pack, unaware how long it would take to complete the passage. By 8 January, shortly after 7:00 A.M., the ship reached end of the ice pack, and open water lay ahead to the south. On that day the last of the sheep were killed and hung in the aft rigging (along with the carcasses of several seals being preserved for food). Later that evening the crew celebrated the triumph over the ice pack by splicing the main brace on the mess deck and with champagne in the wardroom. The festivities had no sooner finished when more good news came from the deck: Land was in sight. In the far distance was the nearest outcropping of the Antarctic continent, Cape Adare.[16]

The *Discovery* approached Cape Adare in the early hours of 9 January 1902. In the distance Bernacchi could see clearly his home of recent months. After the crew dropped anchor a half mile offshore, boats were sent ashore. Bernacchi, Barne, and Armitage left the ship to take magnetic observations, a process that took most of the day. The other scientists, save Hodgson, soon landed on the peninsula. Eventually, half the crew was allowed to go ashore.

Two items on the peninsula attracted the men's attention: the hut left from the *Southern Cross* expedition, which had wintered there in 1899[17]; and the penguin rookery, the first the *Discovery* crew had encountered. Borchgrevink's expedition actually had two buildings, a hut and a store house. Both were found in good repair, except that the roof of the store house was missing because Borchgrevink took it off in a half-baked plan to move the structure to the area around Mount Erebus. The design of the hut generally impressed these new visitors, although the hut seemed small quarters for such a long winter. Skelton noted with interest that the building was well anchored and had withstood the storms of the area well. The chief engineer was interested also in the "whaler design," having doors on the bunks to allow the inhabitants some privacy. Attached to one of the bunks was a note to a leader of a future expedition, in which Borchgrevink listed the achievements of the expedition, including a claim to the discovery of a new seal (untrue) and a new island, the Duke of York Island. The tone of the letter amused the readers from the *Discovery*, and the several mistakes in punctuation and grammar gave them further reason to denigrate Borchgrevink's achievements.[18]

Although the hut itself was in good order, a good deal of debris was scattered about outside. Included in the materials at the base were fifteen tons of coal.[19] The men searched through the rubble and took what they thought might be of use. From inside the hut they took a case of Bovril's lime juice crystals and several Union Jacks. Outside was a collection of items ranging from extra clothing to coal and dynamite.

Even before the men arrived on Cape Adare, they had gained an olfactory impression of the Adélie penguin rookery with its thousands of inhabitants, as the smell of guano wafted offshore and greeted the men as they approached.[20] On landing, the noise of birds added to the stench to

5. Adélie penguin.
Drawing by Kim Crosbie.

create a lasting impression. "It simply stunk like hell,"[21] was one reaction. Others were surprised that it was actually tolerable, noting, "the penguins don't smell particularly sweet, but it is not half as bad as one might expect because all the guano is either blown away or runs into the sea."[22] The explorers arrived when the chicks were largely at the crèche stage, at which time the young chicks huddle together in a rough circle with an occasional adult bird seemingly guarding them against predators, especially the wily skuas. The birds were so thick on the ground that, aimed at a small petrel, the same shot killed five penguins.[23]

The magnetic observers finished at about nine in the evening, and then

Bernacchi was free to visit the grave of his old comrade, Nikolai Hanson, who had died on the *Southern Cross* expedition. Earlier in the day a party had tried to find the grave without success, but Bernacchi went directly to it. Several members of the ship's party went with him. Gilbert Scott, the young marine, took a stone from the grave as a souvenir.[24]

Before departing, the crew left behind in the hut two cylinders, one with the official letters of the expedition and the other with private correspondence. These dispatches were to be the first of several mail cairns left by the *Discovery* as a guide to those in the relief ship that might come to rescue them the following year.[25] Markham's nineteenth-century British Arctic experience, dominated by the tragedy of the Franklin expedition, prompted this predetermination of sites where messages were to be left for the relief expedition.

Their activities completed at Cape Adare, the *Discovery* weighed anchor about 3:00 A.M. on 10 January and headed south. Armitage, who had been up nearly twenty-four hours when he returned to the ship, turned in but was shortly awakened by Scott, who did not like the looks of the ice conditions. Armitage went aloft to guide the ship through the pack ice in the direction of Coulman Island, work he accomplished with what Scott called "admirable patience."[26] The ship was prevented by a good deal of pack ice from staying as close to shore as the crew would have liked, and the trip down to Coulman took much longer because of an intense storm. The better part of a day was spent in the lee of Coulman Island, with the engines working hard to maintain the ship's position against the storm. A break in the storm on the evening of the thirteenth allowed a dredge to be put over the side, and the results were spectacular, the best they had had to this point. Hodgson was ecstatic as nearly seventy different species were removed from the dredge. Because so many of the creatures were new to science, the other officers and scientists readily shared Hodgson's enthusiasm.[27]

Pushing on to Coulman Island through winds that had again become stronger, the ship was eventually able to reach Cape Wadworth — named by Ross for the country home of his wife's uncle — which forms the northern end of Coulman Island. Coulman was Ross's father-in-law. Scott and Ferrar were taken ashore in a whaler, the latter to gather geological specimens while Scott supervised the erection of another mail cairn. Scott, who was to this point keeping his plans for the current summer and coming winter very much to himself, failed to notify the others in time for all to leave letters at the cape. The cairn was a tin affixed to a pole and placed near a large rock (all three were painted red), which was twenty or thirty feet above sea level. While Scott was ashore, Hodgson used the opportunity to dredge again.[28]

From there the ship headed toward Lady Newnes Bay.[29] Sailing into the bay, Scott found it free of ice with towering cliffs on either side and pronounced it a possible excellent wintering place.[30] Some emperor penguins and seals were found, and Scott decided to kill thirty seals for food, a chore that occupied five of the men for the rest of the day. Skelton and Shackleton went ashore to look around and climbed to the top of the ice foot. Returning, they found that Scott had ordered the ship watered. The men worked until 2:30 the next morning at this task and, after a break for cocoa, continued working throughout the night until 7:00 that morning.[31]

While these activities were taking place, a potentially dangerous situation had been playing out elsewhere in the bay. Wilson and Ferrar had gained permission to go out onto the floes with two of the bluejackets to retrieve ten emperor penguins that had been killed earlier in the day. By proceeding from one piece of ice to the next, the two scientists were able to secure the birds and pull them back to where some men were at work skinning seals. Having moved their seals and penguins onto one floe of several hundred acres, the four men discovered that the ice they were on was separated from the ship and was drifting to sea. Fortunately, the men had sunny and relatively warm weather (Ferrar had fallen in the water and had gotten part of one leg wet), and they were able to walk around to keep warm. The officer of the watch was aware of them but did not take action to rescue them, thinking the work with the seals and watering the ship would soon be over. As it turned out, the rescue of the men did not begin until after the ship finished the other work about 7:30 A.M. Not until 8:00 A.M. were the four rescued. Bad weather — always a potential problem in Antarctica — might have made the situation the second disaster of the expedition, but Wilson and the others were fortunate, and the only damage was the "overhauling" of the officer of the watch by Scott.[32]

Once under way again, Scott ordered the men to take the day off as the ship continued its southward voyage. Throughout the sixteenth and seventeenth of January the *Discovery* proceeded in beautifully clear weather along the shore of Victoria Land. The seal meat had been hung in the mizzen mast to freeze, while Skelton had started to render some of the blubber into oil for use in lighting and lubricating to extend the supplies of oils aboard.[33] Armitage spent a good deal of his time in the crow's nest to find the best path through the ice, a pastime he described as a sport that would appeal to many if they could experience it.

It always seemed to me that I had more absolute control of the ship when I was in that situation than in any other. Beneath one is the ship herself, her whole upper contour sharply and gracefully delineated; and one feels, as it were, quite separated from her, and yet directing her every motion. Ahead and all around is a vast, illimitable field of ice, which in the farthest distance appears to be absolutely impervious to attack. Somewhat closer are to be seen thin black-looking streaks of water, and still closer to the ship, the weak places in the line of defense thrown out from the inhospitable land which we are determined to reach, are easily seen; and one is able to guide the ship from one lead to the other by the least line of resistance.[34]

As the ship proceeded toward Wood Bay, the temperature had dropped temporarily, and pancake ice had begun to form. Wood Bay had been thought of as a likely place to winter the ship, based in part on the impression Bernacchi gave to Markham and Scott before the expedition departed, and thus, when the *Discovery* pushed its way into the bay full of heavy ice, some disappointment ensued. Scott believed that the bay might clear with the next gale but decided not to use further time and coal exploring it and instead to continue south toward Mount Erebus.

On 20 January 1902 the vessel came into Granite Harbour, another promising wintering site. A landing party explored the area and found some lichen and insects that were living in moss, both findings pleasing Koettlitz. The inlet seemed to Scott to be "the most excellent spot for wintering, completely land locked and well sheltered from the wind."[35]

Yet the very next day another potential wintering spot appeared to offer even greater potential. Scott headed his ship into what he at first called McMurdo Bay, because he saw what appeared to be continuous land at the outer perimeter of the water. Further investigation proved that the body of water was not a bay but a sound, McMurdo Sound.[36] As the ship moved into the sound, no mountains appeared off in the distance beyond the water, and Scott hoped that it might mean an open path to the South, either by land or sea.[37] Hopes that it might go on a long distance were soon dashed, and Scott ordered the ship to head out of McMurdo Sound again.

By 22 January the ship had proceeded to Cape Crozier, one of the prearranged places for a message about the fate of the *Discovery* to be left for the relief ship. Scott led a large party ashore, including all the scientists, except Hodgson, who stayed aboard to dredge. The approach to shore involved winding one's way through icebergs either grounded or moving. Many were worn, and as the men passed close to bergs that were eroding and resembled fanciful images they were greatly impressed. The colors of blue were particularly unforgettable. Once ashore Barne helped Bernacchi take magnetic observations, while the others explored the area and erected the mail cairn, which contained both official records and private letters from the staff. At least one member of the crew speculated on whether the letters would ever reach home.[38] While that effort was getting started, Ferrar and Koettlitz used the opportunity to gather specimens. Wilson and Royds joined Scott on a walk up a nearby rise to gain a view over what was then known as the Great Ice Barrier, now called the Ross Ice Shelf. What a sight! A sheet of ice larger than France stretched out before them, from an angle never before seen by humans.[39]

On the way back to the boats, the three passed through a penguin rookery, giving additional opportunity to observe the behavior of Adélie penguins, including feeding chases in which two or three hungry young chicks chase an adult in the hope of being fed. Eventually, one is usually successful and receives a regurgitated meal from the parent. These birds were at this point not well studied, and the *Discovery* staff added a great deal to the understanding of Adélies.

The men then returned to the ship. During the shore party's activities Armitage had stayed aboard and swung the ship again and had taken magnetic observations. The ship then proceeded eastward. By 6:00 A.M. on 23 January 1902 the *Discovery* approached, and the rest of the crew was given a first sight of what was at the time the most famous of Antarctic landmarks, the Great Ice Barrier. Curiously, aboard the *Discovery* the reaction to this great wonder was less than overwhelming. Wilson thought it "not stupendous in any way," while Skelton, who had been awakened to see it, thought it "a bit exaggerated."[40] Reaction below decks was similar — Gilbert Scott was "greatly disappointed" in its appearance.[41] Strange that this immense wall of ice standing up at a hundred or more feet above sea level and which had dazzled Ross and his men had such mixed reactions among members of the *Discovery*.

For more than a week the vessel moved eastward along the Great Barrier, which formed a large wall of ice ranging in height from 240 feet to as little as 2 feet. As the ship progressed along the barrier, the weather was generally good, "all that can be desired." Frequent soundings were taken; the depth along the edge ranged from 100 to 482 fathoms. Dozens of large bergs were passed en route. On 26 January 1902 the *Discovery* established a new farthest south for a vessel, 78°34'30" S.[42] By the seventh day many aboard were convinced that the end of the barrier was near, as it was becoming lower and closer to the water. All aboard believed in the possibility of finding new land at the end. Bad weather disappointed the land watchers throughout the thirtieth, but late in the day, about 6:30 P.M., the weather cleared enough for Shackleton to get a glimpse of what he was certain was land. Thus the expedition first saw King Edward VII Land, one of the two most important geographical discoveries of the expedition.[43]

The next day the weather cleared, and Scott ordered that the ship be watered. Emperor penguins appeared in abundance, which led to speculation that a rookery was nearby. No one had yet discovered one, and at this point no emperor penguin egg had been located. From the crow's nest a rookery might have been seen, but the staff was unable to confirm this. Wilson wanted very much to try to reach a rookery and confirm its existence, but the conditions of the ice were increasingly making that impossible. As the ship was being watered, fresh ice was forming in the bay, and Scott was concerned lest the ship be caught in the ice without the protection of a harbor. Already the ship was pushing through dense ice pack. Unaware that such freezing might occur, only to be followed by the scattering of the ice and the opening of ice-free water, Scott ordered that the ship return to McMurdo Sound. He much regretted having to miss the chance of pushing a little farther to the east, as observations indicated the presence of high land beyond where they were. Thus the *Discovery* departed for the west. Scott speculated in his diary that pushing farther east might be "noble work for the third season," although at that time funding did not allow for such a third season.[44]

The first day westward, 1 February 1902, the officers on watch had difficulty in keeping their bearing, and the ship eventually sailed in a circle, arriving back at the spot where it had been watered. The ice was forming rapidly near the ship, providing the crew with a few anxious moments.[45]

Ice encrusted the ropes as the vessel steamed westward at a good pace on 2 February, for Scott was now in a hurry.[46] That evening Scott held a meeting in the wardroom to explain, at long last, his plans for the remainder of the season and the voyage. The ship would return to McMurdo Sound as quickly as possible and winter there as far south as was feasible. The entire company was to winter over on the ship.[47] Thus for the first time, everyone knew what had been virtually a done deal for the past year, that the *Discovery*, not a small wintering party, would remain on the ice.

With the return of spring, three parties were to engage in sledging trips.

The main one would proceed south, although no definite goal, including the Pole, was mentioned. A second group of sledging trips would be made exploring in the vicinity of Mounts Erebus and Terror. Then, once the relief ship arrived, it would depot part of its coal and then take Armitage and a party to Wood Bay where they would embark on a journey to the South Magnetic Pole, which unlike the geographical pole, was of real scientific merit and interest. The relief ship would rendezvous with Armitage and return him to New Zealand. Thus at this point Armitage still could clearly hope to play a major role in the accomplishments of the expedition. Meanwhile, the *Discovery* would have waited the return of the southern party (no mention was made of whom that party might consist) and explore from Cape Adare to Cape North and on to Wilkes Land, ending up in New Zealand to join the relief ship for the winter.[48]

The following spring (assuming funding) the *Discovery* would sail south, to the east end of the Great Ice Barrier and explore eastward from there until March, when it would turn home via Cape Horn, arriving in England about July 1904.[49]

Armitage later wrote that he believed his appointment was independent of Scott's and that Markham had promised that he would be landed with a hut and men for two years but that this had not been fulfilled although such a program was "quite feasible.[50] The possibility that Markham encouraged Armitage to believe this is not out of the question, nor can one omit the possibility that Armitage, who eventually came to see this expedition as not living up to his expectations, saw Markham's promise as another example of his reasons for disappointment.

By 3 February 1902 the ship had arrived at a break in the barrier, which came to be known on this expedition as balloon bight but later had the name Bay of Whales attached to it by Shackleton's *Nimrod* expedition. The barque was tied up to the edge of the barrier at about four o'clock in the afternoon.

Armitage gained permission to lead a small party south, and shortly thereafter he, Bernacchi, Joyce, Crean, and Handsley, were trudging off across the barrier, manhauling. As the wind came up late in the afternoon, Scott decided to wait until morning for more favorable conditions for the balloon launching.[51] Late in the day Scott, accompanied by Skelton and Shackleton, went out on skis to investigate the region to the south, finding in the process a Weddell seal rookery. The surface of the barrier was found to be good for traveling, although the sastrugi — undulations in the ice, resembling waves on the ocean — were found to be difficult to travel over. Returning from the brief sojourn, Skelton described the surface in his journal and how a good sledge party should be able to make "fifteen miles a day even without dogs." Moreover, the engineer added, "I have an idea that a motor car driven by petroleum could be constructed to do very good work on it [the barrier]; of course, the design would have to be greatly different from ordinary cars especially in the matter of wheels, and the body would have to be a van to use as a hut, precautions would have to be taken in case of a breakdown to take sledges."[52] Skelton's thoughts described an idea that continued to fascinate explorers throughout the Heroic Era — traveling by motorcar to the South Pole. Later that evening Skelton mentioned his idea to Armitage, who said that he had considered polar travel with a different form of transport — Siberian ponies. Armitage influenced both Shackleton and Scott with this idea, and both took ponies on subsequent expeditions, Shackleton in 1907 and Scott in 1910.[53]

After dinner on the evening of 3 February, the officers played the men in a football match, almost certainly the first staged on the Ross Ice Shelf. The next morning the weather improved somewhat, and preparations were made to inflate the balloon. The idea for a balloon had first been suggested by Sir Joseph Hooker. Scott had made a significant effort to add a balloon to the expedition's equipment, although its exact purpose was never explained. Skelton was essentially in charge of the group responsible for the balloon, although Shackleton, Kennar, Heald, and Lashly had all been to Aldershot for a short course of instruction (one to seven days) in how to inflate and operate the mechanism.[54]

The balloon was part of the army's arsenal of weapons at the turn of the century and had been constructed from the gut of bullocks, sewn by women working under top-secret conditions. Ordinarily, sixteen cylinders of gas inflated it, but on the ice nineteen were required. Tethered to the ground by a one-inch wire (which Skelton thought a bit too heavy), the apparatus was ready to go late in the morning. Lashly, one of the lead stokers and known to be an exceptionally intelligent bluejacket, took a leading role in this effort. Preparing the balloon was cold work, and the temperature and the newness of the apparatus made the inflation more difficult. Twice while filling, the balloon was torn and had to be repaired. Scott, although he had not been through the course at Aldershot and knew nothing at all about the operation of the balloon, assumed his right as commander to be the first to ascend in the south polar regions. He went up about 550 feet, rather quickly. Once up he looked around for a short time, pronouncing the view "magnificent," and then began to descend, again, rather quickly. Hurriedly, he tossed out handfuls of ballast, but when that did not seem to alter the downward momentum, he threw overboard an entire bag of ballast. His ground crew admonished him not to be so extravagant with ballast, and after a few more harrowing moments, Scott was again safe on the terra firma.[55]

Shackleton was next up and with his camera took the first aerial photographs in Antarctica. From his vantage point 650 feet above the surface he could see the sledging party returning from their effort, but as far to the south as he looked, he could see no land (at that point the mountains were several hundred miles away). He returned, and his place was taken by Heald, who went up for a short time before lunch. In the afternoon Koettlitz and Hodgson were allowed up for short solo flights. By then the balloon was discovered to have a serious leak and a faulty valve and was ordered stowed for a future opportunity. That process was very difficult, as the wind complicated the situation. The balloon was never used again.[56]

Skelton did not think the effort had produced much result, and Wilson was extremely critical of the operation, noting that Scott went up and came down and "through no fault of his own came down safely." The young zoologist thought it "perfect madness to allow novices to risk their lives in this silly way, merely for the sake of novel sensation when so much depends on the life of each one of us for the success of the expedition."[57]

While some men were involved in the balloon adventure, others killed and brought to the ship eighteen seal carcasses, an arduous task given the distance from the rookery to the ship. Thomas Feather, the boatswain, was singled out by Scott for special praise for fine work done under difficult conditions.[58]

Meanwhile, Armitage's sledging party had returned after a twenty-hour adventure. As it turned out the men had had some difficulties with their cooker — they had set out without determining if anyone knew how to use it. Both Bernacchi and Armitage had assumed that they could operate it; they could not. Thus they could not cook their food. Armitage's group had marched out approximately seven miles and turned in for the night; unfortunately, they had a three-man tent and six men. They tried squeezing in together, but Bernacchi gave up and slept outside. In the morning Armitage and three companions pushed farther south before turning back to the ship. In the process they may have inadvertently made a new farthest south, eclipsing Borchgrevink's 1900 effort by a few thousand yards. Scott noted with pride that, typical of the fine man that Jacob Cross was, he no sooner returned from this short but exhausting trip that his first thought was to exercise his dog.[59]

In the early evening the vessel steamed out of the inlet and once in more open water proceeded under sail at about six knots, a good speed for the *Discovery*. Skelton was glad for the opportunity to save valuable coal. Two days of sailing brought the crew back to McMurdo Sound. Before entering the sound, Armitage again swung the ship to determine the magnetic variations. Scott directed the ship into the sound, and it soon came to a possible landing sight. Scott hoped for a place in McMurdo Sound, because it was a good deal farther south than Granite Harbor, another possible wintering place. Moreover, McCormick, a member of Ross's expedition, had mentioned McMurdo Sound as possible winter quarters. On 8 February 1902 the *Discovery* had arrived at what appeared to be a strong possibility for winter quarters. Scott and Armitage went ashore to look at it. Scott's first reaction was that it looked "bleak," but he ordered the ship tied up with ice anchors. Lashly agreed with the assessment, noting that it "looks like a dreary place to spend twelve months." The next morning the site's appearance was much better, and Scott could detect no signs of potentially damaging ice pressure. The water was shallow (as the crew had discovered when they had come around the end of the point and of which they were reminded when they eventually tried to steam out). Scott hoped the shallow water would protect them from drifting bergs. The site also had the advantage of being near Cape Crozier, one of the mail cairns the relief ship would be expected to find. That afternoon a small storm arose and the ice anchors dragged, putting the ship into potential danger. Skelton's staff had steam up, and in fourteen minutes the engines were ready and the difficulty was averted.[60]

On the afternoon of the ninth, Skelton joined the captain for a walk. Observation Hill was named, and on their excursion they discovered a large seal rookery, with more than a hundred potential additions to the larder.[61] Wilson and Barne went for a walk that opening day, and they, too, took pleasure at seeing the seals, which Wilson thought "practically puts scurvy out of the question."[62] The crew of the *Discovery* was home for the winter.

Scott's decision to winter the ship was one that reflected the goals of his mentor, Sir Clements, and clearly was in Scott's mind from the beginning. Scott was looking for a place to winter the ship all along the route down the coast and along the barrier. At first he thought Cape Adare would be a good location.[63] The mail cairns left en route were further evidence that Scott intended to winter, although they were of potential use should the ship sink. Despite this, in his published account Scott indicated that the original intent had not been to overwinter the ship — but having found suitable quarters, the captain opted to winter.[64]

The process of settling in began on 10 February 1902. An attempt was made to dislodge some fast ice to bring the ship around to a better place, but the explosion of the charges showed the great strength of the ice — a small hole was the only result, "practically nil."[65] Thus from the beginning Scott had an idea that explosives would not necessarily extricate a ship from an ice-bound condition. A sight was chosen for the main hut and for the observation huts on the land near the ship. That night homecoming was celebrated with a football game.

Although officers and men might compete on the playing field, Scott would tolerate no breech in naval conduct. The cook, Brett, had been insolent to Shackleton, and when brought before the captain, had been similarly rude to him. Scott had the man put in irons. A struggle ensued as the man did not go willingly. "Eight hours brought him to his senses," and he was released, although Scott's assessment of Brett was that he was "a wretched specimen of humanity."[66]

Building the hut was a considerable task. The dogs were used, for the first time, to help bring up some of the sections of the prefabricated structure, but Scott thought the dogs "young and untrained and haven't any idea of their duty." Scott's sense of naval order ran afoul of the dogs, who were "a terrible drawback to anything like cleanliness and render the condition of life aboard almost unsanitary."[67]

Scott's initial prejudices against skis were also evident in the process of setting up camp, as he noted that although the men had found a splendid ski run which was good fun, the ski "will be of little use for men dragging." Eventually and grudgingly, over the next nine years Scott moderated his views on skiing.[68]

Erecting the hut demonstrated the degree to which the structure was not a particularly well-designed building. The intent was to construct it on supports dug several feet into the ground, but digging holes even a few inches into the frozen soil was an arduous task. The hut had been built in Australia to J. W. Gregory's design and "was more suitable for a colonial shooting-lodge than for a polar dwelling." Thirty-six feet square, with a veranda around the outside, the original design called for interior partitions, but only one was installed, at what came to be known as Hut Point.

Beautifully situated, the dwelling was "most imposing outside and looks palatial within, certainly the largest hut ever used by explorers and designed for one of the smallest exploring parties." The hut's original purpose was eliminated when the *Discovery* overwintered. During the *Discovery* expedition the structure served as a store room and place to dry clothes and hold entertainment. Eventually, the hut was stocked with eight months' provisions and oil and fifteen tons of coal.[69]

Equally important was the erection of the prefabricated magnetic huts that were vital to the scientific program. One of them was soon found to be terribly warped, because the structure was made of unseasoned wood; still the carpenter managed to erect both it and the other.[70]

Work and recreation went on apace that opening week. Football was played on the ice a couple of days before the ice wore down. The games were well played. Sides were chosen at random or by some combination— officers versus men, for example. Several of the men were accomplished players. Still, the officers managed to hold their own, Dailey and Royds being good players. Neither Wilson nor Ferrar played. In one game an additional player attempted to take the field. An Adélie penguin attracted to the curious display on the ice attempted "to join in and going in for rather rough play, [and] it had to be removed from the field."[71]

Scott was pleased with the progress of the men in learning to ski and thought he might put up a competition to encourage them. Unfortunately, the crew soon learned the downside of downhill when Ford, one of the stewards, broke his leg. Skelton considered Ford a very clumsy sort of person and ventured that no one else could have broken his leg in such a manner. Although annoyed with the accident, "a great nuisance at this time," Scott commended Buckridge for his good sense and the care he took with the victim, covering him with his waistcoat and coat and building a little snow shelter until Ford could be moved. Both doctors went out and put a splint on his leg and brought him back to the ship in a rather frozen condition.[72]

Thus the opening weeks were passed in a mixture of hard work and some play. The scientists had already begun to investigate the area, and already Hodgson showed early signs of the determination and hard work that characterized his contributions on the expedition. That he was always, in these early weeks, able to find a volunteer crew to man the whaler was an indication that the workload was not overly taxing and, perhaps more telling, provided some insight into the quality of the bluejackets and their appreciation of the need to volunteer for duty.[73]

Every Sunday the entire party assembled for church. Scott read the service; Koettlitz, befitting his position as the token head of the scientific staff, read the lesson. Royds played the pianola. The image of the men standing on deck in the bitter Antarctic autumn, with the sound of their hymns resounding over Hut Point, was a picture of Edwardian England.

On 16 February 1902 the sun dipped below the horizon for the first time. Fall was turning to winter, and much had to be done before the arrival of the days of darkness.

Scott decided to send a small sledging party to reconnoiter to the south. That he chose Shackleton to lead it may be instructive of his estimate of the merits of his young third officer. Shackleton had turned his hand to every task, had been enthusiastic about every aspect of the expedition, including his own primitive contributions to the scientific program, and had shown his pluck with his tireless work, especially most recently in restowing in an orderly and efficient manner the entire ship in New Zealand. To accompany him, Scott chose Wilson and Ferrar. They were to take provisions for three weeks, a pram to cross or guard against being caught by open water, and a sledge.[74]

Winds prevented their departure on 18 February 1902, but the following day they set out on their adventure. Meanwhile, the hut was nearing completion.

A tragedy was narrowly avoided on 21 February. While working aft, Royds fell into the icy (29° F) water near the ship when the area of ice on which he was working gave way. No one heard him, and Royds was forced to extricate himself. Fortunately, he kept his wits about him, and being a good swimmer, swam to a rope ladder that was fortunately hanging over the stern, and pulled himself back on deck. Once again, the expedition had narrowly missed having its second fatality.[75]

The next day Scott had Koettlitz address the men on the need to be careful in general and of frostbite in particular. Koettlitz's remarks were rather dry and did not have a tone designed to instill in the men a strong sense of the dangers. He concentrated on describing the symptoms, more from a medical perspective than to create in his audience a real appreciation for the hazards of the extreme cold temperature and how quickly a dangerous situation could turn into a fatal one. Scott wished that Koettlitz had quoted more cases of death and amputations and frightened the men more. Skelton noted how dry and lifeless Koettlitz had made the lecture when it might have been presented as exciting material.[76]

The topic could hardly have been more timely, for no sooner had people begun to retire for the night when Shackleton's sledging party returned. The loquacious Shackleton let loose a torrent of description regarding their activities. The others could scarcely manage to interject a comment. But here at least was real experience, not idle speculation about the conditions that faced them in future forays.

Shackleton's party had departed on 19 February 1902, being accompanied to the first little hill by Koettlitz and Hodgson; from that point their apprenticeship began. True to the nineteenth-century Arctic origins of the expedition, Markham had insisted that each officer have a sledging flag, just as had been the case in the Arctic. Thus the three men marched south with their individual sledging flags flying. As they headed toward the island, their goal for the day's journey, the novices soon got a lesson in judging distance in the crisp, clear air of the Antarctic. Their destination seemed only a few miles away, and yet after several hours of pulling their sledge and pram they were startled to note that their goal still appeared several miles away. A brief lunch break interrupted their hike. No sooner had they resumed their march when Wilson felt an excruciating pain in his right big toe, a symptom he recognized as frostbite. Circulation was soon restored to the toe, but it continued to hurt as the party continued south.[77]

Shortly thereafter the weather deteriorated, and they found themselves heading into a blizzard. In Antarctica blizzards can become so severe that whiteout conditions develop, and one has no idea of direction; becoming lost is virtually a certainty. Ignorant of the extreme danger of whiteout conditions, the party pushed on. Soon the storm obscured sight of their island goal. By 11:30 P.M., having been sledging for twelve hours, with only a slight break for lunch, they realized they must camp.[78]

Shackleton and Ferrar, like Wilson, were also frostbitten. Their fatigue and inexperience made erecting the tent more difficult. Once inside the tent the trio assessed their health. All three had frostbite, mostly on hands and faces, and each discovered that his socks were frozen to his boots. The three men put on their fur boots for the tent and began to cook supper — pemmican, cocoa, biscuit, jam, and butter. After the meal they snuggled up and slept in the small tent. Ferrar, who was most exhausted, was given the inner and most warm location.[79]

Up at 3:30 A.M., they broke camp and continued on toward the island but by 7:30 A.M. were at a place where their path was blocked by unsafe ice; they camped and slept until 4:00 P.M. While stopping for a meal, Wilson sketched the area and Shackleton took observations. Leaving their gear behind, they headed for the island about a mile or two distant. The last bit before reaching land involved crossing some difficult ice, but at last Wilson, Shackleton, and Ferrar arrived and succeeded in climbing to the summit, which was the goal of their journey.[80]

The pilgrims had a wondrous sight — as far as the eye could see: a level ice plain, "the true Great Barrier surface." Picnicking on nearly frozen tea and bits of Bovril chocolate, they could justifiably feel satisfied with their accomplishment.[81]

After returning to their tent, they ate a meal and slept for eight hours, waking for another meal, and then preparing to explore the area further. The trio investigated in the direction of the southwest end of the island for the next five hours and then returned to camp for the night.[82]

The next morning, 22 February, the men broke camp and turned back to the ship. By late afternoon they thought they were near enough to risk an attempt to make it back that evening and so stopped only for dinner. As they made their way back they discovered that the ice had gone out on part of their route, which necessitated an exasperating detour. By 10:00 P.M. the trio was within a half an hour's march of home and, leaving their gear, walked the last leg back to the ship, arriving at 10:30 P.M. Thus ended the first sledging journey of the expedition.[83]

Writing after the expedition, Scott noted how primitive was their planning and how limited was their expertise at the outset: "Strange now to look back on these first essays at sledging, and to see how terribly hampered we were by want of experience."[84]

In another respect the first effort of Shackleton's group showed how much they would eventually learn. Returning from this brief sojourn, all three men had pronounced the pemmican inedible — far too rich. The pemmican soup, which, in this instance had been made to the specifications of the planners of the expedition and contained sixty percent lard for that extra little fuel in cold weather, was too strange to the palate. Once the sledging became really intense and the conditions more horrible than even these three could imagine, the pemmican was found to be wonderfully delightful because the body craved the high fat content.[85]

Having been in winter quarters a month, a routine was beginning to develop. Church services on Sunday were followed by an afternoon of rest. For the remainder of the week the scientists were engaged in their activities, usually assisted by one or two of the men. On Saturdays the men cleaned and on Sunday mornings before church stood for inspection by the captain.

The main hut, which came to be known as "Professor Gregory's Villa," was nearly completed. The magnetic hut was ready in time for Bernacchi to begin his regular observations on 1 March 1902. Skelton and his staff worked to assemble the windmill that had been brought from England to provide electricity for lighting through the winter. From the beginning Skelton was skeptical of its value, and in the end his engineer's opinion was proven correct.

To Scott's surprise the ice had still not frozen in around the ship; indeed, had he known, he would have had another month of exploring before he actually had to return to base. Scott relied on Ross's experience from the 1840s, although he did note that the crew of the *Southern Cross*, when it had departed in early March (almost a month after the *Discovery* went into winter quarters), thought they were just escaping being trapped by the ice.[86] Moreover, Scott had discovered some local disturbances in the weather that were not reassuring — that they were anchored in an area with considerably more wind than other places in the immediate area.[87]

In view of additional information about the location of the *Discovery* that would be of use to the relief expedition, Scott decided to lead a party to Cape Crozier to update the information contained in the mail cairn there. As February was coming to a close, he began to make preparations for that sojourn. He would take Royds, Skelton, Koettlitz, eight men, and eight dogs and journey overland to Cape Crozier.

Meanwhile, football and skiing formed the main outdoor recreational activities. As virtually none of the officers had any experience before arriving in the south polar regions and as no real ski expert was aboard, the learning process involved the occasional accident.

Scott learned this all too painfully on 28 February when he sprained his right knee while skiing near the ship. At first he hoped it would not interfere with the trip to Cape Crozier, but the following days proved his initial assessment to be too optimistic. Scott was forced to turn the leadership of the Crozier trip over to Royds, which meant forgoing a valuable learning experience that Scott recognized he would need to make the most of during the following spring's efforts. Scott noted, "to miss such an opportunity of gaining experience was terribly trying."[88] Although Scott held out hope of a last-minute recovery, Royds became the leader, and Barne was added as the fourth officer, a change of plans that subsequently contributed to tragedy.[89]

Scott was unable to make the rounds or conduct services on Sunday, 2 March 1904, an indication of the slow state of his recovery. Armitage took his place in both responsibilities.[90]

Preparations for the sledging trip went ahead with a change of personnel. Shackleton busied himself with the hundreds of details of preparing food and equipment for the sledging party—weighing out the parcels of food and putting them in separate canvas bags.[91]

On 4 March 1902 Royds led his party away from the ship for the purpose of leaving additional information for the relief ship at Cape Crozier. In selecting the men for the journey, Scott had opted to take a proportional number of men from each rating, meaning that he balanced the party by rank, rather than taking what might have been considered the best members of the expedition. Divided into two groups, Royds and Koettlitz led Arthur Quartly, William Weller, Wild, and Vince, while Barnes and Skelton's team included Edgar Evans, Heald, Plumley, and Hare.[92]

Scott had known Edgar Evans when the latter had served on the HMS *Majestic*. Evans was a man of Herculean strength and had been a physical education instructor in the Royal Navy. He was a boxer with well-muscled arms, but his pugilistic skills were matched by a kind spirit and good nature.[93]

Arthur Quartly was the only American aboard the *Discovery*, although he had entered the expedition as a member of the Royal Navy, transferring from the HMS *Majestic*. Six feet tall and regarded along with Evans as one of the two strongest men in the party, Quartly, known as "Ginger" on the expedition, was one of the leading stokers in Skelton's crew and was described as the "handsomest figure amongst the ship's company."[94]

William J. Weller was an able-bodied seaman who had come to the *Discovery* from the merchant marine. Weller was in charge of the dogs, having accompanied them to New Zealand where he and his charges boarded the ship.[95]

Scott wanted Royds's party to proceed directly to Cape Crozier, leave the additional information, and return. If the party had not returned in fourteen days, the ship would be sent to search for them. On the morning of 4 March 1902, they departed. As the two teams left the ship, the men and the dogs were harnessed together. That the dogs did not perform well may have been due to this inefficient method of working them. The team put in a long opening day and camped for the evening. As the Royds's party was having trouble with the primus stove (because, Skelton thought, the men were heavy-handed with the equipment), Barne's group did the cooking for everyone.[96]

They continued on the second day, noting the improvements needed to be made in equipment. The officers who led had the roughest part, breaking the trail and keeping the course, but the day was without incident. By the end of the second day, in which they made five miles, the party was fourteen miles from the ship. Following dinner, Skelton and Barne went over to Royds's tent for a smoke before turning in for the night.[97]

The third day they managed seven miles. By the fourth day the exhausting work of leading was passed from Skelton and Barne to Heald and Evans. That evening the four officers met to discuss the situation. Royds and Barne were in favor of turning back, while Skelton and Koettlitz thought it best to try to continue on to the goal. Koettlitz suggested that the four officers go on while the men were to be sent back.[98]

As this was the first major sledging party, a brief description of life on the trail is in order. Awakened by the senior officer, the rest of the party struggled out of their sleeping bags and then changed into their daytime outfits, meaning they put on their outer windsuits. Following breakfast the group usually got started at about 9:30 A.M., the late start caused by the difficulty of dressing, eating, and breaking camp. After a morning's sledging they stopped for lunch, and then they either erected a tent or, occasionally, pushed on through the afternoon.[99]

Setting up camp at the end of the day was even more difficult than the morning routine. First, one took off the harness and set it aside. Erecting the tent was tricky even in calm weather, but when the wind was blowing the difficulties multiplied. One man spread the bamboo legs, while another arranged the tent cloth over the poles and piled snow up all around it for protection against the elements and to keep it in place. An oiled canvas cloth served as the floor inside the tent. Light green in color, the tents withstood more wind than anyone would have imagined.[100]

Once the tent was set up, the cook for the day began the process of making the evening meal and melting ice or snow for water, tea, or cocoa. The others fed the dogs and then looked after their own gear. Using a primus and a Nansen cooker, the water was brought to a boil. Meanwhile, others had passed to the cook the provisions of the day. When the water boiled, the pemmican was dropped into it, along with seasoning (which included soup cubes) and anything else within reach. By the time the men got inside, the meal was ready, and the stew or "hoosh" as it came to be known, was placed in each man's pannikin. A good hoosh was too thick to drink and had to be eaten with a spoon. In a really good hoosh, the spoon would stand.[101]

While the cook maneuvered, the men worked quickly to get their windsuits off and change footgear from the daily kit to the nighttime attire, which included sleeping socks that were carried next to the skin during the day to keep them from freezing. Unlacing the burberry leggings and boots had to be done with bare fingers; it could not be accomplished otherwise. Over the evening socks went fur boots that reached to the knees. By that time fingers were painfully cold. After socks and boots, fur jumpers and trousers were put on, an easy task the first day, but subsequently, when encrusted with ice, they were stiff and bitterly cold to the touch. Finally, the head was covered by a kind of helmet for sleeping; it might be the same device used throughout the day. Royds never took his helmet off on the entire trip to Cape Crozier. Next, one had to shape the day boots, just taken off, into a form so that they would freeze in a shape that one could get a foot into the next morning.[102]

By the time the clothing change was finished, the men hoped, the evening meal was ready. As the men ate their food, the Nansen cooker was put back into service to melt ice for cocoa, the usual evening drink. Ideally, cocoa was supposed to be the same thickness as the hoosh.

While the warmth of the meal surged through their bodies, the men crawled into their sleeping bags, which varied from single-person ones to those for three men. Some preferred the latter because they tended to be warmer. Then came the final activities of the evening: a pipe and perhaps a little journal writing. The pipe had to be carried in a pocket during the day; otherwise the stem froze. Then perchance to sleep, easier done if one had the middle spot in the tent with someone on either side to provide insulation.[103]

On 8 March 1902 Royds suggested to Skelton that he and Koettlitz go on together while Barne was sent back with the men. Skelton agreed to the plan, and the next morning, with the sledges repacked, a quick check determined that each party could manage its load, and the two set off in opposite directions. The outward-bound party had a good day, twelve and a half miles.[104] As they progressed, Skelton was surprised to find how easy pulling sledges on skis was, quite contrary to the opinions of others before this journey began.[105]

Days of eight, fourteen, and six miles followed as the trio worked their way toward Cape Crozier. A blizzard held them up on the morning of 13 March. By the next morning they were aware that their time was limited, because they had to either complete their mission or run the risk of having a rescue party sent out for them. Royds's men reached Crozier the following day and worked their way down to the shore in deteriorating weather. There they discovered that, despite having been there by ship, they were unable to find the cairn. Retreating to their base camp, they barely got back to the tent before the weather closed in. They had spent eight hours in a howling blizzard.[106]

The next morning the weather made another attempt on Crozier unthinkable, and the three men decided to abandon the attempt and return to the ship. Returning that day, they were able to pick up their outbound tracks and made eighteen miles in the direction of home. Overnight, the temperature dropped to $-42°$ F, and the trio spent a bad night shivering in their tent. A long day brought them nearly sixteen miles closer to the ship, leaving thirty more. Blizzard conditions and snow blindness reduced their progress on the seventeenth, and the full day's efforts brought them only three to four miles closer to their destination.[107]

The final two days were tough. A change from pemmican to beef plasmon rations — a fortified milk product — left them hungry and unsatisfied. Koettlitz said that the nutritional value was the same as pemmican and that one could go all day on a few ounces of it, to which Skelton replied, "the fewer ounces the better."[108] On their last day on the trail, the three men managed eight miles by lunch and by 5:00 P.M. were at Pram Point and pushed on, arriving at the *Discovery* in the evening.[109]

Their return was not as they expected. The warmth of their welcome was heartfelt but tempered by the disaster that had struck the other party in their absence.

The first day after the parties split, Barne's group made good progress, but problems began on 11 March 1902. They had turned from Castle Rock in the direction of the ship when the harshness of the weather forced Barne to order a halt and the tent erected to provide some protection from the weather. Unable to heat food to restore their energy because the stoves were out of order by that time, they ate biscuits and frozen pemmican for lunch.[110]

Meanwhile, young Vince was having trouble with his feet, which had become very cold in his leather ski boots, so he took the boots off inside the tent to try to restore the circulation. Vince accepted Quartly's offer of his fur boots, which he had been carrying inside his clothes. Before they left, Quartly told Vince to change back into leather ski boots as the fur ones would be hard to walk in, and Quartly also took the responsibility of warning the men in his tent to dress as warmly as possible for the blizzard seemed to be worsening.[111]

Recklessly pushing on into the teeth of the blizzard, Barne turned the dogs loose to find their own way home while his party moved cautiously along the slopes, which he presumed led to the *Discovery*. Like Vince, Hare was in fur boots, and the two had great difficulty in maintaining their footing. The other men helped the two that were having trouble with their footing along the path. At that point Hare decided to go back to the tent to get his leather boots, and although Heald told him to wait, the young man took off on his own and soon disappeared into the swirling snow. The others attempted to find Hare but failed, and while attempting this, Evans lost his footing and fell down a steep slope and disappeared. Showing perhaps more courage than careful reason, Barne immediately threw himself over the same slope to help Evans.[112]

Nothing happened for a few minutes; then Quartly told the others that he, too, would go over the slope in an attempt to find the first two. Over he went, and after a few seconds of flying through the void he found himself sprawled in a small snow field. Looking up he found Barne and Evans.[113] Trying to return to the other men was impossible, given the slippery nature of the slope, and so they carefully made their way in the direction of the ship. At one point Quartly called out to Barne, who stopped inches from a void that led directly down into the sea and certain death. Quartly, not presuming to lead in the presence of an officer, asked his superior if Barne had a compass (yes, but out of order) and if he thought he knew the way to the ship (no), and together the three men walked and crawled in what they hoped was the right direction until they spied Castle Rock. From that point they moved in the direction of the ship, aided by the ship's siren, which was blaring out over the frozen wastes. In another moment they came upon a search party, led by Armitage. Seeing them but unable to identify them in the light and in their headgear, the Pilot asked which was Barne. When he did not answer, perhaps dulled by fatigue and cold, Quartly spoke up and identified the trio.[114] The three were "in a dazed condition."[115] Barne was in bad shape; he had lost his mittens early in the ordeal and his hands were badly frostbitten. Armitage sent them home under the direction of Ferrar, who was familiar with the area through his geological work.[116]

What had happened to the other six men? When Quartly disappeared over the slope, Hare was already missing and the other five waited a few minutes before trying a diagonal descent, but almost immediately they found the footing impossible and began to glissade downward. Fortunately, they came to a small drift terrace, where, thanks to the grip of their leather ski boots, four of the men were able to stop. Vince in his fur boots was not so fortunate and shot past the others in the darkness and was carried over the edge down into the sea. For a few minutes the group waited, listening for any sign of Vince, then Wild asserted his leadership of the group and got them to proceed cautiously in the assumed direction of the ship. None of them knew exactly where they were, but by carefully moving forward as a group they eventually got to familiar landmarks and made for the *Discovery*.[117] Wild's leadership was critical in saving the lives of the rest of the men in his party.

Wild's group was the first to reach the ship. The alarm was immediately raised. Scott, naturally, wanted to lead the rescue attempt but was persuaded by his colleagues that he would only handicap the effort.[118] Immediately, all the men and officers volunteered, and within thirty minutes Armitage was out the door leading a search party. Dellbridge thought he could raise steam and suggested to the captain that the siren be used, quick thinking that contributed to the rescue of the three officers by alerting them to the location of the ship. Courageously, Wild, though extremely tired from his ordeal, offered to guide Armitage's group back to where the disaster had occurred.[119]

The snow was blowing so intensely that progress and navigation were difficult as Armitage's party moved out. Wild could not be certain of the location of recent events but did a credible job of getting the party back to the scene. They found the camp and, after searching, came across the three officers who were sent back with Ferrar. Armitage's party continued searching for Hare and Vince, but no trace was found of either man and eventually the group returned to the ship around two o'clock in the morning.[120]

While Armitage's group was out, the thought that Vince might have landed on the shore wherein a rescue could be effected by sea was mooted. Shackleton asked and received permission to lead another group of volunteers who took one of the whalers out for a harrowing six-hour ride.[121] Unable to discover anything in the area of Vince's fall, the crew had been driven offshore by a gale and had to row the last four hours under extremely difficult circumstances.[122] A second close call on this harrowing night.

The next day Wilson was put in charge of another search party, leading Ferrar, Bernacchi, Hodgson, and six of the men. At that point in the expedition Wilson and Ferrar were among those who knew the area best because of their excursions. The intense cold made a stay outdoors very difficult, and several of the party soon suffered from frostbite. Wilson determined that he needed to send some of the men back to the *Discovery* and did so, under Ferrar and Hodgson, while he continued on with Bernacchi and Jacob Cross, one of the petty officers. All three had ice axes and some alpine rope and thus were better prepared for searching. They were also wearing crampons on their boots, although Cross's were ones he had taken from the *Southern Cross* hut and were not as good as the ones the other two were wearing. After five hours Wilson believed further searching was impossible and returned to the ship. Vince and Hare were given up as dead.[123]

While Wilson had been out with his party the captain ordered steam up, and Dellbridge, in Skelton's absence, did a fine job of managing, although much of the machinery had been below freezing point for some time, but the search by ship turned up nothing. Seeing the area in clear weather proved how treacherous the place was and its likelihood as a spot for disaster.[124]

The next morning, 14 March 1902, was a forlorn one on the *Discovery*. Both Hare and Vince had joined the expedition after it had left England but had become extremely popular with their messmates and all aboard. Assessing the health of the survivors, most had a little frostbite, some severe. Edgar Evans had had his ears badly frostbitten, the first of a regular pattern of frostbitten ears that dogged his polar experience until his final journey from the Pole in 1912. Barne's injuries were most serious. Wilson feared that Barne would lose his fingers.[125]

At about 10:30 on that same morning those below heard the quartermaster call out that someone was approaching. Because no one had left the ship that morning, the immediate hope was that it was one of the lost men, and the whole company rushed to the shore to find Hare making his way toward the *Discovery*. His story was wondrous. Finding the going impossible in fur boots, he returned to the tent to get his leather ones. Having done that, he tried to retrace his steps to find his companions but became lost. He wandered around trying to find his way until he became quite exhausted and laid down in the snow, apparently pulling his arms inside his jersey. He awoke, unaware of how long he had slept. He tried to walk but could not stand and so went on hands and knees until his stiffened body would allow him to stand and then walked back to the ship. Hare apparently slept thirty-six hours and was kept from freezing by the insulation of the snow, despite a temperature of −30° F. When Wilson examined him, Hare was found to be quite fit and after a reasonable amount of bed rest, resumed his duties, with no lasting effects.[126]

Two days later, on Sunday evening, with the crew still in a state of mourning, the burial service was read.

Publicly, no guilt was assigned in Vince's death. Privately, Scott placed responsibility for the death of Vince with the officer in charge. Writing in his journal, Scott faulted Barne for not taking adequate care to ensure that his men were properly dressed. The captain called the decision to allow them to be in fur boots "a most grievous and obvious mistake." Not to have made an attempt, at lunch, to recuperate by getting out the sleeping bags and setting up the tent was "most rash." But the final irresponsible act was to abandon the equipment and push on through a heavy blizzard. Had the party stayed in camp and waited the storm out, all would have been well.[127] Although Scott felt the loss of Vince very keenly, he realized that it could easily have been worse — all nine men might have been lost given the combination of events and misjudgments. That the disaster had not been worse was largely due to the efforts of Frank Wild.[128]

Vince's death subdued the party for a week or so, but the daily activities went on as the scientific program required daily effort. Although the end of March was approaching, the *Discovery* was still not frozen in for the winter. Several weeks that might have been used for exploring or taking observations at sea — what the ship had been built for — were lost.

Scott was determined to try to lay a series of depots to the south before the winter precluded such movement. The experiences of the Crozier party prompted some alterations to equipment and plans. Sleeping bags had not been adequate for the low temperatures on that trip, and the southern depot laying party could expect worse conditions and lower temperatures. Snow shoes were improvised out of packing boxes, clothing was made more secure, and sleeping bags were made warmer.[129] General preparations had to be made, but, in addition, each man had to see to his own equipment, a time-consuming but very important effort.[130] Scott hoped to leave before the end of the month but at the same time was hesitant to go until the ship was frozen in for the winter.[131]

Good Friday services were held the morning of 28 March 1902. To celebrate the occasion the cook, whose reputation for incompetence was rapidly being established, baked the traditional hot cross buns, "or bricks, could hardly tell which." That afternoon and the next day the sledges were loaded. On Saturday Scott led a small team that traveled several miles as a preliminary effort. En route, about three miles from the ship, Scott, who was accompanied by Hodgson and Shackleton, came upon a group of emperor penguins. At the turn of the century these birds were largely a mystery to science, and each encounter with them in the early stages of the expedition sparked much speculation. How, for example, were they going to get back to the edge of the pack ice? Scott speculated — but the idea seemed too incredulous — that perhaps these creatures wintered in these regions. Skelton, who did not see this particular group of twenty-eight or so (considered a large number at this time of year), thought it might mean that open water existed to the south and that the birds were migrating north from it or that they were merely walking along in a general northerly direction and passed near the winter quarters of the *Discovery*.[132]

The dogs pulled well on this occasion, and Scott stated his conviction that they would be "of the greatest use to us on our trip."[133] In other respects, Scott was still puzzled by the sledge dogs, animals he did not understand well. Their behavior he often anthropomorphized, which led to disappointment with the creatures. When the Cape Crozier party returned, the dogs at the ship had been allowed largely to run freely around the area. With the return of dogs from the Crozier trip, problems developed. The newly returned dogs were not accepted back into the pack, and two of them were suddenly killed. The dogs' pattern of singling out and killing bothered and puzzled Scott and the other men in his party. Only Bernacchi and Armitage had experience with such animals.

Easter services were celebrated on 30 March 1902, a beautifully sunny day. The southern party departed the following day, twelve men, eighteen dogs, and four sledges, flying the sledge flags of the officers. Four days on the trail gave the men an indication of the horrors of sledging. Morning temperatures were −26° to −40° F, and the winds made every step an effort. The dogs "almost refused to work," and the men found that simple chores such as making and breaking camp took an inordinately long time. The deep cold made every piece of metal a potential weapon — burning exposed skin like hot iron. During the day the surface caused extraordinary drag on the runners, and the dogs could barely pull the loads given them and did so with "a dispirited and downcast mien." Scott concluded that although both men and dogs liked a light load, men were much less easily dispirited by a heavy one. Five hard hours on the trail yielded five miles toward their goal. The shortness of the days contributed to the difficulties on the trail. In the evenings they found that their sleeping bags were increasingly difficult to get into because of the frozen moisture from the previous night's sleep. At night the men shivered while the "dogs whined piteously."[134]

Several of the dogs refused to pull and had to be dragged along. By the third day, 2 April, Scott, having consulted with Armitage, decided to turn back.[135] Wilson thought that a party of officers could have pushed on through such conditions but that the men were too careless with their equipment and thus suffered more from the cold. Once they depoted their provisions and turned homeward, the dogs pulled splendidly and the party covered in one day what they had taken three to manage in their outward effort.[136] The autumn temperatures had proven horrendous; what parallels could be drawn with the spring, Scott wondered. Although they had managed to get their supplies only a short distance south of the ship, Scott, in his initial real firsthand sledging effort, had had his eyes opened to the hardiness that would be required of his men the following spring. If the temperature could reach −50° F on the Barrier in the fall, what would winter be like?[137]

Returning to the ship, the sledging party had been seen at a distance and was greeted by Skelton, who was carrying a flask of brandy for medicinal purposes. The party looked fairly done in, and Scott's decision to return early seemed a sensible one, both for the men's sake and for the dogs, about which some concern for their safety had been expressed.[138]

Fall was nearing an end, with only a "poor apology for daylight even at noon."[139] Concern for his men prompted Scott to order all men to take daily exercise, especially those least likely to take it on their own, the cooks and the servants.[140] Skelton, too, worried about the men in his charge, although most were intelligent and curious enough to get out on their own for exercise. The exception was William Hubert (one of the men from the merchant marine), who had injured his back and did not like to go out. Skelton saw Hubert's carelessness with his own health a further indication that Hubert was an ignorant cockney and a general misfit.[141] Hubert was the donkeyman, in charge of the donkey boiler, the smaller unit that could quickly be brought into service or used for smaller tasks. As a member of the crew from the merchant marine, he felt somewhat estranged from his messmates.

Scott was also concerned about the scientific program. Lacking a civilian scientific leader, Scott became his own, and quite a good one. He kept a hand in the overall work of his scientists and fretted when the amount of work exceeded the number of skilled hands, requiring some delay in implementing the full range of observations and activities. Royds had charge of the meteorological observations. He took note of conditions every two hours during the day, making the trip to the screen where the instruments were housed. Overnight this chore fell to the officers, who each took turns staying up overnight to accomplish this task. In addition to the official recording station, Shackleton and Wilson had an informal one on top of nearby Crater Hill, where they kept a spirit minimum thermometer and an aneroid barometer. In this way the two men who fast were becoming friends had some scientific purpose to their ambling on their daily walks.[142]

In addition to regular observations the occasional serendipitous scientific opportunity came to the expedition. One evening, just at dinner, word came that thirty emperor penguins had been sighted near the ship, and Wilson — joined by Kennar, Barne, and Cross — went out, rounded them up, and herded them back to the ship, trying to get them into a suitable pen. The birds did not cooperate and kept breaking out. Finally, Wilson decided that they must kill the ones that they needed, and soon the entire troop was set upon and dispatched. The men discovered that birds able to survive the harshest of breeding conditions, in the depth of the Antarctic winter, were hard to kill. Emperors withstood blows that could reasonably be expected to kill them. Furthermore, to avoid spoiling them as specimens, the best way was to drive a sharp implement into the back of their brain, assumed both humane and less likely to get blood on the feathers.[143] One of the birds weighed eighty-seven pounds. Although the specimens were for Wilson, Skelton asked for and received two for himself. As glad as the men were to have full-grown birds, the real prize would be to find the first egg.[144] This was the largest group of emperors the expedition had yet encountered.[145] The next morning a few stragglers remained and were easily captured. The captain noted, "they were lost without their comrades."[146]

Besides science a daily routine of activities occurred. Water had to be gathered almost daily, and the freezing and opening of the water around the ship made getting ashore more difficult. Skelton's engineering staff were constantly busy with a myriad of chores — mending broken instruments, designing items not thought of before they arrived in winter quarters, or maintaining anything vaguely resembling machinery aboard ship, from the engines to the wardroom stove. Dellbridge and Lashly proved superb assistants. Dellbridge, for example, designed a small stove for the engine room which allowed both for that area to be heated and for staff to wash and dry clothes and take a regular bath. Lashly could turn his talents to anything and corrected design defects in the heating system of the ship.[147]

Meanwhile, another activity was taking place on the ship, as Shackleton and others — principally Wilson — were busy working on a literary maga-zine regarding the expedition. An editorial office was arranged in one of the holds. Shackleton rigged it with a door that had a rope attached, allow-ing him to admit or refuse a visitor.[148] Shackleton had edited a similar mag-azine when working on a ship taking troops to the South African War. Sim-ilar efforts had been part of British nineteenth-century Arctic expeditions and Nansen's *Fram* (1893–96). The editor worked to make the proposed deadline — the first day of winter. Wilson provided most of the illustra-tions; the articles were contributed by both officers and men.

One of Scott's pet projects collapsed, literally, on 13 April 1902, when the windmill went down in high winds. The windmill had been designed to provide electrical power — without expending the limited supplies of coal or oil — especially for lighting during the long winter. Made of galvanized steel, the structure was twenty feet high and had a driving wheel twelve feet in diameter and was expected to produce the equivalent of three horse-power in a fifteen-mile-per-hour wind. Designed by Arthur Bergtheil, a London engineer, the machinery was intended to provide a steady supply of electricity even in a variable wind.[149] The *Fram*, on its Arctic ocean drift, had had such a device, as did the *Gauss*.

Quartly came down from the deck and announced that the windmill was breaking up. Dellbridge responded immediately and reported that the shaft seemed all right but that the blades were "a complete wreck." Scott angrily set on Dellbridge, saying that Dellbridge should have been more careful. This incensed Skelton, who believed that if Scott had a complaint the appropriate action was for Scott to complain to Skelton, not to take it out on one of Skelton's men.[150]

That night as the officers were coming into the wardroom for dinner someone commented on the windmill, and Scott noted that the incident was the result of "sheer carelessness." Skelton retorted that he did not think it carelessness in any way. The two then let the issue drop for the mo-ment. Skelton knew the windmill was a pet project of the captain and as-sumed that Scott would calm down about it after a while. Skelton's distrust of the whole apparatus was based on the windmill being an untried exper-iment and something he regarded as an "extravagant expense." The chief engineer detested the amount of work involved, because it kept him and his staff from doing other work that he considered more valuable.[151]

The following day Scott had calmed somewhat but had not altered his opinion. He asked Skelton for an assessment of the situation, and the en-gineer responded that he thought the windmill not worth repairing; Scott disagreed and the captain's orders prevailed. The project promised to be difficult work, as in those temperatures the bare metal burned the hands.[152]

Skelton had never had much faith in the apparatus, nor did one of the men who devoted so much time and attention to it, Lashly.[153] But Scott was determined to have it operate, and over the next month a great deal of engineering staff time was devoted to trying to make it function. Scott's obstinacy is not difficult to understand. He thought the windmill had been broken through carelessness, and he intended to "give the engine room staff plenty of employment in trying to repair it even if it is too far gone."[154] Repeated breakage and repairs did not soften his attitude, even though he knew that Skelton was skeptical about its value.[155] Lashly believed that the problem was the inability of the machinery to withstand the strong and boisterous winds.[156] For Skelton, the windmill became a mill stone, and the relationship between him and Scott was occasionally strained by their differences over the continued value of this machinery.

For the most part, few disagreements were apparent among the contented staff. The officers and men had regularly assigned duties that occupied their time. Hodgson was regularly out and about working his fish traps, seeking specimens, and helped by Barne or another officer or one of the men. Ferrar was kept busy exploring the area from a geological point of view. The other officers were busy as well and had bluejackets who assisted them.

Winter was now approaching. An awning was put up on the deck of the *Discovery* to provide shelter and some warmth during the dark months that lay ahead.

The hours of daylight dwindled until only a few minutes of direct sunshine was visible at midday. On 22 April 1902 even that little bit of light and warmth came to an end. Beginning the next day, no sun would shine on the men at Hut Point for more than one hundred days. The Antarctic night, which only two other expeditions, the *Belgica* and the *Southern Cross* had endured, was upon the men of the *Discovery*.

8

The Winter

In 1902 the staff of the *Discovery* wintered five hundred miles farther south than any previous party in polar history. As such the scientists expected to have an entirely new field to study and analyze. August twenty-third was the first day without the sun. The occasion was marked in the mess deck by splicing the main brace and in the wardroom with champagne, liquors, and a luxurious dinner, followed by the presentation of the first issue of the *South Polar Times*.

Regardless of one's assessment of the men who sailed aboard the *Discovery* as explorers—and at times their determination to maintain their amateur status has been frustrating to those who fail to keep in mind the context of their times—as polar literateurs they have seldom been matched. Following the example of the nineteenth-century British Arctic and other expeditions, the decision was made to publish six issues of a magazine, one per month during the winter, to be named the *South Polar Times*, a title chosen by a vote.[1] Shackleton was the editor, but he was assisted by a number of people, most notably Barne and Wilson, who did most of the illustrations, often original watercolors or pencil sketches. Even during the winter, Scott talked of publishing the volume when the ship returned to England and even speculated that its publication in 1903 might help raise funds to allow a third year of exploring. Eventually issued in a limited edition, the reproduction did not capture the vividness of the illustrations of the original, which is today in the possession of the Royal Geographical Society in London.[2]

Contributions came from the wardroom and the mess deck, and men from both groups showed great talent; Scott believed that some of the best articles came from the bluejackets. As editor, to Shackleton fell the unpleasant task of rejecting some copy, but he was determined to uphold the highest standards of writing and decency. Each issue contained not only humorous pieces but significant nonfiction accounts of whales or plant life. Barne contributed delightful caricatures of everyone and also did the cover. Scott's acrostics were extremely popular, sparking contests to provide the first solution.[3]

Armitage wrote of his Arctic experiences, and each member of the scientific staff contributed articles on his area of expertise. Shackleton and others wrote poetry for the periodical.[4] Frank Wild's articles reflected a mind better trained and more agile than many on the lower deck.[5]

Apart from Shackleton and Wilson, the first person to see each issue was the captain, who was given a private preview before officially receiving it in the wardroom at dinner. Each issue appeared as a single copy, typed on Shackleton's machine by Ford, the chief steward. The first issue of the *South Polar Times* was a great success.[6] Other issues appeared at regular intervals throughout the winter, reporting on the various activities of the crew. Royds was asked to read out the best parts while all crowded around.[7]

Although the *South Polar Times* had the largest circulation of any periodical south of the Antarctic convergence, the journal had a rival. The *Blizzard* appeared in a solitary issue as an alternative for material not up to the editorial standards of the *South Polar Times* and to provide more of an outlet for the writing of the less talented who had had their work rejected by the *South Polar Times*. Shackleton supervised the production. This publication contained a good deal of poetry, an indication that before the First World War, poetry was still the province of all classes. Fifty copies of the *Blizzard* were published, using an Edison mimeograph onboard.[8] For a variety of reasons, though, the *Blizzard* did not survive beyond its first issue.

The activities of daily life aboard ship in the winter started very early in the morning when Royds woke the cook's mate, who lit the fires in the galley to begin the day's cooking. Shortly thereafter, a small party of the men was aroused to perform the daily chore of gathering water. The process was to quarry for water by cutting ice from a nearby glacier. Snow was less satisfactory than ice, as the latter required less fuel to melt it. The process involved pickaxes and shovels and took about half an hour before the men returned to the ship and unloaded the frozen chunks.[9]

Although the winter routine was different for the officers than for the men, Scott believed it important that both share the same food, albeit at different times and locations. The men were roused at 7:00 A.M. Breakfast at 8:30 A.M. was porridge and bread and jam. Twice a week this fare was supplemented by seal liver, a prized food in both the mess deck and the wardroom — so much so that at one point Scott considered killing seals just for their liver, an idea he rejected as wasteful.[10]

Both officers and men suffered from the absence of a vital person on a polar expedition — a good cook. Scott dismissed their cook in New Zealand when he got "too big for his boots." Apparently, the choices for a replacement in the colony were limited, as the man hired, Henry R. Brett, proved a disaster. Unimaginative in his cooking, he had the unforgivable sin of being dirty. Moreover, Scott regarded him as a "thorough knave." The men hated him. About the only thing Brett excelled in was tall tales. Given the many incidents he claimed to have packed into one life, the men of the mess deck estimated Brett to be over 590 years old.[11]

Following breakfast the mess deck was cleared, and at 9:15 A.M. the men had prayers before setting out on the day's work. Royds assigned the men their tasks. Returning to the ship at 1:00 P.M., the men had their dinner — their main meal of the day — consisting of a soup, a meat (tinned or fresh), and some sort of dessert — the cook's mate was particularly adept at baking. Seals continued to appear at holes throughout the winter, providing meat three meals a week. One seal fed the ship's company for two days. Both messes missed fresh vegetables, and in general the canned vegetables were the least satisfactory of the foods aboard; "a few fresh vegetables would be acceptable." Following the noon meal, per naval tradition, the men were served their ration of grog. The men received issues of rum at regular intervals, a practice that Scott did not think really necessary and gladly would have eliminated.[12]

Afternoon work followed from 2:00 to 5:00 P.M., when tea with bread, jam, and cheese was served.[13] Occasionally, some food left over from dinner was added. All aboard had fresh bread every day.[14] As the winter wore on, the afternoon work period was omitted.[15]

The men had their evenings free and occupied their time with games, cards, and other forms of entertainment, and by making items such as models, as sailors have for centuries. The craft skill evidenced by the bluejackets was amazing.[16] Mrs. Longstaff, wife of the patron of the expedition, supplied a number of games, which were much appreciated.[17] Reading was a regular pastime, with books like *Fights for the Flag* and *Deeds That Won the Empire* being typical popular titles.[18] Writing, either for the *South Polar Times* or journal writing, also occupied much time.[19] The men had debates and music of their own, and all seemed, at least to the officers, content.[20] For a time an antiswearing club operated, but it died a damnable death.[21]

The mess deck was much more habitable than the wardroom; in terms of warmth, rarely did the temperature fall below 50° F. Better insulated and without the structural problems that developed in the officers' quarters, the mess deck provided reasonably good living conditions. That this deck was generally dry throughout the winter and not plagued by dampness was another healthy benefit of the men's quarters.[22]

At 10:00 P.M. hammocks were hung in the mess deck, and the men retired for the night. The idea of cabins for the men had been argued at one point, but, once in the South, Scott was convinced that this system allowed more open space for the men.[23]

While the officers and scientists were busy with their own work, the men found themselves with more free time. Scott contemplated how to fill it. In the nineteenth-century Arctic voyages, a school had been created for the men in which they were taught to read and other practical skills. With the improvements in education such instruction seemed less appropriate — most of the men could read and write quite well — and the captain wondered what kind of program could be constructed that would meet their needs.[24] Occasionally, lectures were given by the scientists or officers, but these were less to entertain than to inform.[25]

The men's work routine altered with the coming of the winter. Scott declared that the men would work from 8:00 A.M. until 1:00 P.M. After that the crew was free for the remainder of the day. Exercise was to be taken in the afternoon and after the evening meal.[26]

Daily life for the officers followed a slightly different pattern. Wilson was usually among the first up, because he had the responsibility of testing the milk each morning. The chief steward, Ford, awakened Wilson with, "Doctor Wilson, sir, milk inspection, sir." Having found seven acceptable tins, Wilson inspected any tins of meat or fish to be used that day. Then Wilson would open the skylight in the wardroom to let in fresh air. Several discussions, at times acrimonious, took place over the degree to which fresh air was beneficial. Even the medical practitioners disagreed, as Koettlitz opposed too much fresh air while Wilson, perhaps owing to his stay at Davos, Switzerland, for his tuberculosis, argued that fresh air was needed. Wilson found the foul air of enclosed quarters with so many smokers detestable and a high temperature of sixty degrees "his limit." Wilson saved special wrath for the "beastly ass who gave the officers' mess enough cigars to last the winter."[27]

Wilson's thoroughness in bringing in the crisp Antarctic air was sometimes met with protest by his colleagues, who were known to appear at breakfast wearing their fur mitts. Koettlitz was more direct; one morning when he appeared in the wardroom and, noticing the temperature to be less than he desired, ordered the servant to close the skylights. The servant objected, saying that Wilson had just ordered them opened on the captain's request. Koettlitz went directly to Wilson, who defended his position on the matter. Subsequently, Scott issued specific orders on when the skylights were to be opened in the morning.[28]

The wardroom was colder than the mess deck because the insulation in the deck below the former had fallen away, and leaks of cold air from the bunkers below were halted only by the linoleum that covered the floor.

Breakfast for the officers was from 9:00 to 10:00 A.M. and consisted of the same fare as the men's. Most were prompt to arrive, but some others, including Scott, tended to be perennial latecomers to this meal. Following breakfast the wardroom inhabitants scattered to do their work. Some, like Hodgson, stayed out all day, but most returned at 2:00 P.M. for tea, an informal meal found to be "the most enjoyable meal of the day." Nearly everyone made toast on the wardroom stove and smothered it with gobs of butter.[29]

Much of the scientific work of the expedition — skinning and preserving specimens — was done in the wardroom. After a day's work, the officers returning to the wardroom could detect from the variety of foul smells involved in the various work of their colleagues who had been hardest at work.[30]

Back at the ship for the 6:00 P.M. evening meal, a more formal affair, the officers sat at a table under the direction of one member who was president for a week and who enforced order, decency, and the wardroom dinner rules, including no betting, no contradicting the president, and no consulting of reference books (discussions sometimes were fierce). Transgressors were fined; no appeal of the president's decision was allowed. Usually, the fines included buying the table a round of wine. The bills were meticulously kept by Wilson, who loathed the task that he regarded as a colossal waste of time. The meal began with grace (latecomers had to apologize to the president for their tardiness) and ended with table cleaning and grace again, followed by a toast to the king's health, which closed the ceremony.[31]

Conversations at dinner never flagged throughout the winter, an indication that these were men of wide and varied interests. So often in the winters on expeditions in this period conversation slackened as the months wore on, everyone having exhausted their supply of new stories to tell.[32]

After dinner often the first move was to the reference works to check data related to discussions that had just occurred. The lack of an *Encyclopaedia Britannica* had already been noted but was repeatedly brought to mind in these postdinner searches for answers. How the ship could have sailed without the *Britannica* cannot be explained!

Evening pastimes went through phases in the wardroom, as in the mess deck. For a while bridge held sway, and nightly sessions went on for weeks. In turn though, whist — the great card game of the sixteenth through nineteenth century — had pride of place. Early in the winter chess was popular but faded. Scott, Koettlitz, Armitage, and Bernacchi were among the chess aficionados. Virtually all the wardroom occupants smoked, and by the end of the evening, visibility was limited, much to the annoyance of those who did not smoke. Generally, the evening went on until eleven o'clock or midnight, though some, including Scott, stayed up later.[33]

The temperature in the cabins of the wardroom ranged from 40° to 60° F in the daytime and was 33° F at night. The temperature on the floor was considerably colder, and the captain solved the problem of cold feet by keeping his feet in a box of hay. However, nothing could solve the problem of ice forming on the floors and in the corners of the cabins. Bolts that went through the ship's hull from the outside were a major cause of the difficulties of dampness and ice in the cabins. Condensation led to droplets that became ice, although some relief was brought by having felt nailed to the walls.[34]

Part of the scientific program involved taking regular meteorological observations every two hours around the clock. For the night observations Scott suggested that the officers and scientists each take an evening in turn. At first Armitage and Koettlitz were hesitant but had little choice but to volunteer at the captain's suggestion.[35]

The person on duty at night had thirteen different observations to take every two hours, including noting air temperature, cloud cover, weather outside, and the temperatures aboard. Also the observer noted aurora. The whole operation took twenty minutes to perform in good conditions. Often the session took a good deal longer.[36]

The officer was notified by one of the three quartermasters — David Allan, Thomas Kennar, and William MacFarlane — five minutes before the time to go for the observation. In bad weather or good the observer made his way to the screen where the instruments were housed. In bad weather the quartermaster on duty went along for safety. A complete set of observations was kept until 18 July, when a severe storm prevented anyone from leaving the ship.[37]

How people occupied themselves on these nightly rituals varied from officer to officer. Scott scheduled his laundry washing for this time, scrubbing his clothing in a tub until he was either finished or had a back that ached too much to continue. Others used the time to read or catch up on their journal writing, fortifying themselves with toasted cheese sandwiches or other delicacies.[38]

Nearly everyone on overnight duty treated himself to the tin of sardines that was his sinecure. Most liked them fried, and a few took such an interest in this culinary activity that they would wake one another to sample an especially fine result.[39]

Officers and men wore the same clothing, with slight variations. Over woolen underwear they wore a flannel or wool shirt and pilot-cloth trousers. Indoors, the men also wore a turtleneck wool jersey; officers dressed in a brown cardigan. The men tended to wear boots purchased for the expedition in Russia and modified to include a stronger sole. Outdoors, footwear was changed depending on the individual's sense of fashion and comfort to boots, either English, Norwegian, or reindeer fur boots called finneskoes. Over the body was worn a windproof suit of waterproof gabardine made by Burberry.[40]

Neck gear and headgear were much more individualized, as each person of the expedition sought some way of protecting his head, especially his nose and ears from the stings of frostbite.[41]

Unlike other explorers of the time, Scott did not think furs were necessary for clothing. He complained that the men were careless with their garments, resulting in more frostbite and a short life for the clothing, but assumed that in difficult circumstances the bluejackets would manage somehow. The men changed their underwear once a month, or more often if they desired.[42]

From Monday to Friday the routine was much the same. Saturdays the men devoted some of their time to a general cleanup in preparation for inspection. Sunday morning after breakfast Royds announced, "All ready for rounds," and the captain formally inspected the ship. The mess deck was empty because the men were on deck, awaiting inspection. The awning protected the men from light snowfall, but nothing could protect them from the wind and cold. Scott eventually appeared on deck and inspected his men, who were lined up in two ranks. In the depths of winter, Feather, the boatswain, had to precede the captain with a lantern to make it possible for him to see.[43]

Following inspection the mess deck was made ready for church services. Scott read the service. Three hymns were heartily sung, and announcements by the captain to the entire crew formed part of the ceremonies. On at least one occasion the officers and men had different opinions of the services. In early August Scott kept the men on deck waiting two hours while he was going on his rounds. Duncan reflected, "we are treated just as if we were children." Following services the entire company was dismissed from work for the day.[44]

Sunday was a much anticipated day, not for the leisure, but for the mutton. Those carcasses that had hung in the rigging of the ship from the time of the butchering en route south now formed the centerpiece of each Sunday dinner. By thus rationing this delicacy the cook was able to make it last until early spring, 20 October 1902. Both the wardroom and the lower deck looked forward to this meal; in the latter's quarters a toast was often offered to the New Zealand farmers.[45]

The normal activities of life went on, chores such as bathing were attended to, and Scott, concerned for the welfare and cleanliness of his men, made a schedule for the men's washing (by rating) so that each man could have a weekly bath. He announced this, as was his custom, at the Sunday services. He also decreed that long hair and beards were conducive to dirt and would not be allowed, and was prepared to take action if conditions merited. A weekly bath was all they could manage, as it required such an effort to carry a large amount of ice aboard to melt into enough water for a bath. The men bathed on the mess deck, while those in the engineering staff were able to rig a comfortable bath in the engine room. Skelton and his men each had a weekly bath there. The officers bathed in their cabins. Even though the moisture from the bath water made the cabins damp, the effort was made, unlike — Skelton speculated — foreign expeditions during which such cleanliness seemed, in his mind, to be absent.[46]

After dinner in the first part of the winter, usually on Tuesdays, a debate was held. At first two debates a week were held, but when enthusiasm waned, one a week was held. Bernacchi may have been the instigator of the practice.[47] Lots were drawn to determine who would preside each week.[48] The topics of the debates reflected contemporary British concerns. Scott decided that it would be best to alter scientific and nonscientific topics.[49]

A survey of the topics provides an idea of their scope. Scott chaired the first debate, held on 26 April 1902, on the subject, "Is the Great Ice Barrier afloat?" Everyone had twelve minutes to offer an opinion. Scott argued that the barrier was floating, was formed in situ, and was not moving. On the question of whether the barrier was afloat the vote was five in favor, six opposed. Scott voted in the affirmative and noted that his side included "the more thoughtful portion" of the staff.[50]

The second issue debated was women's rights, with Armitage in the chair amid great amusement at several of the speeches. Every man spoke for twelve minutes, long enough to "cram as much nonsense as he could think of in that space of time."[51] On the question, "Do women suffer any disabilities at the present day?" the vote was 10–1, with Hodgson, who had spoken against women's rights, voting in the negative.[52]

Other debates followed on topics such as, "Is our commercial supremacy maintaining its lead or not and are we taking proper steps to maintain it?" After this debate, it was decided to have one per week rather than two.[53]

Subsequent sessions covered the issue of "Conscription, would it be beneficial to the British Empire?" for which the vote was 5–5. The 27 May 1902 debate was on seals and penguins, but the first half of the subject took up so much time that the officers had to leave penguins for another evening. Wilson had the lion's share of the effort in this debate, which lasted four and a half hours. Wilson gained a lot from the experience, as the remarks of the others helped clarify thoughts in his mind about his work in this area. At the end, despite much talk, the only question they could think to put forth was, "Do the Weddell seals migrate north or not as the sea freezes over?" to which the vote was four ayes, two nays.[54]

Spiritualism was another issue discussed. To prepare for the event, Wilson had spent the day before reading on the subject. Again, all contributed to the debate, but none was listened to with more interest than Royds, who was a superstitious sort and related his tale of a fortune teller in Edinburgh who divined that Royds would be going to Antarctica.[55]

Reflecting an important but still unsettled question, one session dealt with "the existence or not of an Antarctic continent," with Shackleton in the chair. Armitage made rather a fool of himself and seemed to make a sneering remark at Scott, which Skelton thought was in "singularly bad taste." Wilson agreed. In the end six voted for a continent, five against.[56]

The next topic offered was, "Is sport good for the nation?" Hodgson came out against all compulsory games and thought that football matches only led to exhibitions of drunkenness.[57] Other issues included sledging and ice navigation. As the winter continued attendance at the debates flagged.[58] Wilson and others were tiring of them and the time that they took, noting that the winter was slipping away.[59]

The debates provided entertainment — and the length of some of them (four hours) showed their popularity at first with participants — but the officers were so occupied with work that these efforts eventually died out. The dialogues had been useful by occasionally providing new ideas, helping to clarify a scientific point, and setting out the problems more clearly.[60]

In addition to the debates, one evening Bernacchi and Shackleton paired off in a contest to defend their favorite poets, Tennyson and Robert Browning, respectively. Each held forth on the relative merits of his man, but in the end the vote favored Bernacchi by a single vote.[61]

In the winter lectures were occasionally offered. Armitage spoke to the men on 13 August 1902 on the use of the prismatic compass and other details of sledging, and he included some slides from his Jackson-Harmsworth adventures in Franz Josef Land. He concluded his remarks by showing them the picture of Nansen that he carried with him to show them "what might be done by a man determined to succeed."[62]

Throughout the winter, at regular intervals, the scientists spoke to the mess deck about their field of interest. Ferrar spoke on geology and wireless telegraphy, Hodgson on biology, and Scott on sledging. All seemed to help pass the time as well as inform.[63] Although some of the officers were concerned that the material might have missed the mark, the men appeared to have enjoyed them. Hodgson's comments gave "great satisfaction," while Ferrar's remarks were "very interesting to all of us."[64]

Scott recognized early the need for regular exercise, both for the physical and emotional health of his men. Few needed prompting to take regular exercise, both because they saw the benefit to their health and because it provided a break to the day.

Few experiences match winter in the Antarctic. Walking out on a cold ($-37°$ F) winter afternoon, the ambler was greeted by the loud, rifle-like reports of the rigging as it contracted in intense cold.[65]

Skiing was also a popular pastime, and besides improving their skills for the coming sledging season the men found it fun. Skelton noted, "Coming down the ski slope I had such a good run that I had to go up again and take another run down."[66] Meanwhile, Wilson and Shackleton kept up their daily walk, a two hour amble during which the friendship of the two men developed.[67]

Football remained a popular pastime when the moon was sufficiently bright. Throughout the winter and into the spring the men continued to play on the ice.[68] Some games were played in temperatures as low as −31° F.[69]

Regular monthly medical examinations were undertaken by the two physicians. Each month Koettlitz took blood samples from the entire crew.[70] Royds and Wilson took measurements of everyone on the mess deck, which caused great amusement among the men as biceps, waist, and lung capacity measurements were subject to jibes from the other sailors.[71]

The *Discovery* was designed without suitable latrines for wintering, and during the first weeks of winter, the carpenter was busy constructing two, officers on starboard, men on port side.[72]

In the decade before the Heroic Era much speculation existed about the weather conditions of Antarctica. Some presumed that the weather would be substantially milder in the South than in the Arctic. Although that did not prove to be the case, Hut Point was not one of the worst places to spend the winter in the south polar regions.

Before the arrival of winter, the crew of the *Discovery* had little idea how to anticipate the onset of a storm. After a particularly heavy one, Bernacchi reported that in the twelve hours before the storm he had recorded an increase in electrometer readings, and some speculation existed that this might serve as a predictor of impending severe weather.[73]

Among the worst storms was one in early May — Scott thought it was the worst during their stay in McMurdo Sound — which lasted for several days, with eighty-mile-per-hour winds and true whiteout conditions. This gale finally finished the windmill, which had been made operational again.[74] The whole machinery was blown off its shaft, which snapped "like a rotten carrot" during the storm.[75] Skelton hoped that this would be the end of the project.[76] As it turned out, this was the case, and Skelton was greatly relieved that he could get back to other work, citing that "it is a jolly good thing the windmill is done for, we should never have had a moment's peace."[77] Wilson was sympathetic to the amount of work required for repair of the windmill and agreed with Skelton's opinion of its value.[78] In his official account of the expedition Scott noted his comfort at knowing "that this last breakdown could not have been prevented; it reveals a radical weakness in the windmill itself, and entirely supports the opinion expressed to the expert who fitted it."[79] Moreover, Scott added that "we never overestimated the possibility of success" with the windmill.[80] Privately, Scott had written at the time that the windmill was a failure and that the subcontractor on the project had not taken the care required. Scott's keenness on the windmill was based largely on his hope that it would save coal over the winter months.[81]

The long winter presented a number of problems, not the least of which was lighting. With the windmill's failure, the crew was forced back to other means, principally kerosene lamps. On the upper deck of the ship were stored fifteen hundred gallons of this fuel, specially formulated to have a low flash point to remain liquid at lower than normal temperatures.[82]

Scott had been alerted to a kerosene lamp that used a wind-up fan rather than chimney to function. Candles were also available. Although stocks were limited — and might be more so in the event of an unexpected second winter — Scott opted not to impose rigid conservation of candles during the dark months.[83]

An aside on tobacco will put this pastime into context on the expedition. Few smoked outdoors, for the wind helped make that difficult, and no restrictions were placed on smoking indoors. Scott was such an avid pipe smoker that, while onshore, he had a regular routine. He spoke to himself before leaving home, "Pipe, money, baccy, matches."[84]

Of eleven officers in the wardroom, three were constant smokers, four were moderate ones, and four were practically nonsmokers. Perhaps a statistic will bring into focus the fog-like atmosphere evident at times in the wardroom. The wardroom smoked about six or seven pounds of tobacco a month.[85]

The mess deck contained mostly smokers; only a few did not smoke. The stronger tobacco used by the wardroom residents created another class distinction between them and the officers.[86] Some of the men chewed tobacco, which Scott objected to, especially when doing so while working. He felt certain that chewing tobacco would detract from their stamina on the sledging parties.[87]

Turning from vice to future virtue, although the days of successful motorized transport in Antarctica were in the future, Skelton had been the first to see the possibilities, as noted in the previous chapter. In the short run though, the winter offered the first real experiment. Shackleton designed a "rum cask car" made of two rum casks and a frame that he and Barne constructed with the help of James Duncan.[88] The initial run was met with derisive laughter by the fellow officers. A subsequent version rigged with a sail did no better.[89] Still, an idea was planted in the minds of both Shackleton and Scott, and both attempted motorized transport on their later expeditions.[90]

Other transport-related problems plagued the expedition. At the onset of winter the boats had been put out on the floe as had been the custom in the Arctic and had been well banked with snow; Scott assumed that they would be safe. Early in the fall Bernacchi had pointed out to Scott the danger of leaving them on the ice, but the scientist had been told at that point to stick to his area of specialization. Over the course of the next several months the boats were found to have become buried in drifts, and when the men began to dig them out on 22 July 1902, the boats were found to be full of frozen water. Although scientific experiments were being conducted on the weight of snow pressing down on the surface of the ice, the significance of leaving the boats out on the ice was missed by the officers.[91]

In his official account of the expedition Scott indicated that he had ordered men to dig out the boats, with "no feeling of anxiety, but rather to provide occupation."[92]

Others were not so casual about the threat represented by the loss of all the boats. They might be needed for a rescue near winter quarters or in the case of the loss of the ship en route back to New Zealand. Nor were the observers mindless of the criticism the loss of the boats would incite in England.[93]

Eventually, Scott joined the chorus of those greatly disturbed by these developments, noting "our stupidity has landed us in a pretty bad hole, for we may have to leave this spot without a single boat in the ship."[94]

Once the seriousness of the problem was apparent Scott determined that they should be dug out and made secure. Thus began a six-month intermittent struggle by the men to recover the snow- and ice-filled boats. The diaries of the men attested to this demanding and tiresome work, "all hands on the boats," "boats hard and fast," and "still some hope of getting the boats." At one point Scott gave up all hope of ever getting the boats out, noting it was a lesson "dearly learned" if they had failed to recover the boats. Meanwhile, the men continued their task, which was "bad as ever, endless job." At various times cracks appeared in the floe where the whalers were situated, and some concern was expressed that they would be damaged. The whole experience seemed, in retrospect, to the captain to be an act of "extreme foolishness." By December the boats were freed from the ice. Even then, Bernacchi noted, the miracle was not that it took six months to dig them out but that the job was eventually accomplished.[95]

Fire aboard ship was a serious danger. The initial experience, en route to New Zealand, sharpened everyone's awareness of the results of losing the ship in such utterly isolated conditions. During the winter the ship's pumps froze, requiring at least twenty minutes of warming with a blow torch to be at a temperature to work. Clearly, with fire raging in the ship, twenty minutes was too long. Still, Scott opted not to keep a fire hole open in the ice near the ship.[96]

Fire fighting plans during the winter called for smothering the flames with cloth or sand. Boxes of sand were placed strategically around the ship. Making the men conscious of the dangers of fire aboard ship was the best safeguard.[97]

Throughout the winter, seals continued to appear in cracks and holes that Hodgson made in the ice for his scientific work. Thus fresh meat was continually added to the larder. Seals knew no enemy on land, and dispatching them was fairly simple. After stunning them with a blunt object, the animals were killed with a knife to the heart.

From time to time, as would be expected with a large group of people, problems arose with men getting lost. Given the changeable Antarctic conditions, anyone caught in bad weather was in a potentially fatal situation. Dellbridge and Feather went out on 17 May 1902, thinking they could walk around Castle Rock and perhaps around the whole island — an impossible task, given the distance — having told only their messmates where they had gone. To do so without permission was against orders. The men did not return by 8:00 P.M., and during the time they were gone a storm with heavy drift arose. Eventually, some of the crew reported their absence. Immediately, a search party was organized, but before one could be dispatched the lost men returned, frostbitten and exhausted. For their foolishness the captain gave Dellbridge and Feather a severe lecture the following day. Wilson was surprised at the stupidity of these men, especially because they were warrant officers and were expected to know better. Among their peers, Lashly criticized the foolish behavior, noting that it was very dangerous to be caught out in bad weather.[98]

Eight days later, 25 May 1902, three men asked Royds for permission to journey to Castle Rock. Royds refused but gave them leave to go for a short walk. Five hours later they returned, one with a badly frostbitten toe. Eventually, the problem of lost men was addressed by establishing a regular set of guidelines, although these were still not always followed.[99]

Another problem during the winter was Petty Officer Smythe, whose mental state for a period concerned the captain. Apparently, Smythe had been in charge of a watch but had been replaced by Evans and harbored some grievance against the latter as a result. Alcohol may have been a contributing factor in the problem, and at one point Scott noted that the situation was "alarming." Scott kept a watchful eye on Smythe, and soon Smythe's mood seemed to improve. "Trouble to overcome difficulties in this climate are quite sufficient without the additional internal discomfort of this sort." Taking Smythe aside, Scott had a long talk with him. The captain found him a simple, ignorant man, prone to imagine injuries. Following the conversation, Scott felt confident that the situation was solved. Scott continued to take care with Smythe and gave him little tasks, "as though he were selected on merit for them." Scott was able to note later that Smythe was much improved.[100]

Scott had wisely assigned each dog to the care of an individual man. Not only did this assure that the dogs would get attention and care, but the men gained positive benefits as well from working with the animals, as has been demonstrated in modern studies. The men often took the dogs on walks with them, although the beasts were sufficiently wild that they had to be kept on leashes.[101]

As the winter wore on the dogs' kennels were moved alongside the ship for more protection from the elements, but even so, after a major storm the kennels often had to be dug out from beneath the drifting snow.[102] Generally, the dogs preferred to remain outdoors during storms, curling up beside their kennels, allowing drifting snow to act as a cover, rather than being confined inside the man-made structures. Scott feared that they were having a hard time, but after each storm the dogs emerged, none the worse for their experience of being snowed over.[103]

Although the dogs were bothered on a preliminary depot-laying trip by shedding their coats in the late fall, a time when in the northern hemisphere this would have been the natural process, by May they all had developed fine winter coats and seemed to be adjusting to the southern winter.[104]

From time to time in the winter one of the dogs would be singled out by the others and marked for death. Sometimes the men noted this behavior, and at other times the first indication was finding a dog's body in the morning. These events disturbed the men, especially those officers who anthropomorphized about the dogs.[105] Scott was not the only one who expressed such feelings when one of the dogs, "Paddy" had been found dead, apparently killed by "Nigger," who had slipped his collar in the night. Typical of his reactions to such instances was Scott's puzzlement at the incident: "The curious thing is that 'Paddy' appeared to be 'Nigger's' sole and only friend; their kennels were adjacent, and as 'Paddy' was always content to play second fiddle, there seemed no chance of a rupture."[106] On another level, the loss of the dogs meant a lessening of the chances for success by the southern party, as the *Discovery* expedition had none to spare.[107]

Thus when a dog died in early July the captain had Wilson investigate the situation. Wilson found that many of the animals had sores on their forelegs and subsequently seemed to lose weight. For the success of the southern party, the dogs had to be kept alive and well.[108]

Fortunately, the number of dogs grew through new litters. Armitage's dog, from the Jackson-Harmsworth expedition, had puppies as did several of the others. By the end of the winter the expedition had nearly as many puppies as it had had dogs at the outset of the voyage.[109]

Relationships among the crew were not always as serviceable as associations between a dog and its guardian. Although contemporary published accounts self-censored any suggestion of disagreement, such dissensions occurred as one might expect under the restrictive and severe circumstances of early Antarctic exploration.

Skelton and Scott twice found themselves in conflict. Once Scott, on ordering Lashly to fix the stoves, intruded on Skelton's prerogative to give orders to Lashly. Fortunately for Skelton, his men, especially Lashly, trained to a proper sense of naval discipline, did not proceed with repairs before consulting him. On another occasion Scott provoked Skelton when he reprimanded one of the engineer's men for breaking a sledge; Scott should have left the responsibility for the actions of the engineer's men with Skelton, where it rightly belonged. Even if Scott may have overreacted to the mishap with the sledge, Skelton wisely let the matter drop.[110]

Naturally, at times, the men wearied of one another. One day Wilson got "deadly sick with everyone" and went for a solitary walk to Crater Hill but returned in an "angelic temper." For Wilson the long winter months exposed the difficulties of men living together alone, separated from the "better half of humanity." He noted that while some of the men seemed decent enough at the outset, the mask had come off and they were unpleasant now. Another time Wilson railed against the naval mentality and all who possessed it.[111]

In general though, few fractious events occurred. The fairly strict separation between the messes was maintained as royal naval custom demanded. The relations among the officers and scientists and the bluejackets were cordial. On occasion members of the wardroom would journey to the mess deck, especially the area boarded off for the warrant officers, to visit. In this way new tales were heard, and yarns that had ceased through repetition to interest fellow mess mates took on a new life with a different audience.[112]

The impression held by the officers that the men were happy and content with their lot in the winter months, while true for the most part, was not always borne out by the comments of some from the lower deck. Unlike the officers and scientists, who had a great deal of interesting work to do for the most part, the men did not share in that enthusiasm.[113] Some men who were given regular work with a given scientist or had other routine assignments, such as the cook, were more likely to escape minor depression. Clearly, the worst days were those with bad weather, when outside activities were restricted or prohibited. Also, for many of the men the companionship and responsibility of a pet was vital to a sustained positive attitude during the long solitude of the Antarctic night. Each caretaker, despite the often ferocious and murderous disposition of his charge, found the animals a bolster against depressed spirits. A man and dog walking together was a common scene during the winter, but still monotony remained a problem for the mess deck inhabitants.[114]

Polar accounts, especially published ones, tended to discount or deny any quarrels in the party unless such disputes defended the author's position on an issue. Similarly, the published accounts of the *Discovery* made little mention of any disagreements; clearly, some existed. Keep in mind that in such circumstances, many people react by being less emotional, downplaying that side of their character. For the most part the *Discovery* was "a happy ship" (Scott's published phrase), and no discredit is cast upon the members of the expedition when a closer look at the sources reveals the occasional spat. William Smythe's perceived sense of injury from Edgar Evans has been noted. On several occasions, fisticuffs settled minor disputes. John Walker made the mistake of crossing William MacFarlane one day and was knocked unconscious for his efforts. Still, given the close quarters for such a long period of time, the *Discovery* was fortunate in the good relations among the men and officers.[115]

The crew of Scott's vessel were not without entertainment. In late April an announcement was posted indicating that a production would take place on 1 May at Professor Gregory's Villa Residence. That evening's entertainment included a slide show by Royds on the construction of the ship and a singsong, despite Skelton's assessment that "there isn't much musical talent aboard." Clarke, the cook's mate, had the best reception with one of his songs. The program ended with the singing of "God Save the King." Even Scott, whose devotion to his men was both admirable and well-founded, was forced to admit that his crew had not been chosen for their musical talents.[116]

On 25 June another theatrical performance occurred, a production of "Ticket of Leave." Grease paints had been provided by a patron and were used to fine advantage. The whole event was great fun. The lack of musical talent or sense of timing was again demonstrated — Kennar was especially singled out in this category — but that only added to the humor of the situation. Of special note was the success of the "ladies" in the play — Gilbert Scott and Buckridge were extremely convincing in their roles, a moment that perhaps resembled the scene in Jean Renoir's film *Grand Illusion* in which the prisoners see "girls" for the first time in two years.[117]

The sixth of August 1902 was the one-year anniversary of their departure from England, although to some it seemed longer.[118] Following dinner the officers and men were treated to another performance at the Royal Terror Theatre, Gregory Lodge, this time for a performance of the Dishcover [*sic*] Minstrel Troupe, a black-face musical. Thirteen of the men sang in this ambitious production; some, including Allan, Page, Kennar, and Pilbeam, were very good. Royds, despite not feeling well, played the piano throughout. The lyrics were written by the crew and contained a good deal of local humor. Koettlitz was chided for his thirst for blood (the monthly examination), while Armitage's penchant for staying indoors was satirized. One very well-received bit of mirth was the question, "What vegetable did the *Discovery* bring from England?" The answer was "The Dundee leak."[119]

While all other pastimes waxed and waned in popularity, one thing retained its appeal — the beauty of Antarctica. To go out on a still winter evening to appreciate total silence, as if on a dead planet, was a profound experience. Occupants of the wardroom and lower deck were affected by the natural phenomenon. Seeing the moon rise in the winter, James Duncan thought, was "one of the finest sights" he had ever seen.[120]

The men passed the dark months preceding the return of the sun in a variety of individual occupations. Each member of the crew contributed to the success of the expedition.

Throughout the winter Scott was occupied with the details of leading the expedition and the planning for the coming season. Given the actual number of hours worked in the winter, in retrospect the task does not seem as onerous as the working hours of professionals in the late twentieth century. Scott had to plan out the various details of sledging with remarkably little data available to him.

In planning, Scott could draw on his instruction from McClintock, whom Markham regarded as the initiator of Arctic manhauling and "our highest polar authority." Before departing England, Scott had received instructions in sledging from both McClintock and Nansen,[121] but McClintock's experience was of limited value in Scott's current circumstances.

Scott made use of the ship's library to learn about the experiences of other polar explorers, though he was distressed to find that no copy of Nansen's *Farthest North* was aboard. Luckily, Wilson had taken some notes on Nansen's book, and these were put to use by the captain.[122]

Moreover, Scott served as de facto head of the scientific staff. Scott's interest in science was evidenced in his willingness not only to participate in the normal activities of science but also to maintain his own little research project. He had Skelton rig up an electrical device with two thermometers, one up the mast and the other over the stern, both of which could be read from Scott's cabin.[123] Moreover, Scott was a fine director of scientists in that he often devised new ideas for his scientists to pursue.[124]

In particular, Scott was fascinated with questions related to ice, and he regretted not having someone with expertise equal to the task. So keenly was this lack felt on this expedition that on his second expedition, Scott enlisted the services of a young physicist (Charles Wright) whose pioneering work helped initiate the science of glaciology.[125]

Armitage was known to all aboard as the Pilot, a title that indicated his role as the experienced ice navigator. This role also took him out of the regular line of authority, allowing Royds, a Royal Navy officer, to direct the daily activities of the ship under Scott.

Armitage is something of an enigma. Clearly, he was appointed for the supposed range of his experience, based on his work on the Jackson-Harmsworth expedition. His career with the P. & O. Steamship Company had been interrupted for four years by that endeavor, and he had resumed his work when he returned from the Arctic.[126] Armitage, perceived by some as direct and by others as brusque, tended to keep indoors to his own work.[127]

Relieved of some duties by Royds, who assumed the overall supervision of the ship and crew, Armitage may well have felt isolated among his peers. Although he had a fairly adventuresome life before and after the *Discovery*, Armitage's dissatisfaction with this expedition may be sensed from the fact that only sixteen pages of a three-hundred-page autobiography were devoted to the *Discovery* expedition.

Much of Armitage's time in the winter was spent taking measurements related to the location of the ship and the area surrounding the winter quarters. Among other things, his measurements demonstrated how deceptive judging distance was in the Antarctic.[128] In this assignment he was often helped by Scott or Wilson, who recorded times while Armitage did the figures.[129]

Much of the efficient running of the daily operation of the ship was due to the skills and attention of Charles Royds, known in the wardroom as "Charlie." He arranged all the men's work and was in charge of day-to-day operations aboard ship.[130]

From the outset Markham had wanted a limited civilian scientific staff. As originally planned, the *Discovery* would have carried fewer scientists than either of the two Antarctic expeditions of the 1890s, the *Belgica* or the *Southern Cross*. Markham believed that the science could be handled by the naval officers aboard, thus increasing the value of a naval expedition; officers could sail the ship and then do the science.

During the winter Royds's primary scientific obligation was to keep the daytime meteorological record. Generally, Wilson took the reading at eight in the morning for Royds. To Royds also fell the work of maintaining the weather screens, a constant problem.[131] The steadfastness of Royds's work in these endeavors, in all weather, spoke well of his determination.

Royds also contributed much through his musical talent, which he shared generously. At services he played the harmonium. Another contribution of Royds, although not one that appeared in the scientific record of the expedition, was his nightly musical offering to his friends in the wardroom. Arriving some time before dinner, Royds would play the piano, which he did with some skill. Scott said that this was an important factor in having everyone in such a fine mood at dinner. Certainly, the music brought back thoughts of home, of England, and all that makes the world civilized.[132]

Royds was bothered during the winter with health problems. In April 1902, when one of Royds's legs developed a problem, Wilson ordered him to bed and assumed the responsibility for meteorological observations during the day.[133]

On 1 August Royds was ill again with rheumatism. Wilson suspected that Royds's cabin was a factor, as it was the coldest and dampest. Also, Koettlitz removed a cyst from Royds's cheek on a makeshift operating table in the wardroom. Royds carried the little scar for the rest of his life.[134]

The work of the chief engineer continued throughout the dark months. Skelton and his crew, principally Dellbridge, tore the engine down and found it had survived the outbound voyage in fine shape. Skelton thought the engine was the best piece of construction in the ship. From his point of view, Skelton had a hard time concentrating on the most essential machinery of the ship because he and his staff were constantly in demand to forge every manner of equipment — including an iron weather vane for Royds's meteorological station. Skelton repaired meteorological instruments, cameras, clocks, electric thermometers, and even Shackleton's typewriter when the third lieutenant came to Skelton in great despair. Skelton thought the Remington a "most cunning little mechanical contrivance." Regardless of the task, whether the boatswain's equipment, Bernacchi's instrument, the only Dyne recording anemometer, or designing a sledge meter for measuring distances covered, Skelton could be relied on to accomplish thejob.[135]

Of particular importance for the *Discovery* was the sledge meter, because an accurate means of measuring distance on the trail had not been addressed before the expedition left England. Skelton designed and built a prototype of a sledge meter; in his diary he noted that he believed it was accurate within 1 percent over a mile. Having perfected the design, he made a series of them for all the sledging parties.[136] Scott's overall assessment of Skelton was that "it would be impossible to have a more clear level-headed one for the many important instrumental adjustments that come into his hands."[137]

In addition, Scott asked Skelton to supervise the coal and oil consumption aboard and to report weekly. One major consumer of oil was Koettlitz's bacteria incubator, which was heated by a lamp. Now jealously guarding oil consumption, Skelton was skeptical of this use. Typical of the attention paid to the British Arctic experiences, Skelton compared oil consumption on the *Discovery* with that on the *Alert* in 1875 and found that his expedition was using far more. He cited the galley as being a culprit in extra oil consumption.[138]

Skelton was also the designated principal photographer and was often called on by the captain to take official photographs. Skelton spent long hours in the darkroom developing photographs ("doing photos all day"), often annoyed at some other scientist who used the equipment but did not leave the darkroom shipshape. Befitting his desire for order, Skelton also devoted much time to cataloging all the photographs made on the expedition.[139]

Still, despite what seemed like the heaviest load of work around the ship, Skelton found time to read, occasionally commenting on the books in his diary. Reading polar literature allowed Skelton to argue more effectively on certain subjects. Once he believed he bested Armitage on a point regarding skiing by quoting Nansen's *The First Crossing of Greenland*. Skelton particularly liked Nansen's account, although he wished it had been one rather than two volumes. Still, "even his padding is good and worth reading," was the engineer's assessment.[140]

Skelton was a good superior officer in that he protected his men, particularly the second engineer, Dellbridge, from potentially excessive demands. Dellbridge, "the handiest of handy men," was busy with the same projects as Skelton and a few of his own. To Dellbridge fell much of the work on the dreaded windmill, which he patiently reconstructed, making both structural and design changes. Despite Skelton's belief that the "game is not worth the candle,"[141] Dellbridge managed to get the device working again.

Among his other accomplishments during the winter, Dellbridge made a pipe for the tide gauge, a very nice copper tobacco box for Barne, and for Skelton, an ice ax, "a splendid job, one of the best pieces of small forging I have ever seen."[142]

Koettlitz, the senior physician, had two obligations on board, medicine and science. Although Koettlitz was fortunate in the good health of those aboard the *Discovery*, he had a number of responsibilities related to his position as senior medical officer. Each month he took an extensive series of measurements on both officers and men — weight, chest measurement, grip strength — and blood samples, which he studied to determine changes in the color and "richness" of the blood, keeping meticulous records. Scott questioned the aim of all the blood work and speculated that the doctor was not clear on its purpose either. Yet Scott was reassured by the blood tests that assured him that scurvy was unlikely.[143] The blood samples were the butt of jokes and were satirized in the *South Polar Times*.

Koettlitz or Wilson continued to inspect every tin of food because of the lingering assumption that scurvy was caused by poorly tinned foods.

One senses though that Koettlitz's real joy was in his work as bacteriologist. Before he left England, students at Guy's Hospital (where he had studied twenty years earlier) had given him a set of bacteriology instruments, and the medical officer spent hours in Antarctica tracking down any microbe. Koettlitz studied the intestines of penguins and seals in search of data on bacteria, and from time to time he would come out of his cabin to show one of his favorites in the wardroom the latest discovery revealed by his microscope work.[144]

Koettlitz also maintained one thermometer at his own station, which gave him an outdoor occupation, but he was often found in his cabin working on specimens, or writing his voluminous diary.[145]

Koettlitz did not always fit in with the other members of the wardroom. He may have felt some handicap by his lack of a university education, but Koettlitz was separated from the others by a personality that cared not at all for the public school pranks and prattle that occasionally surrounded him.

Koettlitz was often the butt of jokes. For example, he was fond of a particular tea, grown in India by his brother and sent by him for the expedition. Koettlitz often took tea in his cabin, occasionally inviting certain people to join him, selecting those currently in favor. One day Barne, being the chosen one, switched cups with Koettlitz and substituted some ordinary tea. Everyone in the wardroom was in on the gag, but when the steward switched cups Barne failed to get one that matched the one Koettlitz had been using, and so Koettlitz noticed the difference. The original cup was brought back, but Koettlitz suspected another prank and refused to accept it as his own tea. Shackleton, breaking into laughter, did nothing to convince Koettlitz of the origins of his tea. The whole episode ended with the senior surgeon in a tiff, and neither side showed an appreciation for the other's point of view.[146]

For another prank Bernacchi put two chairs together in the wardroom and bet Koettlitz that he could take off his shoes and jump over them; then Bernacchi jumped over his shoes. Koettlitz was "speechless with disgust" and refused to pay up on the bet.[147]

At times Koettlitz inadvertently was the cause of mirth. At the wardroom table a discussion on whether flying fish actually fly was winding down as the meal was ending. Scott noted, "I have no opinion on the matter," at precisely the same time that Koettlitz was about to profess the meal-closing prayer, cutting off the captain in midsentence with "thank God. . . ." The table, save Koettlitz, broke into raucous laughter.[148]

Koettlitz reacted badly to these childish public school pranks, losing patience with his fellow officers. This behavior must be seen in light of similar behavior in other fields of endeavor populated by former British public school boys at the turn of the century. Even in London's financial district outbursts such as throwing water-filled balloons were not uncommon.[149]

Koettlitz did not endure well the ribbing he suffered and would punish an offender by not showing the transgressor the next curious beast discovered in Koettlitz's microscope. Alternatively, the offender would find himself barred from tea in Koettlitz's cabin. Whether a man was invited to tea was an indication of his standing at that moment with the senior surgeon. For the offenders Koettlitz created the "Order of the Ass" with various gradations thereof depending on the severity of the offense.[150]

The biologist, T. V. Hodgson, was more of a loner than some. Hodgson spent much of the winter cutting and maintaining a series of holes in the ice to allow him to catch fish for study. Departing usually right after breakfast, "Muggins," as he was universally known, went off to net specimens. It was cold, lonely work but much to his taste. Hodgson thought before he left England that he would not find much work in the winter months, not expecting to continue to gather specimens. Eventually, Weller, one of the men, began to help him, but the sailor reported that the assistance consisted mostly of watching Hodgson work. Periodically, Barne also accompanied Hodgson.[151]

Processing specimens was time-consuming, and Hodgson's cabin displayed a vast collection of little bottles. He was always at work. Among the creatures Hodgson brought back were a variety of sea urchins, worms, spider-like creatures (including a five-legged one that caused great excitement as one had not before been seen), and sponges with long tentacles. Hodgson and Koettlitz shared specimens. Hodgson used the seal specimens, taking fish and crustaceans from their stomachs, while Koettlitz utilized other parts.[152]

Some insight into the seriousness of Hodgson's approach to his work might be gained from a comment he made in his journal during the stay in Cape Town: "Here I saw the finest sight I have seen for a long time, a small tide pool, a few inches deep and about 5 or 6 yards round on a granite bed, crammed full of sea anemones of every conceivable colour, all in beautiful condition."[153]

Although Hodgson was continually at his work throughout the winter, he suffered at times from a shortness of breath, which eventually prevented him from joining the spring sledging parties. Koettlitz and Wilson both agreed that Hodgson should not be involved in sledging, especially in the early weeks when the temperatures could be expected to be the worst.[154]

Another who tended to leave after breakfast and not return until the dinner hour was Michael Barne. His scientific assignment was to measure seawater temperatures, which he did throughout the winter. Scott questioned how valuable this research could be, given that the temperatures at various locations and depths rarely varied more than a tenth of a degree.[155]

The most experienced Antarctican aboard the ship was Louis Bernacchi, who was back in the Antarctic after only a brief break in England. Bernacchi was in charge of gravity, electrometer, auroral, and seismic observations. Having performed some of the same work on the *Southern Cross* expedition, he was well acquainted with his subject and did good work. His instruments required a constant temperature above freezing, the reason why he was a major consumer of oil in his observation huts.[156]

Bernacchi had two term days, the first and fifteenth of the month when he did observations every two hours. This meant that although under severe conditions others might not venture outdoors, his work required him to make regular runs to his observation hut even in the most dreadful weather, resulting in a regular series of frostbites.[157]

In addition to his regular work, in late July Bernacchi began his pendulum observations. Skelton helped him, as the equipment was very heavy and required being heated with lamps before it could function.[158] Because of difficulties Bernacchi decided to take two observations hourly instead of four. Besides, he was having trouble with the vacuum on his apparatus despite Skelton's efforts to repair it.[159] Eventually, Bernacchi was able to make the observations on 31 July and 1 August, although the experience nearly proved fatal. On the former date the weather began to deteriorate as they were finishing up. When the two tried to return to the ship, a matter of less than one quarter of a mile, the men lost the guide rope that had been allowed to sag between poles and therefore was buried beneath the snow. After spending an hour and a half wandering around in the severe weather Bernacchi's face was frostbitten. The situation was made worse by the lack of windproof clothing, which the pair had failed to don because the weather had been clear when they left the ship.[160] To have been so close to the ship the entire time and yet to be so close to death demonstrated Antarctica's unforgiving nature.[161] Wilson, remarking on the incident, noted, "I know nothing so utterly bewildering as the white darkness of this roaring drift. It is the easiest thing in the world to be lost in it and remain lost in the close vicinity of the ship. You can see nothing and barely open your eyes."[162]

That same evening Royds and some of the men had been in Gregory Lodge rehearsing an upcoming musical and had left after Skelton and Bernacchi. The returning musicians, too, lost their way but, being a larger party, were able to join hands and sweep along the ice until they found the guide rope that led them back to the ship. Curiously, a corn cob pipe that dropped from Skelton's pocket that night was found two months later.[163]

Bernacchi was not fortunate in his attempts to study the total eclipse of the moon on 23 April, as cloudy weather prevailed. But he was able to use his equipment for other enterprises.[164]

Bernacchi's workload prevented him from taking on other studies related to physical science, a lack Scott in his role as quasi-scientific leader regretted.[165]

Unlike the other scientists, H. T. Ferrar had his quarters (and his lab) forward in the ship. Consequently, he had less contact with the other members of the wardroom, aside from meals. Ferrar, an enthusiastic worker, was never happier than when scrambling over the rocky areas near winter quarters. Few could match his knowledge of the immediate area.[166]

Finding answers related to the questions surrounding the Great Ice Barrier was one of the missions of the *Discovery* expedition. Ferrar put out stakes in an area of the barrier near Hut Point to note any movement, even though all expected the movement to be slight.[167]

For Ernest Shackleton the idea of wintering in the Antarctic in 1902 would hardly have occurred to him several years before. Although subsequently one of the three greatest Antarctic explorers of his age, Shackleton had originally joined the *Discovery* because it was "an opportunity and nothing more."[168]

Scott was well pleased with his third officer, describing him as an "indefatigable worker." Shackleton was in charge of all the food aboard and issued it to the cooks. He was also editor of the *South Polar Times* and continued his salinity work throughout the winter. Shackleton was in charge of preparing the sledge rations for the coming season.[169]

The *South Polar Times* work brought Wilson and Shackleton together many hours each week, ensconced in the little office that Shackleton maintained in one of the holds. Their daily walks continued throughout the winter. The two became "fast friends," according to Shackleton's first biographer, H. R. Mill, who also noted that "a walk with Billy" was a common phrase in Shackleton's diary. Considerate of his friends, one evening, Shackleton, seeing that Wilson was asleep, took the midnight observation and let his friend sleep until 2:00 A.M. Shackleton found time to help others despite his workload and was often out with Hodgson helping him dig his ice holes.[170]

At the outset of winter Shackleton had laid out a program of study for the dark months, but the range of his other responsibilities kept him so busy that he found no time for extended study.[171] Shackleton was thoroughly liked by nearly all the officers and had a strong following among the men.

The *Discovery* officers were diligent in their duty, but none distinguished himself more for consistent hard work than did Billy Wilson. Scott noted that Wilson was always at work, performing a hundred and one kindly duties for men and officer.[172] His popularity with all aboard was described by Mill: "He had the finest mind and the most attractive personality of the whole ship's company, and was a universal favorite, loved and trusted by all."[173]

The winter months were extremely busy ones for Wilson. He had dozens of bird specimens to skin, and in this work he was fortunate in securing some help from Skelton and others, but most especially from Jacob Cross, who became a first-rate taxidermist. Help was needed because each emperor penguin took about six hours to skin. First, the bird had to be thawed, and then great care had to be taken to remove all the fat from the skin. As thawing was often done in the wardroom, one can imagine the smell.[174] Regrettably, much of the early taxidermy work that Wilson did was lost because he had stored his specimens in the former coal bunker and the skins became covered with coal dust and soot and were ruined.[175]

Throughout the expedition Wilson's skills as an artist were in demand whenever a subject was too dark or too fleeting for photography. Over the winter Wilson completed water color paintings based on drawings. In doing so he often gave himself numbered guides to the colors he should use when later painting from the monochrome sketch. His artistic work formed a vital part of the *South Polar Times*, although he occasionally regretted the amount of time it took from the rest of his serious work.

Wilson's diary of the expedition — admirably edited by Ann Savours and published in 1966 — betrays the amount of time that Wilson devoted to his writing. That even Wilson fell behind in his diary is an indication that the officers and scientists were kept busy during the winter.[176]

Added to his other activities, Wilson found time to read and keep up with medical studies on a regular basis.[177] As second physician he had the occasional medical problem to attend to — a tooth or a slight injury — but on the whole this work was slight, as the men remained remarkably healthy throughout the winter.[178]

Similar to everyone else, Wilson spent time on the details of life, washing clothing and keeping his cabin clean, but in midwinter he got a wonderful reward for the latter activity. While rummaging through his cabin he found a box he had not opened at Christmas in which were several letters and photographs, including some from his wedding that he had not seen.[179]

Engaged in many of the same tasks as other bluejackets, Tom Crean passed the winter. He was ill in early June with "dropsical" symptoms and lost nearly twenty pounds in a month.[180] The doctors assured Scott that the illness was not scurvy.[181] For a time it appeared that the mysterious problem with his legs would prevent Crean from taking part in the spring sledging work.[182]

The boatswain, Thomas Feather, was a quiet, determined man, who under Royds carried on much of the ship's work. The success of an expedition depends on the contented nature of the crew, and, apart from Royds, no one was more important in providing such an environment aboard ship as Feather.[183]

William Lashly was one of the most fortunate additions to the crew. Extremely popular with all aboard, he was a quiet man of good cheer who was never happier than when employed. Lashly could turn his hand to anything.[184]

Lashly was a nonsmoker and a teetotaler who was as fastidious about his person and attire as polar conditions would allow. He wore a little cross around his neck and was generally clean-shaven. Being clean in living and in speech were other ways Lashly stood out from his peers.[185]

Every day brought a new job. Among his winter projects, Lashly tinkered with the stoves in the mess deck and got them working. Part of the problem with the stoves was that they were designed to burn anthracite coal, but the manufacturers had assured the expedition planners that the devices would burn ship's coal equally well, a promise that seems to have been exaggerated. The draft had to be altered to burn ship's coal, which resulted in the stoves smoking more. Moreover, because the stoves were in the metal-free area needed for magnetic observations, the heaters were made of phosphor bronze, which wore out quickly.[186]

The mess stoves had been smoking a great deal whenever a storm blew outside, and Lashly was able to correct the operation of the stoves so that they worked efficiently. Lashly was a superb cobbler and kept the ship's company supplied in this respect.[187]

Lashly made a convenient little bracket for Skelton's cabin that was used for capturing the heat from the lamp to boil water and for holding a candle while reading in bed.[188] Clearly, Lashly was not idle, noting that "we still get plenty of work to do to help pass the time away, which is a good thing as it would be very trying with nothing to do."[189]

Lashly seemed content with his lot, though thoughts of home crept in from time to time. On the anniversary of joining the ship in London, Lashly wrote, "I wonder how my wife and child is [sic] getting on."[190]

The chief steward, Ford, had a remarkable number of tasks to accomplish each day throughout the winter, all of which he performed with a singular attention to detail. Under Shackleton's supervision Ford was in charge of all food supplies to be consumed onboard, and the smooth operation of the wardroom greatly facilitated the scientific program of the expedition.[191]

James Duncan was kept busy throughout the winter with a variety of projects, including putting felt in the wardroom cabins to improve insulation, helping correct a leak in the bow, or helping build the stage for the theatrical productions. He also made the commemorative cross for Vince.[192]

By the winter Frank Wild had clearly demonstrated that he was a cut above many of the other members of the mess deck and so was made an assistant in taking the sea-temperature experiments.[193]

Although he participated in the same full range of activities as the other men, Jacob Cross devoted much of his time to helping Wilson skin and prepare bird specimens. He enjoyed the work and became extremely adept at it.[194] Cross also had the only sewing machine aboard, a Singer, and was kept busy in this area.[195]

Part of the activities of the officers and men was the celebration of holidays, especially in the winter. No holiday went uncelebrated. A glance at some of the events of May 1902 gives an indication of the pattern. The fourteenth was honored as the anniversary of the ship's steam trial. The following day was Lady Markham's birthday, a cause for a second passing of the wine in the wardroom. Victoria Day was celebrated on the queen's birthday, 24 May 1902, with an extra toast at dinner, and the men spliced the main brace. The second edition of the *South Polar Times* also appeared on that day.[196]

When no holiday existed, however contrived, the men resorted to inventing one. The first day of June was celebrated, and two glasses of wine were downed in the festivities.[197] Skelton's birthday was the same as the Duke of York's, another chance for a second pass of the wine and one of liqueur.[198]

Scott's birthday was celebrated 6 June, and because that was also the anniversary of the arrival of the *Discovery* in London, the officers had extra liqueur all around.[199] The sixteenth of July was the first anniversary of Wilson's marriage, and leading up to the day (which was noted on Markham's calendar for all to see) Wilson received some gentle ribbing about the anniversary.[200] A week later, on 23 July, Wilson's birthday was celebrated. Wilson noted the event in his diary, "thirty years old today, and still as childish as ever."[201]

Because Midwinter day fell on a Sunday, the holiday was celebrated on

Monday. Traditionally, the most festive date in the south polar winter and celebrated like Christmas, the entire ship was decorated and among the men each mess competed with the others to provide the best possible decorations. The men had their favorite photographs on the tables, and the stoker's table even had an ice sculpture of Neptune. At 12:30 P.M. Scott led the officers through the men's quarters to exchange greetings of the season and to distribute gifts. Mrs. Royds, mother of the lieutenant, had sent a personal gift to each man on the *Discovery*, a small but well-appreciated gesture. Officers and men also had other little presents to open that they had brought from loved ones in England. H. R. Mill, that special friend of the expedition, had sent each man a Christmas card for the occasion. To record the event Skelton took an official photograph of each mess.[202]

Dinner in the mess deck consisted of real turtle soup, boiled ham, kidney beans, and potatoes, plus each man had a small bottle of Bass. The men's toast was "God bless the New Zealand farmers." The crew nearly missed their Christmas pudding, as it had been temporarily misplaced.[203]

In the evening the festivities continued with the men having tea cakes and sweets. Grog was served, but when some of the men approached Scott about having more, the captain told them to go to bed.[204]

In the wardroom the officers and scientists had assembled at 6:00 P.M. for a repast that included turtle soup, mutton, plum pudding, mince pies, and jellies. An excellent dry champagne, a gift of J. J. Kinsey, the expedition's agent in New Zealand, followed. Markham had arranged for a small number of bottles of wine to be aboard that had been taken with Sir George Nares to the Arctic in 1875, and one of these was uncorked for the special occasion. Speeches and a little singing followed dinner. At the close of the meal the officers toasted the captain's health, and then they sang in his honor, "For He's a Jolly Good Fellow."[205] After dinner many of the officers went on deck to take in the aurora of the southern sky.[206] All in all, for both officers and men midwinter had been a grand day.

To Scott fell the responsibility for the summer 1902–3 program. By early June his thinking was sufficiently advanced to brief Wilson about it. Scott's decision to take Wilson into his confidence was quickly apparent as Scott went through the details.

In his cabin Scott explained to Wilson that the southern party for the coming summer must be a small one, with only two or three people taking all the dogs, and that he had reserved this polar attempt for himself. Scott then asked the stunned Wilson if he would like to be the second person in that group.[207] Wilson immediately replied that his bill of health had not been clear when he joined the expedition. Scott was unconcerned. Wilson then argued for a three-man party for safety reasons — that two men might be able to get an injured man back when a single healthy one would fail. Scott found the argument persuasive and asked Wilson's choice for the third person. Wilson demurred, saying that the decision was Scott's, although both men knew that Wilson's first choice would be Shackleton. Scott agreed, and Shackleton's ambition to be on the polar party appeared to be fulfilled.[208]

The next day Scott called Shackleton into his cabin and told him that he was to be the third man in the southern party, but he asked Shackleton not to speak of the matter openly yet. Before the announcement could be made, Scott indicated a thorough medical examination would be undertaken.[209]

The goal of the southern party was to push over the Great Ice Barrier as far as possible, ideally to the Pole. Two support parties would accompany the three men briefly, but the bulk of the journey — one hundred days — was to fall to the southern party on their own. En route south Shackleton was to have charge of the dogs for the journey.[210]

The other arrangements for the summer included Barne being in charge of laying depots for the southern party.[211] Aside from the southern party, two major trips would be made. In the first Royds, Skelton, and Koettlitz were to go east to Cape Crozier to leave mail and to make natural history notes and to climb Mount Terror. Royds wanted this assignment, as he knew the way to Cape Crozier and the journey suited him.[212] This party had to be back in time for Skelton to ready the ship for sea. Skelton had hoped to be part of the southern party, but Scott explained to Skelton that he could not take him on that journey as Skelton was needed to ready the ship for sea in January 1903.[213] However, Skelton would be allowed to go with Armitage and the Western party.[214] Although disappointed not to be included in the preeminent sledging trip, Skelton understood Scott's reasons. In general, Skelton thought the captain's ideas about the coming season were practical and sensible.[215]

Early in the season Armitage was to lead a party to survey westward from winter quarters in the direction of what is today Minna Bluff. Later, another team would go west, also led by Armitage (and probably including Ferrar, Hodgson, and Koettlitz). In this second major trip Armitage's team would be taken by the relief ship to Wood Bay and from there attempt to reach the South Magnetic Pole. The relief ship would await their return and then proceed to New Zealand.[216]

Meanwhile, once the southern party had returned, the *Discovery* would sail around Cape North and explore in that region, as far as coal and time would allow.

The spring and summer plans having been made by Scott, the crew waited for the end of winter to begin to implement this program.

The return of the sun on 22 August 1902 was witnessed by a number of members of the crew who went to Crater Hill to gain an early glimpse of the returning orb. Wilson and Shackleton trekked up to Arrival Heights to see "the sun, the whole sun, and nothing but the sun," and pronounced the event a great joy.[217] Scott was among those who made the pilgrimage and reported that the view "dazzled the eye with its brilliance.[218] To celebrate the event, the mess deck was given a bottle of Bass per man at dinner.[219]

The fifth issue of the *South Polar Times* came out 26 August 1902. Wilson thought it the best so far.[220] This last issue of the winter signaled the close of the crew's period of relative confinement.

The men of the *Discovery* had survived the winter without the depression that had been such a sad feature of other polar expeditions. Most recently in the Antarctic, among the crew of the *Belgica* in 1898, several men suffered greatly from depression, and one even lost his mind from polar anemia.

Moreover, the crew of the *Discovery* distinguished themselves for their good cheer and determination to keep to the work at hand. Neither mess deck nor wardroom was populated with saints, but their ability to cooperate with one another for the benefit of science and for the honor of their flag casts great credit on the whole company.[221]

Originally, Scott hoped to be able to begin the spring sledging season at the end of September. By August the weather appeared to have improved sufficiently that the captain thought at one point that a late August start might have been possible.[222]

One unsettled question was the possibility of a third summer, 1903–4. Scott knew when he sailed that the funding for that extra time did not exist, but he was hopeful that Markham and other friends of the expedition would have made it possible. Thus he planned on wintering in 1903 in New Zealand and returning to explore the Antarctic coastline, west from Cook's farthest point back around to King Edward VII Land. Not everyone believed that funding would be forthcoming, Royds among them.[223]

Skelton, who kept track of coal stocks, was concerned that if the relief ship did not arrive the *Discovery* had sufficient coal only to get around Cape

North and go a little farther before it would have to turn north to New Zealand.[224]

Many people contributed to the preparations for the spring sledging season. Wilson gave a talk on the medical kit to be carried with each sledging expedition. Dellbridge and Lashly turned their attention to getting primus stoves, pots, and sledging harnesses ready. Shackleton was kept busy throughout the winter preparing for the spring sledging season, weighing supplies and dividing them up into weekly or daily rations. Aided by several of the men, everything that was to be used by the sledging parties was weighed and measured, put in little linen sacks, and made ready for the day of departure.[225]

The lack of experience with dogs was evident in the preparations for sledging. With no trained dog handler, the task of fashioning dog harnesses fell to the boatswain. Elementary progress was made in designing gear for dog sledging. Nor was it certain how best to use the dogs — alone or working in tandem with men pulling the same sledge.[226]

Among the problems that the autumn sledging had uncovered was the need for more protection from the cold for the face. A variety of blinders and coverings were tried with mixed success. Regrettably, the *Discovery* did not carry glycerine, as the *Southern Cross* had, to protect skin against the harsh elements.[227]

Preparations went on to the last minute, until the departure of the first sledge parties. Scott decided to make a short sledging trip with five others to survey the coast to the north of winter quarters. On the afternoon of 2 September 1902 Scott's party started out. Spring had arrived in earnest.

9

Summer 1902–1903

The return of the sun and the preparations that had been going on for some weeks signaled the beginning of spring and the sledging season. Scott knew when he left England that the expedition only had funds sufficient to last to the end of that summer, and that then he would have to return to New Zealand.[1] Thus this summer was expected to be the only complete one of the endeavor unless additional funding was forthcoming. By that time Markham hoped he would have raised enough money for a third summer, one which had a tentative route that might lead to a number of significant geographical discoveries.

The summer of 1902–3 was to be the main season for scientific work. The centerpiece was the southern party's attempt to establish a new farthest south and perhaps discover some great inland feature. All operations that summer were planned around this all-important effort, even though the possibilities for scientific discovery might not be as great as other itineraries.

The inexperience of the *Discovery* staff had been clear in the previous autumn's sledging efforts. The lack of preparation regarding transport handicapped their activities, and manhauling proved difficult.

The previous autumn the dogs had been moderately successful. Regrettably, Scott was not in a position to make better use of the animals, either because of his own sentimentality toward dogs or because his mentor, Markham, was so deeply prejudiced against them. In this respect the *Discovery* was a retreat from the advances made by Borchgrevink's *Southern Cross* expedition in which the value of dogs in the Antarctic had been demonstrated.

Scott had to wrestle with other dog transport issues besides the prejudice against them. Markham failed to assume that the ice in Antarctica would be different from that in the Arctic Sea region, where vast fields of rafted ice often made dog travel difficult. In the South the broad expanses of continental ice without masses of pressure ridges made ideal conditions for dogs. Moreover, Scott had brought the wrong kind of animal. Although Eastern Siberian and Canadian dogs were thought at the time to be more suitable for use, Western Siberian dogs had been chosen, in Bernacchi's understanding, to save time. Also, insufficient numbers of animals were aboard the *Discovery* at the outset, twenty-four dogs versus the seventy-five on the *Southern Cross* expedition. Too little attention had been paid to the accouterments of dog driving, and throughout the winter and into the spring sledging season various members of the staff—who had essentially no prior experience with dogs—were trying to improvise apparatus, such as the harness, instead of making the best use of established and proven equipment. Finally, and perhaps most significantly, no one from the staff had any real experience with dog handling, a skill that takes years to master. Markham assumed any officer could muddle through when the time came. These initial difficulties meant that except for the southern party, manhauling was to be the principal form of transport in the 1902–3 season.[2]

Scott led a small preliminary party to explore land near winter quarters and to gain experience with his two companions for the southern party. Thus on 2 September 1902 he led Wilson, Shackleton, Skelton, Feather, and Ferrar beyond Glacier Tongue, to the north of winter quarters. Wilson had asked to be excused so that he could remain at the ship to continue his work, but Scott insisted that he join this group. Departing late in the day Scott's party went for three hours before camping for the night. As an experiment men and dogs were harnessed to the same sledge, an idea that did not prove viable. Some of the dogs pulled well; others were termed "sooners," as they would sooner do anything than pull. Other experiments included sleeping arrangements: Scott, Wilson, and Shackleton shared a three-man sleeping bag while the others had single bags.[3]

On the second day out, Scott put Skelton in charge of the dogs, even though he was less experienced with the animals than his captain was. The party investigated Turtle Island and just beyond. Even a short trek such as this demonstrated some of the problems involving sledging—difficulty sleeping, largely constant discomfort, and work at a pace that demanded large quantities of food.[4] Also, this journey gave each man an appreciation of the daily habits of sledging. Wilson described them:

When you turn in at night you have taken your fur boots off and turned them inside out, a very easy thing to do because they are wet and warm and merely wash leather reindeer skin with the hair on [*sic*]. The hair which has been outside all day is now inside. Then you take off two thick pair of wool socks, leaving one third pair on, all wet through and these you tuck up inside your chest against your shirt to dry where your night socks have been all day. The latter come out now of course and are put on, and over them the finnesko inside out, i.e., fur inside.[5]

Scott determined that his group had done enough and on 5 September decided that the men should turn back after lunch. Once pointed toward home, the dogs pulled so well that they could barely be restrained. The first sledging trip of the season was a success, and all returned safely. Ferrar had been able to do some geological work, Skelton had field-tested his sledge meter, and new dog harnesses had been tried. Scott noted that the value of dogs had been "abundantly proven."[6]

Scott was still trying to determine the ideal size of a sledging party. Three seemed like a good number because small parties could go farther on the supplies carried. Still, he wondered if his men would do as well in distances as the British Arctic explorers of the nineteenth century. Scott realized that his predecessors had one advantage over his men. Scott's men had accurate sledge meters that recorded their actual distance, while the old Arctic explorers went by dead reckoning and were more likely to err by accidentally overestimating the miles accomplished.[7]

Scott also sent Armitage on a short journey to retrieve the depot of supplies put out the previous autumn. Armitage returned two days later, having accomplished his mission.[8]

On 10 September 1902, Royds, accompanied by Koettlitz, Lashly, Quartly, Evans, and Wild — what Skelton thought was "the best you could get" — departed on a reconnaissance trip to the bay north of Mount Discovery.[9] The mess deck had a similar high opinion of these men, calling them the "guarantee party," meaning that they could go anywhere and do anything. While Royds was gone, the meteorological observations, which were now in the capable hands of the quartermasters, were to be supervised by Wilson. Royds headed toward the mainland, planning to search for a way through the mountains, and was expected to be away for fourteen days. Instead, the men encountered very cold weather, temperatures as low as $-53°$ F, and several blizzards. They returned on the nineteenth of September because Lashly's sleeping bag had been blown away in a blizzard.[10]

Armitage left one day later than Royds, 11 September 1902, in the company of Ferrar, Cross, Gilbert Scott, Walker, and Heald. Armitage, who had been a steady opponent of skis, surprised some members of the expedition by beginning the trip on skis, the first sledging party to do so.[11] By this time Scott was convinced that skis could be of use in soft snow but still reserved judgment as to their value in hard snow. In addition, Scott thought skis were usable only in pulling loads of a given weight. Curiously, the men, rather than the officers, were early converts, believing that it made the pulling easier.[12] Armitage was also responsible for finding a path through the mountains. Suspecting a path might be found on the Ferrar Glacier, Armitage was allowed to pursue that track. Aided by a sail to propel the sledge, they made nine miles on the first day.[13]

Six days later though, Armitage's party was only twenty-nine miles from the ship, held up one whole day by storms. Progress was further delayed by the ill health of the men. One member was suffering from pains in his lower limbs, another had a sprained ankle, and a third had sore gums. Leaving part of his group, Cross and Blissett, at the base, Armitage took the remainder of the men up the valley, which he hoped would be the road to the interior of Victoria Land. Two more men became ill, and Armitage felt it unwise to continue, although in getting as far as he did Armitage discovered a route later used for farther inland exploration. On the eleventh day out of winter quarters Armitage decided to turn back.[14]

Meanwhile, at the ship, work continued. With the return of daylight, the awning on deck was removed and clearly showed the degree of filth in the wardroom — everything was sooty.[15] With many men away on sledging parties, fewer remained to maintain the daily activities of the expedition. Wilson found himself especially busy with supervising the meteorological observations for Royds and looking after Koettlitz's work while attempting to carry on his own research, one important aspect of which was collecting seal specimens. Wilson was trying to get specimens of all ages, and during this period in the early spring he was able to add to his collection several young seal pups, including a stillborn one.[16] Wilson wanted to gather a series of seal embryos at various stages of development.[17] He also took every opportunity to examine penguins that came close to the ship. Emperors continued to puzzle him. Noting the brooding patch on the abdomen of his specimens, the zoologist assumed that the birds would soon be laying their eggs.[18] When Wilson saw a group of sixty-five emperors heading south in late September, he thought they were deceived by the temperatures, and he surmised that the birds were going toward the barrier and starvation. Further investigation proved several of Wilson's conclusions wrong.[19]

Royds's party returned from Mount Discovery earlier than expected, but not the first group to do so. Scott had set out on 17 September but returned on 19 September. Before starting on the seventeenth, the captain had had to delay his departure on a day-to-day basis because of cold and unpredictable weather. Bemoaning the delay caused by the dogs and the need for heavier loads, Scott noted that with men alone he might start in such weather.[20] This time Wilson's request to remain behind and do zoological work was granted; Barne went in his place.[21] When Scott's party left the ship the temperature was −43° F, but they managed to get in a good day searching for the best path south. Overnight, a blizzard hit, confining the men to their tents all day and causing them to go thirty hours without hot food. The storm was so severe that for a while some concern developed that their tent might be blown away.[22] Scott, surprised by the extreme and unexpectedly low temperatures (nothing in the Arctic or Antarctic experiences had led him to expect such low temperatures at this time of year), turned back and returned to the ship on 19 September 1902.[23] Many in the ship's company went out to greet them and help with the sledges. "They looked like warriors, all covered in ice and snow."[24] Shackleton and Barne were both frostbitten, and Skelton believed that Shackleton had been eager to return, which the engineer thought displayed a lack of determination. Skelton thought that the effort was "not altogether a success."[25]

On Scott's second effort Barne's fingers had been so badly frostbitten that he had to remain onboard ship while the captain led Shackleton and Feather on Scott's third sledging expedition, which departed the vessel 24 September 1902. This team did eighteen and a half miles before stopping for the night. The next day began all right, but by afternoon the weather had deteriorated sufficiently to cause them to camp early. Two good days followed, and then on 28 September Scott's party awoke to find a howling blizzard. Impatient to be on the move, Scott pushed on with the two teams following in his wake. Trying, unsuccessfully, to watch for crevasses as he drove forward, Scott suddenly heard a cry behind him and turned around to see that Feather had disappeared. He was soon pulled out, and the party resumed the march. Another sledge disappeared down a hole but fortunately was sufficiently well packed that it survived intact the jerk of the rope. The party pushed forward, now roped together, to the end of the day. In his published account Scott freely admitted that the decision to go on in a blizzard was foolish, but once again the pilgrims bought their lesson cheaply — Feather was fine, the sledge survived, and no one was lost.[26]

By this time the captain's group was east of Minna Bluff, and on the first of October they depoted their supplies — six weeks' provisions for three men — roughly sixty miles from the ship. Turning back with minimum loads, they were able to return to the *Discovery*, averaging twenty miles a day, arriving on 3 October.[27]

While Scott was still away on this third preliminary trip, Armitage was overdue. Armitage's men had food for fourteen days, and when they did not return on the fifteenth day, a relief effort was organized. Fortunately, on 26 September the group returned to the vessel, having pushed on over-night because Armitage feared that the health problems with his men were serious. During this sledging journey, Armitage had discovered what appeared to be a glacier that ran up to the inland ice toward the mag-netic Pole.[28]

The experience of sledging had not been a pleasant one for Ferrar. Armi-tage was inclined to believe that Ferrar was not suitable for sledging, ap-parently also taking into consideration the possibility that Ferrar was be-ing bothered by scurvy. At one point during the journey, when Ferrar had been away from the camp, he became exhausted and wanted to sleep, but Bill Heald saved his life and brought him back to the base. With a temper-ature of −45° F, Ferrar most likely would have perished without Heald's in-tervention. Armitage had nothing but praise for Heald and Cross, whose work had been first-rate. Presiding at services the following Sunday, Ar-mitage singled out Heald for special recognition.[29]

But a far greater problem than Ferrar's unsuitability for sledge travel de-veloped on Armitage's sledging trip — scurvy. Heald and Cross joined Fer-rar as victims. Wilson examined the men and feared that "history is evi-dently going to repeat itself in the south," a reference to the disasters of British Arctic exploration in the nineteenth century. Wilson was also fear-ful for the sledging parties still out in the field. At first the situation may have been hushed up.[30]

As Scott was still out sledging, Armitage became the senior officer pres-ent. The outbreak of scurvy gave Armitage his one real chance to demon-strate his leadership potential. From his experience in the Arctic he knew the seriousness of the disease. He took immediate action to help those in-flicted and, more importantly, took steps to prevent the spread of the out-break. How was it possible that the disease took hold when the men had been eating seal over the winter? In part, the answer lay with one person: the cook. His lackadaisical, uninspired cooking of seal meat had diminished its appeal, and apparently the men were not getting as much of its antiscor-butic benefits as Scott assumed. Armitage immediately ordered fresh meat and lime juice for the entire company.[31] Then Armitage, in a dressing-down regrettably not recorded, put the fear of God (or at least of Armitage) into the cook. After that conversation Brett was a changed man. Seal appeared on the menu every day, but — far more importantly — the meat was deliciously prepared. Suddenly, Brett could cook, a possibility that had vaguely occurred to the men but now, thanks to Armitage's "encouragement," became a reality.[32]

Scott had thought that by taking such thorough watch over the tinned foods (having one of the physicians inspect each tin before serving) he would avoid scurvy. In his published remarks Scott pointed out that the best tinned foods had been chosen, within the time allotted before departure. At the time of the publication of The Voyage of the "Discovery" Scott still believed ptomaine poisoning to be the cause of scurvy. Yet on the expedition the men were aware of the preventive power of fresh meat, and the captain put it on the menu for that purpose. Wilson, too, found the outbreak surprising, and although the tinned food origin had been assumed to be true, the junior surgeon found it difficult to square that notion with the extant facts. Koettlitz was unable to suggest a cause. In the end though, Scott suggested in his published account that future Antarctic expeditions should not have any problem with scurvy as the Discovery expedition had proven the preventative value of fresh food available in Antarctica. He neglected to mention that the Southern Cross expedition had proven that conclusion before the Discovery sailed.[33]

When Scott returned on 3 October he had immediately sensed a change in Armitage's manner. After dinner Armitage explained the situation, which the captain regarded as "indeed a shock!" Writing in his diary, Scott praised Armitage's handling of the situation and noted that a most significant improvement had been made in the cook to whom, Scott surmised, Armitage must have spoken with uncommon inspiration, for the improvement in the seal fare was a marvel. Now the most appetizing seal dishes were being served, including a liberal supply of livers, hearts, and kidneys. Wilson thought that seal liver was as good as any dish he had ever eaten. All tinned meat consumption ended. Demand for seal food led to more intensive hunting near the ship. A hole through the ice was dug near the Discovery in the hopes of enticing seals to surface nearby. In addition, regular scouting parties went out to bring back even more seals now.[34]

Concerned that the health of his men might be affected by the condition of the vessel, in early October Scott ordered a massive general cleanup of the ship — drying damp spaces in the holds, cleaning and disinfecting bilges, continuing the work that Armitage had begun. To relieve the crowding in the mess deck Scott ordered some of the men to sleep in the hut each week. Continuing the ban on canned meats, Scott vigorously insisted on exercise for all aboard. He ordered his officers to watch for any signs of fatigue, which could indicate scurvy. By these actions Scott hoped to prevent further spread of the disease. From the captain's point of view, Armitage's handling of the scurvy matter gave Scott great confidence that in his absence on the southern party, Armitage would be an able commander.[35]

Other short trips were undertaken. Koettlitz led Bernacchi and Dailey out for eight days, starting 24 September, during which Koettlitz worked largely on his own and was able to accomplish much. Koettlitz had asked Skelton to go on this trip and he wanted very much to accompany the physician, but Bernacchi had already spoken to the captain about the trip and was given the nod. In their time away the party did significant work, in Skelton's estimate, far more than Royds's party had done under similar circumstances.[36]

Wilson, with two men, led a small excursion to the northwest to investigate a report of open water. The plan called for Royds's party to pick up Wilson and take him on with them, while sending Lashly back with the other two men.[37]

In addition to dealing with the major problem of scurvy, Armitage, in his role as commander, also took charge of the weekly church service in Scott's absence. In the place of Koettlitz, Wilson read the lesson, a task he thoroughly enjoyed. At one service Armitage's sermon was direct and short. He noted that Galatians chapter 6 was as good a lesson on sledging as the men would ever hear: "Be brothers and live together in unity and be unselfish and help one another." Well might the sledger think of Galatians chapter 6, verse 5, "For each one shall bear his own load."[38]

During this time two mysteries appeared, one solved and one unsolved. The emperor penguins continued to puzzle. At least twice in the early spring groups of them were heading south. With no open water anywhere to the south, the scientists could not figure out why the birds were headed in that direction. Had the men been able to determine the sex of the birds, the mystery might have deepened, as it is likely that they were all female.[39]

What the scientists did not know in 1902 was that the emperor penguins' breeding cycle is one of the strangest on earth. After pairing off, the female lays a single egg, which the male then scoops up and carries on his feet (a fold of skin goes over the egg) and then incubates for sixty-two to sixty-four days. Through the long and bitterly cold Antarctic winter the males guard the egg. Meanwhile, the females leave to feed in the sea. In the spring they return in time (a day or two before) for the egg to hatch. Then both parents are involved in feeding the single chick. The details of this life cycle were as yet unknown to the scientists of the *Discovery*, but their puzzlement helps explain why unlocking the mystery of the emperor penguin was so appealing and led to the great winter journey on Scott's second expedition, 1910–13.[40]

6. Emperor penguins. Drawing by Kim Crosbie.

The second incident, though strange, was explicable. Two dogs disappeared and were gone for three weeks. The men assumed them lost. Instead, while taking a walk to Turtle Island, two of the men came across the dogs. A seal, attacked by the dogs, had apparently fallen dead on the remains of the chain of one of the dogs and pinned the dog to the spot. The second dog had remained with the trapped one, both feeding off the seal in the meantime to survive until rescued by the men.[41]

One of the more important efforts of the summer was the trip to Cape Crozier to investigate penguins and to update dispatches for the relief ship. Departing on 4 October 1902, under the command of Royds, the team comprised Skelton, Lashly, Evans, Quartly, and Wild, with two sledges and provisions for one month.

Traveling on the sea ice, the party arrived at Cape Crozier a week later. On 11 October Royds, having sprained an ankle, turned over the mission of reaching the mail cairn to Skelton, who took Evans and Quartly and started out. They found the cairn with little difficulty, as the mail drop was the most prominent feature of the shore.[42]

In addition to leaving mail the party was to ascertain if a route to the barrier could be found from the slopes of Mount Terror. The men encountered harsh conditions with temperatures as low as −58.6° F. From the thirteenth to the seventeenth work was interrupted by a five-day blizzard, during which time the men were confined to their sleeping bags and unable to cook, surviving on biscuits and sugar.[43] Skelton resumed what eventually became a formidable natural history report on penguins, which Scott and Wilson highly praised.[44] Certainly, his report included early descriptions of what is now familiar behavior by these birds—the loud squawking and parents chasing after stray chicks to replace a lost chick of their own. In addition to the study of Adélies, the party found the first known emperor penguin rookery. As a result of his study at Cape Crozier, Skelton was first to suggest, on the basis of evidence, that the birds either wintered at the rookery or more likely (though incorrectly) that the penguins had arrived very early in the spring. Skelton also noted the high mortality rate of the chicks, estimating that perhaps as few as ten percent survived.[45]

Wilson and Hodgson had been out to Cape Armitage on 24 October 1902 to check the thermometer there and to field-test a new pair of wind pants for the men of the southern journey. While there, they spied the Royds party approaching. Muggins (Hodgson) returned to the ship to announce the return, and the zoologist went out to greet them on the trail. Much concern had been expressed while they were away because the weather had been particularly fearsome during their absence. The appearance of Royds's party on 24 October was such a surprise that after seeing them, Scott feared some tragedy had befallen the group.[46]

After the men returned to the vessel after twenty days on the trail a bath was a great luxury. Usually, they arrived with ravenous appetites, and the first few meals aboard the *Discovery* were seen as particularly good, no doubt from the change of diet. Returning sledgers consumed everything set before them, and having finished the meal found themselves half an hour later searching around for bread and butter or chocolate. Moreover, the return to a warm, dry bed was most welcome, because after a few days on the trail the sleeping bags became icy and wet from the perspiration of the men at night. Getting into the bags at that point was a cold and unpleasant activity. When the group got back from this Crozier trip, Skelton weighed his three-man sleeping bag. At the outset it was forty-five pounds, but by the end, with the encrusted ice collected en route, the bag weighed seventy-six pounds.[47]

The return of Royds and his team was celebrated with champagne; however, the celebration did not last long. The meager results of Royds's party were noted by the captain, and he called Skelton into his cabin to question him. Scott wanted to know why the party was back so early and why more had not been done. Coming back a week early with the only apparent result being the visit to the emperor penguin rookery seemed meager. Skelton mentioned the five-day blizzard but indicated that Royds had not seemed enthusiastic about the work; indeed, Skelton told Scott that he did not think Royds was cut out for sledging work. This supported the report from Koettlitz that the captain had previously sought. Despite his personal impressions, Skelton tried to protect his fellow officer as much as he could, leaving out the incident of the sprained ankle, about which Skelton was skeptical.[48]

Royds was called into Scott's cabin where Scott criticized his work. Later, Royds went to both Koettlitz and Skelton to try to determine what each had said about him. Royds suspected the information had come from Koettlitz and Skelton but no doubt did not appreciate that Skelton's remarks to the captain had been restrained. In his journal Skelton's opinion was less so: "Though he [Royds] does not actually funk sledging, he is next door to it and in fact is never feeling happy, too girlish and certainly has very little brains and no observing powers at all for scientific or interesting matter."[49] Nothing was mentioned in the published account of Royds's behavior on this sojourn.[50]

The criticism of Royds seems harsh. Royds worked diligently at all the many tasks assigned to him by his captain. Royds was unusual in that he was very straightforward about sledging in his diary. Royds was one of the few officers who had no illusions about the amount of suffering one had to endure. Sledging was no picnic, and Royds at times saw the whole experience in Antarctica as a duty to be fulfilled, perhaps as a tribute to his family. His uncle, Wyatt Rawson, had served in the Arctic, and Royds believed that he had to keep up the family tradition and honor.

Back from the Cape Crozier trip, Skelton noted what he thought were slight signs of scurvy. His stamina for walking seemed diminished, but he hoped that he would soon improve with a fresh seal meat diet. Wilson and Koettlitz examined him, but they thought the condition no reason for concern.[51]

A number of other short sledging sojourns were made in the first half of the 1902–3 season. Most were to gather food or for limited investigations of particular phenomena. On one such seal-hunting expedition, Wilson noted that the flags placed on the glacier snout during the previous trip had indeed moved. Wilson believed it the first proof of movement in Antarctic glaciers.[52] These seal-killing forays were messy affairs. One got covered with blood in the process, and the intense cold meant that one had to be extremely careful with every action. The men's felt mitts froze in whatever shape they were in, and to get them off or on the men often had to thaw them in the still-warm seal's blood.[53]

On one of these short journeys Wilson faulted Barne's behavior. The surgeon believed Barne was careless in that he overworked his men and did not listen to Wilson on such matters. Furthermore, Wilson was annoyed that although the men knew the situation to be unsuitable, their naval training required them to obey Barne's orders and to ignore Wilson. In his diary, in reaction to this journey, Wilson described Barne as a "thoughtless youth, a good many years one's junior, whom I consider quite incompetent to be in charge of men, and whose main idea seemed to be to show that he was able to do as he chose." Subsequently, Wilson discussed the situation with some of the other officers and was persuaded that his duty was to report Barne's action to the captain, who investigated the situation. Wilson was hesitant to bring the matter to Scott's attention but feared that because Barne would be in charge of the depot-laying trip and perhaps others, Scott needed to know. After being reprimanded by Scott, Barne became cooler toward Wilson.[54]

Meanwhile, preparations for the southern party were going ahead. Barne had charge of the supporting party, which left on 30 October 1902 to help carry additional provisions as far south as possible. Scott had determined that with a twelve-man supporting party the southern party could travel one-third more distance than they could carrying all their own equipment and supplies from the ship.[55] As the manhauling explorers departed the *Discovery*, their sledges were decorated with sledging flags declaring, "Hope On, Hope Ever," "The Ocean Cavalry," and "No Dogs Admitted." The rest of the men had the day off, and many accompanied Barne's group for the first few miles.[56]

Among the last-minute changes for the southern party made by the captain on the eve of departure was to substitute some freshly cooked seal meat for pemmican for the southern journey in an attempt to stave off scurvy. To remove the water the meat was cooked again and again.[57]

Before departing for the southern trip, Scott had directed Armitage to lead a party westward, taking whomever the Pilot chose. Also, in the event of Scott's failure to return in time for the sailing of the *Discovery* north, Armitage was to take the vessel back to New Zealand.[58]

Anticipating a 1 November start, on 31 October a celebration dinner was held for the trio. Although excited for the southern party in the days leading to their departure, at the least Shackleton had been annoying at times with his constant prattle about the forthcoming trip. Skelton, for one, found his patience sapped and at one point described Shackleton as a "gas bag." But the dinner was very pleasant, with a champagne toast wishing them luck. Shackleton knew fortune was a factor, and although he hoped to reach the Pole and return to England in triumph, he also realized that failure was a possibility. He spent the night before departure writing letters "in case."[59]

Bad weather delayed the departure by a day. While waiting on the first, Koettlitz had a special treat during tea — he harvested his mustard and cress crop and served it, the first fresh green food for thirteen months. Finally, on the next day, 2 November 1902, the southern party was able to depart at about ten o'clock A.M. The dogs started well, and soon Shackleton and the dogs left the others far behind. Several men accompanied them for a while but in the end waved their good-byes. Although no figure was set as a goal, 80° seemed a realistic line for which to aim.[60]

The next day two other groups departed. Royds led another party to Cape Crozier. They were away from the ship from 3 November to 17 November. Royds hated the idea but had to volunteer to do so. With him he took Blissett and Plumley and provisions for fifteen days.[61]

The second sledging party consisted of Koettlitz, Skelton, and Hare. The first day they made for Razorback Island, near a group of seals. Thinking that seal calf's liver would taste good, the men acted on their thoughts and soon had boiled liver and heart with their pemmican. The rest of the seal was brought along for future meals. On that first day the party noted that flags that had been put on the glacier snout to determine its movement were now out of line by nearly nine feet in sixty days.[62]

A hearty breakfast of fresh seal kidney, liver, heart, and sweetbread started the next day. Koettlitz's team arrived at the supposed locale of an Adélie penguin rookery but found no sign of a rookery save for some dead chicks. When the men reached their farthest north point they could see open water. The next day both Skelton and Koettlitz felt ill, and Hare, too, had a cough. They departed for Turtle Rock and the ship and arrived home on 5 November, about eight in the evening. Returning to the *Discovery*, the men found others were bothered with catarrh, which may have been caused by the spring cleaning of the vessel stirring up germs that then attacked the men.[63]

The summer was not all work. Armitage organized a series of games to celebrate the king's birthday on 8 November. The day was fine and clear, and in honor of the occasion, the Union Jack was flown for the first time in winter quarters. Flags that had flown on the *Alert* and the old *Discovery* in the Arctic in 1875, gifts of Sir George Nares, were hoisted. Armitage betrayed his lack of royal naval practice when he arranged to have a single gun fire as the flag was raised, which would have been the signal for a court-martial. As chance would have it, the gun did not fire. In the forenoon Koettlitz served more mustard and cress, which he had grown in the wardroom skylight. In addition, he had some lettuce and radishes, which were served to all hands.[64]

Among the day's events were tobogganing, tug-of-war, sledge pulling, and downhill ski running. Skelton won the latter, while Quartly's team won the tug-of-war. Armitage oversaw the entire event, apparently enjoying his opportunity to be in charge. Prizes, small silver medals brought from England for such a possible competition, were distributed by a princess.[65] In reality, the princess was Gilbert Scott dressed up as a girl, and "an uncommonly pretty one too."[66]

A week later the second part of the events took place, including a ski race of two miles. Although some thought Duncan or Walker might win, in the end the stamina of Edgar Evans proved the deciding factor and he came in first. Two possible challengers were away — Scott and Quartly. The shooting contest was marred by faulty sights on the rifles. That night the men joined the officers in the wardroom for a concert, and Armitage distributed the remainder of the prizes. The evening ended with "God Save the King" being sung by the entire company. The whole event was a great success and demonstrated that Armitage had a knack for making himself popular when the mood struck him.[67]

Two days later the Royds party to Cape Crozier returned. Gone for two weeks, the party arrived with a great triumph, an emperor penguin egg that had been found by Blissett.[68] They had also visited an Adélie penguin rookery and brought back eggs. These had their shells blown for scientific purposes, and then the contents were turned into scrambled eggs. Each man was allotted one from the stock brought back; officers received two.[69]

By this time some concern was felt for Dailey's support party, which had gone out with the southern party and was several days overdue. Plans for a relief expedition were under way when Dailey returned on 21 November 1902, having traveled eight days since turning back. Dailey's party arrived hungry — their provisions had given out — but otherwise were in fine shape.[70]

Two days later during church services, Dellbridge interrupted to say that Barne's party had been sighted, and a group from the ship went out to greet them and help them bring back their gear. Barne had made it to 79°15′ S before turning back. At that point the barrier still stretched on endlessly; no land was in sight. When Barne departed the dogs were still pulling well, although one, Blanco, had been sent back as unfit. Blanco returned to the ship and her puppies.[71]

Meanwhile, preparations were under way for the last great sledging expedition of the summer season. Armitage's western party was charged with studying the western mountains and perhaps getting as far as the South Magnetic Pole, although this was extremely unlikely.[72] Departing on 29 November 1902, the men did not return until 19 January 1903.

Although some had placed hopes on a pass being found in the area of New Harbour, Armitage surmised that the valley south of the Ferrar Glacier would lead up into the mountains and allow his party to penetrate the interior.[73] As they proceeded Armitage took magnetic observations, as one aspect of this journey was to proceed roughly in the direction of the South Magnetic Pole.

The main party had been supported by a second subsidiary group, which turned back under the direction of Dr. Koettlitz. Before departing he warned Armitage that although his men were apparently fit they still showed some signs of scurvy.[74]

Twelve days out the party altered course. Several times they were delayed by storms, including a four-day one. The party spent Christmas in camp, unable to move because of storms. Christmas dinner was fried cheese and bacon with horseradish, and most of the day was spent playing euchre. After a thirty-six-hour delay caused by bad weather, Armitage noted upon starting out again that some of his men were weakening.[75]

The new year arrived with a gale from the west, which held the men up for a day. The next day, able to move again, Armitage saw one of the petty officers in the second party fall. MacFarlane, evidently quite ill, was having difficulty breathing. Armitage feared MacFarlane was dying. Finding several other members of the team done in—including Wild, whose tentmates complained that the loud beating of his heart at night was keeping them awake — Armitage ordered this group to camp under the direction of David Allan, one of the petty officers. Armitage was keen to get to the top before sending this party back and hoped to rest them before doing so.[76]

Armitage pushed on to the top of the Ferrar Glacier and on 4 January 1903 made the most outward camp at the summit of the ice cap in that area of Victoria Land.[77] Unable to proceed owing to the condition of MacFarlane and the others, Armitage was forced to turn back. Had he kept going, he would have found the route inland to the area behind the mountains of Victoria Land.

Returning to Allan's camp, Armitage saw two of his men walking near it. He called out to warn them of crevasses, when suddenly the surface disappeared beneath him and Armitage was himself plunged into an icy void. Fortunately, his harness held, and Skelton soon had a line down to him, by which Armitage was able to regain the surface.[78]

En route back they reached the base of the Royal Society Range without mishap. At one point on the way out Ferrar had laid out a line of sticks on a glacier, and after returning twenty-three days later the party found that the markers had moved two feet, nine inches.[79]

MacFarlane felt well enough on the way back to ski along behind the sledges, but unfortunately even this was too much of a strain and he collapsed.[80] Regaining the coast, the men feasted on seals, which were found lying along the ice, a meal greatly appreciated.[81] A final effort brought Armitage's group back to the *Discovery* 19 January 1903, ending the fifty-two day mission.[82]

While Armitage had been away the rest of the ship's company had celebrated Christmas (with reduced company) with a magic lantern show. Several small sledging trips had been made.

With all the sledging parties save the southern party back from their various assignments, some thought was turned to the possible arrival of the relief ship. However, even if such a vessel were to arrive, no possibility existed of it sailing up to winter quarters in the night, for the *Discovery* was frozen solid and twelve miles of ice separated it from open water and freedom.[83]

Being caught in the ice was and is a major danger for ships in the polar regions. The *Belgica* in 1898 had been caught in the pack ice and drifted for months before being freed. The contemporaneous German expedition, the *Gauss*, unbeknownst to the men at Hut Point, had also been nipped by the ice and had spent eleven months trapped in its grip. What the staff of the *Discovery* did begin to realize by January 1903 was that their ship was miles from open water and that nothing they could do could free it. Only the forces of nature could break up the ice and open a channel to the open sea and New Zealand, where the men were expected in April 1903. On the matter of the ice going out of McMurdo Sound, Skelton was suspicious, noting on 21 January 1903 that "I think it might be a little late this year." [84]

As if listening to Skelton, a storm arose the next day, and after a furious blow some of the ice between the *Discovery* and open water was blown out but nine miles of it remained.[85] Still, preparations had to begin to ready the barque to depart. Anticipating the relief vessel, men began climbing to Arrival Heights to get a good view. Just after midnight on the twenty-fourth, the announcement was made that the relief ship, the *Morning*, was in sight, ten miles off, as close as it could get.[86] After more than a year of isolation, morning brought the outside world to winter quarters.

10

The Attempt on the Pole

Although other sledging excursions were made in the summer of 1902–3, the most important was the attempt on the South Pole. Scott opted to lead this party himself and chose as his two companions Wilson and Shackleton. Both men were good selections. Wilson was hard working, indefatigable, and a physician. From the outbound voyage Scott had been impressed by his young zoologist. Wilson was well liked by his colleagues, and he could be counted on to be level-headed in a crisis.

For his part Shackleton had proved himself adept at every task assigned. Early on, Scott had also been favorably inclined toward his third officer. Whether supervising the ship's stores or editing the *South Polar Times*, Shackleton tackled his work with great enthusiasm. Scott's confidence was evident when he asked Shackleton to lead the first short sledging party in February 1902. Besides, Shackleton was an interesting fellow, not an inconsequential factor to consider when one thinks of being tentmates with someone for weeks at a time. Shackleton was flattered to be chosen and extremely excited to be going.

The same could not be said for Wilson, who viewed the southern trip with mixed emotions. Naturally, he was flattered to be chosen for this most important and potentially most rigorous assignment of the expedition (especially given the state of his health at the outset of the expedition), but Wilson was also aware of the drawbacks. His real work, in zoology and art, would be better served by other endeavors — the southern trip was unlikely to uncover any wildlife and perhaps not even sight any landscape to sketch. He would have preferred to have drawn the new coastline to the southwest of winter quarters.[1]

Preparations went on throughout the winter and grew more feverish as the projected date of departure approached. The overall plan was for Barne to lead a group of twelve to carry extra supplies for depots en route. Scott's trio would follow with the dogs, and at a predetermined point Barne and the others would turn back north, leaving the southern party to march on alone.

At the outset wild speculation among the staff caused them to hope for a successful trip — if not to the Pole, then perhaps close. Indeed, the lack of a defined destination was a factor in the planning. Given the amount of sledging done to that point, one might have assumed that Scott would have set out a clear goal. The others on the ship expected a good southern record, and several maintained hope that the Pole itself could be reached.[2]

Barne's group departed 30 October 1902. The sledges were decorated with various banners: a Union Jack and several sledging flags in the tradition of nineteenth-century British Arctic experience. Among the banners in evidence were ones that reflected the mood of the party and their attitudes about the effort in general. "Hope On, Hope Ever" and "No Dogs Admitted" were two of the themes promoted.[3]

Barne's progress was slow. Manhauling even in the best of circumstances could not compete with fresh dogs, and the three-day head start would not allow them to keep the lead for long. Barne's party also experienced bad weather for the first three days and were confined to their tents for a considerable part of that time.[4]

Scott hoped to leave 1 November. He was impatient to be off and was unhappy when a blizzard prevented departure. The three men waited throughout the day for the weather to clear, but no break in the weather appeared. The distraught party had one bright spot that day: the plate of fresh cut mustard and cress prepared by Koettlitz for the southern party, a welcome bit of fresh food before the departure.[5]

The long-awaited farewell came the next day. The trio had their photographs taken with the nineteen dogs who were to provide important transport.[6] Then, with most of the ship's company tagging along for the first few miles, Scott's team departed, members of the escort gradually dropping off one by one until only three men continued on the trail.[7]

Shackleton was the dog driver despite his lack of experience before the expedition; he had no less expertise than the others, however, neither of whom had ever worked with the animals. Still, the pilgrims set off south at a dash — the men could keep pace with the dogs only by a great effort, even though the animals were pulling a heavy load. Unable to keep up comfortably, two men rode on the sledge to retard the pace of the dogs. Among the equipment on the sledges were skis for Barne's men, who had left without them. At the last minute Scott figured that perhaps Barne's team would make better progress with skis.[8]

The first day's travel proved the efficiency of dogs over manhauling— Scott's party caught Barne by 5:00 P.M. of the opening day despite Barne's three-day head start. Scott took some equipment from Barne to lessen the support group's load, but still, for the next week or so, the southern party made slower progress owing to Scott's desire to stay with the support team.[9] Passing Barne's party, Scott's trio pushed on, but while on the trail, one of the dogs, Nellie, slipped her collar and bolted for the ship where her new pups waited. Scott bemoaned the loss of one of his few animals, but Wilson was more resigned to such events. In any case, Barne's party caught the animal and returned it to the team the following day.[10]

Barne, working with a different schedule, passed the southern party, but the next afternoon Scott and the dogs again overtook his supporting party. Markham's admonitions that dogs would not be appropriate for such a trip over the barrier were proven inaccurate again. While Barne's team was having a difficult time with the surface, the dogs breezed across the ice. Scott took another 150 pounds from Barne's group and told them to travel independent of the southern party.[11]

The two parties continued south, usually in sight of one another, although the undulation of the barrier surface temporarily put one party out of view from the other. On the third day Scott and Wilson put on their skis. To that point they had been slogging along on foot, and they found the skis a great relief, especially Wilson, who was feeling the strain in his legs.[12]

The fifth of November began modestly well, but within a few hours the wind began to gust, forcing Scott to stop for the day with barely three miles traveled. The men spent the rest of the day confined to their tent, where Wilson read aloud from *The Origin of Species*, the book chosen as reading material for the southern journey.[13] Fortunately, the weather cleared the next day, and both parties continued south. Barne left two hours earlier than Scott, but the latter caught up within a couple of hours and continued ahead of the supporting team. That night, when Scott's party camped, Wilson noted that although his own head cold had cleared up, Shackleton had a "most persistent and annoying cough."[14]

The following day a blizzard kept Scott's team in their bags, this time with Shackleton reading aloud. However, the weather cleared enough for them to push on in the afternoon and into the evening, but the following day found them again confined by a storm. The first week ended with the southern party having traveled only fifty miles, a disappointing beginning for a trip that hoped to reach the Pole. The first day of the second week brought no progress; the men were confined the entire day to their sleeping bags. Being Sunday, Wilson read the Psalms and gospel for the day.[15]

In the meantime, Barne had pushed on through part of the storm, and by marching all night, he caught up with Scott on 10 November and camped. While the other party slept, Scott's team pushed ahead the ten miles to Depot A, the stockpile of food established the previous spring by Scott, Shackleton, and Feather. From this supply the southern party filled their sledges to capacity before pushing southward. On this march Scott, for the first time, noted that the dogs seemed to have been tiring.[16]

Much has been made of Scott's anthropomorphizing about the dogs, which he did along with others on the expedition. That alone would not explain his attitude toward the animals. Scott also used anthropomorphic terms in describing inanimate objects. Too much can easily be made of this attitude. The key to Scott's hesitation to use these animals lies elsewhere. In the first place, Scott's attitudes were strongly influenced by those of his mentor, Sir Clements R. Markham, whose inaccurate ideas about the incapacities of dogs Scott appears to have adopted. Of greater significance was Scott's inability to recognize the need to acquire dog driving skills before the southern party. Moreover, although his journal has numerous examples of what he might have been learning about dog sledging, he gave little indication that he was profiting from his own experience during the 1902–3 southern journey. On his second expedition in 1910, Scott worked to correct the mistakes he made on this southern journey. For example, his journal contains a number of references about the dogs pulling better when someone or something was in front of them. But nowhere does Scott state that he *put* someone in front to encourage the dogs.[17]

Scott waited at Depot A for the arrival of the support party. While there the dogs alerted the men to visiting snow petrels, what naturalist Larry Hobbs called the "ghost birds of the Antarctic" and what Wilson referred to as "snow-white doves."[18] The morning of the eleventh was spent waiting; finally, late in the afternoon Barne appeared.

Although still on full rations the men's appetites were constant and enormous. The next morning the two parties started out together, but to make it possible for Barne's twelve to keep up, the dogs were given additional weight. Nine hours on the trail gained them ten miles. Even with the additional load the animals pulled so well that the men "could scarcely hold the dogs," and the men were better able to keep up with them now that they were pulling reduced loads. Indeed the dogs were pulling so well that Scott altered his plans and intended to send half of Barne's party home the next morning. They camped that night at a new farthest south — a tremendous sense of satisfaction for the fifteen men involved.[19] A photograph was taken of the whole company, with sledge flags flying.[20] Dailey and five men turned back, while Barne and the other half continued on with Scott's trio. Despite the heavy loads — over two thousand pounds — the dogs pulled easily with Barne's party leading the way. Barne dined with the other officers on the evening of the fourteenth and on the following day departed with his men to the north.[21]

When the supporting group turned homeward, hope was high that Scott would achieve a great farthest south mark, but, very quickly, circumstances dictated a reevaluation. The first morning on their own, Scott's party found that the dogs could not budge the entire load owing to a change in the snow surface. Any alteration of temperature, moisture, snowfall, or even wind can alter the surface and the friction between it and the sledge runners. Thus on 16 November the trio was forced to begin relaying. For the next thirty-one days they had to take half their equipment a distance, then return for the second load. Thus they were forced to do three miles for every one made to the south.[22] The first day yielded five miles progress.

The following two days of relaying were equally tough, and Scott's trio managed only five and six miles southward, respectively. Scott worried that the dogs might prematurely tire and considered giving them a day of rest. Moreover, on the eighteenth he mooted in his diary a problem with the dogs' diet. Despite the ready availability of seals near winter quarters, Scott fed his animals dried fish. At first on the trail, this food seemed to bother the dogs, but Scott comforted himself that they had adjusted. That would prove untrue.[23]

Even at this point the men were pulling with the dogs. The relay work was exhausting both man and beast, and the next few days of marching fifteen miles to gain five to the south was wearing on all. Scott considered resting his animals. On 20 November the captain's team made a shorter day of it — hours of brutal work brought them only three and a half miles closer to the Pole. Hope for a great southern mark was "steadily melting away."[24]

On 21 November Scott altered the course slightly. He wanted to move closer to the land to leave a depot of part of the equipment to lighten their loads. The strain of relaying was beginning to wear on the men. Their noses and lips were red and sore from the gelid conditions, and they found their amateurish attempts to drive the dogs an unpleasant effort. The men were increasingly forced to drive the dogs forward with shouts and whip, a job Scott found "horribly tiresome."[25] Wilson noted in his journal the decision to turn toward land was a good one, because it allowed the men to survey the new area and it was better than marching across an ice plain "simply to beat a southern record."[26]

To this point the men were on full rations. Breakfast was bacon fried with biscuit and tea. At lunchtime they had biscuits and Bovril chocolate. Dinner was the main meal — a hoosh of pemmican, with seasonings and cheese, followed by hot cocoa. For all but the toughest circumstances, the ration was sufficient, but in this instance, the food was inadequate. They began to dream about food, an indication that their bodies craved more calories than they were getting.[27]

Half loads relaying continued through the twenty-fourth, but Scott noted that the dogs were tiring. The men opted for a change in their work schedule: Three pulled until lunch; one remained behind to set up the tent, while the other two returned for the remainder of the equipment. In the afternoon another man remained behind at the second stop to set up the tent and prepare dinner. After another day similar to the previous one, Scott decided to rest his dogs for a day, believing that they needed that more than food.[28]

The next morning nature reinforced the decision to rest the dogs: the men awoke to a thick and flowing snowfall, so they returned to their sleeping bags and passed the day reading aloud from *The Origin of Species*. When the weather cleared Scott began to think that the dogs were bothered by the heat of the day and resolved to travel at night, an experiment that began on 28 November 1902. The idea seemed to work. They continued relaying, and the progress came easier for the next two days, although Wilson and Scott nearly lost their way en route to the second camp because of drifting snow. By the end of the month, though, Scott realized that the dogs were becoming exhausted and required ever more shouting and beating to continue.[29]

The dogs were weakening, no doubt due to a lack of adequate food — both in quantity and quality. Scott suspected as much, and by the time he published his account of the expedition he realized that the dried fish must have spoiled, presumably on the long voyage through the tropics, adversely affecting the animals.[30]

For their part the men decided to go on reduced rations on 1 December. In the hope of pushing a little farther south, some portion of the week's food allotment was held back to extend the time on the trail.[31] Land was visible south of them, and the trio was eager to get as close to it as possible before being forced to turn back. The landscape was as yet unclear, but the mountains the men spied appeared to be part of a vast range; in fact, Scott did not realize that he was gazing on the Trans-Antarctic Mountains, a stretch of high land that continues south from Cape Adare.

The dogs began to falter. By the first of December several of the dogs were noticeably weaker and not pulling. Gains of as little as four miles became increasingly difficult. Food problems increased. The team discovered that some kerosene had leaked onto the week's supply of pemmican, leaving a noticeable taste, but given their physical condition, the men were not discouraged enough not to eat it. Fuel shortages prompted greater efficiency. Not only did this dwindling fuel supply necessitate a rigid time limit on the cooking of each meal (and they worked hard to shorten the time involved from lighting to extinguishing the burner), but the problem limited their liquid intake, as all water had to be melted. Dehydration was a terrible danger for sledgers, diminishing reason and increasing fatigue.[32] Less fuel meant that they would have to forgo a warm meal at lunchtime and substitute a cold repast of dried seal's liver.

The situation worsened. One of the dogs got into the food supply and ate a week's worth of seal meat. Now even less food was available, an especially devastating loss given the antiscorbutic value of the seal meat.[33] Fortunately, Wilson's regular medical checkup showed that the men were still in good shape, considering their circumstances.[34]

The same could not be said of the dogs. Increasingly, they were unable to work. The first one died on 9 December, and the others appeared to be faltering. The animals were suffering from an intestinal ailment — several were seen passing blood. No one could mistake their weakened condition. Once, when one of the dogs fell in his traces, Scott lifted it onto the sledge and discovered how painfully emaciated it was — mere skin and bones beneath its fur. One benefit, however, accrued to the surviving dogs. Their dead former comrades were cut up and served in the evening meals.

En route south the men saw no sign of life from the time the last snow petrels departed until the day after they killed the first dog. Suddenly, the dogs in the traces became alive with excitement — a skua had appeared, drawn many dozens of miles by the scent of the dead animals' blood.[35]

The men, too, continued to be plagued by hunger. Each suffered the agony of slow starvation during the day followed by tempting dreams of great meals at night. Often the trio dreamed that they were at a banquet, but the waiters would not bring them any food. Wilson once dreamed that he had found a cake intended for the family tea but, overcome by hunger, had eaten the whole thing. Later, everyone kept asking, "what happened to the cake?"[36]

Given the trying conditions, dividing the food as equally as possible was of vital importance. The one dividing felt obliged to take the smallest-looking portion; the other two, despite what they knew about the character of their companion, had to resist believing they were being cheated. Shackleton came up with a solution: "shut eye." The appointed divider made three portions and then asked another man, whose back was turned, "Whose is this?" Unless one has been in such trying emotional situations, it is difficult to understand what a relief finding this solution was for the trio.[37]

Hunger and the condition of the dogs were the dominant issues of their lives. Wilson suspected that the dried fish was the cause of the problem with the dogs, a solution Scott later endorsed. In addition to the plentiful seal meat not taken, there remained back at the hut a supply of Spratt's dog biscuits. In all likelihood the dogs were being slowly starved while simultaneously being poisoned by their food.[38] As the dogs died, sometimes while pulling in the traces, Wilson acted as the butcher to prepare the carcasses for the other dogs' food.[39] Wilson was originally chosen on the assumption that as the physician he would most humanely kill the animal. Although Shackleton performed the dreaded duty on occasion, Scott never did. To his credit, the captain in his published account admitted his reticence in the matter.[40]

On 14 December 1902 the trio reached a point where they believed they could establish a depot with some assurance of finding it again. The work was taking its toll. Scott thought that they could not go on many more days as they had been with full loads, for the weakening of the dogs, the fatiguing of the men, and the difficult surface on which they were working combined to make the days leading to the depot particularly difficult. Exploring near Depot B, as they called this cache, the trio found their way stopped by ice blocks and crevasses. When the weather deteriorated they had some difficulty in finding their way back to the depot.[41]

When the party resumed the journey south, just before midnight of 16 December, for the first time in a month they were able to move all their equipment without relaying. Now, days of seven or eight miles of marching meant they actually gained that distance toward the south. They left the depot pulling supplies for four weeks' worth of food for men and dogs and had left behind three weeks' worth of provisions to carry them back to Depot A. All this planning counted on fairly decent weather. After seven weeks on the trail they had made 330 geographical (380 statute miles) to the south.[42]

Another week of putting one foot in front of the other followed. Although new land was in sight, often the men could not see it, as snow blindness was a persistent problem. Almost every day one or more of the men were in pain from inadequate care of their eyes. The usual cure, a solution of cocaine, helped for a short while, but the constant reapplication was an indication both of the intense pain and the short-lived properties of the relief. Meanwhile, Scott had adopted the policy of feeding the nine strongest dogs with the remains of the dead ones, in hopes of keeping a few of the animals alive as along as possible. For a while the change of diet helped, but nothing short of adequate food would help the dogs recover. The men were not better off. Wilson began saving a piece of his supper biscuit to eat when hunger pangs awoke him in the middle of the night; otherwise he found it impossible to fall back to sleep.[43] In the early stages of the trip, Scott believed that his pipe helped him stave off hunger pangs, but by mid-December, his tobacco supply was so low that he resorted to smoking tea leaves with "horrid" results.[44]

Despite the problems Scott's men pushed southward. They found the unmerciful driving of the dogs intolerable. By this time the dogs would not move without prompting by the whip. Beating dogs on the verge of death sickened the trio. As each dog died or was killed by Wilson, out of the sight of the others, the men marked the passing of their animals by name in their diaries. The horror, day after day, of having to force the animals forward at every step did nothing to win the trio over to dog travel. Still, they pushed on, determined not to head north until their planned turning date, dictated by the consumption of half the food taken beyond Depot B.[45]

Sometime around 21 December 1902, Wilson's routine medical examination of the trio turned up ominous news — signs of scurvy. In his published account Scott noted that this report was made to him on 21 December by Wilson, but in Wilson's diary no mention was made of an examination on that date. Wilson noted an examination on 24 December and remarked that both Shackleton and Scott showed slight scurvy signs — suspicious looking gums. Scott indicated that neither he nor Wilson told Shackleton of his condition, but they dropped bacon from the menu after the first mention of the problem and substituted seal meat in hopes of fighting scurvy. The possibility of one sick man bringing disaster to the party was inherently obvious. But Scott felt safe in continuing south.[46]

Christmas was now approaching. For weeks conversation on the trail centered on food, but now, for the first time in twenty-five days, the men anticipated a full day's supply of food. They discussed the Christmas meal in infinite detail; each spoke to a rapt audience. At last the day came.

Christmas in the Antarctic, especially on sledging parties, had often been a brief moment of surfeit with near-starvation on either side of that day. Scott's party awoke, exchanged "a merry Christmas," and then prepared for the day's march. What made this day's work significantly different was the fuller rations. Fuel shortages had dictated the most rigid economy in this regard. Normally, the time the stove was going was rigidly measured, but on this day they kept it going longer. The men also had a warm lunch, and supper was a grand feast.[47]

In his journal Wilson described breakfast in detail: seal liver and bacon, fried up with biscuit crumbs, a full pannikin of tea, and afterward, from the only tin that they carried south with them, a spoonful of blackberry jam.[48] The evening meal was even more memorable: They even washed before supper.

The festivities began with a hoosh with "a double whack of everything," so thick that a spoon would stand in it. Cocoa followed. Meanwhile, Shackleton had produced from a spare sock (pray a clean one) a small plum-pudding, which they heated in the cocoa.[49] For decoration Shackleton had brought a piece of artificial holly, which gave their tent a festive air. They crawled into their sleeping bags without being hungry. After his second pipe, Scott described the scene after dinner: "We have been chattering away gaily, and not once has the conversation turned to food. We have been wondering what Christmas is like in England—probably very damp, gloomy, and unpleasant, we think; we have been wondering, too how our friends picture us. They will guess that we are away on our sledge journey, and will perhaps think of us on plains of snow; but few, I think, will imagine the truth, that for us this has been the reddest of red-letter days."[50]

More significant than the culinary joys of the day, the party made ten miles in less than seven hours that day. The effect of an adequate supply was immediately felt. This lesson was the key to reaching the Pole.

With Christmas behind them and at least two of them showing signs of scurvy, the decision to turn back could not be long delayed. Scott's assessment was that after Christmas they were gradually wearing down, unable to maintain themselves on the meager rations on which they were living.[51]

Scott's published account offered a marvelous look at the daily drudgery of sledging. The mind focused on the most trivial, which, because of circumstances, assumed untoward importance. The men marched along counting footsteps, unable to prevent thoughts of how much would be in the evening's hoosh — would it be a fraction of an ounce larger or smaller than the previous dinner? Then another sudden memory jolt — the sledger remembered a meal once eaten, or a dessert passed up at some point in the past: "How could I have been so foolish?"[52]

These thoughts dominated, despite the daily appearance of undiscovered land, never before seen by humans. For some time the trio had trudged along in the sight of the coastline that separated the barrier from the mountains. Southward they continued.

The day after Christmas brought Wilson the most painful bout of snow blindness of the trip. Seeing Wilson's discomfort, Scott stopped early for the day. All night long, despite steady drops of cocaine solution, Wilson lay in his bag, his body shaking from the pain that he described as a stabbing and burning of the eyeball. Finally, he gave himself a dose of morphia and was able to sleep. The next day he pulled on skis, his eyes blindfolded to protect them from the pain that light would cause.[53]

By 28 December the party was beyond the eighty-second parallel, a barrier the party psychologically was glad to cross. Scott planned to make one more partial day's march to the south to establish his record for the journey. Wilson, barely recovered, removed his eye bandages to sketch quickly the new land they had discovered. By this time, Scott had decided to name the two loftiest mountains after his principal patrons, Mount Longstaff and Mount Markham.[54]

Instead of a last day's march, the next morning brought a blizzard, and Scott's group was forced to remain tent-bound. The weather was no better on the thirtieth, and although Wilson and Scott made a ski run to get a closer look at the distant land, the fog obscured not only their view but made it hard to find their way back to the tent. Such was the men's hunger that the scanty supper did not satisfy, Scott noting in his diary that he felt almost as hungry as before dinner. The men's hunger made them feel the cold all the more.[55]

Scott resolved that this would be his last camp and that on 31 December the trio would turn north. The mark achieved was 82°17' S, a reasonable record given what they had endured since the supporting party left, but a disappointing one in terms of the expectations when Scott departed the ship.[56]

The next morning as they broke camp they could barely see the tantalizing image of an inlet opening to the south, for fog continued to limit their view. An attempt to move through the crevassed area to gain a different angle of observation was unsuccessful. They returned to their camp. That evening, at dinner, a moment of sheer horror occurred: Shackleton upset the hoosh pot. A careful scraping of the contents of the pan from the tent floor back into the pot followed. "It was a soup so didn't suffer much," was Wilson's assessment.[57]

The new year brought a new direction — north. The party must have looked pitiful. The dogs could barely stand, let alone pull. They no longer responded enthusiastically, as they once did, to the announcement of the end of the day and food. The men were deeply sunburned, their lips and nostrils raw from exposure to the elements. A bright side was that with the wind to their backs now they were able to rig a sail. By the end of the day, Mounts Markham and Longstaff were already fading in the distance.[58] The men's future lay ahead: Depot B had to be reached by 17 January before the food supply was exhausted. From the outset the margin was close.[59]

Uncertainty complicated their situation. They had no previous explorer to give them a hint of weather or surface conditions on the barrier in the late summer. Moreover, the trio had not yet managed to pull their entire load without the assistance of the dogs, and yet, certainly, with the dogs dying off at a steady pace, manhauling would soon be their only option. When the new year began only eleven dogs remained.[60]

The party's pace in the first few days northward was not encouraging, eight and a half, eight, nine and a half, and eight miles were the results of the efforts of the first days of the new year. The survival margin for Scott's party was desperately narrow, so much so that he was certain they could not afford to stop even for storms and must keep pushing forward under all circumstances. Scott also realized that given their position, all three men would be in desperate straits if one of them became ill or injured.[61]

In those four days, three of eleven dogs had perished; those that remained were "good for no work at all." Scott, deciding that carrying extra dog food was senseless, began distributing it liberally to the surviving dogs. Although this might appear to be a practice of limited value if one assumes that the dried fish was poisoning them, at least two of the dogs quickly responded to additional food and were noticeably stronger the next day. Nevertheless, the demoralizing pattern of vicious dog driving continued much to their disgust. Scott noted that progress could only be made with "monotonous certainty by shouting, pulling, and, I fear, some swearing."[62]

Lack of food remained the principal problem of the trio, who were reduced to a cold lunch of a biscuit and a half, eight lumps of sugar, and a piece of seal meat.[63] A glance at their daily meal practice at this point gives an indication of conditions on the trail.

Wilson had breakfast down to a fine art by this time and was rewarded by being made the sole cook at this meal. Fuel consumption was critical: Wilson could manage the whole meal in twenty minutes, from lighting to extinguishing the primus. Into the inner and outer parts of the Nansen cooker went snow, and as the water began to boil tea was added to the outer part. When the water in the inner part approached boiling, Wilson would pop in the ground biscuit and seal meat. Almost immediately the primus was snuffed.[64]

Lunch was distributed at breakfast, and each man carried his own close to his skin to thaw it a bit. How difficult these extremely willful men found resisting the temptation to dip into their lunch during the morning's march! Supper, which passed for a main meal, came in several guises: fried seal meat and biscuit or a hoosh. The latter was preferred, as it seemed to be more filling. In either case the men had only one pannikin full. So keen were the men on conserving oil that they tried not to remove the lid to stir any more than they had to, as they knew this cost fuel. The meal was completed with cocoa with plasmon, a milk-fortified powder well liked by all the sledgers of the *Discovery*.[65]

Days averaging eight miles followed. The dogs were now doing little, and the men did virtually all of the pulling from 5 January 1903. Indeed part of the time the dogs were tied to the back of the sledges and pulled along or at least kept pace. For the most part the trio continued to march rather than ski, either because of the surface or their own lack of expertise on difficult surfaces. Scott and Wilson, by this expedition's standards, were fairly good skiers; Shackleton was acknowledged as one of the poorest from the ship. Even at this late date Scott pondered if the benefits of skis were enough to excuse their weight on the sledge.[66]

The last four marches before arriving at Depot B were difficult, made more so by the men's anxiety of reaching their supplies in time. At least without the dogs pulling, the men could converse on the trail, something they had found difficult when driving the dogs. Among the topics discussed was whether they could afford a really big meal once they got to the depot; even the thought of such a prospect helped them to sleep. A blizzard overtook them on the tenth, but they pushed on through it, the first time they had tried such an effort. At least the wind propelled the sail-rigged sledge forward. Running to keep up with the sledge, an irregular path determined by the wind, and the difficulty of steering tired them out worse than any other march. All three were exhausted, Shackleton the worst.[67]

On 11 January 1903 Scott speculated that they were only ten miles from the depot, but discouraging surfaces and then a blizzard the following night caused him to assess the stark realities. They had a five-day supply of provisions that could be stretched to eight if necessary, plus two remaining dogs, if all other food became exhausted.[68] Finding the depot might be difficult; after all, although marked by a flag, the whole pile stood on a vast, undulating snow field and might easily be missed. Overshooting the depot was a disaster too great to consider.[69]

The bad surface continued. The men stripped the silver facing from the sledge runners to make hauling easier. Even with greatly reduced weights (the food bag, Scott noted, was a "mere trifle"), the men could barely make the minimum miles needed to carry them safely to each depot in turn. What would happen when they reached the depot and had to depart it with much heavier loads? At least the sledge without the silver runners pulled more easily.[70]

But fortune smiled on the pilgrims again at lunch on the thirteenth. After a particularly harrowing morning of bad surface, Scott spied the depot flag in the distance. He called out the news to his companions in the tent, who shouted their approval, a situation that when translated into print was retold by Scott, "We are not a demonstrative party, but I think we excused ourselves for the wild cheer that greeted this announcement."[71]

But all was not well in the party. Signs of scurvy were apparent, with Shackleton the worst affected. Even before arriving at the depot Scott had confided in his journal that the change in his companion's condition prompted him to double the seal meat allotment beyond what they had consumed the previous two weeks.[72] While at the depot Wilson undertook a medical examination of the group, the results of which were not encouraging.

In his published account Scott indicated that all of them were plagued with symptoms of scurvy but that he and Wilson felt fit and well. In his diary he was not as optimistic, noting that he was having trouble with his right foot but would not mention it because nothing more could be done now. Shackleton suffered most, for not only did he have bad gums, he was also coughing badly, spitting blood during the day, and at night found it difficult to breathe. Shackleton's health had been noticeably worse since the blizzard of the tenth. Apparently, the strain of that day had been too much. Scott realized the gravity of Shackleton's health and took action. Shackleton was relieved of all camp work and was not to pull hard during the day. Clearly, Scott was worried, noting in his diary that "Shackleton . . . is our weak point."[73]

The party also changed their diet, removing bacon for fear it had something to do with the scurvy as the current ptomaine theory on the disease might have suggested. Scott also decided to kill the two remaining dogs to eliminate the need to haul twenty-five pounds of animal food. Wilson thought it unlikely that the canines would survive the trip back to the ship in any case. That day the party had found a green substance inside the bundle of dog food, an indication of some foreign substance that might have been injurious to the animals. The next day the dogs were killed before the party left camp.[74]

An effort was made to pare down equipment before departing Depot B. Excess clothing, sledges, and dog food were all jettisoned. They left behind their skis, save for one pair for emergencies in case one man had to go ahead for relief from the ship.[75]

Fortunately, when they departed, Scott's party was able to pull the sledge. Shackleton helped pull on the first day, but a bad night of coughing and great trouble breathing with little sleep followed. Still attempting to pull in the traces, Shackleton fell into a crevasse and was badly shaken. Scott, too, had fallen, but the lieutenant's inability to recover quickly showed his fragile state of health. The following day Shackleton again fell into a crevasse, to ill effect, and Scott noted that by lunchtime on the sixteenth Shackleton seemed groggy. Even though he was not allowed to work, either in camp or on the trail, at the end of the day Shackleton was "panting, dizzy, and exhausted." Already Scott was contemplating the possibility that his lieutenant would have to be carried on the sledge. Wilson feared that they would not have the strength for such an arduous task.[76]

Shackleton's health was the barometer of the mood of the party. With the increased seal meat intake, all three men looked and felt better. Wilson and Scott were clearly gaining strength, but Shackleton had a series of days that alternated between improvement and relapse. From 17–20 January progress was made on three days, but on the other one the team had had to stop early because Shackleton was too tired to continue. Scott lamented the lost opportunity to push on and privately feared that "we must inevitably be prepared to carry him as a lame duck sooner or later."[77]

Scott's medical opinion at this point is worth noting. Scott, like Wilson, believed that scurvy was caused by tainted food. Both attributed, in part, the recovery they made in mid-January to eliminating bacon from the diet. Moreover, Scott thought that scurvy attacked the weakest part of the body, in Shackleton's case his chest. Is it reasonable to assume that Scott was forming an opinion about Shackleton's fitness for polar work?[78]

Meanwhile, a comparatively trivial issue remained a problem. One or another of the three men continued to be plagued by snow blindness. At various times each of the three men had to march blindfolded. The weather contributed to their problem because in dull overcast weather in which the horizon disappears, the absence of objects on which to focus causes great eye strain.[79]

By the twentieth Shackleton had improved enough to be allowed to cook supper while the others worked outside. The next day, he resumed his place in the traces, helping to pull, although on that day the sail was propelling the sledge along so fast that Scott had Shackleton ride on the sledge for a while. Scott's published account is unintentionally misleading when it stated that "Shackleton was carried on the sledges."[80] Actually, the captain wanted the sail-powered vehicle slowed and steered; however, the potential to allow Shackleton to rest was also a factor. Later in the day, Shackleton returned to ski, and a good pace was maintained. Scott believed Shackleton was improving.[81]

The next day (22 January) Shackleton skied alongside while his two companions pulled the sledge. His improvement was seen by Scott as a sign for less need for anxiety. For the next three days, Shackleton was healthy enough to go ahead of the party and guide them on the path. Shackleton even helped pull while on skis.[82]

By 25 January Mount Erebus came into view, a hopeful sign but counterbalanced by a deterioration of the surface. Scott joined Wilson in regretting the decision to jettison the skis, as they slogged along while Shackleton skied calmly over the surface of the snow.[83] Wilson and Scott were responding well to the increase in food allotment since leaving Depot B.[84] Both Wilson and Scott allowed their thoughts to wander to the idea of homecoming on the ship and the comfort that would mean.[85] When they arrived at Depot A on 28 January the situation brightened — ample food to make it back to the ship and the possibility of increasing the daily food allowance.[86] Luxuries such as sardines, raisins, port, and chocolate were all found in the depot. More important, Scott's men found adequate supplies of fuel; dire conservation was behind them. By this time Scott was more confident that they were going to make it.[87]

Not only were the prospects of their return excellent, the news found in the depot was also uplifting. Scott read of the progress in the various sledging expeditions, of the finding of the emperor penguin egg, and the especially good news that scurvy had not reappeared at the *Discovery*.[88]

The huge meal on 28 January left Scott with a terrible stomachache from overeating after such a long period of privation. Forced out of the tent to walk it off, the captain passed several hours in this condition, to the amusement of the other two. Apparently, when Scott's stomach settled, Wilson's intestines took it as a signal to start, and the physician replaced the captain on the path circumnavigating the tent.[89]

Then on 29 January Shackleton took another turn for the worse; his cough and his breathlessness had returned. Now, any illusions of doing anything on the way home, other than dashing to the ship, were shattered. Fortunately, a blizzard that day kept them in the tent, with Wilson and Scott reading Darwin, and allowed Shackleton needed rest.[90] The team had adequate food and fuel for the proposed trip even if it took longer than expected.

On the thirtieth Shackleton awoke in poor shape having had another very bad night. The lieutenant had to be helped onto his skis, and then he skied along at his own pace. The healthy pair dragged the sledge for nine hours. Wilson's diary makes no mention of the situation, but both Scott's diary and published account relate that two hours into the march that morning, Shackleton was so ill that Scott thought it best to seat him on the sledge again, where, with the help of the sail, he was carried until lunch. That night in his diary Scott described Shackleton as "our invalid" and "asthmatic."[91] More familiar landmarks by now were visible, and Scott hoped to be at the ship within a few days.

On the last day of the month, after a peaceful night's sleep, Shackleton was clearly improved. He skied on independently of the others, and the party made good progress. Wilson's knee was bothering him greatly, but he pluckily kept at it, no doubt aided by the supply of luxuries and adequate food supplies they had had since leaving Depot A.[92]

February opened with a successful march. Shackleton improved steadily, while Wilson continued to march despite his knee, which continued to bother him. Indeed Shackleton was so much improved that Scott remarked in his published account that, "our invalid . . . certainly has great recuperative powers."[93] In his diary that night Scott had noted merely that Shackleton "is rapidly improving."[94] By the end of the day Castle Rock was in sight, and the travelers could expect to return to the ship the following day.[95]

The next day they pushed on but could not make it back to the ship and camped one more night. Shackleton was better, according to Scott, and all were excited at the prospect of arriving on the third.[96] Scott's published account related that he had no confidence in Shackleton's continued good health, but no such comment appeared in the diary.[97]

On the morning of 3 February 1903 the party began, confident of arrival that day. Within three hours of marching, two figures appeared in the distance — Skelton and Bernacchi, who had come out to greet them. Scott learned of the arrival of the *Morning* and the news that the *Discovery* was still beset in ice, eight miles from open water, but this did not seem a major concern as some weeks remained in the summer season.[98] At Cape Armitage the party was met by a "stream of people," and on arriving at the ship Scott was overwhelmed to find the vessel decked out in flags. The trio returned to the hearty cheers of the officers and men on deck.

Scott's party came aboard the *Discovery*, so familiar but so vastly different from the world they had just left. Food, a bath, and letters from home followed in a blurred succession of happiness and relief.

One thing had puzzled the men as they saw the trio approach the ship — no dogs. Almost all the contemporary diary accounts made much of their surprise that none of the dogs survived. Perhaps that was in part due to the nature of the dogs as special pets of individual men. In two cases Scott's party brought back the fangs of a favorite dog, and in the case of Bernacchi, whose dog Joe had been born in the Antarctic during the *Southern Cross* expedition, a bit of a fable went with the souvenir. Bernacchi was told that Joe had struggled on, valiantly pulling, stubbornly refusing to yield, like the anthropomorphized creature he was. Joe had died in the name of science, doing his duty to the end.

11

The Relief Expedition

Few aspects of the *Discovery* expedition demonstrate so clearly that the roots of this endeavor can be traced to the Royal Navy's nineteenth-century Arctic experiences as the *Morning* relief expedition, 1902–3. Not only did this voyage play an integral role in the whole enterprise's second summer in the south polar regions, but in the end this relief effort had an enormous impact on the fate of the entire project.

Publicly, the launching of the relief effort had begun by the time the *Discovery* sailed from London on 31 July 1901.[1] Privately, the scheme genuinely might have started in 1847, twenty-one years before Robert Falcon Scott was born. In that year, Sir John Franklin was reported lost in the Arctic. His disappearance spawned a virtual growth industry: the search for Franklin. Many at the time, and most significantly Sir Clements Markham, believed that the fate of Franklin had been sealed by the failure to send out an immediate and timely relief expedition. Like so many things Markham believed, this idea may have been an illusion.[2] That Markham believed the idea that Franklin died for lack of rescue was the key to understanding both the need for the *Morning* undertaking and ultimately the disaster of 1903 — as Markham viewed the events of May of that year.[3]

Once again the controversy that had nearly driven the expedition on the shoals before the first sail was set — the question of the captain's control of the enterprise rather than the scientific director commanding — seems to be an essential element of the *Discovery* saga. With the settlement of the question of the captain's control, which led to the departure of J. W. Gregory and established the tenor of the expedition, the strong likelihood that the ship would overwinter had been decided.[4] Once one understands how critical were the results of that 1901 victory by Markham over the leadership of the Royal Society, the reason for and direction of the *Morning* comes into clear focus.

As early as 1897 Markham decided that if the vessel wintered, a ship would have to be sent the following year to relieve and resupply the men. Although this decision was never made clear to his partners in the Royal Society, nor even mooted in the 1899 deputation's meeting with A. J. Balfour when the government became involved in underwriting the endeavor, Markham was certain enough in his own mind of the project that as early as 1897 he began to go to Norway to look at possible relief ships. That search, part of the supposed investigation for a suitable principal ship for the expedition, tied the decision to build the *Discovery*, along with the ensuing implications so important for British Antarctic work in the Heroic Era, into the relief expeditions — for a second was eventually launched. All these developments led ultimately to the decisions of May 1903, which wrested control of the entire enterprise from Markham's hands. A careful observer in 1901 might have noted that in the instructions to the captain, he was directed to leave messages at specific places indicating where he was planning to establish a land base, assuming, as one knows Markham had intended by that time, that the ship did overwinter.[5]

Markham was not alone in considering the need for such a second vessel even before the *Discovery* sailed. George Murray, once he became involved in the project as the token scientific leader, suggested to Markham that another ship would be necessary in the 1902–3 summer. Markham and Scott apparently discussed the idea of relief during the second summer before the *Discovery* sailed from England. By his own latter account Markham argued that he began organizing the *Morning* expedition in earnest as soon as Scott sailed.[6]

As was his habit, Markham began with a public announcement to the press, followed by a circular letter calling for financial support and detailing the motivation for this cause. Naturally, he also recommended a relief ship committee, and one was appointed 2 October 1901.[7] The membership included Markham, McClintock, and Longstaff.[8] The public announcement of plans was made later that month.[9]

In his published declaration, Sir Clements clearly related the precedent suggested by the Franklin experience. Markham's first estimate of the cost of such an effort was £10,000, but as the months went on the figure increased to £20,000. In his initial missive Sir Clements suggested the reasons for sending out a second ship. If the expedition were to stay a second winter — although the funds for that were not yet assured — the *Discovery* would need resupply. Leaving aside for the moment whether that statement was true, Sir Clements then averred that relief ships were always dispatched, and he listed all such voyages sent out since 1836. Markham also claimed that the "national credit was at stake." [10]

Preliminary responses to his appeal were good. If Markham was the father of the *Discovery*, Longstaff was the kind godfather. Once again, the RGS backbencher took the lead with a donation of £5,000, even before the appeal became public. Later, during the refitting of the *Morning*, Longstaff paid for new ballast tanks. However, as with the *Discovery* funding, the remainder of the money came in small amounts. Appeals to the city yielded £100 from the Fishmongers Hall, £800 from the Stock Exchange, and Lloyds Underwriters contributed £100, while the Goldsmith Hall sent £20. King Edward VII graciously forwarded £100, and the Prince of Wales added £50. [11]

Still, at the end of 1901 only £9,000 was in hand. As with the appeal of 1899, Sir Clements was disappointed with the lack of money from large contributors and complained when so-called soap millionaires and South African magnates refused to add to the fund. Regarding one donation from a wealthy peer who contributed £2 to the endeavor, Markham minuted, "Ugh!" More than one suggested that the project was "a waste of money" or that this should be a government affair. Others were moved to contribute for the "safety of the expedition." In his annoyance, Sir Clements noted that although the rich did not contribute, the poor did, and cited the example of a schoolboy who was saving for a bicycle and instead contributed his five shillings to the effort. [12]

By the spring, as the time for departure of the *Morning* approached, Markham's rhetoric became more exaggerated, worth noting given what developed in the spring of the following year. Sir Clements decided that the relief expedition was necessary to avoid disaster. He pleaded that "our gallant explorers cannot be left to fate." Continuing in that vein, the RGS president stated that Scott in a letter had indicated "our retreat would be cut off," although the original of that message cannot be traced. Surely, Sir Clements hoped this appeal would "move a heart of stone." [13]

When the appeal did *not* raise adequate funding, in March 1902 Sir Clements again turned to the government. He wrote to A. J. Balfour reminding him that money "has always been granted to such efforts." He explained to the minister that the Treasury had contributed £5,000 to the relief of Benjamin Leigh Smith in 1880 when that explorer appeared to be lost in the Arctic. Perhaps unfortunately, Markham noted that a relief expedition had always been considered "an essential part of the scheme." Suggesting that the cause lacked roughly £8,000, Markham trusted that the government would supply the money, asking, somewhat naively, "Can this aid be withheld?" [14]

Balfour indeed found a way to avoid helping: he refused. Markham first received word privately from F. Sidney Parry, whose behind-the-scenes help had been so crucial in 1899 and who attempted to help here in 1902. In the formal refusal that came in April 1902, Balfour expressed surprise at the request, noting that he understood that after the 1899 grant no further money would be needed. Balfour expressed regrets that no mention had been made of this project when the deputation made its original proposal. In these times of increased demands on the Treasury, no funds could be granted. Balfour suggested that the government was not responsible for the expedition and that the two societies would have to look to their own resources. [15]

Markham's new frantic tone did yield results from private sources. Lady Constance Barne, the lieutenant's mother, suggested a series of concerts; Markham's response was to appoint a Concert Committee. When held, the musical performances yielded not only more than £585 but also further publicity to the effort. For his part Sir Clements continued to travel throughout England, speaking at meetings and passing the hat afterward in the financial interests of his cause, sometimes collecting merely £10 for his efforts. [16]

Of more importance was a donation from Edgar Speyer, who responded to an urgent appeal in *The Times* by contributing £5,000. [17] Although Australia declined to contribute, the government of New Zealand voted £1,000 to the cause. [18]

The final tally raised by Markham was approximately £22,606, sufficient for the expenses of the relief voyage. Most of the money had come from RGS fellows, whose generosity brought great credit on that venerable institution. [19]

In the end Markham again triumphed, but at a cost. In his appeal for the first relief effort he had alienated two critical bodies. The Royal Society early on expressed unhappiness with the tone of the appeal, and although they at first contributed £500 to the project, the RS leadership moved to separate itself from day-to-day operations. [20] The government's patience had been tried in 1902; the next time, in 1903, its toleration snapped.

With assured funding, Sir Clements turned to the question of staff. Markham's hatred of Carsten E. Borchgrevink, commander of the *South-*

ern Cross, was such that one of the worst ways Sir Clements could describe someone was to say the person was like Borchgrevink. Scott inherited the animosity from his mentor. Yet, the loathing the president of the RGS felt toward the *Southern Cross* commander was not visited upon his subordinates. Louis Bernacchi was already on the *Discovery*, and now Markham turned to another of Borchgrevink's staff, William Colbeck, to command the relief ship.

Colbeck was an excellent choice. Having been trained in navigation in his youth, he went to sea and worked his way steadily through the ranks: second mate's certificate in 1890, first mate's in 1892, and master's ticket in 1894. He went to work on passenger vessels for the Wilson Line. The company gave Colbeck a leave of absence to join the *Southern Cross* in 1898 and welcomed him back when he finished that duty.[21]

After Colbeck's return from Antarctica, the RGS had given him the Back award for his scientific and navigational efforts on the expedition. Colbeck wrote Markham personally to thank him for this award. Colbeck's obvious talent did not go unnoticed by Sir Clements, and Colbeck had not been back long with the Wilson Line when he was approached by Markham to be captain of the relief vessel. "I hope you are keen on being selected," Markham began and urged Colbeck to send his testimonials quickly.[22]

Colbeck was interested and as a kind gesture sent to his potential employer a sample of Antarctic vegetation, which Sir Clements much appreciated.[23] Markham, to whom such things meant so much, took great comfort that the name "Colbeck" meant "ship's bulwark."[24]

Once assured of Colbeck's interest Markham worked to secure permission from the Wilson Line. Early in December 1901, approval was in hand. In the meantime, Colbeck had dined with Markham at the latter's house in Eccleston Square to discuss the appointment. Two weeks later Markham officially offered Colbeck the position of captain of the relief ship at a salary of £400 per year. A fortnight later Colbeck accepted the appointment.[25]

Immediately, Colbeck became involved in the preparations for the expedition. At Markham's request Colbeck journeyed to Norway to look at possible ships. On one occasion he took with him the chief engineer of his most recent ship, the *Montevallo*; another time he accompanied Sir Clements.[26] From the outset Colbeck contributed significantly to the success of the relief effort.

For his part, Sir Clements promptly set about helping his new protégé by requesting Colbeck's appointment to lieutenant in the Royal Navy Reserve. Ever seeking to promote his people and the Royal Navy, Markham worked for some months with the Admiralty making a claim, countering the navy's response about lengths of time served in various kinds of ships, and gradually wearing down the men at the Admiralty whom Markham referred to as "very wearisome people." No doubt they had similar thoughts about Markham's tenacity. Although the process took more than a full year, Sir Clements accomplished his purpose.[27]

Markham, with Colbeck's help, now turned to finding a crew. Choosing the men might have been easier had the Wilson Line given permission for the entire *Montevallo* crew to join with Colbeck, for so popular was the chief officer that almost everyone on the ship wanted to remain with him for his next assignment. Although eventually eight of the crew came from the *Montevallo*, the rest were found elsewhere.[28]

As his chief executive Colbeck had originally offered the position to someone who had to decline. Rupert England, appointed in June 1902, was Colbeck's second choice. England took a leave of absence from the Wilson Line. Thus entered into Antarctic service a man who would not only be important on this cruise but would play a crucial role in Shackleton's *Nimrod* expedition (1907–9). England was a fine first officer and earned the respect of those aboard. Markham described him as a steady and attentive man who knows his work and sees that others do too.[29]

The Admiralty had granted permission for two naval officers to join the expedition; one of them signed on as second officer. Edward Ratcliffe Garth Russell Evans (1881–1957) was, according to Markham, an ideal candidate. Royal Navy, athletic, "hard as nails," Evans was an old *Worcester* boy (the Royal Navy's training ship), an institution in which Markham took a great interest. In April 1902 Evans had approached Markham about a place on the relief expedition and was invited to dinner to discuss the matter. Within a month he had applied for leave to serve on the relief effort, and Markham worked behind the scenes to secure permission. Evans had hoped to be appointed the first officer (Rupert England having not yet been chosen), but Markham dissuaded him, arguing that Evans was too young for such an appointment. In praising Evans to Colbeck, Markham noted that the young man was a fine officer and "would take any billet." Evans was duly appointed second officer 28 May 1902. For the navy's purposes he was carried on the books of the *President*. Markham then worked to get him promoted to lieutenant, a task Sir Clements accomplished by the spring of 1903.[30]

More than fifty men applied for the position of third lieutenant, but two had inside advantages. Lieutenant Evans[31] was keenly promoting an old chum of his from his *Worcester* days, Gerald Doorly. Together they had won the two top prizes in their graduating class.[32] Doorly had chosen a career in the merchant service and had recently been promoted by P. & O. Steamships, a company he had joined in April 1901.[33] Evans invited his pal down to London to visit and advised him to contact Sir Clements.

At that interview Doorly was surprised at how much Sir Clements knew about him and his record; obviously, Evans was a good source. Markham was impressed and passed on a good report to Colbeck. Unfortunately, another person also had Markham's attention.[34]

The family of George Francis Arthur Mulock was known to Markham, and the young officer came highly praised. Markham took steps to ask for him as his second naval officer.[35]

With two rival claimants in the field, Lieutenant Evans approached Markham with a solution: take both. Even though the expedition was short of funds, the suggestion of Evans was taken, and Mulock became third officer and Doorly, fourth officer. The Royal Navy and the P. & O. permissions followed, and both men sailed with the ship.[36]

The close cooperation between Colbeck and Markham continued, and occasionally when the former dined at Eccleston Square, he now was joined by his lieutenant, Evans.[37] Colbeck took the lead in selecting the men for the vessel, as most of the remaining places were filled by men from Hull, Colbeck's home area. He knew that the locality produced sound and experienced seamen, and the success of the expedition testifies to the correctness of his decision.

One crew member needs to be identified. A. B. Cheetham, who went on to serve with Shackleton on the *Nimrod* expedition, gained his first Antarctic experience during the relief voyage. A man of exceptional ability, he was early seen as someone who could be entrusted to take one of the watches on ship, a job he eventually assumed.[38]

Although the Ship Committee officially appointed the officers and men, Markham and Colbeck made the decisions. Four other appointments merit attention. J. O. Morrison was appointed chief engineer, which turned out to be an extremely trying position given the equipment aboard the relief ship. Morrison also proved to be a competent poet. George Adam Davidson was appointed ship's surgeon upon the recommendation of Professor Wyllie. A name that was familiar to Markham was added to the crew list as a midshipman. Neville Pepper, the son of Colbeck's old captain on the *Montevallo*, was given the opportunity to gain experience on the voyage. Although seen by Doorly as "a little soft," Pepper seems to have accomplished his work. The fourth person was also a midshipman, Frederick Louis Maitland Somerville, a fifteen-year-old who had met Colbeck in Norway and applied for the position. Markham liked him, in part because of the attractiveness of his person and also because Somerville could trace his ancestry back to Alfred the Great.[39]

The search for a vessel had been ongoing for some time. At least as early as 1899 Markham had agents looking at the *Morgenen*, the one he eventually purchased. Early on, Sir Clements engaged an agent in Christiania, T. Bonnevie (1836–1902). The RGS president also had people investigating ship opportunities in Dundee.[40]

When no options appeared within Britain, the choice fell to the best of the whaling ships available in Norway. The one with the most appeal was the *Morgenen*, a vessel that Markham had considered earlier when it had been on the market for £6,000. Now the price had fallen, although in seeming defiance of basic economics rumor reached Sir Clements that another buyer was hot on the trail.[41] Although Markham later suggested that the Russian government was eager to purchase it, no independent confirmation has been found.[42] Great pressure was exerted not only by Bonnevie but also by H. J. Bull, who became involved in the sale at this point and eventually reaped £400 for his efforts. Bull had been the progenitor of the 1894–95 *Antarctic* expedition that had made the first undisputed landing on the Antarctic continent. He remained over the years a hanger-on in polar circles, and as late as 1901 Bull was trying to go south again, in this instance with William S. Bruce's *Scotia* expedition.[43]

When Markham arrived in Christiania to look at ships, Bull met him at the station. Sir Clements characterized him as a "horrid looking creature."[44] Markham had several opportunities to view the various vessels. When Sir Clements reported later that, under the pressure of the moment, he had bought the *Morgenen* practically sight unseen, he was perhaps stretching a point. What is clear is that Bull urged a quick decision and that the Sven Foyn firm, which owned the vessel, was eager to close the deal. Under the pressure of circumstances, Sir Clements purchased the *Morgenen*, built in 1871 (the boilers, at time of purchase, dated from 1883), on his own responsibility for 70,000 kroner (£3,880).[45]

Anyone searching for proof of Markham's ability to exaggerate or perhaps to self-delude need only read his comment to the press, that the *Morning* was "the strongest whaler ever built."[46] Compare that with Colbeck's assessment in the field that the *Morning* "could not butt a match box."[47]

The reality was that the ship, whose name had been changed by Markham from *Morgenen* to *Morning*, needed a good deal of work before leaving for Antarctica. First, it had to be brought from Norway to Great Britain. Markham took possession of it on 30 October 1901, and some preliminary work was carried out in Norway before a crew sailed it to England at the end of the year, arriving in London 27 December 1901.[48]

Markham had prepared the way for the ship's arrival by arranging for it to be berthed at the Admiralty's Victoria Dock. The *Morning* had no more arrived and the Norwegian crew departed from Sheerness to return home when an alarming report was sent to Markham saying that the vessel was taking on water rapidly. As it turned out, the leak was a small matter, but the incident was a trying way to end the year for Markham and a foreshadowing of difficulties ahead. He wrote to Colbeck urging him not to be concerned about the rumored leak, that the ship was strong and the caulking sound.[49]

Once the vessel was in Britain, Markham secured the services of Green's, a major ship refitter, which had a dry dock and could perform all the necessary repairs, plus the alterations that Sir Clements was ordering.

The first thing a visitor to the *Morning* in Green's dry dock might have noticed was the unmistakable smell of blubber. Decades in the whaling and sealing business had permeated the decks with the by-products of that trade, and the stench continued to ooze out for months. A naval architect's view would have been much more severe. The boiler bed had to be replaced, new iron casting was needed forward, and the masthead was found to be rotten. Markham did not think new ballast tanks were needed but was persuaded to go ahead with the work. The bill for that item, £500, was paid by Longstaff. Colbeck helped oversee the repairs. Altogether Green's final bill ran to thirty-nine pages, repairs having cost £8,017 13/1, more than twice the purchase price.[50]

In addition to all these repairs, Markham wanted a number of alterations, including an ice house on deck and extensive changes to the men's and officers' quarters.[51]

As expected, the furnishings of the officers' and men's quarters were on different scales. The men slept in canvas hammocks and ate on mess tables that could be set up and taken down. The officers lived in nicely appointed cabins and dined on the wardroom table, for which Markham ordered 144 cloth napkins.[52]

A second dry dock stay was necessitated by the discovery that the shaft was damaged and had to be replaced. Although the deadline for sailing seemed threatened, in the end the ship was ready to depart on schedule. When it finally left the dry dock, the *Morning*, which was entered for legal purposes as a yacht with Markham as the owner (an important note as the story developed), flew the ensign of the Royal Corinthian Yacht Club to which Sir Clements had been elected for that purpose.[53]

Colbeck's instructions indicated what the RGS and Markham expected the voyage to accomplish. The *Morning* was to act as the tender to the *Discovery*, bringing supplies and providing rescue help if such was needed. In addition, the relief vessel was expected to conduct a regular program of meteorological observations and undertake a study of ocean fauna. Furthermore, Colbeck was to find the *Discovery* using the agreed on trail of messages left by Scott. Once the two ships were united, Colbeck was to place himself under Scott's command.[54]

If Colbeck failed to find Scott between Cape Adare and McMurdo, the *Morning* was to proceed eastward along the Great Ice Barrier (Ross Ice Shelf) to the point where Borchgrevink (although he was not referred to by name) landed in 1900. Failing to find Scott in either of these two locations, Colbeck was to return to Cape Crozier and establish a depot there. A further cache was to be laid at Wood Bay and a third at Cape Adare. If in the course of his sailing in Antarctic waters, Colbeck should find orders from Scott that ran counter to these directions, Colbeck was to follow Scott's instruction.[55]

Colbeck was then to return to New Zealand and await further orders. The instructions make it clear that both ships were expected to return to Lyttelton together, as funds sufficient to continue beyond the austral summer of 1902–3 were not at hand. Although the instructions were signed by the presidents both of the Royal Society and the RGS, Markham was the dominant voice and wrote the instructions.[56]

A few final details had to be sorted out before departure. As the crew assembled, Markham realized that the ship had no piano and that one was needed both for camaraderie and for religious services. This prompted Sir Clements to scramble around to find one. Failing to do so, at the last minute he ordered his own taken from his home at Eccleston Square, but a problem developed in delivery. Finally, one was purchased at a store near the docks and brought down to the vessel. However, the instrument was too large to fit through the wardroom door. Morrison, the engineer, offered a solution: Cut it in two. Instead, the front part of the keyboard was sawed off and reassembled once inside the wardroom.[57]

The lines of the little black vessel with a white ribbon and a yellow funnel were let go at the East India docks at two o'clock in the afternoon of 9 July 1902 on a mission, Markham assured all, of mercy and succor. The weather did not cooperate, and the journey down the Thames took place in a downpour. Aboard the ship for the first part of the journey were Sir Clements and Lady Markham and a number of other dignitaries, including some wives and daughters of sponsors of the expedition. Doorly, the fourth officer, noted in his diary the soggy clothing of one of the women standing in the rain and noted: "The rain was pouring in torrents and as there were one or two lady passengers the situation was to say the least awkward. . . . My heart gave a sorry throb when I observed the laceful lingerie bedraggled in the dirt."[58] With that strangely surreal moment the expedition was launched.

Steaming along, the underpowered vessel's prop beat the water vigorously to small advantage. After stopping at the mouth of the river the men gathered on deck to hoist the anchor using a machine that one officer thought hearkened back to Noah's ark. Colbeck pointed his ship in the direction of Madeira, the first stop, as the lights of England slowly sank below the horizon.[59]

Eleven days later the *Morning* arrived at Madeira. This stop was much anticipated, especially because of the possibility of receiving mail. Two of the officers, experienced in being away at sea, primed their correspondents with a flurry of letters shortly before departure. Doorly and Evans were well rewarded: fifteen and twenty letters each. Officers and men were given shore leave, and the officers took up residence at the Garnio Hotel, enjoying the luxuries of a bath and meal ashore, followed by cigars on the verandah in the cool breezes of the island. Reading and answering correspondence were the primary activities.[60]

While there, Evans and Doorly met someone who had met and keenly remembered Shackleton when the *Discovery* passed through the year before.[61] The stop here was to take on provisions and coal, but the visit was important for another reason: Colbeck had to deal with the first problem of the voyage.

Several of the sailors concentrated their efforts on the local bars and returned to the ship intoxicated and in a feisty mood. Colbeck reacted sharply to this behavior and canceled further shore leave and ordered that no spirits be brought aboard ship. When the call to raise anchor went out the fireman, F. Taylor, having returned to the *Morning* drunk, refused duty. Colbeck put him in irons and locked him up in a store room. But the fireman broke out and, armed with a large ice pick, threatened anyone who came near him. The bo'sun and Evans wrestled him to the ground, and the guilty party soon found himself lashed to the ship, his hands tied behind him. Left overnight in a position in which he could not sleep, Taylor had a change of heart and begged forgiveness of Colbeck and the others. Released, the fireman declared himself a new man — henceforth to be a teetotaler.[62]

Three days out of Madeira the *Morning* passed a German training ship. Those who would incorrectly assume Britain and Germany somehow to be enemies in the fifteen years before 1914 would have been surprised to have witnessed the encounter. Doorly felt that the German vessel was the "finest sailing ship I have ever seen," a magnificent overabundance of canvas and lines. As it came alongside the small British barque, the band on the training ship gathered on deck and played for the crew of the *Morning*, who responded by dipping their ensign. Then the band struck up "God Save the King" to which again the RNR ensign was dipped. Then the handsome German vessel turned back to its course and sped away.[63]

En route to the South the piano began to get a serious workout. Doorly was an accomplished musician. He had learned a song, "Intrepid Souls," written by Sir Clements. The words capture some of the spirit of the two expeditions, and eventually Doorly taught the men the song.[64]

Also en route the officers, following British Arctic tradition, decided to publish a magazine, which, after some discussion, was called "Aurora Australis." The first edition came out on Colbeck's birthday and was a great success.[65]

As with the *Discovery* voyage, celebrations of other birthdays and events followed in regular order because, as with Scott's vessel, Sir Clements had given the men a calendar marking important dates in the expedition's history.[66] The voyage to New Zealand passed pleasantly as the crew worked well together. Even the fireman, after his night chained to a mast, became enthusiastic. The officers began teaching the crew skills such as semaphore signaling and arithmetic.

The ceremony of crossing the equator was duly observed. Several members of the crew, plus Evans and Mulock, went through the process of being shaved, medically inspected, and dunked. One enterprising sailor took advantage of one of the less astute members of the crew by drawing a line on a binocular and then showing the actual line of the equator to his comrade.[67]

Passing the Cape of Good Hope, the *Morning* encountered a powerful storm. Colbeck showed his cool attitude toward danger and his superb seamanship in these circumstances. All hands were called to take in sails, and what might have been a potentially fatal situation became one that bound the crew together and increased their admiration for their captain. Such situations fixed in Doorly's mind the impression that Colbeck was an ideal type of commander. Bernacchi, who had sailed with him on the *Southern Cross*, thought him quiet, bold, and resourceful.[68]

By the end of August the vessel was far enough south to necessitate issuing winter clothing to the men. The officer's kit was fairly complete.[69] Life aboard ship followed a routine, broken only by special events such as concerts and the occasional high tea, when the men were invited to the wardroom for tea and cigarettes. Doorly and Evans, who regularly did duets at these events and generally took the lead for these performances, sang not only contemporary popular music but also composed topical songs related to the voyage. Evans and Doorly even wrote a musical about the voyage, and a small minstrel show was staged. At one point the ship's cat, a favorite of all, died. The cat's death was celebrated in song, and "The Dirge of the Dead Cat" became a favorite of the men.[70]

During the voyage out Colbeck had an opportunity to observe his officers in action and was well pleased with what he saw. Rupert England had general supervision of the men and the rigging work, while Doorly took the meteorological observations. Mulock was in charge of stores and of the hydrographical research. Morrison spent much of his spare time studying zoology and geology, in preparation for work in Antarctica. Finally, Evans, whom Colbeck described as "indefatigable," assisted in all the work of the ship.[71]

Routine was broken by the occasional storm, such as the one in late September when conditions were so rough that Colbeck ordered two men on the wheel both lashed to it to prevent them from being washed overboard.[72]

By early November the *Morning* was nearing New Zealand; after weeks at sea, the men could smell the land long before it came into view. By the time they reached port, the *Morning*, which early on had been the subject of some biting remarks (for example, the engine was referred to as a "coffee mill"), had won over both the officers and men. They were a contented crew and justifiably proud of their splendid little ship. Finally, on 16 November 1902 New Zealand came into view, and the ship arrived at Lyttelton that day.[73]

The three weeks passed in New Zealand were idyllic ones for the men. Suddenly returned to the civilization of collars, parties ashore, and the

company of women, both officers and men relished the opportunity to relax and recuperate from months at sea. Both officers and men received free
railroad passes and used them to commute between Lyttelton and Christchurch. A round of entertainment occupied the entire crew, similar to that
which the men of the *Discovery* had enjoyed.

The *Morning* went into dry dock, but as no repairs were needed, it remained there only forty-eight hours, a radical difference from the experience of the *Discovery*. To prepare for departure the vessel took on eight
months of supplies for Scott, twenty months' provisions for its own crew,
and roughly three hundred tons of coal. Before departing, Colbeck informed Markham that he expected to return early next year, but should he
fail to do so, no undue concern should be taken as Colbeck had great confidence in his ship's ability to withstand an overwintering.[74]

Thanks in part to the superb and generous help of the people of New
Zealand, Colbeck was able to steam out of Lyttelton harbor at a much earlier date than Scott had the previous year. On 6 December 1902 the *Morning* slipped its moorings and steamed southward. Its captain's previous
Antarctic experience must have been a comfort to the group of mostly
Yorkshire men who formed the crew of the relief ship. On 22 December
1902 the crew sighted its first ice at 62°05′ S, 175° E. Doorly was so excited
and elated that he rushed below to play "Christians Awake to the Morn"
on the piano.[75] Continuing on, the vessel crossed the Antarctic Circle on
Christmas day.[76]

That same day Lieutenant Evans made a major discovery—a new island
not previously charted. A second smaller island was also sighted. The larger
of the two Colbeck originally called Markham Island, a basaltic rock about
one mile long and three-quarters of a mile wide. Rising to a height of
270 feet, the land mass could hardly be seen to be the promised land, but
it was a discovery, and, given the geographical discovery results of the entire *Discovery* expedition, this find was important. A landing was made by
Colbeck, Davidson, Mulock, and Morrison; geological samples were obtained; and a record was left. The second island, eventually named Hag-
gitt's Pillar, was more circular in shape, about 200 feet in diameter and
about 250 feet high. Thousands of birds inhabited the two islands. While
the others were landing, England used the tow net and made a good haul.
Mulock sketched both islands.[77] Subsequently, the name of the large island
was changed to Scott Island.

The following day the *Morning* entered the ice pack that surrounds
the continent. The crossing was quick, a mere five days, most of it spent in

heavy fog, and the experience was impressive enough for Doorly to comment that in the process the "world stood still."[78] Actually, Colbeck managed to traverse most of the pack in three days but was forced to seek refuge in the pack when the vessel encountered a heavy gale just south of it. For six days the storm buffeted the little ship and, once again, Colbeck's superb seamanship prevented a potentially dangerous situation. At one point the crew had to man the deck to push off blocks of ice as they bore down on the *Morning*.[79]

Victoria Land was spied on 3 January, and by 8 January 1903 the men were off Cape Adare, the first place where the *Discovery* was to have left a message. Colbeck led a party ashore where they were greeted by thousands of penguins. The first thing the men saw was the *Discovery* record, which must have been a relief as this marker was the first indication that Scott's party had survived the voyage down, never a certainty in those waters. Borchgrevink's hut stood nearby in fine condition, another indication of the good planning of the Anglo-Norwegian. An inspection was made of the interior. Colbeck left a message in the record cylinder, describing the voyage to that point, and then the party returned to the ship.[80]

Given the relatively easy passage through the ice pack, Colbeck hoped to make a quick voyage along the coast of Victoria Land, but within a few hours after leaving Cape Adare the captain realized that he had been overly optimistic. Proceeding to the Possession Islands, a boat was put ashore but found no record. Leaving a message in a conspicuous place, the *Morning* continued toward Wood Bay.[81]

The men were disappointed at their next stop, for the entrance to Wood Bay was impossible to enter, being entirely blocked by ice. Colbeck decided not to attempt to send a party over the ice but to continue to Franklin Island. There Rupert England landed with a party but could find no sign of a record from Scott. Here again England left a message of the ship's progress. Because no record was found at Franklin Island, Colbeck assumed that Scott was not in Wood Bay, or he would have been able to place a mail cairn at Franklin Island.[82]

The *Morning* had open water from there all the way to Cape Crozier, which was reached 17 January 1903. About one in the morning Colbeck led a party ashore and quickly spied the *Discovery* record left by Royds a mere three months earlier. Colbeck immediately signaled his crew that the message indicated where Scott was. Adding a note to the cylinder, indicating that he would now sail for McMurdo, Colbeck reboarded his vessel.[83]

Three days later Colbeck's crew was making good progress when the

Morning was overtaken by a storm, which could be heard thirty minutes before it hit the ship. Fortunately, the gale was brief. The next morning the weather was ideal, but later in the day another storm, with force ten winds, bore down on Colbeck's men. Fortunately, this too was a short interlude. The next day, 23 January 1903, the relief ship rounded Cape Bird, continuing south, and at 11:40 P.M. the top of the masts of the *Discovery* came into view. The moment of elation quickly evaporated as Colbeck then saw the ice edge. Ten miles of solid ice separated him from Scott.[84] The *Morning* fired rockets, and the *Discovery* responded. Colbeck had found his quarry.

For the next thirty-eight days the *Morning* was moored on the ice edge in hopes of joining the *Discovery* in returning to New Zealand, a goal prevented by the elements.

Without question the men of Scott's ship were elated at the arrival of the relief ship. "Glorious day," was Lashly's reaction to the news, and everyone else shared in this sentiment.[85] Aboard the *Morning* one entire cabin was devoted to mail for the men of the *Discovery*, and the keenest desire of the men was to receive the letters and parcels.

While Armitage previously had shown some interest in being a popular commander, regarding the mails he incurred considerable wrath from his men. As soon as the relief ship was sighted, Armitage led a sledging party over to the visitors to retrieve the mail. Instead of returning immediately, however, he tarried. A day passed, and back on the *Discovery* the men were grumbling. By the evening of 26 January 1903 the grousing had become quite vocal and was only ended when Skelton, who had been sent back while Armitage remained on the *Morning*, arrived at 11:30 P.M. with the first shipment of letters. Skelton had urged Armitage to return with the mail on the twenty-fifth and thought Armitage most inconsiderate. Armitage did not return to the *Discovery* until 29 January, bringing with him a load of fresh mutton.[86]

The return of Scott and the southern party on 3 February 1903 brought into focus the question of the condition of the ice and the chances of the ship gaining its release during this summer. Royds had been busy since early January preparing the *Discovery* for sea, and the vessel was ready if a channel opened in the ice. In early January the odds of getting out still looked good, but as each day passed the chances diminished. By 1 February ten miles of ice still separated the two vessels. The *Morning* attempted to smash its way through, with no success. Armitage described the relief vessel as "so underpowered, it had to stop the engine to blow the whistle."[87]

Even before the return of the southern party Armitage and Royds had tried blasting, to no effect. This should not have surprised them; as when the party first arrived at Hut Point in February 1902, Scott had tried to blast away a small amount of ice to give the ship a better anchorage, but in that instance too the ice was unmoved. In a rare change of attitude, by early February 1903 the men were hoping for something unusual, a storm. Only a major gale could break up that much ice.[88]

As the month wore on Scott decided to transfer as much of the coal and provisions as possible by manhauling them across the ice that separated the vessels. Two parties a day set out from one ship and were relieved at the halfway point by a team from the other vessel.[89]

Among the items Scott had requested before leaving New Zealand in 1901 the most important were coal and additional meat. The former he needed if he were to accomplish any significant exploring by sea in the 1902–3 season. The size of the *Morning* meant that very little was left over after allowing for its own use in steaming down from and back to New Zealand. Colbeck was able to give Scott some coal, a portion of which, given the limited time remaining before the *Morning* was set to sail, was left on the Glacier Tongue near to where the relief ship was moored. As to the meat, the *Morning* carried six thousand pounds for the men of the *Discovery*.[90]

How important were the supplies brought out in 1902–3 by the relief ship? Later, Scott publicly declared that "nothing brought out was essential for our existence." Certain luxury goods added to the comfort of the men for a second winter, but other essential items, such as fuel for lamps and candles, were omitted from the supply manifest. Before the *Morning* arrived Scott's party was short of vegetables and sauces, and these items were resupplied. Several members of the crew reported that the additional food brought by the relief ship added greatly to the crew's comfort in the second winter. With the additional provisions brought by the relief vessel, Scott estimated that the *Discovery* could survive another two or three years.[91]

All eyes were on the ice. The optimism of January and early February began to fade by the middle of the latter month. By that time signs that summer was fading fast were evident — the sun dipped below the horizon for the first time on 17 February.[92] Although Scott maintained hope for another month that the *Discovery* would be freed, his opinion was not widely shared. Colbeck, Morrison, and Doorly all thought escape was not likely that season.[93] Lashly thought some hope existed of getting out, but it was doubtful.[94]

With the possibility looming large for a second unexpected (and unplanned for) winter in the offing, Scott decided to reduce the size of the company to remain. He put a sign up in the mess deck announcing that anyone wishing to return with the relief ship should notify Royds of the desire to leave. Scott had certain people in mind to send home, a decision that has been the subject of some discussion since that time.[95]

Understandably, Scott wanted to be rid of some of the men he considered undesirable. Several men, a majority of whom were merchant seamen, found life on the expedition not to their liking and went to Royds to explain their reasons for leaving. Most were straightforward — they desired a new assignment. Merchant men were used to regular changes of ship, and, after a year and a half, many were ready to move on to other surroundings. Some of the merchant men left because they found life under naval regime foreign to their lives and were not happy with such regulations. Because most of the crew were bluejackets, the merchant men felt out of place, and both groups suffered from being in close quarters. In any event, Scott took satisfaction that the ones he most wanted to be rid of volunteered to leave. A single exception was Clarence Hare; Royds was sorry to see him depart. Some of the men were sent home for health reasons: Page, Peters, and MacFarlane. Peters had not applied to return, but Scott considered him idle, and although Peters was not happy with the decision, he went. Scott was well pleased to be rid of "all the crocks."[96] Before the men left the ship, they were paid off. Even at this point Hubert, a merchant marine seaman, caused a row by refusing to sign off, in a dispute with Scott over wages.[97]

The crucial issue was Scott's decision to invalid Shackleton home. Without question Shackleton's health had failed him on the southern journey, and on the surface sending him back seemed appropriate. However, the question was more complex than a superficial motivation would answer. Other reasons have been suggested.

Roland Huntford, in his biography of Shackleton, offered another version. Having cited a number of instances in which Shackleton and Scott had had disagreements, Huntford viewed this decision as based in large part on Scott's animosity toward his junior officer, a motivation Huntford broadly hints was based on a fear that the charismatic Shackleton was a threat to the captain's leadership. From Huntford's account, one can infer Scott's desire to have Shackleton medically examined by Koettlitz as an attempt to influence the medical officer's opinion by suggesting that the orders were "formal, in writing."[98]

Yet anyone familiar with the body of Huntford's work knows well to read with care regarding the subject of Scott. That Scott asked for an opinion formally and in writing was his approach to most things on the expedition. The answer requires a broader view than that.

Scott's decision to send Shackleton home must be understood in the circumstances of the time. True to his mentor's desires, Scott wished for an all-naval affair and did nothing to discourage the merchant men from leaving. He urged Armitage (not Royal Navy) to return for the good reason that Scott felt Armitage had personal reasons to return. Armitage refused. When the merchant men volunteered to leave, Scott noted that these were the very men who he had hoped would return. Thus, although the captain was glad to be commanding a more nearly all-naval endeavor, the theory that Shackleton was leaving as part of clearing the ship of merchant men is not convincing.

Was the medical decision that Scott gave as his official reason — and to which he was consistent in public addresses after the expedition — borne out by a wider reading of the primary source material? Contemporary accounts of the southern party's condition on their return indicate that all three men were badly affected by the experience. Returning to the ship 3 February 1903, Shackleton and Wilson were clearly worse than their leader. Yet when the reaction from being safely back aboard set in, all three men appeared much worse than the original estimates. How quickly they recovered provided further insight. Wilson's leg was particularly bad and continued so even after the captain and his third lieutenant were up and about again.[99] Additionally, as late as 1 March Wilson was not well enough to visit the relief ship, yet on 16 February 1903 Shackleton led a party bringing stores from the *Morning* to the *Discovery*.[100] No indication of a relapse on Shackleton's part after that date appears in the existing record. Consider also that the commander kept T. V. Hodgson, even though he did not have a clean bill of health for sledging work. Perhaps with a scientist Scott could make a different policy — and it would have been an exception in his requirements for his scientists — but for one of his officers he would not make such an exception.[101]

While none of the contemporary observers stated that Scott sent his third lieutenant home because of personal animosity, or as Huntford suggested because Scott feared Shackleton's potential as a rival, both Ferrar and Armitage suggested that factors other than medical were involved. Armitage, in later years, wrote that he protested Shackleton's being invalided home.[102] Royds, on learning of Shackleton's departure, noted in his diary nothing about health but did suggest that perhaps it was "for the best."[103] Huntford was convinced of the rivalry theory, but not all would be. Also of note, in his diary Scott stated that he was hesitant to send Shackleton home and that Shackleton fails only in constitution, hardly a hard-bitten statement about ridding one's self of a rival.[104]

At least as important as the two previous arguments was the idea that Scott felt that Shackleton had been tried and found wanting in the field, a failure not so much of stamina but of will, and what might well have been called at the time, pluck. Further suggestions of this arose in the controversy that engulfed the two men in 1907 over Shackleton's plan to use McMurdo as the base of his Nimrod expedition. At that point, Scott wrote that Shackleton lacked not just the ability to lead men in dangerous situations such as the Antarctic but more significantly the will to carry through a long sledging trip. By comparison Wilson, who was in early March worse off than Shackleton, had "no bottom to his pluck."[105]

Regardless of which of the conclusions one assumes motivated the decision to send Shackleton home, the young lieutenant was clearly unhappy about it. Bernacchi noted that Shackleton was deeply disappointed and wanted very much to stay.[106] Imagine the scene the day before departure from the ship when the two men met for the captain to pay off his third lieutenant and have him sign off in the log book!

In a similar vein, what prompted Armitage to stay another year is an interesting question. The Pilot may have been motivated by a combination of wanting to remain at his post and not to be seen as sent home in the middle of the expedition with the possible implication that he somehow did not have the stuff to survive. Perhaps Armitage still held out hopes that Scott would allow Armitage to make one great sledging trip that would bring credit upon himself and somehow redeem a phase of his life which he no longer believed was a stellar one. Another possible explanation, although not supported by primary source material, was Armitage's stubborn refusal to allow Scott to be so easily rid of him. Armitage had a strange, difficult streak in him, and this might have been a factor.

To replace Shackleton, Scott asked Colbeck for Mulock, who had already shown his value by helping Armitage with the surveying work. Colbeck consented to his young naval sublieutenant being transferred to the *Discovery*.[107]

The season was advancing, and the *Morning* needed to leave. The underpowered vessel ran risks with delay, for the possibility of encountering ice that it could not penetrate was a very real one. Scott, prudently, set the date of departure for the first of March.

On 1 March the *Discovery* men, excluding Wilson who was still not up for such a journey, sledged across the ice to the *Morning*. As Shackleton departed he was cheered by the men.[108] The night before the departure of the relief ship most of the officers and men of the *Discovery* went over for a last farewell. The men's celebration involved considerable drink, and while returning to the ship, both Wild and Smythe had to be tied to the sledge to get them back safely.[109]

On 2 March 1903 Colbeck ordered the lines cast off and the little vessel turned north as a few men from the *Discovery* looked on and waved. Despite the attempt to remain optimistic about getting out themselves, the next day Scott ordered that seals be killed and their meat laid in for winter food. Optimism about getting free from the ice had given way to reality: a second winter.

12

Red Sunset of Noon Is Vanishing Fast

For some time after the departure of the *Morning*, Scott and others hoped that the ten miles of ice that separated the *Discovery* from the relief ship on the day the latter sailed would be driven out in a storm. Aware of possible difficulties, Scott acted even before the *Morning* sailed to fend off criticism for his choice of winter quarters. He argued that most years the ice cleared out, without explaining why he had risked wintering given those odds.

The lack of money for this second winter was a concern for Scott as was his belief that a second winter would be "a waste of time."[1] Markham's message to Scott, delivered by Colbeck, was that funds had not been raised for a third season. What Scott did not know was that Markham had sent him a letter to await his arrival in New Zealand that clearly detailed the problem. Only £3,858 remained in the expedition coffers, an amount sufficient to bring the two ships back to England in the spring of 1903, but just barely. Both Markham and Scott had originally hoped that funds could be raised while the expedition was south to extend it for another year, but this had not proven to be the case.[2] Even with the limited information at hand in March 1903, Scott knew that grave financial problems would result from the inability to extricate the ship from its icy lodging. Moreover, Scott may have been concerned about the degree to which a further delay in returning would affect his naval career. Exploring was a mere sidelight; he expected to return to the navy, ideally with his standing enhanced by the polar experience.

Although Scott continued to hope, at least until April, that a freak storm would allow the *Discovery* to break out of winter quarters, no such disturbance occurred.[3] At no point in the summer of 1902–3 did the ice edge come closer than four to five miles from the ship. Wilson hoped that the ship would be freed in order to do some of the important exploring work that originally had been intended. Even if the ship were beset farther north, at least the party would have a new base of operations.[4]

If Scott was concerned about these matters at least he had a happier, if much more subdued, crew for the second winter. Both officers and men were glad to be rid of most of the departed crew members. Only three non–Royal Navy men among the nonscientists were left in the party: Armitage, Weller, and Clarke, all regarded as superb fellows. Inspections went better, and life was easier for the bluejackets now that everyone aboard understood and ascribed to the routine of a naval vessel. The mess deck was especially glad about the departure of Page and Hubert, both of whom were seen as unpleasant or unsavory fellows who did not get along well with their messmates. Scott thought the departure of the ne'er-do-wells was a factor in having no problems in the second winter. Even Hodgson, hardly at the center of naval issues, noted the improvement. Although the officers had reason to be concerned that, with the departure of Hare, they were reduced to only two servants, they managed to make it through the winter on that number.[5]

Assessing the work of the 1902–3 season, Scott was proud of what had been accomplished. The most notable lack to that point was in oceanographic work. In retrospect Scott thought the expectations may have been too high in this regard because the ship could not be both at sea and in winter quarters. Also, he was annoyed that the scientists had been able to accomplish so little in the area of physical properties of ice. Time and library resources for background material were cited as the principal reasons for the failure of the expedition regarding ice issues.[6]

Despite the benefits brought by the relief expedition, virtually as soon as that vessel left, the lack of candles and materials for lighting was keenly felt. Officers and men carefully saved up drippings, and many hours were spent making candles over the winter. Each person got one candle per day, but because the candles burned eight hours, most men were able to manage with this allotment. Everyone jealously guarded his supply, and even the usually unaffected Wilson was prompted to wonder where Skelton got his supply of candles. Hodgson also was puzzled by Skelton's supply. In fact, Skelton had gotten them from Colbeck shortly before the *Morning* sailed.[7]

A problem is an opportunity for an engineer, and Skelton soon was working on a solution. Within a week he had suggested the possibility of acetylene light and turned his attention to rigging a system on the ship. Neither he nor his crew could devote their whole attention to this matter, as other jobs were constantly being presented to the engineering department, from repairing pots damaged by the careless and now departed cook to making candlesticks and bookshelves for the officers.[8]

Within a month the experimental power station was ready for a test in the wardroom. Two hours of fairly constant light resulted. Refinements continued, and by 14 April 1903 Skelton presented his fellow wardroom dwellers with ten hours of bright acetylene illumination each day. Once the flaws were corrected in the operation, Dellbridge extended the system to the mess deck, where light was provided for the men's evenings, even though the mess deck was too large for the single burner to be as effective as in the wardroom. Given the difficulties of the *Belgica* expedition and Frederick A. Cook's light cure, the health benefits of such bright light in winter may be important, but without question it added immeasurably to the comfort of all aboard.[9]

Oil was another problem, one that Skelton could never overcome. Oil was needed both for illumination and heating in the observation huts, and each week the chief engineer presented his captain with an account of how much oil had been used and how much remained. The coal situation was another cause of concern. At the time of the *Morning*'s departure, the *Discovery* had only 84 tons of coal left aboard, well below the 150 to 200 Scott had hoped to have available for exploration in the spring.[10]

Winter set in quickly in the fall of 1903, and Scott took the precaution of gathering a large supply of seal meat and skuas for the larder. Later on, fish traps were set in the open areas of water that appeared during the winter. At first the men caught a good number, but later, inexplicably, the numbers declined. The fish were a welcome change in the breakfast menu. When the fish became scarce, the officers on occasion did without so that the mess deck could enjoy them. In general the food situation was much improved in the second winter. Although Scott was aware that Brett, the cook during the first winter, was incompetent, the quality of the food the second winter was a pleasant surprise. Clarke, who had been the cook's assistant, became the acting cook and was helped on a regular basis by Cross. The meals were tasty, appetizing, and, with the predominance of seal meat in the diet, much healthier. With the improvement in presentation the men much preferred the seal, and for the one day a week they dined on tinned meat, several men saved some of their seal meat from the previous day's supper to eat instead of the tinned food. That the crew was essentially free of illness during the second winter is an indication of the quality of Clarke's efforts. The physicians had regular inspections for scurvy, but none appeared this season. Because the workload of the two cooks was much heavier than that of the other men, the officers had a cold meal once a week to give the cooks a rest.[11]

Both officers and men spent more time reading in the dark months. Fewer diversions were scheduled in this season despite Scott's earlier comment that if a second winter were necessary more entertainment would have to be offered. In this winter no concerts or musicals were staged. Fewer other programs were presented, although the occasional lecture was scheduled. Armitage, for example, read a two-hour-long paper on the western party trip he led the summer before. Hodgson thought the presentation boring and tedious, but at least one member of the lower deck thought the experience very interesting. Skelton gave a magic lantern show to the warrant officers and the members of the mess deck. Bernacchi addressed the mess deck on several occasions, speaking about aurora and astronomy.[12]

Some of the officers offered instruction to the men in various subjects; for example, Hodgson started teaching Clarke arithmetic and soon found himself with two additional willing (and apparently able) students.[13]

Other entertainment resurfaced with the coming of the fall. Field hockey again enjoyed a surge of popularity despite being played in temperatures as low as $-39°$ F. Various combinations were used: officers versus men, fossils versus colts (men over and under age twenty-eight), and married against the singles. In addition to the pleasure of the game, playing provided much needed exercise for the general health of the crew. The men played every day that they could until failing light ended the season; it resumed in the spring. Injuries did occur. Scott got a nasty cut over his eye and was "knocked silly" for several minutes. Several officers noted the improvement of the men's play as they became smarter at the game and added their intellectual abilities to their athletic ones. Field hockey also provided at least one example of the concept of Antarctic history as Edwardian society in action. In a close game Royds managed to score a goal but in doing so noticed that he was offside when he scored. No one else caught the infraction, but Royds stopped and insisted that the credited goal be disallowed: one must play the game! Other things besides standards did not change: Hodgson still was not a threat at hockey. He played, but it "made no difference."[14]

Officers and men occupied themselves with other games. In the wardroom the popularity of bridge and chess waxed and waned. Scott, Skelton, and Royds were excellent players and Armitage nearly so. Occasionally,

Royds went to play bridge with the warrant officers. A chess tournament was also held. Several of the officers never played cards: Mulock, Barne, Hodgson, and Wilson. Whether one considers it a game or poor sportsmanship, a continuing favorite pastime was playing jokes on Koettlitz. One day during the winter Barne dressed up in wolf skin furs, and Bernacchi played dead in a snowbank near the ship. Koettlitz came upon the scene in the low light of winter, torch in hand, was startled by the wolf, and may or may not have taken flight, depending on the version believed.[15]

The men also engaged in other activities to pass the time. In the centuries-old tradition of seafarers, many were extremely talented artists and craftsmen. Lashly, who could turn his hand to anything, demonstrated his considerable artistic skill by making for Skelton a model of a sledge out of the German silver runners that had been taken off the sledges and discarded.[16] Cross made a similar one for Wilson, who was delighted at the "very pretty souvenir."[17] Many of the men were avid readers and could "give their opinion on the books of any recent novel writer you like to mention."[18]

Walking was at least as popular as it had been the season before. Scott often took a dog or two with him when he went out. These animals were the puppies born the previous winter. Scott noted his surprise at how steady the dogs were on the steep slopes.[19]

In the wardroom an election was held for the editorship of the *South Polar Times*, and Bernacchi emerged the winner. A series of issues appeared in due course throughout the winter. Bernacchi did not have the literary finesse of Shackleton, however. The second volume still provided amusement, although Scott thought the second year's issues not as rich in reading material.[20] Bernacchi was ably assisted by Wilson and Ford, who did most of the work.[21]

The routine the second winter was similar to that of the first. Royds scheduled all the officers, except Scott, Armitage, and Koettlitz, to take the nightly round of meteorological readings, a practice that went on throughout the winter. The meteorological record established through the efforts of Royds and the others was one of the most important scientific results of the expedition. Of particular value was the second complete year of meteorological records that gave far different results than the first had. Regrettably, Bernacchi ran short of paper for the Eschenhagen instrument, but he used what he had for the most interesting conditions.[22]

Although the second winter had not been planned, it added immeasurably to the quality of the entire scientific program. Scientists in each department had both improved the methods of their research and added substantially more to the body of scientific data than could have been imagined at the close of the 1902–3 summer.[23]

The men were employed in various tasks. Among the routine work was the gathering of ice for water. In addition, Royds kept everyone busy preparing for the coming sledging season, making and repairing equipment. Tents and sleeping bags had been badly worn in the previous season, and the men were forced to improvise, to some degree, to provide sufficient shelter for the sledging parties in the forthcoming season. Still, little could disguise that insufficient work existed for the entire party, even though now reduced in numbers from the previous winter. The men's work schedule reinforced this conclusion. They were awakened at 7:30 A.M. and had breakfast at 8:30 A.M. They worked from nine o'clock in the morning to one in the afternoon when they stopped for dinner. After that the men were free for the rest of the day. Supper was at 17:30, and again the crew had no evening work.[24]

The quartermasters continued their tasks, which included maintaining the fires and helping with the overnight observations. The quartermasters made sure that the officers were reminded to take the observations and accompanied them in inclement weather.[25]

The engineering staff had a wide range of activities. In addition to maintaining the lighting, Skelton and his crew took apart and overhauled the engine over the winter. When not occupied with those two tasks they were constantly called on to make right anything that broke or needed fixing. Pots had to be mended; metallic equipment for the sledging parties generally came to Skelton's department for servicing.

Mulock proved himself a valuable addition, spending much of his time working on the surveying data gathered up to that time. Mulock had a drawing table in Scott's cabin, and from this experience Scott learned a great deal about the kind of information that sledging parties needed to gather during the coming season. Barne spent much of the winter out on his own each day, in the field with his sail-power-assisted sledge taking soundings and other scientific measurements. Indeed, all the members of the wardroom were remarkably busy throughout the winter. Wilson indicated that rarely did one find someone taking an afternoon nap.[26]

Two final items need to be mentioned. Without question, much of the daily excitement of the newness of the Antarctic was gone in the second winter and, combined with other factors, contributed to a decline in the quality and quantity of the journal writing.[27] Men such as Skelton, who rarely missed a day of writing the first year, now skipped two or three weeks at a time. Monotony was a much greater factor in both the wardroom and the mess deck. The second issue of note was the degree to which these men maintained their unfailing cheerfulness throughout. Scott noted it and credited this characteristic as being critical for the healthy survival of all through the tedium of the long winter. Royds reflected on this issue in his journal on one occasion and made it very clear that although one had such down feelings, the important thing was not to let them show and to keep up a brave face and upbeat countenance for the sake of the others.[28]

Disturbances did surface more in the second winter. At one point Armitage and Scott were not speaking to one another, a condition that lasted for a short while but the repercussions of which stretched into the second season. Whether a factor or not, Armitage, who had played a large role in the sledging in the 1902–3 season, did almost nothing in that regard the following summer.[29]

For his part Armitage was not happy. In retrospect, Skelton remembered Armitage as not fitting in as well as the rest of the party. Armitage was not popular in the expedition and felt unappreciated. Given the degree to which his opinion had been valued at the outset of his association with the expedition, advising on all manner of things and seeing himself as the one sent along to watch over Scott, the reality of his two years can easily be seen as disappointing. Armitage's surveying and magnetic tasks allowed him the opportunity to work on his own. In the first winter he seldom ventured outdoors, a habit satirized in the *South Polar Times*. The second winter, he did on occasion go walking with Mulock, with whom he worked on the surveying. Mulock was something of an outsider in the party also because his personality did not lend itself to the camaraderie of the wardroom.[30] In later years Armitage was clearly bitter at what he thought was a breech of promise by Markham in not being allowed a more independent field of action.

Another indication of the petty squabbles one can reasonably expect under such confined quarters occurred when Koettlitz became annoyed with Scott for what the medical officer thought was the captain's rather childish behavior over bridge. Scott was not terribly difficult to live with, but he was overly sensitive, which meant that he did occasionally overreact in situations such as card games. The low-key nature of the second winter was also reflected in the way the disappearance of the sun was treated. The day was not marked with great ceremony as it had been the year before, although below decks the men did splice the main brace. Midwinter was celebrated in a similar vein. Although the warrant officers were invited to dine in the wardroom, the day was less extravagantly celebrated. Gone were the special items brought along for the purpose of decorating each mess; the celebration was a more matter-of-fact affair in 1903. "None of the knick-knacks of last year" was the way one bluejacket described it. However, Royds did serve out small bottles of Bass beer, the last on the ship; and Wilson distributed a tin of one thousand cigarettes that had been sent to him via the *Morning*. In the wardroom the last of their best champagne was drunk by the officers.[31]

The winter was colder than the previous one but roughly the same in terms of storms. The first gales did not arrive until June. The lowest temperature recorded this season was −67.7° F.[32]

Shortly after midwinter Scott shared his plans for the coming sledging season. The paramount goal was to free the ship, by whatever means available. To that end he decreed that sawing would be started in December in an attempt to cut a channel from the water's edge to the imprisoned ship. All sledging parties were to return by 15 December to assist in this herculean effort. He stated that further investigation was to take place in the neighborhood of Cape Crozier, in part, in an attempt to learn more about the life cycle of the emperor penguin. A western party to continue the work of Armitage would be undertaken by Scott himself. A third proposed journey would be led by Barne to the southwest. Barne and Scott would lead supported trips, while Royds would take an unsupported sledging party. No further attempt would be made on the South Pole. Scott had carefully worked out the details: without better dogs it was impossible to go any farther south than he had gone in 1902.[33]

The sledging season began early; on 7 September 1903, Royds departed winter quarters for Cape Crozier. Although the *Discovery* had as many dogs aboard as the expedition had started with, the journeys of the spring of 1903 were manhauling affairs. Indeed, in September on the eve of the sledging parties, Scott ordered all the puppies killed as they were of no value.[34]

Among the several reasons for undertaking this adventure was Wilson's desire to learn more about the emperor penguin and its breeding cycle. By the spring of 1903 Wilson had come to believe that the birds must lay their eggs in August. He hoped by getting there in early September to gather samples both of eggs and young chicks. Wilson hoped to make a series of trips to Cape Crozier in the spring to study the development of both the emperor and Adélie penguins.[35]

Royds, who was a realistic rather than an enthusiastic sledger, led his party of five away from the ship 7 September 1903. Wilson hoped to build on the excellent natural history notes on the emperor penguin that Skelton had compiled. The journey was made in the early spring light, and camping duties often had to be done by candlelight. Owing to the expected low temperatures this early in the spring, the party used two three-man sleeping bags, which while marginally warmer, were a great deal more uncomfortable. The confined quarters led to restless sleep, each man being awakened at various times by his bag mates.[36]

Royds reached Cape Crozier 12 September 1903. The group went immediately in search of the emperors but found the topography much changed from the previous visit. Rafted ice blocked the path the men hoped to take, and after an afternoon's work they returned to camp with little accomplished other than to know what route not to take.

Wilson sent three other men to search for the Adélie rookery, while he led a party to that of the emperors, which Wilson estimated contained a thousand birds. Regrettably, Wilson's estimate of the hatching period was incorrect; the chicks were more advanced than he had anticipated. Still, Wilson delighted in the opportunity to study these species, to this point little understood. At that time, Wilson was not sure if the birds returning from the sea fed only the chicks or if they also fed the other adults who had remained at the rookery. Noting the intense instinct to nurture the chicks, the zoologist also surmised perhaps that when adults went to feed, they left their chick with a neighbor.[37]

Wilson noted the high mortality rates of the chicks and correctly deduced that some of the deaths were caused by overzealous adults trying desperately to get possession of a chick to brood. The men gathered eggs and dead chicks for their collection and returned to their camp.[38]

The next day, with their precious cargo of frozen eggs, dead chicks, and a couple of live chicks, Royds and his party headed home. Blissett had a bad frostbite on his face and looked much the worse for wear. The temperatures en route home ranged from −45° F to −61° F, which, combined with the irregular sleeping and hard work, left the men exhausted by the end of the day.[39]

Fortunately, the trip home took only four days, and on 17 September Royds saw in the distance people coming toward him from the ship. The return was a success. Emperor chicks were brought back through the kindness of Cross, who gave up his sleeping jacket to keep the chicks warm en route home.[40]

The chicks provided amusement for some time. Living in Wilson's cabin — and anyone who has observed a penguin rookery can imagine the results of those guests — the chicks amazed the men with the heartiness of their appetites. All participated in their feeding, and the men were stunned at the amount of food consumed. Full of food, the young penguins assumed the shape of a half-full bag of pennies dropped on the floor. Scott viewed them at first as small tanks, then as bottomless caverns; no amount of food seemed to satisfy them. One of the chicks lived quite a while, until the coming of warmer weather.[41]

Wilson made another visit to the rookery departing on 12 October, taking with him Cross, who had been his regular zoological assistant, and Whitfield. The trip took over seven days and was tiring. Some days the party of three was forced to relay its two sledges. Wilson was under some pressure to reach the rookery by 19 October, the date when Skelton had visited it the previous year. The season had clearly advanced, and temperatures now were in the range of $-15°$ F during the day.[42]

Arriving on the eighteenth, the men descended to the sea ice to the emperor rookery and found a large number of chicks. Wilson thought that fewer chicks were present this year, based on Skelton's report. Wilson estimated the mortality rate at seventy-seven percent. He rescued one chick that had fallen into the water in a crack near the rookery. The zoologist commented, "Six adults were fighting over it, though not one had the sense to help it out."[43]

The next day began well — fresh seal liver fried in butter for breakfast. In addition to gathering zoological notes, Wilson was also a postman and took the messages from Scott to the main cairn by the Adélie penguin rookery nearby. Wilson also collected rocks for Ferrar while here.[44]

Bad weather plagued Wilson's attempts. At Cape Crozier the party was confined to its tent for nearly a week, from 22 October to 28 October. Food and oil supplies were inadequate for such additions to their stay, but seals made up for both lacks.[45]

When the storm cleared, Wilson led the others on an egg-collecting foray to the Adélie rookery. They wanted food for themselves and plenty to take back to the ship. Penguin after penguin was pushed off the nest, but no eggs were found. Frustrated, they took three adults back to camp and ate them for dinner.[46] Then another three-day storm arrived.

After digging themselves out on the fourth day, 2 November, Wilson headed for the ship. The party was already overdue, and food supplies were dangerously low. En route home Whitfield was considerably bothered by a bad leg, but Wilson pushed on, assuming that what the injured limb needed was exercise. As Wilson's team was overdue, a search party was being organized, but the zoologist's group returned to the ship on 5 November, before Royds sent anyone out to look for them.[47]

While Royds had been away on his first trip, two other preliminary journeys had begun. In preparation for his western party Scott took out a depot-laying party, which left on 9 September 1903 and returned on 20 September. A cache of supplies was established sixty miles from the ship, on a path up a glacier, which Scott hoped would be a shorter route for the plateau. Scott's party, too, traveled in harsh weather, temperatures in the minus fifties degrees Fahrenheit being the norm.[48]

Barne had engaged in a preliminary sojourn of eight days to establish a depot to the south, in support of his major journey of the season. His group experienced extremely bitter temperatures, to minus sixties degrees Fahrenheit, and Ernest Joyce got his foot badly frostbitten in the effort.[49] Home for a fortnight, Barne and his men departed the ship 6 October to survey land to the south.

For the first three weeks a supporting party accompanied Barne. In the early stages of the trip harsh southwestern winds tore at their faces and made progress slow and painful. The second group turned back on 28 October, and the main party continued on to 80° S, which was reached on 14 November. The men reached their farthest south latitude and turned north, keeping close to the coastline, and returned home 13 December 1903.[50]

Barne's party did excellent surveying work and made an important glaciological discovery. Barne observed that Depot A, which had been clearly marked by a line of transit with two mountains, had moved 608 yards since it had been established. This conclusive proof that the barrier was moving helped to solve the riddle of the Great Ice Barrier.[51]

Three other sledging efforts were made in the spring of 1903. Royds led an unsupported party comprised of Bernacchi, Cross, Clarke, Plumley, and Gilbert Scott that departed on 10 November for the South. The idea for Royds' unsupported party, heading southeast from winter quarters, originated with Bernacchi, who had asked Scott during the winter what proof existed that the barrier continued level to the east. Finding no conclusive proof existed, Scott made this question one that Royds's party was to answer.[52]

For eighteen days Royds's team sledged southward for 155 miles, reaching their turning point on 28 November. Bernacchi made magnetic observations and took a detailed series of temperature measurements en route. The information thus gained provided support for the theory that the Great Ice Barrier was afloat for a considerable distance south of its northern edge. The trip was made under very difficult circumstances, without support, and Scott praised the party for their efforts.[53]

Armitage was planning to leave for Mount Discovery with Wilson and Ferrar, but the latter became injured and Heald took his place. Ferrar was left in charge of the little emperor penguin chick, which he fed chalk and cod liver oil. Departing 23 November Armitage surveyed the glacier that runs into McMurdo Sound from Mount Discovery. The team returned on 12 December.[54]

The major effort of the spring was the one that departed on 12 October 1903 and was led by Scott to the west to investigate the area beyond the coast of Victoria Land. Attached to this party at the outset was a three-man team led by Ferrar, which intended to do geological work and stayed with Scott until 11 November.

Setting out, Scott was plagued by bad weather and tough sledging surfaces. Scott, however, was determined "that from first to last . . . there should be hard marching."[55] On the thirteenth the group cleared Butter Point, so named because Scott left a tin of butter there, anticipating that this was the first place on the return that the group was likely to encounter seals and would need butter in which to cook them. Dailey and Williamson soon showed the strain of the marching. Meanwhile, Plumley managed to cut off part of his thumb while chopping frozen pemmican. He showed it to people as a curio. Proceeding up the valley, by 16 October they had reached the depot that was placed under Cathedral Rocks. In six days Scott had managed to reach Knob Head Moraine, which had taken Armitage twenty-seven days to reach the previous year.[56]

Now Scott's party was hampered by technical problems. The German silver that covered the runners of their sledges was reported as split first on one and then on another sledge. On normal snow surfaces this flaw would not have been critical, but on hard ice the wood quickly splintered and disintegrated. Thus Scott had no choice but to return to the ship. Leaving a depot of materials, Scott turned toward the *Discovery*, determined to make a good march of the distance. He covered eighty-seven miles in three days, an amazing accomplishment. On the second day back the captain told his other team, which was showing some signs of wear, to return at their own pace, but the support party too made a determined effort and set a speed record, thirty-seven miles in a single day to reach the ship.[57]

By 26 October Scott was ready to return to the trail. By the twenty-ninth the captain's party was at Knob Head Moraine again. The next morning a sudden wind swept down on them while they were breaking camp and blew away loose items such as gloves and sleeping bags. After a few frantic minutes most of the items were retrieved. However, among the things apparently lost at this time was Scott's copy of *Hints for Travellers.* Because this volume contained the tables to assist in finding latitude and longitude, the loss was crucial. Scott was determined to continue and eventually worked out his own system for determining his position, one that, when checked later, proved to be remarkably accurate.[58]

Moving up the valley, Scott's party found that their crampons, which had been manufactured on the ship and had been used without difficulty the previous year, were now causing blisters. Skelton took the matter at hand on the trail and with Feather's help soon had produced a revised item that worked without mishap.[59]

By the first of November three of the four sledges had badly damaged runners, so again the chief engineer went to work. This time assisted by one of his own engine team, Lashly, he established a makeshift repair shop at the camp and was able to remake the silver runners in a workable fashion.[60]

Fighting their way into the teeth of the wind, the party pushed on, assuming that this was a normal condition of the area and that waiting would accomplish nothing. By 4 November they were at seventy-two hundred feet when they were overtaken suddenly by a violent storm. Searching quickly for some snowy place on which to camp, Scott spied one and tried to dig out snow blocks for the tent. The snow was too hard, but Feather arrived at a convenient time and, with greater skill, had more success in chipping out snow for the tent.[61]

The storm lasted six days during which time the men were confined to their tents in what they termed "Desolation Camp." Scott thought it one of the most miserable weeks of his life. Fortunately, the party had a book with them, Darwin's *Voyage of the "Beagle,"* to pass away the time. The men took turns reading aloud until "their freezing fingers refused to turn the page."[62]

By the fifth day of imprisonment the sleeping bags were becoming wet, and the men complained that they were having trouble keeping their circulation working in the confined quarters. Scott was determined to try to leave the sixth day, despite horrific conditions. Ten minutes into the experiment, the party retreated to their sleeping bags, with several frostbitten toes and feet to show for their effort.[63]

On 11 November, impatient to be away, Scott departed in marginal weather, while Ferrar's party, which included Kennar and Weller, split off to do geological work. Scott's party pushed on to the summit by 13 November and had five weeks provisions in hand.[64]

Ferrar's party turned back down the glacier valley to do geology work. On this carefully planned and executed trip he found fossil plant remains, an important discovery. C. A. Larsen, who was in 1893 credited, incorrectly, with being the first to find fossils in Antarctica, found them on an island off the Antarctic peninsula, and Ferrar's find was the first on the continent.[65] Ferrar's discovery occurred at a high altitude and contributed to the knowledge of the history of the earth's climate. The young scientist made a thorough geological survey of the area and determined that the glacier had receded considerably over the centuries. The geologist noted that the glacier was about eighty miles long and rose to a height of nine thousand feet.[66] Ferrar's team returned to the ship 11 December 1903.

Meanwhile, Scott continued moving ever westward. Some men in Scott's six-man party began to tire. Temperatures on the plateau dropped to −44° F, and the wind was relentless. The men were forced to relay, and then Handsley began to have chest pains. Faced with the probability of several of his men faltering, Scott elected to split the party, sending three men home under Skelton, while he continued with only Lashly and Evans. Handsley believed he was the cause of the decision and approached his captain to plead with Scott not to think ill of him. Scott reassured him that that was not his intention.[67]

Scott kept Lashly and Evans with him and sent Handsley and Feather (who was suffering in silence with back problems) back under the command of Skelton. Skelton took it easy while heading back to the ship and arrived on 16 December after a reasonably uneventful journey. En route home Skelton conducted some observations and as the semiofficial photographer of the expedition added to the photographic record of the *Discovery*.[68]

Scott and the two bluejackets renewed the struggle to gain distance to the west. Scott knew he had a strong party and was determined to make a good show of the journey. Scott praised the herculean strength of Evans and noted that Lashly was deceptively powerful, healthy in habit (he neither smoked nor drank), and possessed good sense and intelligence.[69]

For three more weeks Scott's men muscled their way westward at a surprising rate. Roland Huntford saw this journey as important to Scott in other ways. Sharing a three-man bag with his two companions, Scott learned a great deal more about the lives of his bluejackets than years in naval service had taught him.[70]

The wind was the beast of the hour. Literally a cutting wind, airborne ice particles and the lack of humidity ripped at their flesh. Each man suffered, so much so that Scott noted that it was painful to laugh. Still, Scott had earlier decided not to turn until the end of the month, but on 30 November he called a halt to their outward progress.[71]

Scott later recalled his month spent on the Victoria Land plateau as being of "some vivid but evil dream." The desolate landscape offered no respite for the eye; no feature broke the unchanging scene.[72]

When the trio turned, they had fourteen days of food and a somewhat smaller supply of fuel. Indeed, fuel concerned Scott greatly. Being roughly seventeen days' march away from the glacier depot, he began to consider the need either to extend the marches or face reduced rations. The latter option seemed unwise, as the men were already ravaged by hunger, reflected by the vividness of their dreams about food.[73] When Scott's party was halted by lack of visibility on 2 December, they were forced to stop at midday to rest, rather than try to continue over the uneven surface, which caused them to stumble and fall. Correctly, Scott feared what an injury from a fall might mean; his experience of the southern party made him hesitant to repeat the experience of traveling with a disabled man. Although the weather had not cleared, Scott's men rigged their sail and pushed on over the wasteland; Scott felt blessed that he had such tremendously strong companions.[74]

Alarmed by the increased shortage of oil, Scott determined the need to eke out an extra half hour of marching before stopping at the end of each day. The slim margin for error demanded such a change, and his two companions agreed. Recent snowfall had changed the surface over which they had traveled only days before and made the pulling harder. At times even with a significantly lighter sledge the trio could sustain only one mile per hour.[75]

Rare for his style of leadership, Scott consulted his bluejackets about the difficulties of their circumstances. All three agreed that given their situation they had to push on an extra hour each day to be assured of reaching the depot before their food was exhausted. Evans did not fancy cold lunches but agreed. Additionally, Lashly agreed to take on all the cooking for the time being, as he was the most competent cook and could operate the primus to its greatest efficiency, proving again that he was a man who could turn his hand to anything.[76]

Scott watched as hunger caused his men to waste away before his eyes.

This constant reminder that their survival hung in the balance prompted all three to the maximum effort. Another critical shortage appeared: Evans and Scott were out of tobacco. Reduced for some time to half a pipe a day, by 12 December even that respite ended.[77]

Conditions worsened on the thirteenth, and after a series of falls caused by poor visibility and harsh winds, Scott was forced to call for tea breaks to revive his men and to stave off the ravages of frostbite. Evans's nose was a continual victim of the winds and assumed most curious guises as it went through the various stages of frostbite and recovery. But the fourteenth was undoubtedly the worst day, one the men nearly did not survive.[78]

The day began on a good note. The stormy conditions cleared in the morning, and the men were able to set off with decent visibility for a change. After days of limited visibility and without the lost book of navigation tables, Scott confessed that he was not certain exactly where they were. Proceeding carefully downhill, Scott had his two men behind the sledge to guide it. Suddenly, the steepness of the incline increased, and the trio found themselves unable to break the downhill movement of the sledge. Then Lashly slipped, and Evans fell immediately thereafter. Scott looked up to see the sledge and his two companions fly past him. He, too, was swept off his feet, and for a terrible few minutes they were all sliding down the slope, out of control. Scott instantly perceived the danger of a broken limb and could only hope that none would result. Fortune smiled on them, as they were brought up before disaster occurred. Halted by the surface, Scott looked up to see Evans and Lashly pulling themselves up on their feet, unhurt.[79]

Bruised but mobile, Scott discovered another reason to rejoice: The glacier appeared to them in the distance. They were uninjured and now knew where they were. In the fall the sledge had capsized, scattering food and supplies along the path. Within minutes all provisions were restowed, and so the group moved on. But the dangers of the day were not yet behind them.

Perhaps dulled by the exhaustion of the day, they moved unknowingly into a crevassed area. Scott had ordered Lashly to move a little to his left when suddenly the snow beneath the captain's feet gave way. His next realization was that he was in a crevasse, hanging by his harness. Looking up he saw that Evans, too, had fallen into the hole. Scott asked if Evans was all right, and the quiet, matter-of-fact tone of the petty officer's response reassured the captain. The whole sledging expedition might have ended at that moment but for the quick and steady action of Lashly.[80]

Lashly had reacted instinctively to keep the sledge from following the men into the crevasse. With one hand still gripping the line that suspended his two companions, he grabbed Scott's ski sticks, still on the surface, and wedged them under the suspended sledge to brace it and prevent it from tumbling farther. That was all he could do. He dared not leave his precarious perch to assist the two to the surface.[81]

Hanging by his traces, Scott swung around at the end of his rope. The slick surface of the walls of the crevasse offered no grip, but he managed to find a small pinnacle on which to brace himself. He knew Lashly could not help, and so the captain took off his gloves in the subzero temperature of the ice opening and contemplated how long it had been since he had climbed up a rope. No other alternative loomed. Scott made his way up the rope, past the hanging Evans, until he reached the surface by which time his hands were numb with cold. Only when he reached the surface did he realize how desperate Lashly's situation was.[82]

Several minutes expired while Scott strived to restore feeling and action to his hands. Then he lowered his line to Evans. Together, the pair worked to get the nearly two-hundred-pound man to the surface. They did it. No one spoke for a brief time, so exhausted were they all from the exertion, then Evans broke the silence with "Well, I'm blowed." They were alive.[83]

Bruised and battered, they camped for the night. Lashly, ever irrepressible, began to sing while he cooked the evening meal. From time to time Evans would mutter something about the day's events, finally noting quietly, "My word, but that was a close call." The next day they reached the Nunatak depot, which contained food to carry them to the next food cache. At Nunatak they also found welcome news, small notes from Skelton and Ferrar indicating that they had passed this way and that all had been well with them.[84]

On 16 December 1903 they reached the next depot, which contained adequate provisions to ease their minds about their situation. Scott's party took a day's break from marching to explore the ice-free Taylor Valley in which the men found themselves — a welcome change. By the twentieth they were at the depot by Cathedral Rocks, where they could see the sea for the first time in many weeks. Butter Point was their next stop. There the team found fresh meat left for them by a thoughtful Skelton and had seal steaks cooked in butter.[85]

By 23 December the trio was nearing their goal, and on Christmas Eve the masts of the *Discovery* became visible in the distance. Scott and his men arrived at the ship that evening and slept for the first time in weeks in their own quarters. They were home for Christmas.

Thus ended the second most difficult sledging effort of the expedition. Scott could feel justifiably proud of having made both of them himself and was generous in his praise of the two men who had shared the second journey. They had been on the trail for eighty-one days, instead of the sixty-five he had planned. They had traveled 725 miles in the fifty-nine days since their second departure, averaging 14½ miles each day in that time.[86]

Only four men were aboard when Scott returned; the rest were following the orders Scott had left before departing and were at a sawing camp near the edge of the ice trying to cut a channel that would allow the *Discovery* free access to the sea.

Scott and his party rested for nearly a week before venturing down to the sawing camp. In the meantime Armitage had been endeavoring to carry out the orders to cut a path to the sea. Scott had indicated that the sawing was to begin shortly after 18 December 1903 at a place near the ice edge.

Armitage established the tent city, with officers and men sleeping in separate sections of the makeshift quarters. The Pilot divided the entire crew into three shifts so that the work could go on round the clock. The men slept about a mile and a half from the job sight and marched out and back at every shift. Laboring four hours on and a few hours off, the bluejackets were joined by the officers and scientists in the task. The men were constantly at it, barely having time to venture out and back, work, eat a quick meal, and turn in for a bit of rest before being awakened to start the whole process again eight hours later. Even Wilson became downhearted. The ice was seven to eight feet thick, and the drudgery was brutal.[87]

On average the shifts managed to cut about forty feet in four hours. When one party laid down the tools the next group immediately took them up. A sense of competition developed between the parties, each trying to cut farther than the previous ones. Despite all this, within a day or two everyone cutting knew that the whole process was a complete waste of time.[88]

What motivated Armitage to continue the futile attempt is hard to understand. Perhaps he was determined to show the folly of the entire operation by continuing with naval pigheadedness, to show that he too could drive the men as well as a naval officer. For whatever reason, the bluejackets demonstrated that Markham's confidence in them, that they could do anything — even the futile — was well founded.

At the rate of progress the men were maintaining, sawing a channel to the ship would take approximately 220 days, that is, throughout the remainder of the summer and into the following winter. Nineteen miles of solid ice separated the ship from open water. To make matters worse, once the ice was cut loose, often no place existed for the loose material to be floated out of the way of the work. In addition, on cold days the newly opened channels quickly froze over again. The ice saws often became frozen in place, and at least one shift spent the entire four hours trying to get the saws free so that the work could continue. Everyone knew that the moment the captain arrived, Scott would see the futility of the effort and call a halt to the fiasco. The men grumbled but kept at the task.[89]

Unfortunately, the official reports that were coming back to the ship from the camp indicated that all was going as planned, and Scott, exhausted from the western party sledging trip, remained at the ship for a week before venturing down to see the operation firsthand. Strangely, the camp and ship were in daily contact with one another. Dell had blood poisoning in his left arm and thus was invalided. He was put in charge of the dogs at the ship and managed to turn them into a fairly effective team, proving himself a capable driver. Scott finally visited the sawing camp on New Year's Eve. He saw immediately how hopeless the task was that his dutiful crew had been attempting and declared a day off for 1 January 1904. Scott slept in his own tent for the night, although he was joined by Wilson, with whom he no doubt discussed the entire matter.[90]

When work was resumed, Scott watched for an hour and then ordered the fiasco abandoned and sent the men back to the *Discovery*, determined to try to renew the cutting nearer the ship where a better chance to do some good seemed possible. In his official report of the effort, Scott justifiably praised his crew, who labored, shift after shift, despite "the hopeless nature . . . obvious to everyone."[91]

Scott did not return to the ship immediately. He and Wilson went off for a period of rest and to study a nearby Adélie penguin rookery. Scott was suffering badly from indigestion and needed a break from the company on the *Discovery*. The ice showed no sign of breaking up, and the possibility of a third winter loomed large. Unless news from home made it impossible, Scott asked Wilson to stay another winter. While encamped there Scott and Wilson were sitting on their sleeping bags with the tent door open when Scott exclaimed, "Why, there's the *Morning*!" Both men emerged to get a better look. Seeing the ship meant that sufficient supplies would be at hand, in the event of a forced delay of a year, and also meant that some men could be sent home if needed.[92]

While looking out at the *Morning*, Wilson and Scott saw something that startled and puzzled them — a second ship. What could this mean? Why was a second ship bearing down on their position? What Scott soon came to understand was the saga of the relief expedition since Colbeck had sailed away the previous March, a story that brought the *Discovery* to the point where Scott essentially lost control of his own destiny in the South.

13

The Grand Old Man Falters

When the relief vessel *Morning* had departed the ice edge roughly five miles from the *Discovery* on 2 March 1903, the men left behind to over-winter cheered and waved until Colbeck's ship began to move out of sight. Seen from the decks of the *Morning*, those who were remaining seemed a forlorn lot. As the party began to sledge back to their ship, Scott's men turned and gave one last wave before disappearing into the mist. Doorly was moved to write a song about the experience. One phrase reflects prevalent contemporary Edwardian mores: "Doing their duty, not counting the cost."[1]

Colbeck had not sailed far north before conditions indicated he had pushed his luck to have waited so long. He could not expect his under-powered ship to crush its way through ice as the *Discovery* might have done in similar circumstances. Within thirty-six hours of departing, the *Morning* was stopped by the ice. The vessel could not cut a path. Wintering at this point might have proven disastrous. The possibility of having the ship crushed by the ice was a real one, and having given Scott's party virtually all their oil, candles, and matches, the winter would have been dark and depressing.

Thus Colbeck took a gamble. Spying a blizzard bearing down on them from the south, he determined to set sail and drive through the ice. When the storm arrived the engine was set full speed forward. The sails billowed and then stretched, and soon the masts could be seen straining under the intense pressure of the wind. The *Morning* groaned and bent but did not falter. Still, despite the fury of the storm and the modest help of the engines, a curious result occurred: The boat was driven backward by the strong currents. Eventually, though, Colbeck's plan proved successful, and the ship broke through the belt of ice and was able to continue northward.[2]

All along the coast of Victoria Land Colbeck had to wind his way through ice. Pancake ice was forming everywhere, an indication of the need to retreat before the winter. While still sailing along this coast, the ship hit something: perhaps a whale, asleep on the water.[3]

By the time the vessel had passed Cape Adare the ice danger was largely passed, but then the ship was stricken by a series of very severe storms. From 12 March to 20 March 1903 gale after gale buffeted the ship. Often the vessel shipped a great deal of water as the winds drove the ship leeward for hours at a time.[4]

Meanwhile, although the men were crowded aboard ship, they were as content as weather conditions would allow. Shackleton recovered a great deal on this voyage, and by the time he arrived in New Zealand he seemed in fine health. The three-week voyage neared an end when land was sighted 24 March 1903.[5]

In the morning hours of 25 March the *Morning* steamed up into Lyttelton. By a strange twist of fate, another vessel was making its way into port at the same time, and aboard that steamer was Mrs. Wilson, Bill's bride, who had journeyed out from England to greet her husband. She would have to wait another year.[6]

A cheering crowd greeted the rescuers, and another round of social activities occupied the next few weeks. True to the not uncommon experience of Antarctic heroes returning from the South to the gentle hospitality of New Zealanders, within weeks three of the men became engaged.[7]

Colbeck had orders from Markham not to speak with the press for forty-eight hours. Instead, Colbeck was to send a five-hundred-word telegram reporting the situation to the RGS president, which he did. When the officers and crew did speak to the press, they indicated their belief that this had been an especially severe summer and that nobody held any hope that the *Discovery* would be freed that year.[8]

No sooner had word of the voyage of the *Morning* reached England than Markham began to distribute the information to the press, shaping the story to his own perceptions. Without question Colbeck had accomplished all he had set out to do. Without his considerable seamanship the voyage might have had a far different and less fortunate outcome. Well might Sir Clements report that the RGS council was pleased with his work.[9]

The interpretation of other facts betrayed Markham's ideas. According to the RGS president, before the relief ship had arrived, Scott's men had "experienced some privation owing to part of the supplies having gone bad."[10] The arrival of the relief ship was described as "providential," but

Sir Clements now made it clear that Scott only had sufficient provisions until January 1904, thereby planting the seed of a second voyage by the *Morning*. Such a subsequent voyage was "absolutely necessary for the safety of our countrymen."[11] None of Markham's premises for a second voyage was correct.

Naturally, Markham's estimates of food supply ignored the reality that seals and penguins could sustain a party of thirty-seven men indefinitely. Markham was now in a terrible bind. Having had difficulty raising funds for his first rescue effort, he now had to find more money. Moreover, he knew he was short approximately £8,000 in meeting the wages and other commitments of the *Morning* and the *Discovery*.[12]

From Markham's orders, which awaited his arrival in New Zealand, Colbeck learned that if he returned without the *Discovery* he was to remain in New Zealand. Markham informed him that Scott had requested further stores in the coming season. At this point the RGS president was hopeful that, in addition to the tinned foods already in Christchurch, supplies would be obtained either from local Kiwi sources or from Harrods. Sir Clements suggested that Shackleton could be of assistance in preparing for the resupply of the *Discovery*.[13]

Even at this early date Markham recognized the possibility that Scott might have to return without his ship the following summer. If that were the case sixty men would have to be crammed into the tiny *Morning*. Undaunted by this prospect, Markham reminded Colbeck that that was the usual number on polar ships in former times. Ruminating further on the possibility, Markham suggested that accommodation could be found by having a larger night watch, freeing up several hammocks, and by using the deck house for accommodation. Markham requested Colbeck's thoughts on the matter.[14] Again, regarding all the men returning in the *Morning*, Sir Clements allowed his desires to alter his perception of reality.

For the moment, the first requirement was that Colbeck keep his costs for the winter in New Zealand to an absolute minimum, for now that the *Discovery* was known to be imprisoned, Markham knew a second relief effort would have to be made. Colbeck proved himself as good an administrator as captain and survived the winter on a tightly controlled budget.[15]

What Colbeck could not know was that the relationship between the Royal Society and the RGS had been deteriorating. When the first relief expedition had been proposed, the Royal Society early had indicated its willingness to leave the matter in the hands of the RGS. The RS contributed £500 but had little effective input into the affair.

Now in London, in the spring of 1903 Markham launched a campaign to raise money for a second relief effort. At first Markham spoke of needing £6,000, then £8,000, and later closer to £15,000. The previous year, when his first efforts were not successful, Markham's rhetoric had become increasingly inflammatory. In 1903 he reached that level much more quickly.[16]

At first Markham's appeal was a straightforward effort to persuade donors to come forth and help in the relief effort. When they did not do so in sufficient numbers, Sir Clements changed the tenor of his appeal. Now, the first voyage of the *Morning* had saved the men of the *Discovery* with the food they brought.

Markham again turned to the Royal Society and persuaded it to draft a joint letter to Prime Minister A. J. Balfour, asking for funding to send out the second relief expedition. A letter was sent on 24 April 1903 to F. Sidney Parry, the Royal Society friend at the Treasury, to gain some advice regarding Balfour's views. The answer was not promising.[17] Responding to the points raised in the unofficial reply, Markham stated two things that do not match the facts in the case. Sir Clements argued that the *Discovery* was a national endeavor and that Parliament, representing the nation, was responsible. Then in response to another point, he prevaricated that a relief ship had not been part of the scheme of the two societies at the time. If one defined time as the exact moment of the 1899 deputation, a element of truth is present, otherwise not.[18]

Perhaps Sir Clements believed that he could persuade the government, in part by creating a groundswell of indignation, that the government was standing by, doing nothing, while brave men perished, for on 19 May 1903, over the signatures of the presidents of both the Royal Society and the RGS, he dispatched a formal request for funds from the government for the second relief effort. The letter outlined the reasoning behind the request. Anyone familiar with the details of the *Discovery* expedition from 1893 to 1901 may find the following description strange: "H. M. Government were not entirely prepared to organise such an expedition themselves." Because no one knew what had happened to Scott, a relief ship was sent out to reprovision and offer help if needed. In describing the much-needed food brought out by the relief ship, Markham implied that scurvy might have been caused by defective tins, part of the number that were condemned, thus reducing the supply of food available.[19]

The president's letter called for the government to come to the aid of the thirty-seven officers and men of the *Discovery* by taking out provisions and, if need be, bringing Scott's party back, even if it meant abandoning their ship. Markham reminded the government that the two societies had raised £22,600, beyond what was needed for the matching grant of 1899. To arrive at this figure, Markham conveniently lumped together the money raised for the *Morning* expedition with that for the *Discovery*, even though separate accounts were kept for the two enterprises.[20]

Using the same trump card that may have swayed the government in 1899, Markham reminded Balfour that the *Gauss* was overdue and that the German government had voted funds for its relief. Then, pointing out the potential dangers to ships, only five of which had been in those waters, the two presidents suggested the possibility that a second relief vessel might be prudent. The £12,000 requested was a modest sum for a single vessel, but if the government chose the safer option of having two ships, the amount needed would be £25,000. The two presidents offered to lead a deputation to see Balfour if he desired.[21]

While the government was considering the request, Markham's comments about the situation perhaps reflected his anticipation of a negative answer and the need to stir the public to action. Markham averred that without the *Morning* relief voyage "there would have been a serious and perhaps fatal disaster."[22] Even supporters such as Longhurst, the expedition's secretary, noted that Sir Clements was not always too careful in what he said. The situation continued to deteriorate when Markham, while addressing a meeting at Liverpool, alluded to the "wickedness of the government leaving such splendid fellows to perish for want of a few thousand pounds."[23]

The entire episode came to a head in the House of Commons when Colonel Royds asked the prime minister at question time if Mr. Balfour intended to take action on the request of the two societies to come to the aid of the men of the *Discovery*. Given Balfour's usual detachment from political animosity, the answer was remarkably direct. He regretted the course of action taken by the two societies and noted that his confidence in them had been "rudely shaken."[24]

Responding to the charges, Markham explained in a memo to his council that Balfour was "gravely misinformed." The 1899 estimates were not intended as definite, as such data had not then been available. He added that the entire operation had been accomplished within budget. For example, he had estimated the price of the ship at £39,000, and the actual cost had been £38,624. To make the figures come out favorably in this instance Sir Clements merely omitted the £11,000 the engine cost.[25]

Although at least one editorial endorsed the efforts of Colonel Royds, the Royal Society was horrified. The RS moved to assure Balfour privately that the Society had had nothing to do with any subterfuge about a possible future relief expedition. The RS representatives informed Balfour that the RS knew nothing about a relief expedition when the deputation met with him in 1899. Balfour believed them.[26]

When Sir Clements was told what the Royal Society had done, he too wrote to Balfour's secretary to explain that the RGS had nothing to do with any misinformation but that if blame were to be assessed it should fall on Markham alone. He acknowledged that the thought of a relief ship was in his mind in 1899 and assumed other people were thinking the same thing. He then reiterated how critical the previous year's relief expedition had been.[27]

The government's response to the request and to the escalating rhetoric was not known until Francis Mowatt wrote the two presidents on behalf of Mr. Balfour. The news was stunning.[28]

The government would come to the rescue of the stranded men — but for a price. Balfour's government demanded that, in return for rescuing Scott's party, the two societies must turn over all control for the relief expeditions to the government, including the ownership of the *Morning*. Mowatt requested an immediate reply as the time was short to effect a rescue in the 1903–4 season. The two societies were assured that the government did not mean to reflect on the conduct of the original *Discovery* expedition.[29]

The Royal Society quickly agreed to the government's terms but Markham, understandably, adamantly refused to hand over the *Morning* permanently to the government. In Markham's opinion, Balfour had acted with bad grace and had written a most insolent letter to the two presidents. For a time it appeared that a deadlock would result, for Sir Clements believed that surrendering the relief vessel was a "breach of trust." Then, while Markham was out of the country, the RGS council voted to agree to the government's plans. When he returned, Markham was persuaded that he had to sign over the *Morning*, for, as he put it, the government had a "pistol to our heads." Markham signed but did so "under protest."[30]

In one of the strangest interpretations of events of this four-year expedition, Markham wrote to Colbeck describing the circumstances of the government appeal, the refusal, and then the offer to help in return for control of the relief effort. Markham wrote that after the government's "brutal refusal," he and the Royal Society wrote again, but no reply was forthcoming. Markham stated that he then got the press to work and "seeing the feeling of the country, Balfour was obliged to crawl down."[31]

Others saw the situation differently. Longhurst thought that Markham had been badly treated: "It is not fair on Sir Clements. He has worked like a slave for the expedition and now practically at the end of it he gets his ship, the *Morning*, stolen from him and other people such as Sir William Wharton who have been anything but friends to the expedition stepping in and putting on the finishing touches to the work he has done."[32] The assessment of H. R. Mill, the preeminent polar historian of the early twentieth century, was that "if he [Markham] had only been a little quieter in asking for the money in the spring he would have saved himself a world of trouble and remained to reap his deserved reward." Markham was badly shaken by this turn of events. Mill understood that the fiasco had aged Sir Clements terribly and that his health had been badly damaged by it all.[33]

If Balfour thought he might save money by assuming control, he turned the entire affair over to the wrong people, a committee of naval men. Admiral Pelham Aldrich chaired the committee, which included Admiral Bays and someone who had been in opposition to Sir Clements throughout the period of the expedition, the Royal Navy's hydrographer, Sir William Wharton. Although Aldrich was the nominal leader, Wharton dominated the proceedings. Markham had hoped that Aldrich would be a more effective block to Wharton's plans but was disappointed in this expectation.[34]

The committee bought a second ship, the *Terra Nova*, a sturdy whaling vessel destined to be remembered as the ship Scott took to Antarctica on his last expedition. Built in 1884 at Dundee, the barque measured 187 feet long and had a beam of 31 feet. With a 120 horsepower engine the vessel was considered much more powerful than the *Morning*. Bernacchi considered it the best whaler afloat, an opinion others shared. Wharton purchased the second ship to accommodate Scott's crew in the event of the *Discovery* not being freed in the coming summer. The ship was completely refitted in naval yards at an undetermined cost. Shackleton became involved in the refitting of the *Terra Nova* and worked "with terrific enthusiasm." Wharton too praised the contribution of Scott's former lieutenant. Mill hoped that Shackleton would be given the command of the second relief vessel, but the committee chose a whaling master, Henry McKay.[35]

After four weeks of extensive refitting, which included a significant improvement to the engines to increase the power and speed of the vessel, the *Terra Nova* was ready for its trial. The ship performed well, making seven and a half knots in a preliminary run.[36]

In the meantime, invited by Sir Clements, Colbeck had decided to return to England to consult with his superiors. In England Colbeck went to the Admiralty and met with Wharton, and although the hydrographer's treatment of Colbeck was faulted by several people at the time — Markham described it as "niggardly" — the outcome was satisfactory. Colbeck was to remain as captain of the *Morning* and to have overall command of the two-ship expedition. Markham urged his commander to be firm with the hydrographer; any sign of weakness would be fatal. Markham wanted Colbeck to come over to Norway to consult with him, but the Admiralty would not allow the expense. But Colbeck did send a copy of his orders from the Admiralty to his former supervisor. Markham thanked Colbeck for this and reminded him that the captain of the *Morning* was responsible to the country and not to those "wretched jacks-in-office."[37]

Colbeck's orders from the Admiralty were to take the *Morning* to Hobart, Australia, where he would meet the *Terra Nova*. From there, after 1 December 1903, the two ships under his command would proceed together if possible to the ice to relieve Scott. He was to take eighteen months' provisions with him. All the men of the expedition, with or without the *Discovery*, were to return to Lyttelton at the end of the cruise.[38]

Markham spared no venom in his description of Wharton and his action. Sir Clements saw Wharton as "a terrible blunderer" who contributed nothing but obstruction and red tape.[39] The RGS president criticized several aspects of the hydrographer's ideas, principally the decision to send the relief expedition from Hobart, which Markham saw as Wharton's "foolish and spiteful" plan.[40] Given the need to coordinate magnetic observations with the observatory in Lyttelton, the *Discovery* would have to return there.[41] Sir Clements also ridiculed the "abominably bad English" in which the orders were written.[42] Markham once again changed his story about the cost of the relief expedition as he would have supervised it and determined that under the Royal Navy committee the effort cost nearly ten times as much. One of the few good things that came from the government takeover, Markham assured the captain of the *Morning*, was that with the command of two ships he was now a brevet commander.[43]

Finally, Sir Clements wrote a satirical poem about Colbeck's orders, which merits reading in full.

Proceed now to join the *Morning*
No report yet rec'd on her state
This is mentioned to give you a warning
So be sure that you are not too late.

A second ship comes out well launched
To fill both you must bear in mind

If the holds are exceedingly crowded
Why you can leave plenty behind.

Together both ships should be started
If both cannot go then let one
But yet they must never be parted
Though one is much better than none.

Keep company! 'tis all important
But not if you're stopped in the pack
To leave one you certainly oughtn't
So fail not to bring them all back.

The route through the ice must be taken
That you have once taken before
For we know of no other to mention
So cannot propose any more.

And when you return to New Zealand
To Plymouth you are to return
How to do it you'll ask Billy Wharton
'Tis a riddle you really must learn.[44]

As Colbeck prepared to depart for the South, Sir Clements reminded him that he and his people "belong to us" and wrote that now that he was rid of Wharton all would be better.[45] Markham credited Colbeck's firm handling of Wharton a reason for the success of the second rescue effort.[46] How wonderful it will be, Sir Clements thought, for Colbeck when he has once more forced his way under the shadow of Mount Erebus to "grasp Scott and his companions by the hand."[47]

To speed the rescue Wharton ordered an unprecedented action — the *Terra Nova* was to be towed most of the way to New Zealand by naval vessels, another hidden cost of the second relief expedition. Three men-of-war took shifts in towing her from England. As a result the ship from Great Britain to Australia was faster than most mail steamers.[48]

Captain McKay was regarded as one of the most experienced old Arctic hands and was considered by many to be an authority on Arctic matters. His long experience in polar regions had been gained whaling and sealing. Known as a quick and careful thinker, he was extremely popular with his crews. In Arctic whaling the crew drew most of their pay through a system of shares, that is, the men received a percentage of the profits. McKay's reputation for always being able to find seals and whales was based on his willingness to take calculated risks. McKay was said never to have had a cruise in which he lost money for his owners, a rare captain indeed.[49]

McKay was ordered to stay with Colbeck, and the two were to sail their vessels to Cape Crozier. If separated, the two ships were to rendezvous there. If on arrival the *Morning* was not yet there, McKay was to contact Scott, sledging over the ice if necessary to do so.[50]

McKay's crew was entirely civilian and composed of rough and handy men. Most of the thirty-seven aboard hailed from Dundee and had Arctic experience. Indeed, two members of the crew joined the ship directly from Arctic cruises.[51]

Colbeck took his ship out of Lyttelton Harbor 24 October, bound for Hobart to join the *Terra Nova*. Appropriately for several members of the crew, the band played at their departure, "The Girl I Left Behind." Rupert England had to be carried aboard, having injured his foot performing an act of kindness. Apparently he was a bit clumsy — during the winter in New Zealand he destroyed three bicycles and fell overboard trying to leave the ship for a formal dinner. The mishap with his foot was caused by his good-naturedly volunteering to clear something blocking a gutter at the hotel in which he was staying. A few minutes later the good Samaritan had fallen through the hotel's skylight, scattering glass everywhere. The uneventful voyage to Hobart ended 4 November 1903.[52]

By 1903 Hobart had played an important role in polar exploration. Ross had sailed from here in 1840. More recently, but little mentioned by members of Markham's expeditions, in 1898 Borchgrevink had sailed from Hobart en route to the first intentional Antarctic overwintering. The people of Hobart repeated the kind reception that Markham's ships had received previously in Christchurch.

The friendly relations between the two crews and the townspeople were not duplicated in their interactions with one another, however. The hostility deteriorated to fisticuffs on at least one occasion. One evening one tough old hand from the *Terra Nova* came down the wharf to tout the men of the *Morning*, and when Evans and Doorly approached him to urge him to return to his own vessel, the sailor pulled a knife. The Doorvan Twins (as they were known collectively in New Zealand) sprang into action and quickly — and without much attention to gentleness — subdued the man. They tied him up and took him back to the *Terra Nova*, where they turned him over to Captain McKay, who locked the man up for the rest of the night.[53] Subsequently, as the two crews proceeded south and struggled against a common enemy, the ice, they lost their animosity toward one another. By the time they arrived at McMurdo they operated as one team.

The *Terra Nova* had brought out a great number of supplies, courtesy of the Admiralty committee for the *Discovery*. Fully loaded, the two ships sailed from Hobart on 5 December 1903 and, after a day at anchor to allow the *Terra Nova* to rearrange its cargo, headed for south polar waters 6 December. Following orders, the two ships made a determined effort to stay together. Despite the different sailing qualities of the two ships, they did remarkably well at staying close. McKay's barque was considerably faster under steam than was Colbeck's, but under sail Colbeck's ship could zip past that of the Scotsman. Thus whichever method of propulsion was used, one or the other vessel had to proceed more slowly than it would if it had been alone. Both vessels sailed as much as they could to save coal.[54]

The voyage proceeded virtually without incident. One exception was on 17 December when the *Terra Nova* bore down on the *Morning* and, failing to break off as it should have, as the Scottish vessel was the weather ship, nearly hit the bowsprit of the other vessel. A moment of careless overzealousness that might have been disastrous passed with minimal damage.[55]

By Christmas the two vessels were in the ice pack, earlier and farther north than the year before. McKay and his first officer, A. P. Jackson, visited the *Morning* for Christmas dinner, and the *Terra Nova* captain entertained his companions with great stories from his Arctic adventures. He had been first mate on the *Terra Nova* twenty years earlier and had gone on to be the master of his own vessels for the past fifteen years. Two days later Colbeck returned the courtesy visit.[56]

As the two ships passed through the ice pack, Colbeck dropped behind McKay, for the latter's vessel was so much stronger. At times the *Morning* had trouble even following because of the amount of ice in the other's wake. At one point the two vessels were forced to stop and wait for the ice to clear.[57]

As the *Morning* and the *Terra Nova* ventured through the ice pack, the two parties had an opportunity to gather some scientific specimens. They shot a leopard seal and managed to find three examples of the even-then rare Ross seal.[58]

Even in the ice pack affairs of the heart have their moments. Before they had departed New Zealand, Evans's fiancée had entrusted to Doorly a series of letters that the latter was to deliver on specific days throughout the voyage. Doorly attempted to deliver them to Evans indirectly to keep him from guessing who the source was, although Evans probably knew. Later on in the season when Evans was out on a sledging journey, Doorly asked one of the seamen to play the postman. The letter was delivered on time.[59]

When the new year opened, the two crews spied Cape Adare one hundred miles in the distance; they were nearing their goal. Cruising down the coast of Victoria Land, by 4 January 1904 the two vessels arrived at Franklin Island. A party landed, but although a new record was left they had been unable to find the one deposited the year before. The penguins were so thick on the ground that the explorers had to kick them out of the way to make their way across the island. That same day one of the boilers on the *Morning* began to leak, the beginning of a series of serious engine problems that were to plague the ship for the rest of the voyage. Engineer Morrison was scalded in the incident but recovered.[60]

Knowing that the *Morning* was nearing the *Discovery*, Doorly climbed early one morning to the crow's nest to be the first to sight Scott's ship and nearly six hours later was rewarded by being the first to see the object of the journey. Shortly thereafter the two rescue ships found their progress blocked by impenetrable ice. When the *Morning* had departed the previous March the ice edge was five miles from Scott's winter quarters; now eighteen miles of thick ice separated the two ships from the *Discovery*.[61]

Meanwhile, Scott and Wilson had seen the two vessels and had gone to investigate. The two came aboard at four in the afternoon and began to learn the story of the expedition over the past ten months. A prearranged signal was sent to the *Discovery* to announce the relief ship's arrival, and Heald brought the word back to Scott's barque that two vessels were at the ice edge. Everyone aboard was wild with excitement. Royds noted in his diary that it was "ripping to know tomorrow we'll have mail." The men spliced the main brace in celebration.[62]

Aboard Scott's ship the speculation as to the identity of the second ship ran wild. The *Gauss*, the *Scotia*, or a man-o-war were among the favorite choices. The following day both the answer to that question and the first installment of the mails arrived, having been brought over by Dell and the dog team. The officers and men also began to glean some details about the political situation in which they found themselves. Royds complained about the amount of detail on the government takeover, but his correspondents gave him the essential outline: Markham had been nasty, and the government had taken over in response.[63]

Back at the *Morning* Wilson spent the day reading the large stack of mail awaiting him, and Scott read, rested, and thought about the newly defined circumstances in which he found himself. Among the letters that Scott received was one that stunned him: his orders from the Admiralty. He waited several days before announcing the orders to his crews. The message was direct and specific. Meanwhile, Doorly and Evans went off on a lark to visit the newly abandoned camp that Scott had been using at Cape Royds.[64]

By 8 January 1904 Scott's officers understood the outline of the Admiralty's orders, and on the tenth Scott addressed the men on the mess deck, to inform them. He told his crew that he had been ordered to abandon the *Discovery* if it could not be freed from the ice this summer. He related that the rest of his orders specifically outlined what he was to do. All present realized how stringently framed the orders were and the unprecedented manner in which they afforded no leeway to their captain. "The captain is much cut up and says he cannot yet realize abandoning the ship," was the comment of C. R. Ford.[65] Scott thanked the men for their loyal and devoted service. Seeing their captain's state, the men responded by giving him three cheers and "there's doubt he deserved it if ever a man does."[66]

Scott was "brokenhearted" by his orders. He had already begun plans for a third winter. Before the relief ship arrived, he had cut back on certain foods that he knew would be in short supply in coming months if the *Morning* did not return that year. He had also begun to ask for volunteers for the third winter. Because he estimated that he had up to five years supplies aboard ship and because scurvy had not reappeared — which he still believed was because of the abandonment of tinned meats — Scott could reasonably expect to survive another winter.[67]

On 10 January the *Discovery* was still eighteen miles from the ice edge. The previous year the distance had been one third of that, and yet the ship was never freed. Scott did what he could over the next three weeks in a series of desperate attempts to free his ship. He did not fail to see when something was not working: sawing at the ship was abandoned by 12 January, having been determined hopelessly futile.[68]

From the moment that the two relief ships arrived in McMurdo, the chances of the *Discovery* getting free looked infinitesimally small. At his most optimistic, H. R. Mill had hoped that Scott might already have broken free early in the summer and be there to "rescue the relief ships."[69] No such early breakout occurred.

If one searched for an optimistic detail in what seemed like a fairly hopeless situation, the thickness of the ice might have been a reason for hope. The previous year it had been fourteen feet thick between the two vessels; this year it was only ten feet.[70]

Scott ordered blasting to begin both near the ship under the direction of Royds and at the ice edge wherein he himself took charge. The relief ships brought out a good supply of gun cotton, but despite more than two weeks of intermittent blasting, the effect was negligible. Man-made efforts were insufficient; what was needed was a series of natural events that could break up and carry off the ice.

In preparation for abandoning his ship, Scott ordered that the scientific collections, instruments, and personal items of the officers and staff be transferred to the relief ships, with the *Terra Nova* receiving most of the material. The items moved were carried halfway by the *Discovery* men, and then the relief ship crews arrived and took the sledges back with them. Some provisions were taken in the other direction.[71]

The relief ship did bring a number of provisions, which were welcomed by the men. Royds issued tobacco from the new supplies to the men. Among foods, the return of fresh vegetables was most appreciated — "how one glories in fresh vegetables."[72]

The work of transferring instruments and specimens to the relief ships continued. At times this effort was backbreaking; one day it took six hours to drag the sledges two miles over a particularly difficult surface.[73] The two relief ships were doing their best to break through the ice and reach the *Discovery*.

This laborious process of trying to break through went on from the tenth through the eighteenth with slow progress. The *Terra Nova* would move back several hundred yards from the ice edge and then with full speed ahead ram into the ice. Sometimes the barque crushed a full ship's length into the barrier; other times the results were significantly less. The relief ship crews tried sawing again. The result was six feet progress in two hours. The backbreaking work was called off after a day. Blasting was also tried and still found wanting. Holes were dug, and sixteen to forty-eight pounds of gun cotton were lowered in and detonated. The resulting hole was not large, and no significant cracking of the ice resulted.[74]

On 19 January the weather cooperated. Ironically, the blizzard that arrived that day and called a halt to the man-made efforts accomplished more than previous activity had.

By 22 January the gap between the ships had narrowed to fourteen miles, better but hardly a reason to be optimistic. Then the next day the news changed: The relief ships sent word to Scott that the ice was going out rapidly. The ships were moving closer to one another.[75]

By 25 January the ships were separated by about a ten mile barrier, approximately four miles having gone out in the previous week. Two days later the temperature shot up to $+7°$ F, and more ice began to move away.[76]

A heavy snowfall on the twenty-sixth was thought by many on the three ships to put pressure on the ice, which would encourage it to break up and float away. By the end of January hopeful signs were appearing at both ends of the struggle. Cracks were noticeable in the ice near the *Discovery*; perhaps the blasting efforts of Royds were paying some dividend. Near the *Terra Nova* the ice continued to go out. Indeed, the decision to shift the half-way camp was made just in time, as the ice around the old one became broken and dangerous. Moreover, the ice near Scott's ship was melting. Still, Scott was justifiably cautious; the ice was not going out fast enough for him.[77]

On the last day of January eight miles of ice remained, but for the first time the swell of the sea was felt at Scott's ship. The work of transferring equipment continued, and one observer thought it painful to see the tearing down and carting away at Scott's vessel.[78]

Ford, the steward, celebrated his birthday on 4 February and noted in his diary, "My last birthday in the Antarctic, please God!" The blasting at Hut Point continued; now roughly only six miles of gelid barrier remained.[79] As late as 9 February the opinion in the wardroom was that chances were very slim that they would get out. Although down from eighteen to six miles, the previous year only five miles of ice blocked them and the ship was never freed. Scott was noticeably downhearted about the realities of having to abandon his ship.[80]

Even while all this was occurring, the ship had another lesson in the constant dangers that life in the Antarctic presents. Tom Crean was working near the ship when he fell into the water. Immediately unable to haul himself out because of the paralyzing effects of the icy water, his life hung in the balance. Fortunately, his cries for help were heard, and Allan and Smythe got a bowline around him and pulled him to safety. Crean was not a careless man, but one gets a sense of the risks involved in working around unstable ice, because after changing clothes Crean returned to work and fell in a second time and had to be rescued again.[81]

Although Royds had succeeded in opening some water near the ship, on 10 February Scott posted the orders for the abandonment of the *Discovery*. He also determined that regardless of the outcome, the *Morning* would sail on 27 February, as the danger of the smaller vessel waiting longer was too great. Part of the *Discovery* crew would sail with Colbeck at that time.

The *Terra Nova*, being a much more powerful ship, could risk delaying its departure a little longer.[82]

The wind picked up noticeably on the tenth. An indication of the state of mind of the men at this point was a key phrase written in one of the men's diaries, "weather bad, or should I say good." The hope for a storm, a rare thing for a sailor to wish for, was prompted by the belief that with the season so advanced, only a major storm could free the *Discovery*. As a result of the gale force winds, by midnight on 11 February only two miles separated the *Terra Nova* and the *Discovery*, but Scott's ship still remained encased in ice seven feet thick.[83]

More hands were put on the blasting detail. The *Terra Nova* continued to ram the ice with the *Morning* following rather meekly in its wake. Dawn of 14 February 1904 showed the progress that had been made but no one could be certain of anything. Close to the goal now but still perhaps hopelessly blocked, McKay was attempting to rally his men despite his own lingering doubts. At that point one of the sailors remarked that although they were not going to break through, a certain Captain Jackman could do it. McKay's ire was stirred, and throughout the day the ship feverishly butted the ice, the crew sallying as it charged into the remaining barrier.[84] Colbeck's vessel joined in, and to the men on the *Discovery* it looked almost like a race.[85]

By six o'clock in the evening McKay was within half a mile of Scott, the men of the whalers exhausting themselves sallying the ship, while the old barque ground away at the ice. By 11:00 P.M., with a mighty push the *Terra Nova* broke into the pool of water near the *Discovery*. Just after midnight, determined to free his ship from the block of ice that imprisoned it, Scott set off a series of blasts that shook the ship so violently that Hodgson was blown out of his bed. The explosions continued all day, but Scott's ship was still held by a sizable piece of ice.[86]

In the early hours of 16 February, with the ice showing signs of cracking from the relentless attack by the gun cotton, Scott tried another pair of massive charges. The retort was enormous, and then the ship shuddered and floated free. The men went crazy. Cheer after cheer from all three ships shattered the Antarctic stillness. Now Scott's vessel would not have to be left behind as some ghastly memorial to the terribly strong forces of the Antarctic climate. The *Discovery* was free.[87]

14

From Ice to Champagne

After two winters' confinement, on 16 February 1904 the *Discovery* was at last free and floating again. Yet within thirty-six hours of its liberation, Scott's vessel was nearly lost by a clear and present danger.

Everything happened so quickly on 16 February that some of the men from the blasting detail were still on the ice, digging holes for explosives, when the ship floated free, and they had to be rescued.[1] Before leaving the sight of his winter quarters Scott decided to have a short memorial service for Vince, who had lost his life in March 1902. A memorial cross was erected on the hillside above winter quarters. That took place at 5:00 P.M.[2]

To celebrate his ship's liberation Scott invited McKay and Colbeck to dine on the *Discovery*, and both joined the wardroom members of the *Discovery* in a joyous celebration. Singing was under way when the wind began to freshen. Soon a gale was blowing outside, and McKay scrambled to get back to his ship. Colbeck did not have a boat readily available and was delayed in returning to the *Morning*. Some men visiting from the *Terra Nova* were similarly caught on Scott's ship.[3]

The two relief ships headed out into safer water. Once in the severity of the storm the ships were driven miles from Scott's winter quarters. The gale was so severe that Rupert England was unable to bring his ship around until he had been blown past Cape Bird.[4] Scott kept his ship in the area of the anchorage.

The following morning Colbeck and two of his officers, having slept overnight on the *Discovery*, returned to their ship. Then a little before noon Scott gave orders to cast off, to take his ship around Hut Point. Then disaster struck. The winds were severe as the *Discovery* began to move, and Scott and his men were powerless to stop the leeward drift of their ship.

Within minutes the vessel had been driven onto the shoal on which the ship had struck bottom when it arrived at winter quarters.[5]

Once again the splendid scholarship of A. G. E. Jones provides significant insight into an aspect of Antarctic history. The whole episode occurred so fast that the officers had insufficient time to react. Wind and tide combined to fix the vessel more firmly on the shoal. Eight hours of agony followed as the *Discovery* was buffeted by the wind, waves, and sea bottom. Large sections of the false keel were ripped from beneath the barque and were seen floating to the surface. The ship's timbers were cracking with the helpless bumping of the vessel. The door jams on the cabins were so warped that the doors would not close correctly.[6]

The men worked to try to free the ship, using the engines and sails, but to no effect. Soaked to the skin, the men, including the extra hands from the *Terra Nova*, worked in the driving snow to try to save the *Discovery*, which seemed on the verge of breaking up. For a time several thought the back of the ship would break and it would be utterly destroyed. At one point during the afternoon Royds believed that Scott had given the ship up for lost.[7]

The decks of the helpless *Discovery* rose and fell; how the ship "buckled and bent was too awful for words."[8] As the day wore on nothing the crew did seemed to help. At a break for the evening meal the officers sat in silence, their anxiety increased with every creak and jolt of the ship. "Never was there a more despondent party than that which sat down to dinner," was Scott's assessment. He added that he was extremely dispirited.[9]

At six o'clock the wind had been at force 5–8 but an hour later had dropped to force 4–6. The direction also changed from south to south by southeast and then to southeast. At the same time the tidal current reversed its direction and began to run south. Then at 7:50 P.M. the ship began to work astern. The news of this latest change was brought down to the wardroom by an excited Mulock, and all scrambled to the deck to take advantage of the situation. Scott ordered the men to sally the ship, and with engines running full speed astern the *Discovery* began to move off the shoal and back into safer, deeper water.[10] Seeing the result, the men gave "three heartfelt cheers," and elation replaced desperation in an instant.[11]

Soon Scott's vessel was steaming up toward the *Terra Nova*, six miles away and tied up alongside preparatory to coaling from McKay's barque. At last the officers and men could breathe easy. Of the events of 17 February Royds wrote, "Never do I want another day like today." He added,

"Never do I want to go onshore in a vessel again, especially in these remote regions. The horrible thoughts that crowd through one's brain, and there above us, Vince's grave."[12]

The two ships were soon joined by the *Morning*. England indicated that he had seen the dangerous situation the *Discovery* had been in but, of course, he was helpless to assist. McKay added that he had been unable to see from where he was, but even if he had, nothing could have been done to help Scott's vessel.[13]

Looking back at their winter quarters from a different perspective than the one of the past two years, Royds noted how odd it looked. Then he added, "Yesterday's experience has driven what little regret there was away from me and for my part I was decidedly glad to know that we were seeing it and its surroundings for the last time."[14]

Despite the exhausting efforts of the day before, Scott ordered the ships to proceed to transfer stores and to coal. The coal issue was a particularly sensitive and important one for Scott. At first it appeared that the *Morning* could spare no coal, which struck Scott as curious for a relief ship. Colbeck reconsidered the situation and on the eighteenth transferred twenty-five tons of fuel to Scott, although this put the *Morning* at considerable risk in terms of its own supply and, significantly, added to the dangers of it being underballasted for the cruise to New Zealand. McKay next came alongside and transferred fifty tons, an amount Scott considered reflected his captain's "Scottish caution." The *Discovery* also took on seven thousand cases of provisions from the *Terra Nova*.[15]

That task completed, the three ships began moving north toward Wood Bay. Royds was greatly relieved, as he had been very concerned that two sailing ships should be in such quarters — so many bits of rigging to get entangled. As they sailed on, the spirits of all improved greatly, and the return of such pleasures as electric light, which Royds described as "simply ripping," made being at sea seem quite natural again even after two years of confinement.[16]

Scott was prevented by an oncoming storm from watering his ship and now decided to move up the coast to a point where this could be accomplished. Skelton had wanted to do it before leaving winter quarters, but Scott had been impatient to be away. Scott signaled the other ships to "follow me," and the small fleet moved northward. For a day the three vessels kept close company, but under sail alone (to save coal for possible exploration) the *Morning* zipped by the other two slower vessels. On the twentieth Colbeck asked for permission to take advantage of the favorable winds, and Scott signaled Colbeck to proceed on to the rendezvous in the Auckland Islands on his own.[17]

The two ships entered Wood Bay and watered the *Discovery* on 21 February. Royds knew the men were very tired and hoped to be able to rest a day or at least to proceed under steam to eliminate the need for the crew to be at the sails for a day. The first officer was disappointed when Scott impatiently called for sails to be set.[18]

The problems of the *Discovery* were not over. While the ship moved up the coastline the leak returned. At first Skelton was able to handle the problem, but on 22 February the pumps in the engine room became clogged, and the water began to rise. Soon it was up to the stoke hold plates, and Skelton had to let the fires out. Hand pumps kept the trouble at bay for several hours before the donkey boiler was lit, and Skelton's team gained control of the situation again.[19]

That crisis overcome, another more important one developed. The carpenter inadvertently noticed something wrong with the rudder and found that it was badly damaged and held together only "by some miracle."[20] The two ships hauled up in Robertson Bay, and the crew had a long day replacing the old rudder with the spare one. The new device was smaller and much less effective and suggested possible problems with accurate steering.[21]

Immediately after departing from Robertson Bay a strong ice blink indicated the presence of ice to the north. The two ships entered the ice pack and picked their way through it for the next few days.

En route north Scott resumed the series of soundings. He still hoped at this point to be able to go to Cape North to attempt to go beyond the area that Ross had explored in the 1840s. On 28 February 1904 the two ships lost sight of one another in bad weather, and the *Terra Nova* continued on to the Auckland Islands on its own. The storm was a fierce one; the *Discovery* took on a good deal of water. Several wardroom cabins were flooded. Royds, who hated such situations, sarcastically marked his disgust at the turn of events by noting, "Oh, it's real joy this is."[22]

Scott soon realized that his supply of coal was not sufficient for any real exploring and instead proceeded to the Balleny Islands and in the direction of Wilkes Land. Wilkes's sighting of land in a seemingly unlikely area had been contested since his announcement of the find. Scott decided to settle the question.

The *Discovery* reached the Balleny Islands sixty-three years to the day after Ross had been there. Scott was able to fix the location of the islands more accurately and then continued on for Wilkes Land.[23] On 3 March 1904 Scott sailed over the spot on the chart where Wilkes claimed to have seen land. Royds could not imagine how Wilkes could have made such an error. Scott was able to take satisfaction at having put an end to that misconception. At the same time, he decided that despite his desires, his coal supply — by this time about sixty tons — was barely sufficient to reach New Zealand and that he would have to break off exploring and head north. On that same day William S. Bruce made a major discovery on the other side of Antarctica — Coats Land.[24]

On 5 March the *Discovery* crossed the Antarctic Circle, a milestone Royds quietly hoped he would never again see.[25] Two days later the last iceberg was seen, and soon those hallmarks of the southern continent faded in the wake.

The *Discovery* then had a week of bad weather. The first rain in two years was a novelty; not so pleasant was the hail and the onslaught of several storms that followed. The men had a rough time of it, but good-natured humor still appeared in their diaries. Commenting on how they were soaked and miserable, Ford wrote that it was all right as it was all for "King and Empire."[26] On 14 March the Auckland Islands came into view and the following day Scott's ship dropped anchor in Sarah's Bosom, the sailor's popular name for Laurie Harbor.[27] Scott expected to find one or both of his companion vessels in port already, but neither was visible.

Five days passed before the *Terra Nova* came into view after a fairly good voyage. In the meantime Royds had had time to begin preparing the ship for port — painting and a general cleaning. The sight of green stirred the explorers, as did the prospect of fresh meat. Several hunting trips failed to bring in one of the pigs that were on the island, but a bull was found and shot. Shooting such domestic stock was forbidden, but Scott intended to settle with the owner when he got to New Zealand.[28]

Meanwhile, the *Morning* was nowhere to be found. Colbeck had a terrible run after taking leave of the *Discovery*. Gale after gale had hit the little craft on its journey. Water poured into the cabins, leading Doorly to remark wryly, "Who wouldn't want to be a sailor?"[29] On at least one occasion the seas were rough enough to bury the entire bowsprit under the water. In addition, the relief vessel had had a great deal of engine trouble, making sailing a necessity. Relentless winds kept Colbeck off course. The heartbreaking persistence of the winds at one point took the *Morning* closer to New Zealand than its goal in the Auckland Islands. Even when the winds lessened enough to turn in the right direction, the wind prevented

Colbeck from making much progress. At one point he talked openly of turning and running with the wind to New Zealand, but duty prevailed and he continued to his assigned harbor. Finally, tenacity won out, and on 20 March Colbeck brought his ship in to anchor near the *Discovery*.[30]

Another nine days were passed in Laurie Harbor preparing the ships for their return to civilization. The men needed the rest after their arduous voyages, and even though kept busy during the time here they appreciated the break prior to landing in New Zealand.[31] In addition to the men watering and painting the ships, the *Morning* had to take on ballast as it had been seriously under ballasted en route to the rendezvous. Scott also took back the collections and instruments from the *Terra Nova* and saw them safely onto the *Discovery*.[32]

The men of the ships had an unexpected visitor, the *Hinomoa*, a government vessel making its rounds searching the islands for shipwrecks and laying depots for such unfortunates. From the new vessel the news of the world reached Scott's party. World news figured prominently in the discussions, especially the Russo-Japanese War. However, one bit of personal information struck deeply — their old comrade Buckridge, who had returned with the *Morning* in 1903, was dead in a sailing accident. Not everyone was thrilled to see the *Hinomoa*, because it meant that word of imminent arrival would precede them to port and result in even more social engagements.[33] One thing from the visitor no one objected to was fresh potatoes and other vegetables.

On 29 March 1904 the *Discovery* sailed out of the harbor, followed by the other two vessels, and was swung for magnetic variation before setting a course for Lyttelton. Even in this relatively short run the sailing qualities of three ships made it extremely difficult for them to stay together. The *Morning*, now with damaged engines, had no chance of keeping up with the others under steam, and the other two ships were not the sailing vessel that Colbeck's was. Two days later with land in sight Scott remained offshore to avoid being signaled so that all three could enter the port together. On 1 April the trio entered the harbor at Lyttelton, with the *Terra Nova* in the lead, followed by the *Discovery*, and with the *Morning* last, "leaning heavily on the arm of the tug." The ships looked smart after the stay in the Auckland Islands.[34]

To the strains of "Home Sweet Home" played by the band onshore, the three ships came up to the dock. Clean white shirts, long hidden in cabin trunks, were worn by all who had them. A few visitors arrived by tug as the ships steamed up the entrance to the harbor, and the first aboard was

Mrs. Wilson, who had come to greet her husband of three years but had been separated from him for nearly all that time.[35]

As the ships came up to the dock, visitors threw baskets of food and flowers onto the decks. After a brief official welcome, reunions followed. Several of the men were reunited with their fiancées; others were met by friends, either of long standing or which dated from the outbound voyages. One tough, hard-bitten sailor was so overjoyed to see a friend when he came aboard that the bluejacket could not speak.[36]

No one was sorry to be back. After months of enforced emotional control, this Good Friday (as it happened to be) was described by one man as "one of the happiest days of my life."[37] Doorly wrote of the completion of the voyage: "So ends the voyage of the *Morning* to the South Polar regions. May it never be my lot to make such another voyage in such a weak powered vessel. The little *Morning* has had many scrapes and has got out of them in miraculous ways but I should fancy that any more voyages of a like nature would be tempting providence."[38]

The stay in New Zealand lasted more than two months. A round of celebrations, official receptions, and personal vacations occupied the time of the officers and men during their stay. All were given liberty and, judging from the amount of money the men drew from Royds, some must have had a pretty good time. In his diary Royds wrote, "What do the men want all the money for?"[39] Most were content to pursue their private lives, but for Scott the responsibility of leadership involved him in other matters.

One minor point can be quickly covered. That bull that had been shot during their stay in the Auckland Islands became a problem because the owner made a quick settlement impossible. In the end Scott and Royds had to appear in police court to pay a £50 fine. Their lack of concern for the matter was reflected in their next stop after the court: the local golf course.[40]

The second issue was far more serious. Newspaper reports indicated that Scott had been highly critical of the handling of the second relief effort. Two points were paramount: Scott's distress at being thought to have suggested that his men were in dire straits and needed rescue, and that he was quoted as saying that the *Terra Nova* was a terrible waste of money. That it was a terrible waste of money was not of import; what mattered was that officers were ill-advised to criticize the admirals running the Royal Navy.

Scott maintained that he had written nothing to indicate that a fatal disaster would result if succor was not forthcoming. Indeed, since he had first heard of the problem from Colbeck and others when the ships arrived in

January, Scott had received the news as a "bomb shell." Despite all efforts he could not remember a single item of an alarming nature that he had written to any of his correspondents. Newspaper reports published at the time that the ships arrived at Lyttelton did not ease matters. The press reported that Scott had been upset enough with the conduct of the second relief effort that he had refused to take provisions from the *Terra Nova*. That this was inaccurate did not mitigate the reactions in England.[41]

Scott also wrote to Admiral Aldrich, chair of the Admiralty relief committee, to thank him for all the work on behalf of the *Discovery*. In this letter Scott was careful to tell his superior that clearly the expenses could not have been avoided. He also expressed regret that somehow people concluded that the *Discovery*'s situation was serious.[42]

Having been stung by press criticism, Scott turned the fourth estate to his own purposes. Through the London newspapers, Scott denied any criticism of the Admiralty. Privately to his mother, Scott indicated his suspicions regarding who was behind the problem, Sir Clements. Although annoyed with his mentor's actions, Scott understood the goals of Sir Clements and thought he had acted with honorable intentions.[43]

With refitting and revictualing finished, the *Discovery* prepared for sea, and on 8 June 1904 Scott's crew cast off the lines, and the ship proceeded down the harbor to the open sea. Despite the desire to return to England to resume their lives, the hospitality of the people of New Zealand made the parting difficult. One bluejacket summed up the situation for many of his shipmates, "I have never felt so miserable in my life."[44]

One other event had occurred before the *Discovery* sailed from Lyttelton. En route south in 1901, Skelton spent a lot of time with the Meares family. Mrs. Meares was an attractive, appealing woman, and in the course of spending time with her and her husband, also a likable fellow, the chief engineer had met other members of the family. One particularly caught his eye. Before leaving New Zealand Reginald Skelton had become engaged to Sybil Meares.[45]

The route of the *Discovery* was from Lyttelton to South America, continuing the scientific program with soundings en route. While leaving New Zealand the crew were reminded that the farmers of that country had not forgotten them — twenty sheep were penned on deck at departure. Regrettably, the next day sixteen of the sheep drowned in a severe storm.[46]

By 8 July Scott's party arrived at Punta Arenas, Chile, described in the words of one officer as being a "wretched looking place" containing the dregs from other places.[47] From there the ship headed for Port Stanley,

Falkland Islands, which the same officer described as a "God forsaken place," a description no contemporary observer could ascribe to, as today Port Stanley has the manner of a small English village and charms, all despite occasionally uncooperative weather.[48]

In the Falklands the *Morning* caught up with the *Discovery*, but the latter left while Colbeck's ship was still in port. The *Terra Nova* had made an independent voyage home. Departing Port Stanley with another twenty sheep, the bad luck continued: Half their sheep drowned in a storm the following day.[49]

An ongoing problem of the voyage home was the emotional instability of one of the sailors, Whitfield, who had begun to show signs of depression since leaving New Zealand. Both Royds and Scott were involved in attempting to talk with the man and urging him to try to snap out of it. A guard watched his behavior, and although at one point Whitfield seemed suicidal, he improved en route to England.[50]

Pushing ever northward Scott arranged for the distribution of such things as the library, some of the china and silverware, and other trinkets from the ship.[51] A stop was made at Port Delgada, where Scott's men entertained the Prince of Monaco, returning from an oceanographic expedition. The prince was a leading researcher in this field.[52]

A week later the Lizard Lights were in view, and on 10 September 1904 the *Discovery* entered Portsmouth, transferring to London two weeks later. Well-wishers turned out in large numbers in both cities. The *Discovery* went up the Thames and dropped anchor in the East India Docks. Where the voyage had begun, the sailors had now returned.

Conclusion

The *Discovery* expedition was critical both because of the development of British Heroic Era exploration of Antarctica and because of the people introduced to the south polar regions by it. The essential question about the expedition was settled before the first sail was set: adventure triumphed over science to the extent that this was to be the only one of the four contemporaneous national expeditions that was not led by a scientist. Instead, a naval commander was chosen. That result came about because of the steadfast stubbornness of Sir Clements Markham.

In assessing the work of the *Discovery* expedition, several issues should be addressed. The first was whether Robert Falcon Scott was the best possible commander. The expedition might well have accomplished more with Bruce in charge, or at the least, an objective observer might have thought that in 1901. Given Markham's qualifications for the position, Scott probably was a better commander than the expedition deserved, for his ability as a scientific leader emerged as one of his strongest qualities.

Detractors have had a field day with Scott for the past twenty years, since the publication of Roland Huntford's *Scott and Amundsen*. Sadly, for Scott's family and supporters, Huntford's image of Scott is the one that many — perhaps most who have come to know the story since 1979 — have fixed in their minds.[1] By describing Scott on his first command, I have tried to give the reader a balanced view of him, his strengths and weaknesses.

Scott's critics will find more fodder in his actions of 1901–4: leaving New Zealand with more sheep than dogs, nearly losing his ship departing from winter quarters, the loss of Vince on a sledging journey, and his devotion to naval formalities. Indeed, one might well pose the question: What did Scott bring to this expedition that made his presence essential? Armitage could have commanded the ship; Bruce or Koettlitz could have directed the scientific staff.

Remember that Scott's actions during the *Discovery* expedition were severely limited by Markham and the restrictions that the RGS president established. Scott was to a large degree the agent of Markham's will. Scott also operated within the context of his times and his experiences: Britain, while still powerful, was perceptibly in decline relative to other powers; contemporary British hesitation to accept new ideas, especially from foreigners; and the Royal Navy, a conservative and hide-bound institution. Perhaps Scott should have risen above his circumstances more, but he did not always do so.

I have provided the reader with a more balanced view of the whole team of *Discovery* men. Too often in the past the focus has been on Scott and Wilson; splendid though they were, especially during Scott's second expedition, they were not the entire endeavor in 1901 to 1904. Sir Clements believed in the ability of the bluejackets of the Royal Navy to surmount every problem, to endure great suffering, and to do their duty. I hope I have persuaded you that, in this one respect, Markham was completely right.

Clearly, the geographical discovery aspect of this expedition was limited. More details were added to the knowledge of the Great Ice Barrier (Ross Ice Shelf),[2] King Edward VII Land was discovered (though not explored), and, most important, the vastness of the inland ice of East Antarctica was determined.[3] Taken together, hardly a good result for the £51,000 spent on an exploring vessel. The same conclusion applies to the limited oceanographic work in high latitudes.

Every other British expedition in the Heroic Era can trace its roots directly back to the *Discovery*. Indeed, one could make a case that for the entire twenty-one year period, all the important British players figured in Scott's first expedition.

That Scott's party did not accomplish more can be directly attributed to the limitations placed on the expedition by Markham's hand. Yet, for creating an endeavor virtually single-handedly, credit must go to Markham for the very existence of the expedition. The team's collective inexperience led to occasional difficulties, and, although disaster and tragedy did overtake the party, the list of catastrophes might indeed have been far longer given the crew's lack of expertise.

Mindful that the expedition was founded on the failed models of nineteenth-century British Arctic exploration, the accomplishments merit great praise. Setting forth for King and Country, armed with a strong sense of purpose and duty, the men of the *Discovery* accomplished a great deal in terms of science and adventure. Regardless of their individual and occasional collective shortcomings, and given their inexperience at the outset, the expeditions that followed 1904 owed a great deal to these pilgrims on the ice.

Notes

GJ   *Geographical Journal*
JMGS   *Journal of the Manchester Geographical Society*
PR   *Polar Record*
RGS   Royal Geographical Society
RGSCM   Royal Geographical Society Council Minutes
RS   Royal Society
RSCM   Royal Society Council Minutes
SGM   *Scottish Geographical Magazine*
SPRI   Scott Polar Research Institute
VOD   Robert Falcon Scott, *The Voyage of the "Discovery"*, 2 vols. (London: Smith, Elder, & Co., 1907)

PREFACE

1. Alexander William Kinglake, *The Invasion of the Crimea*, vol.1 (London: William Blackwood and Sons, 1877), xxi.

I. TO THE LAND OF UNSURPASSED DESOLATION

The title of this chapter comes from Louis Bernacchi, *To the South Polar Regions* (London: Hurst and Blackett, 1901), 65.

1. James Cook, Journal, February 21, 1775, cited in A. Grenfell Price, ed., *The Explorations of Captain James Cook in the Pacific as Told by Selections of His Own Journals, 1768–1779* (New York: Heritage, n.d.), 186.

2. All claims must be tempered by the realization that from Livingston or Deception Islands in the South Shetlands, on an exceptionally clear day the continent

is distinctly visible. Therefore, early seal hunters must have seen the continent before all three of these explorers.

3. For a full treatment of the issue of who discovered Antarctica, see A. G. E. Jones, *Antarctica Observed: Who Discovered the Antarctic Continent?* (Whitby: Caedmon of Whitby, 1982). A. G. E. Jones has made important contributions to the history of Antarctica and the polar regions.

4. Details of the meeting are disputed. See H. R. Mill, *Siege of the South Pole* (New York: Frederick A. Stokes Company, 1905). Mill's account remains the best introduction to the period before 1890, but a forthcoming work by Michael Rosove, *Let Heroes Speak* (Annapolis MD: Naval Institute Press, 1999), will provide the reader with a wonderful summary of Antarctic exploration to 1922 using, as much as possible, the words of the actual explorer to tell the tale.

5. For further information about the Enderby firm, see several references given in a splendid collection by A. G. E. Jones, *Polar Portraits* (Whitby: Caedmon of Whitby, 1992).

6. For a view of this expedition by one of its members, Lieutenant William Reynolds, see Anne Hoffman Cleaver and E. Jeffrey Stann, *Voyage to the Southern Ocean* (Annapolis MD: Naval Institute Press, 1988).

7. For a fuller treatment of the careers of both Rosses, see M. J. Ross, *Polar Pioneers: John Ross and James Clark Ross* (Montreal: McGill-Queen's University Press, 1994).

8. For a detailed account of the *Challenger* expedition, see Eric Linklater, *The Voyage of the Challenger* (London: John Murray, 1972).

9. For a detailed account of the decade of the 1890s, see T. H. Baughman, *Before the Heroes Came: Antarctica in the 1890s* (Lincoln: University of Nebraska Press, 1994).

10. Dundee *Advertiser*, 6 September 1892.

11. John Murray, "Notes on an Important Geographical Discovery in the Antarctic Regions," sGM 10 (April 1894): 195. Larsen was sent by Christensen, see Baughman, *Heroes*, 33.

12. Baughman, *Heroes*, 33.

13. Mill, *Siege*, 380.

14. To receive credit for an achievement an explorer must do three things: get there, get back, and be able to prove the accomplishment. In this respect the whalers or sealers who might earlier have landed on part of the continent do not meet the basic standards set for explorers.

15. John Murray, "The Renewal of Antarctic Exploration," gJ 3 (January 1894): 1–27.

16. "Antarctic Explorations," *Living Age* 206 (1895): 614–16.

17. "The International Geographical Congress," *SGM* 11 (July 1895): 474; Mill, *Siege*, 384.

18. Mill, *Siege*, 384–85. Although Mill put the motion before the congress, he was acting for and directed by Markham.

19. "Geography at the British Association," *SGM* 10 (July 1894): 473; Bruce to J. S. Keltie, 6 November 1895, 26 February 1896, 11 March 1896, RGS Correspondence.

20. For a detailed account of Borchgrevink's 1896 failed effort, see Baughman, *Heroes*, chapter 4.

21. "Geographical Notes," *SGM* 10 (February 1894): 100.

22. For a survey of the activities of the *Belgica* and for annotations related thereto, see Baughman, *Heroes*.

23. For a detailed account of the Cook-Peary fiasco, see Wally Herbert, *The Noose of Laurels* (New York: Athenaeum, 1989). Robert M. Bryce has published a more recent account, *Cook and Peary: The Polar Controversy Resolved* (Mechanicsburg PA: Stackpole Books, 1997).

24. Peter Kemp, ed., *The Oxford Companion to Ships and the Sea* (London: Oxford University Press, 1976), 767. Wiencke Island in the Antarctic Peninsula was named for the lost sailor. For Roald Amundsen's reaction to the death of Wiencke, see Roland Huntford, *Scott and Amundsen* (New York: G. P. Putnam's Sons, 1980), 57.

25. For a more detailed account of the *Southern Cross* expedition with annotations related thereto, see Baughman, *Heroes*.

2. THE DETERMINED OLD MAN

1. Regrettably, no full-scale biography of Markham exists, although Ann Savours is working on one for the Hakluyt Society. Markham's cousin, Admiral Albert Markham, published a biography in 1917, but Sir Clements deserves a thorough treatment. Recent historians have not always been kind to Sir Clements. Roland Huntford paints an unfavorable picture of him in *Scott and Amundsen*, 137–39, 142–43, and 146–47.

2. *Dictionary of National Biography*, s.v. "Markham, Clements R."

3. John Hemming, interview with the author, November 1994.

4. A. H. Markham, *The Life of Sir Clements Markham* (London: John Murray, 1917); and *Encyclopedia Britannica*, 11th ed., s.v.

5. Clements R. Markham, "The Present Standpoint of Geography," *GJ* 2 (December 1893): 483.

6. Mountstuart E. Grant Duff, "The Annual Address on the Progress of Geography, 1892–93," *GJ* 2 (July 1893): 2.

7. Many were misled by Ross's report of the Great Ice Barrier (Ross Ice Shelf) and thought this insurmountable ice wall surrounded the entire continent. Current scientists believe the ice in parts of the Antarctic is more than twelve thousand feet thick. Duff, "The Annual Address," 16–17, 17 quoted. I am indebted to Colin Bull for his help on this and other ice-related matters.

8. Murray, "The Renewal of Antarctic Exploration," 24.

9. Murray, "The Renewal of Antarctic Exploration," 29.

10. R. Vesey Hamilton, "On Morrell's Antarctic Voyage in the Year 1823, with Remarks on the Advantages Steam Will Confer on Future Antarctic Explorers," *PRGS* (old series), 14 (14 March 1870): 145–52; Murray, "The Renewal of Antarctic Exploration," 31–32.

11. Benjamin Leigh Smith and Murray did not attend the meetings. Markham memorandum, SPRI 1453/2; Clements R. Markham, "Address to the Royal Geographical Society," *GJ* 4 (July 1894): 21–22.

12. Report of the Antarctic Committee, 7 December 1893, RGS Committee Book, 145a–d.

13. *Dictionary of National Biography*, s.v. "Sabine, Sir Edward"; Jack Morrell and Arnold Thackray, *Gentlemen of Science* (Oxford: Clarendon Press, 1981), 353–70, 333 quoted. Morrell and Thackray have done an excellent job of unraveling the details behind the Ross expedition. Northhampton to Minto, 6 January 1839, reprinted in a second volume by Jack Morrell and Arnold Thackray, *Gentlemen of Science: Early Correspondence of the British Association for the Advancement of Science* (London: Royal Historical Society, 1984), 298–99; Clements R. Markham, "The R. G. S.: A Personal History of the Society," 53, RGS 47.

14. RSCM, 24 February 1894, 74.

15. RSCM, 22 February 1894, 74–75; RSCM, 6 December 1894, 132–34; Foster to Markham, 24 February 1894, RGS MS 1/1/4; Foster to Markham 2 November 1894; RSCM, 5 July 1894, 113–14; RGSCM, 5 November 1895, 3; Report of the Antarctic Committee, 1893–94, RGS 1/1/3; RSCM (6 December 1894), 132–33; *Nature*, 12 October 1893, 574.

16. RGSCM (26 November 1894), 1; Markham to the scientific societies of Great Britain and the Empire, 3 December 1894, RGS 1/2/1. The same letter was sent to a broad range of organizations.

17. Zoological Society of London to the RGS, 17 January 1895, RGS, 1/2/4.

18. Clements R. Markham, "Starting the Antarctic Expedition: A Personal Narrative," SPRI 1453/2; RGS Antarctic Committee Report, 5 November 1895, 283–84.

19. Markham to Goschen, 24 November 1896, RGS Expeditions Committee

Minute Book; Clements R. Markham, "Anniversary Address," *GJ* 9 (June 1897): 594–95.

20. Neale to Markham, 6 April 1897, reprinted in RGSCM, 10 May 1897, 1; RGSCM, 10 May 1897, 3, Report of the Expeditions Committee; RGSCM, 10 May 1897, 2.

21. Markham to Salisbury, 25 October 1897, RGS Committee Book, Expeditions Committee, 19 October 1897; "The Monthly Record," *GJ* 12 (July 1898): 75–76.

22. RGS Expedition Committee Report, 10 June 1898, 60.

23. For more on the relationship of the press to polar exploration at the turn of the century see the excellent account by Beau Riffenburgh, *Myth of the Explorer* (London and New York: Belhaven Press, 1993); Sir Clements R. Markham, "Address to the Royal Geographical Society," *GJ* 16 (July 1900): 10.

24. Sir Clements R. Markham, "The Antarctic Expeditions," in *Verhandlungen des Siebenten Internationalen Geographen Kongress* (Berlin: W. H. Kuhl, 1901), 623–24.

25. Markham, "The Antarctic Expeditions," in *Verhandlungen*, 625; the British explorer Edward Whymper (1840–1911) tried using dogs in a Greenland attempt and found them unserviceable.

26. Markham's views of sledging as a manly activity was shared by others. For Charles Beresford's opinion see Murray, "The Renewal of Antarctic Exploration," 33. On the benefits of dogs see Huntford, *Scott and Amundsen*, 100, 425–26; Frederick A. Cook, "The Antarctic's Challenge to the Explorer," *Forum* (May 1894): 512.

27. Markham, "The Antarctic Expeditions," in *Verhandlungen*, 629.

28. Clements R. Markham, "The President's Opening Address, 1898–99," *GJ* 13 (January 1899): 8–9.

29. James Geikie, "Antarctic Exploration," *SGM* 15 (May 1899): 256; "The Monthly Record," *GJ* 15 (March 1900): 287; quote, "The British National Antarctic Expedition," *GJ* 13 (April 1899): 425–26.

30. Markham to Sir Cuthbert Peek, 19 April 1899, RGS 2/2/4, Antarctic Expedition Box 1.

31. Parry to Markham, 10 May 1899, RGS 2/2/6.

32. Parry to Markham, 7 June 1899, RGS 2/2/7.

33. The Joint Committee's letter to the government estimated the cost at £100,000, although an earlier estimate had been placed at £71,000. Markham, Draft proposal of costs of National Antarctic Expedition, RGS 2/3/5; "The National Antarctic Expedition," *GJ* 14 (August 1899): 191–92.

34. Sydney Parry to Markham, 20 June 1899, RGS 2/2/9; quote, Parry to Markham, 16 June 1899, RGS 2/2/8.

35. "The National Antarctic Expedition," *GJ* 14 (August 1899): 193–94.

36. "The National Antarctic Expedition," 200.

37. "The National Antarctic Expedition," 200.

38. Francis Mowat to Lord Lister, president of the RS, 3 July 1899, reprinted in *Nature*, 13 July 1899, 256.

39. Parry to Markham, 3 April 1900, RGS 2/2/14; Parry to Markham, 6 April 1900, RGS 2/2/15.

40. For a detailed account of the era before the Heroic Era, see Baughman, *Heroes*.

41. The Royal Scottish Geographical Society asked for a place on the Joint Committee but was turned down by the RGS and the RS.

42. Clements R. Markham, "Proposed Constitution of the Administration of the Antarctic Expedition," RGS 1/5/1.

43. The other members appointed by the RS were: Lord Lister, A. B. Kempe, Sir Michael Foster, Professor A. W. Rucker, A. Buchan, Sir John Evans, Sir Archibald Geikie, Professor Herdman, and P. L. Sclater. For more information on Hooker, see W. B. Turrill, *Joseph Dalton Hooker: Botanist, Explorer, and Administrator* (London: Nelson, 1963). The RGS also named: Sir Clements Markham, Major Darwin, Mr. Hughes, Somers Cocks, Sir Anthony Hoskins, Rear Admiral Aldrich, Captain A. M. Field, Sir Richard Strachey, and Dr. W. T. Blanford. A curious omission from the RGS was Sir Erasmus Ommanney, the long-standing advocate of Antarctic exploration. Ommanney was miffed at being passed over, but Markham reassured him that no slight was intended, but rather, the decision had been made to spare him a great deal of tiring work. Markham to Ommanney, 18 August 1899, RGS Correspondence.

44. Minutes of the Joint Antarctic Committee, 26 June 1899, 6.

45. Markham, "Memorandum by the President," RGS 1/5/2.

46. Minutes of the Joint Antarctic Committee, 4 November 1899, 1; RGSCM, 2 November 1899, 2–3 and 13 November 1899, 1.

47. Clements R. Markham, "List of Meetings of Committees," RGS 1/9/4.

48. Poulton to the Council of the Royal Society, RS, 548; "The Belgian Antarctic Expedition," SGM 16 (May 1900): 296; H. R. Mill, "On Research in Geographical Science," GJ 18 (August 1904): 409.

49. E. von Drygalski, "The German Antarctic Expedition," GJ 24 (August 1904): 148.

50. William S. Bruce, "The German South Polar Expedition," SGM 17 (September 1901): 461, 466–67; H. R. Mill, "Address to the Geographical Section," SGM 17 (October 1901): 508; "On Research in Geographical Science," GJ 18 (October 1901): 409.

51. "The Swedish Antarctic Expedition," GJ 18 (December 1901): 627.

52. Peter Speak in an interview with the author, November 1988.

53. RGSCM, 18 February 1901; "The British National Antarctic Expedition," *Science* 13 (7 June 1901): 891.

54. Clements R. Markham, "Dates of the Antarctic Expedition," RGS 13/2/12.

55. Sir Clements Markham, *Antarctic Obsession*, Clive Holland, ed. (Alburgh, Harleston, Norfolk: Bluntisham Books, Erskine Press, 1986), 13; RGS 13/2/12.

56. *VOD*, vol.1, 24.

57. Huntford, *Scott and Amundsen*, 129–35. Further complications to Scott's appointment existed. To what degree Scott saw the expedition as an opportunity to advance his naval career is one question as yet unanswered.

58. Markham, "The Starting of the Antarctic Expedition," SPRI MS 1453/2.

59. RGS Committee Minutes, 18 November 1897.

60. The survey department attracted more staid men, whereas torpedo officers were more likely to gain rapid promotion in the navy. To Markham this meant that the latter were more likely to demonstrate the kind of daring needed.

61. Markham, "A Personal History of the Royal Geographical Society," RGS 47.

62. The members who supported Scott were Admiral Sir Anthony Hoskins, Admiral Sir Vesey Hamilton, Admiral Sir Leopold McClintock, Vice Admiral A. H. Markham, Captain May, and Captain Parr. Those opposing Scott's appointment included Admiral Sir William Wharton, Captain T. H. Tizard, Captain E. W. Creak, Captain Field, Admiral Sir George Nares, and Rear Admiral P. Aldrich.

63. Wharton had access to Scott's naval record, part of which has disappeared from the Public Record Office archives. Whether negative reports may have prejudiced Wharton seems to be impossible to know. Conversation with A. G. E. Jones, January 1994.

64. Minutes of the Joint Antarctic Committee, 4 May 1900; 25 May 1900; H. R. Mill, "With the *Discovery* to Madeira," GJ 18, 396; Markham, *Antarctic Obsession*, 129–30.

65. Roland Huntford suggests that Markham may have grown unhappy with his choice of Scott. Huntford, *Scott and Amundsen*, 133–34, 136.

66. RSCM, 28 May 1903; Clements R. Markham, "Objects of the Antarctic Expedition," RGS 1/5/5; Clements R. Markham, "Address to the Royal Geographical Society," GJ 18 (July 1901): 7; for details on the failure to capitalize on the *Southern Cross* experience, see Baughman, *Heroes*, chapter eight.

67. The bibliography, compiled by H. R. Mill, provides an interesting view of what had been written about the Antarctic to 1901.

68. RGS Committee Minutes, 1 May 1901; "Geographical Notes," SGM 19 (February 1903): 102; "The National Antarctic Expedition," GJ 18 (August 1901): 160; Clements R. Markham, "Address to the Royal Geographical Society," GJ 20 (July 1902): 1.

69. Bruce to Keltie, 22 August 1893, RGS Correspondence, W. S. Bruce.

70. Keltie to Bruce, 4 March 1896, RGS Correspondence, W. S. Bruce; Bruce to Keltie, 16 March 1896, RGS Correspondence, W. S. Bruce; Bruce to Keltie, 4 March 1896, RGS Correspondence, W. S. Bruce; Baughman, *Heroes*, 45–50; Mill to Bruce, 6 October 1897, SPRI MS 101/62/1; Mill to Bruce, 5 February 1898, SPRI MS 101/62/2; Mill, *Siege*, 380.

71. Koettlitz to Markham, 15 March 1900, RGS 3/3/18.

72. Bruce to Markham, 21 March 1900, SPRI MS 441/16; Bruce to Markham, 15 April 1899, SPRI MS 441/16.

73. Markham to Bruce, 17 April 1899, SPRI MS 441/16.

74. Mill to Bruce, 5 March 1899, SPRI MS 101/62/4.

75. Peter Speak, interview with the author, November 1988; Mill to Bruce, 5 March 1899, SPRI MS 101/62/4.

76. Mill to Bruce, 23 March 1900, SPRI MS 101/62/6; Markham to Bruce, 23 March 1900, SPRI MS 441/16.

77. The likelihood of more oceanographic work is highly probable, although the accomplishments in geology and geophysics might have been less. In addition, assuming Bruce had not overwintered his ship so far south, the vessel could have done winter surveying work in lower latitudes. For a refinement of this material I thank Colin Bull.

78. Markham, "The Question of an Ice Master for the *Discovery*," RS 548; "The Monthly Record," *GJ* 13 (June 1899): 654; Clements R. Markham, "Address to the Royal Geographical Society," 18 (July 1901): 11; Clements R. Markham, "Address to the Royal Geographical Society," *SGM* 17 (July 1901): 346; Clements R. Markham, "Dates of the Antarctic Expedition," RGS 13/2/12; Sir Thomas Sutherland to Markham, 18 December 1900, RGS 3/3/5. Armitage was close enough to Markham, or politically astute enough, to name his daughter, born 25 October 1901, Cicely Markham Armitage. Albert B. Armitage, *Cadet to Commodore* (London: Cassell and Company, Ltd., 1922), 150–51. Reginald Skelton thought Armitage overstated his importance to the planning and execution of the expedition and that Armitage was unliked on the expedition. Markham to Admiralty, n.d., RGS 3/3/6; Evan MacGregor to Markham, 25 February 1902, RGS Correspondence.

79. Markham memorandum, n.d., RGS 3/3/28; Markham, "The R. G. S.," 47; Markham to Admiralty, 16 June 1900, RGS 3/3/29; Markham to Royds 18 June 1900, RGS Correspondence, notifying him of his appointment; Report of the Executive Committee, 8 June 1900, RS 548; Minutes of the Joint Antarctic Committee, 4 May 1900, 1; Angus Erskine, "The Men of the Discovery," *Naval Review* 57 (1969): 311.

80. Markham to Admiralty, 12 April 1901, RGS 3/3/12; MacGregor to Markham, 19 April 1901, RGS 3/3/13; Markham, Notes on the Expedition, RGS 3/1/22; Min-

utes of the Joint Antarctic Committee, 15 June 1900; Scott to Markham, 12 September 1900, RGS 3/2/10; Erskine, "The Men of the Discovery," 311.

81. H. R. Mill, *The Life of Sir Ernest Shackleton* (Boston: Little, Brown, and Company, 1923), 28.

82. Mill, *Shackleton*, 20.

83. Following the conquest of the Pole by Amundsen and Scott in 1911 and 1912, Shackleton attempted the last great Antarctic geographical feat, the crossing of Antarctica. His *Endurance* expedition was caught in the ice in the Weddell Sea en route to landfall, and against the most extreme odds, Shackleton led his men across ice floes to a safe haven on Elephant Island. Then he sailed eight hundred miles in a small open boat to South Georgia, which he crossed virtually without equipment. Shackleton then returned to rescue the remainder of his men from Elephant Island and bring the entire party under his direct command to safety without a single loss of life. Unable to adjust to life apart from exploring, Shackleton organized the *Quest* expedition and was en route south when he died of a heart attack at South Georgia 5 January 1922. His death marks the end of the Heroic Era.

84. Mill, *Shackleton*, 289.

85. "Speeches at the Unveiling of the Shackleton Memorial," *GJ* 79 (March 1932): 165.

86. Mill, *Shackleton*, 53–55; Roland Huntford, *Shackleton* (New York: Fawcett Columbine, 1985), 25.

87. Mill, *Shackleton*, 53–55.

88. L. C. Bernacchi, *Saga of the Discovery* (London and Glasgow: Blackie & Son, 1938), 213. Huntford indicated that Markham was told to appoint Shackleton by Longstaff. Huntford, *Shackleton*, 29.

89. Report from the Executive Committee, November 1900, 3; Markham, *Antarctic Obsession*, 15, 77–79; Mill, *Shackleton*, 58.

90. Markham, *Antarctic Obsession*, 15.

91. Minutes of the Joint Antarctic Committee, 4 May 1900; *The Argus* (Melbourne), 18 January 1916, 7; Koettlitz to Markham, 3 March 1900, RGS 3/3/16; Geikie to Markham 16 March 1900, RGS 3/3/19; Harmsworth to Markham, 23 March 1900, RGS 3/3/20; Harmsworth to Markham, 26 March 1900, RGS 3/3/21; Vesey Hamilton to Markham, 31 March 1900, RGS 3/3/23; D. W. H. Walton, "Profile: Albert Borlase Armitage," *PR* 140 (May 1985): 515; Markham, "Starting the Antarctic Expedition: A Personal Narrative," SPRI MS 1453/2, 83; Minutes of the Joint Antarctic Committee, 4 December 1899 and 4 May 1900; "Geography at the British Association," *GJ* 14, 549; "Geography at the British Association," *Nature* 61 (2 November 1899): 19.

92. Report on Medical Examinations of Officers, 4 January 1901, RGS 3/1/5; Ann

Savours, ed., *Edward Wilson, Diary of the Discovery Expedition to the Antarctic Regions, 1901–1904* (New York: Humanities Press, 1967), 2 July 1901; Report on Medical Examination of Officers, 4 January 1901, RGS 3/1/4, penciled note in margin in Markham's hand; Report from the Executive Committee, November 1900, H. R. Mill, "A Collection of Unpublished Documents Relating to the National Antarctic Expedition," SPRI MS 367/23.

3. OLD MEN BICKER

1. Hugh Robert Mill, "Antarctic Research," *Nature* 57 (3 March 1898): 416.
2. Markham to Lister, 4 October 1899, RGS 1/6/1; Minutes of the Joint Antarctic Committee, 24 May 1898, 1; RGSCM, 13 March 1899, 7; von Drygalski, "The German Antarctic Expedition," *GJ* 13 (April 1899): 409.
3. Minutes of the Royal Society Antarctic Committee, 24 May 1898; Report of the Executive Committee, May 1900, RGS 1/6/2; von Drygalski, "The German Antarctic Expedition," *GJ* 13 (April 1899): 409; Clements R. Markham, "The Antarctic Expeditions," 14 (November 1899): 480; and "Polar Regions," 16 (December 1900): 689.
4. Markham to the RGS Council, undated, RGS 1/7/2.
5. Clements R. Markham, "Memo on the Joint Committee," RGS 1/7/2.
6. Clements R. Markham, "Memo on the Joint Committee," RGS 1/7/2; Foster to Markham, 3 December 1900, 1/7/4.
7. Markham to Foster, 5 December 1900, RGS 1/7/5; Foster to Markham, 7 December 1900, RGS 1/7/6.
8. Markham, "Plan of Operations for the National Antarctic Expedition," RS 548, 6–8.
9. Markham, "Plan of Operations," 9–11.
10. Markham, "Plan of Operations," 12–14.
11. Markham, "Plan of Operations," 16.
12. Markham, "Plan of Operations," 15–30; Markham, "Objectives of the Antarctic Expedition and Plan of Operations," 1897, RGS 1/5/5.
13. Markham, "Starting the Antarctic Expedition: A Personal Narrative," SPRI MS 1453/2, 138.
14. The characterization that the nineteenth-century British Arctic expeditions were a success is a highly debatable conclusion.
15. Markham, "Starting the Antarctic Expedition," 2.
16. Draft Instructions to the Director of the Scientific Staff, RS 548.

17. Poulton to the Fellows of the Royal Society, 15 May 1901, RS 548; Markham, "Memorandum by the President on Dr. Gregory," RGSCM, 18 February 1901.

18. Markham to Gregory, 30 January 1901, RGS 4/1/10.

19. Gregory to the Royal Society Members of the Joint Committee, 28 January 1901, RS 548.

20. Gregory to Royal Society Representatives of the Joint Committee, 28 January 1901, RS 548; Poulton to Fellows of the Royal Society, 15 May 1901, RS 548.

21. Markham to the Joint Committee, 1 February 1901, RGS 4/1/11.

22. Minutes of the Joint Antarctic Committee, 8 February 1901, RS, 548; "Proposed Amendments to the Instructions for the Director of the Scientific Staff," RS 548; "Proposed Amendments to the Commander's Draft Instructions," RS 548.

23. Markham, *Antarctic Obsession*, 137.

24. Minutes of the Joint Antarctic Committee, 12 February 1901; Poulton to the Fellows of the Royal Society, 15 May 1901.

25. Poulton to the Fellows of the Royal Society, 15 May 1901, RS 548; Minutes of the Joint Antarctic Committee, 12 February 1901, RGS 1/9/1; "Proposed Amendments to the Commander's Draft Instructions," 8 February 1901.

26. Poulton to the Fellows of the Royal Society, 15 May 1901, RS 548; Hoskins to the president of the RGS, 28 February 1901, 1/9/6; Minutes of the Joint Antarctic Committee, 19 February 1901.

27. Hamilton to the president of the RGS, 28 February 1901, RGS 1/9/6.

28. "Memorandum on the Recent Negotiations Concerning the National Antarctic Expedition, Presented to the Council by the Officers," RS 548; Minutes of the Joint Antarctic Committee, 5 March 1901.

29. RGSCM, 27 March 1901, 4.

30. Markham to Huggins, 2 April 1901, letter one. Markham wrote two letters that day, and they are noted as "letter one" and "letter two."

31. Markham to Huggins, 2 April 1901, letter one.

32. Markham to Huggins, 2 April 1901, letter one.

33. Historian Markham qualified his comment owing to an instance on an 1852 Arctic expedition on which the captain had allowed a boat party to proceed on its own under a separate command.

34. Markham to Special Committee, n.d., SPRI MS 367/18.

35. Markham to Huggins, 2 April 1901, letter two.

36. RGS to RS, draft of letter, RGS 1/9/4.

37. Goldie traveled widely in Africa in the last thirty-five years of the nineteenth century. He is often referred to as the founder of Nigeria. As prominent a figure in British colonial affairs as Cecil Rhodes, Goldie had a passion for anonymity, which

he carried to the lengths of burning his personal papers before he died. For details of his life see Dorothy Wellesley, *Sir George Goldie, Founder of Nigeria* (London: Oxford University Press, 1960) and John E. Flint, *Sir George Goldie and the Making of Nigeria* (1960).

38. Markham, *Antarctic Obsession*, 35.

39. "Memorandum on Recent Negotiations," 3.

40. RSCM, 13 June 1901, 205.

41. "Memorandum on Recent Negotiations," 3, 48.

42. RSCM, 13 June 1901, 205.

43. *Nature*, 23 May 1901, 83.

44. For the other, see chapter four on the impact of the *Discovery* on British Antarctic exploration.

45. Royal Society Committee Minutes, 13 June 1901.

4. FROM THE EAST INDIA DOCKS

1. Three previous accounts tell the story of the *Discovery*: Albert B. Armitage, *Two Years in the Antarctic* (London: Edward Allen, 1905); *VOD*; and Ann Savours, *The Voyages of the Discovery: The Illustrated History of Scott's Ship* (London: Virgin Books, 1992). This latter book was published during the time that I was working on this account, and I waited until I had finished the draft of this work before reading it.

2. Markham noted that the "old *Discovery* is rotten," and in his own account of the saga of the *Discovery* Markham made it clear that no other suitable ship existed. Yet other ships — whalers — were available, one of which Markham purchased as a relief ship. Markham, *Antarctic Obsession*, 19; Mill, "A Collection of Unpublished Documents," 26.

3. Markham's own report indicated that whalers existed that could transport the expedition to and from the ice. Of the other ships used in the Heroic Era, only the *Gauss* and Charcot's two ships were purpose built.

4. The *Fram* was built by Fridtjof Nansen for use in his expedition to drift over the Arctic ice pack from 1893 to 1896. The *Fram* is currently on display in Oslo. Nearby is the *Gjoa*, the boat Roald Amundsen used on the first successful voyage through the Northwest Passage. For a detailed account of the *Discovery* by its architect, see W. E. Smith's article in *Proceedings of the Institution of Naval Architects*, April 1905. A good one-page summary can be found in Appendix B of Savours, *Wilson Diary*, 405.

5. For a drawing showing a comparison between the *Discovery* and the *Fram*, see *VOD*, vol.1, 39.

6. Bruce, "The German South Polar Expedition," 460–61.

7. "Proposed Constitution of the Administration of the Antarctic Expedition," RGS 1/5/1; Minutes of the Joint Antarctic Committee, 5 May 1899, 6; 12 December 1899; Markham, "The R. G. S.," 47.

8. George Murray to Markham, 23 February 1901, RGS 4/2/11; Joint Committee Minutes, 12 February 1901, RGS 1/19/1.

9. During his stay in Dundee, Skelton resided in the Queen's Hotel, which today still overlooks the *Discovery*, now moored at Discovery Point. After the initial voyage, the *Discovery* served in a variety of tasks, including additional service in the Antarctic. Eventually, the ship was moored in the Thames for many years and is now berthed at Dundee, Scotland, where the vessel is wonderfully presented and is a centerpiece of Dundee tourism. For a thorough and excellent account of the ship and its story, see Savours, *Voyages*.

10. Scott, Letter of Proceeding number four, December 1900, RS 548; "Polar Regions," *GJ* 19 (January 1902): 97; Robert F. Scott, "The National Antarctic Expedition," *GJ* 24 (July 1904): 29; W. S. Bruce, "The German South Polar Expedition," 250.

11. *The Press* (Christchurch), 21 December 1901, 9; *Lyttelton Times*, 29 November 1901, 5.

12. *Canterbury Times* (Christchurch), 4 December 1901, 46.

13. Bernacchi, *Saga*, 8.

14. "Memorandum by the President," n.d., RGS 1/5/2; Armitage, *Two Years*, 9–10; Bernacchi, *Saga*, 9–10.

15. *The Press* (Christchurch), 29 November 1901, 5; *Lyttelton Times*, 29 November 1901, 5.

16. "The British and German Antarctic Ships," *Nature* 63 (18 April 1901): 591.

17. *Lyttelton Times*, 29 November 1901, 5.

18. *Lyttelton Times*, 29 November 1901, 5.

19. Editorial, *The Times*, 20 March 1901, 13; *Canterbury Times*, 4 December 1901, 45; Bernacchi, *Saga*, 12–13.

20. *Canterbury Times*, 4 December 1904, 46.

21. Savours, *Wilson Diary*, 16.

22. *The Standard*, 7 June 1901, 2.

23. *VOD*, vol.1, 24.

24. Huntford, *Scott and Amundsen*, 123–24, 132–33; A. G. E. Jones, interview with the author, January 1994.

25. Armitage, *Cadet*, 130.

26. On the question of holding a grudge, note Scott's later behavior in the controversy with Shackleton over the location of the latter's expedition base or his ar-

gument with Armitage when after the expedition, Armitage lectured and published a book on the voyage. D. W. H. Walton, "Profile: Albert Borlase Armitage," *PR* 140 (May 1985): 515; Armitage, *Cadet*, 156; for Scott on Borchgrevink, Scott to Keltie, 15 July [1901], RGS 20/50.

27. D. W. H. Walton, "Profile: Albert Borlase Armitage," 516. Roland Huntford described Scott as having a "weak personality" and being "uncertain of himself" at the time of the *Discovery* expedition; see Huntford, *Shackleton*, 31.

28. Armitage, *Cadet*, 130.

29. Armitage, *Two Years*, viii, 33. By that time Armitage was heavily involved in the expedition. The child's godfathers were Markham and Longstaff.

30. Armitage to Markham, 5 June 1900, RGS 7/1/1. Koettlitz agreed on the need for more sugar than one might expect. Koettlitz to Scott, 9 November 1900, RGS 7/1/2.

31. Armitage to Markham, 5 June 1900, RGS 7/1/1. Regrettably, no archive for the Borchgrevink expedition exists to match the material held at the RGS on the *Discovery* expedition. Given the success of the *Southern Cross* commander in terms of materials, the glimpse provided by the *Discovery* planners shows that Borchgrevink deserved much praise for his selections of equipment and foodstuffs.

32. Armitage to Markham, 5 June 1900, RGS 7/1/1; Scott found Nansen "as practical as they make them": see SPRI MS 342/28/6.

33. Armitage to Markham, 5 June 1900, RGS 7/1/1; Markham, "The Antarctic Expeditions," in *Verhandlungen*, 625.

34. Armitage to Markham, 5 June 1900, RGS 7/1/1.

35. Koettlitz was thought by Markham, and others, to be a little unworldly.

36. Koettlitz to Scott, 9 November 1900, RGS 7/1/2, and for not scrimping on provisions see Koettlitz to Scott, 15 November 1900, RGS 7/1/3.

37. Medical Report on Discovery Officers and Scientists, 4 January 1901, RGS 3/1/5.

38. Clive Holland, *Arctic Exploration and Development, c. 500 B.C. to 1915* (New York & London: Garland Publishing, 1994). No scholar working in Arctic or Antarctic history can fail to acknowledge the benefits derived from this splendid and essential work.

39. For example, Skelton might have profited from such an examination, because en route south he had to have dental surgery aboard ship as the doctors removed a tooth and fragments of jaw.

40. "Memorandum on Royal Society-RGS Cooperation," n.d., RS 548, F 7.

41. "Memorandum on Royal Society-RGS Cooperation," F 7; quote, Scott to Keltie, n.d., RGS Correspondence.

42. *VOD*, vol.1, 52. Near the end of the *Discovery* expedition in a letter to Keltie,

Bernacchi wrote of Borchgrevink, noting that the *Southern Cross* commander has "sunk into as deep an oblivion as the builder of Stonehenge," Bernacchi to Keltie, 18 July 1904, RGS Correspondence.

43. C. S. Wright, "The Ross Barrier and the Mechanism of Ice Movement," *GJ* 65 (March 1925): 215.

44. Clements R. Markham, "Dates of the Antarctic Expedition," RGS 13/2/12.

45. Bernacchi, *Saga*, 3.

46. Janet Crawford, "The First Antarctic Winter," SPRI MS 1367, 309.

47. Scott to Keltie, n.d. [1900–1901], RGS Correspondence; Minutes of the Joint Antarctic Committee, 15 June 1900; Janet Crawford, "The First Antarctic Winter," SPRI MS 1367, 353.

48. RGSCM, 26 November 1900.

49. RGSCM, 26 November 1900. Markham was virtually incapable of writing an unbiased account of anything related to polar history.

50. Armitage, *Two Years*, x; Mill to Markham, 1 November 1901, RGS 1/8/6; Borchgrevink to Mill, 23 August 1898, SPRI MS 100/12/3; Koettlitz to Mill, 13 April 1900, SPRI MS 100/59/1; for Scott's appreciation see Scott to Mill, 6 November 1901, SPRI MS 100/100/1 and Scott to Mill, 17 December 1901, SPRI MS 100/100/2; quote, Scott to Mill, 17 December 1901, SPRI MS 100/100/2.

51. Mill, *Shackleton*, viii; quote, SPRI MS 100/106/16.

52. Shackleton to Mill, 24 December 1901, SPRI MS 100/106/1; Shackleton to Mill, undated, SPRI MS 100/16/2; quote, Shackleton to Mill, 15 March 1921, SPRI MS 100/106/17.

53. W. S. Bruce, "Cruise of the *Balaena* and the *Active* in the Antarctic Season, 1892–93," *GJ* 7 (May 1896): 503.

54. Donald to Mill, 20 August 1892, SPRI MS 100/25/1.

55. William Speirs Speak, *The Log of the "Scotia" Expedition, 1902–4*, ed. Peter Speak (Edinburgh: Edinburgh University Press, 1992), 24, 287; Borchgrevink to Mill, 8 October 1897, SPRI MS 100/12/2; Mill to Bruce, 6 October 1897, SPRI MS 100/62/1; Mill to Bruce, 5 February 1898, SPRI 100/62/2.

56. *Morning Post*, 20 August 1898; *St. James Gazette*, 20 August 1898.

57. Hugh B. Evans and A. G. E. Jones, "A Forgotten Explorer: Carsten Egeberg Borchgrevink," *PR* 17 (September 1974): 106, 226.

58. Mill to Bruce, 5 March 1899, SPRI 100/62/4.

59. Speak, *Scotia*, 25.

60. Markham to Mill, 19 October 1901, SPRI 100/70/5.

61. Markham, *Antarctic Obsession*, 25.

62. I have a long-standing admiration for Mill that comes from reading the correspondence to and from him. If time and finances permit, I would like to write a

biography of Mill entitled, "Friend to Heroes: The Life of H. R. Mill," Regrettably, the commercial potential of such a work would be negligible. Instead, I shall try to write a long biographical essay on Mill. No one deserves it more.

63. "The National Antarctic Expedition," *Nature* 64 (20 June 1901): 182–83.

64. *Western Morning News*, 27 August 1901.

65. *Pall Mall Gazette*, 24 July 1901, 7. Armitage was reported to have spent long hours in the crow's nest of the *Windward* during the voyage to Franz Josef Land when the ship's captain was incapacitated. *The Press* (Christchurch), 29 November 1901, 5.

66. *Daily Mail*, 31 July 1901.

67. *The Press* (Christchurch), 29 November 1901. 5; "Question of an Ice Master for the *Discovery*," RS 548, EE, 2.

68. "Question of an Ice Master for the *Discovery*," RS 548, EE, 2–3.

69. *Western Morning News*, 27 August 1901; *Pall Mall Gazette*, 24 July 1901, 7.

70. Scott, Diary, 31 July 1901, SPRI MS 352/1/1.

71. *Pall Mall Gazette*, 1 August 1901, 6.

72. Sir George Goldie to Scott, 29 July 1901, SPRI MS 366/15/10. Markham, of course, was aboard throughout.

73. *Pall Mall Gazette*, 1 August 1901, 6.

74. Savours, *Wilson Diary*, 30 July 1901.

75. *Pall Mall Gazette*, 1 August 1901, 6.

76. Frank Wild, Memoirs, SPRI MS 1139, 16.

77. Savours, *Wilson Diary*, 5 August 1901.

78. *The Press* (Christchurch), 30 November 1901, 8.

79. Savours, *Wilson Diary*, 5 August 1901.

80. *The Press* (Christchurch), 30 November 1901, 8.

5. FROM ENGLAND TO CAPE TOWN

1. The Admiralty had given special permission for the *Discovery* to fly the blue ensign. Technically, England was still visible the next morning.

2. *Pall Mall Gazette*, 1 August 1901, 6.

3. George Murray to Mill, 27 June 1901, SPRI MS 367/9.

4. George Murray to Mill, 26 June 1899, SPRI MS 367/8.

5. George Murray to Mill, 23 October 1900, SPRI MS 367/9.

6. George Murray to Mill, 24 February 1901, SPRI MS 367/9.

7. Mill, "A Collection of Unpublished Documents."

8. George Murray to Mill, 24 February 1901, SPRI MS 367/9.

9. George Murray to Mill, 24 February 1901, SPRI MS 367/9.

10. Markham, "Dates of the Antarctic Expedition," RGS 13/2/12. J. W. Gregory was also on the voyage of the *Oceana* in November 1898.

11. *The Press* (Christchurch), 29 November 1901, 5.

12. In his journal Skelton made special note of successful hauls. Savours, *Wilson Diary*, 8 August 1901.

13. George Murray to H. R. Mill, 23 October 1900, SPRI MS 367/9.

14. *Lyttelton Times*, 7 December 1901, 8; Savours, *Wilson Diary*, 8 September and 30 October 1901. Shackleton to Keltie, 6 November 1901, RGS Correspondence.

15. *The Press* (Christchurch), 29 November 1901, 5.

16. Editorial, *The Times*, 20 March 1901, 13.

17. *The Press* (Christchurch), 29 November 1901, 5; Albert B. Armitage, *Two Years*, 116; Scott, "The National Antarctic Expedition," GJ 18 (September 1901): 277; *Pall Mall Gazette*, 18 July 1901, 2.

18. Markham, *Antarctic Obsession*, 70–93.

19. *The Press* (Christchurch), 29 November 1901, 5.

20. *Pall Mall Gazette*, 18 July 1901, 2.

21. Armitage, *Cadet*, 149.

22. Scott to Keltie, 6 November 1901, RGS Correspondence.

23. Scott, "The National Antarctic Expedition" (1901): 277.

24. Savours, *Wilson Diary*, 16 August 1901.

25. Savours, *Wilson Diary*, 23 July 1901.

26. Ferrar's father was the Durban manager of the Natal Bank. *Canterbury Times*, 4 December 1904, 47; *Lyttelton Times*, 2 December 1901, 5. After the *Discovery* expedition, Ferrar worked in Egypt and New Zealand. He served in the First World War and from 1919 to 1932 was an outstanding figure in the New Zealand scientific community. He died suddenly after a minor operation. Bernacchi, *Saga*, 230–31; *Pall Mall Gazette*, 18 July 1901, 2.

27. Barne, Diary, 26 September 1901.

28. Bernacchi, *Saga*, 22.

29. Savours, *Wilson Diary*, 9 September 1901.

30. Wilson's illustrations are magnificent, and the reader is well advised to seek them out, most readily in Savours, *Wilson Diary*, or one of the Seaver biographies, including George Seaver, *Edward Wilson of the Antarctic* (London: John Murray, 1933) and *Edward Wilson, Nature Lover* (London: John Murray, 1937). Scott Polar Research Institute in Cambridge, England, has an extensive collection of Wilson's work. Cost prohibited including reproductions here, but if I had to choose just one to include it would be "Paraselene."

31. Bernacchi, *Saga*, 226.

32. Sir Charles Wright, in an interview with the author, November 1975.

33. Savours, *Wilson Diary*, 8 August 1901.

34. Armitage, *Two Years*, 125.

35. C. W. Royds, "On the Meteorology of the Part of the Antarctic Where the 'Discovery' Wintered," *GJ* 25 (April 1905): 387; Markham, *Antarctic Obsession*, 21, 64; Bernacchi, *Saga*, 44; Armitage, *Two Years*, 11.

36. Armitage, *Two Years*, 11; Scott to Skelton, 12 October [1900], SPRI MS 342/28/6.

37. Scott, Diary, 18 August 1901, SPRI MS 352/1/1.

38. *VOD*, vol.1, 54.

39. I am indebted to Peter Wadhams and Maria Pia Casarini for helping me obtain permission from the family to use the Heald diary. My special thanks go to Heald's son and his daughter-in-law.

40. Wild, Memoirs, original in Mitchell Library, Sydney. In addition, he wrote a good account of the *Quest*; see Frank Wild, *Shackleton's Last Voyage* (London: Cassell, 1923).

41. Scott, Diary, 12 September 1901, SPRI MS 352/1/1.

42. Armitage to Mill, 13 May 1922, SPRI MS 100/11/4.

43. Hodgson, Diary, 1 October 1901, SPRI 595/1; Gilbert Scott, Diary, 15 August 1901, SPRI MS 1485; Shackleton, Journal, 15 August 1901, SPRI MS 575/2; Mill, *Shackleton*, 70, says the reason for Hodgson's nickname was unknown.

44. Savours, *Wilson Diary*, 16 August 1901.

45. Barne, Diary, 21 August 1901, SPRI MS 1518/1; Scott, Diary, 19 August 1901, SPRI 352/1/1.

46. Gilbert Scott, Diary, 22–24 August 1901, SPRI MS 1485; Scott, Diary, 23–24, 27 August 1901, SPRI MS 352/1/1.

47. Armitage, *Two Years*, 20; Savours, *Wilson Diary*, 31 August 1901; Shackleton, Journal, 31 August 1901, SPRI MS 575/2; Gilbert Scott, Diary, 30 [*sic*] August 1901, SPRI MS 1485.

48. Scott, Diary, 13 September 1901, SPRI MS 352/1/1.

49. Skelton, Diary, 13 September 1901, SPRI MS 342/1/1; *Lyttelton Times*, 30 November 1901, 8; *Canterbury Times*, 4 February 1901, 7.

50. Scott, Diary, 13 September 1901, SPRI MS 352/1/1.

51. Savours, *Wilson Diary*, 13 September 1901.

52. Armitage, *Two Years*, 20.

53. Savours, *Wilson Diary*, 15 September 1901.

54. Gilbert Scott, Diary, 13 September 1901, SPRI MS 1485.

55. Armitage, *Two Years*, 27.

56. Scott, Diary, 19–20 September 1901, SPRI MS 352/1/1; *Cape Times Weekly Edition*, 9 October 1901, 12; Skelton, Diary, 22 September 1901, SPRI MS 342/1/1.

57. Scott, Diary, 27 September 1901, SPRI MS 352/1/1; Savours, *Wilson Diary*, 16, 21–23 September 1901.

58. Scott, Diary, 22, 30 September 1901, SPRI MS 352/1/1.

59. Lashly, 3 October 1901, SPRI MS 890/1; *Cape Times Weekly Edition*, 9 October 1901, 12.

60. Scott, Diary, 23 September 1901, SPRI MS 352/1/1.

61. Professors Beatty and Morrison of Cape University; Skelton, Diary, 3 October 1901, SPRI MS 342/1/1; *VOD*, vol.1, 72.

62. Scott, Diary, 4–5 October 1901, SPRI MS 352/1/1; Skelton, Diary, 4–6 October 1901, SPRI MS 342/1/1.

63. *Cape Argus*, 12 October 1901, 5.

64. Savours, *Wilson Diary*, 5 October 1901.

65. Scott, Diary, 5 October 1901, SPRI MS 352/1/1.

66. Scott, Diary, 7 October 1901, SPRI MS 352/1/1.

67. Skelton, Diary, 5 October 1901, SPRI MS 342/1/1.

68. Scott, Diary, 6–8 October 1901, SPRI MS 352/1/1; Gilbert Scott, Diary, 12 October 1901, SPRI MS 1485; Skelton, Diary, 10–13 October 1901, SPRI MS 342/1/1.

69. Scott, Diary, 10 October 1901, SPRI MS 352/1/1; Savours, *Wilson Diary*, 9 October 1901; Skelton, Diary, 6 October 1901, SPRI MS 342/1/1.

70. Skelton, Diary, 23 October 1901, SPRI MS 342/1/1.

71. Markham, *Antarctic Obsession*, 104.

72. Waterman may have been discharged for syphilis, a not unusual affliction in the Royal Navy of the time.

73. Scott, Diary, 13 October 1901, SPRI MS 352/1/1; quote, Scott, Diary, 14 October 1901, SPRI MS 352/1/1.

6. FROM CAPE TOWN TO NEW ZEALAND

1. *Canterbury Times*, 4 December 1901, 46; Armitage, *Two Years*, 311; *Daily Mail*, 27 July 1901, 3.

2. Armitage, *Two Years*, 311; *Daily Mail*, 27 July 1901, 7; *VOD*, vol.1, 266.

3. Armitage, *Two Years*, 311.

4. Savours, *Wilson Diary*, 19 November 1901; Armitage, *Two Years*, 311.

5. Skelton, Diary, 31 October and 27 November 1901, SPRI MS 342/1/1; Scott, Diary, 28 November 1901, SPRI MS 352/1/1.

6. *VOD*, vol.I, 74.

7. Horace Buckridge's carelessness may have caused the fire, but that cannot be determined for certain. Wild, Memoirs, SPRI MS 1139, 15.

8. Skelton, Diary, 14 November 1901, SPRI MS 342/1/1; Scott, Diary, 14 November 1901, SPRI MS 352/1/1.

9. Savours, *Wilson Diary*, 14 November 1901.

10. *Daily Mail*, 25 February 1902; Savours, *Wilson Diary*, 16 November 1901; Scott, Diary, 15 November 1901, SPRI MS 352/1/1; Gilbert Scott, Diary, 16 November 1901, SPRI MS 1485.

11. Savours, *Wilson Diary*, 16 November 1901; A. R. Ellis, ed., *Under Scott's Command: Lashly's Antarctic Diaries* (London: Victor Gollancz, Ltd., 1969) (hereafter, Ellis, *Lashly*); *VOD*, vol.I, 76.

12. Gilbert Scott, Diary, 16 November 1901, SPRI MS 1485; *VOD*, vol.I, 77; Wilson to Longhurst, 8 July 1906, RGS 13/2/14; Savours, *Wilson Diary*, 19 November.

13. Skelton, Diary, 20 November 1901, SPRI MS 342/1/1.

14. Skelton, Diary, 21 November 1901, SPRI MS 342/1/1.

15. Scott, Diary, 18 and 20 October 1901, SPRI MS 352/1/1.

16. Scott, Diary, 22 November 1901, SPRI MS 352/1/1; Savours, *Wilson Diary*, 22 November 1901.

17. Scott, Diary, 22 November 1901, SPRI 352/1/1.

18. Savours, *Wilson Diary*, 22 November 1901.

19. Scott, Diary, 22 November 1901, SPRI MS 352/1/1.

20. Savours, *Wilson Diary*, 22 November 1901; *The Press* (Christchurch), 30 November 1901, 7.

21. Scott, Diary, 22 November 1901, SPRI MS 352/1/1.

22. Savours, *Wilson Diary*, 22 November 1901.

23. Scott, Diary, 24 November 1901, SPRI MS 352/1/1.

24. Scott, Diary, 25 November 1901, SPRI MS 352/1/1.

25. *Lyttelton Times*, 30 November 1901, 8.

26. Savours, *Wilson Diary*, 26 November 1901.

27. *The Press*, 30 November 1901, 7.

28. *Lyttelton Times*, 30 November 1901, 7–8.

29. *Lyttelton Times*, 30 November 1901, 6.

30. A number of letters appeared in the press offering opinions on the origins of the leak. One anonymous letter writer, who claimed to have been the carpenter on a similarly plagued ship, suggested that the worm holes in the greenheart were likely the cause. *Lyttelton Times*, 7 December 1901, 8; *Lyttelton Times*, 11 December 1901, 8; quote, Scott to Mill, 17 December 1901, SPRI 100/100/2.

31. *VOD*, vol.I, 82; Scott, Diary, 25 December 1901, SPRI MS 352/1/1; Scott, Report on the Condition of the S.S. *Discovery*, 21 December 1901, RGS 12/3/7; Scott, Letter of Proceeding, number 4, 22 December 1901, RGS 12/3/8.

32. *Lyttelton Times*, 7 December 1901, 8.

33. I have grave misgivings about accusing the management of the Dundee Shipbuilding company of negligence both because the evidence is inconclusive and because additional material in the company's defense may no longer be available.

34. *Lyttelton Times*, 11 December 1901, 8.

35. *Lyttelton Times*, 29 November 1901, 6.

36. Scott, Diary, 25 December 1901, SPRI MS 352/1/1; Scott, Letter of Proceeding, number four, 22 December 1901, RGS 12/3/8.

37. Savours, *Wilson Diary*, 1, 4, 17 December 1901.

38. Savours, *Wilson Diary*, 7, 10 December 1901.

39. *Lyttelton Times*, 9 December 1901, 6; 11 December 1901, 8; 12 December, 6; 16 December 1901, 6.

40. *Lyttelton Times*, 12 December 1901, 6.

41. *Lyttelton Times*, 11 December 1901, 8; *The Press* (Christchurch), 11 December 1901, 8.

42. *Lyttelton Times*, 11 December 1901, 8.

43. *Lyttelton Times*, 11 December 1901, 8.

44. Savours, *Wilson Diary*, 11 December 1901.

45. *Lyttelton Times*, 11 December 1901, 8.

46. *Lyttelton Times*, 2 December 1901, 5.

47. Skelton, Diary, 29 November and 3 December 1901, SPRI MS 342/1/1.

48. Skelton, Diary, 4 and 7 December 1901, SPRI MS 342/1/1.

49. Skelton, Diary, 18, 19, and 21 December 1901, SPRI MS 342/1/1.

50. *Lyttelton Times*, 11, 16, and 17 December 1901, 8; *The Press* (Christchurch), 20 December 1901, 5.

51. *VOD*, vol.I, 79–80.

52. *Lyttelton Times*, 11 December 1901, 8.

53. *Lyttelton Times*, 16 December 1901, 6.

54. Scott, Diary, 4 October, 3 and 25 December 1901, SPRI MS 352/1/1; Markham, *Antarctic Obsession*, 104.

55. Scott, Diary, 25 December 1901, SPRI MS 352/1/1.

56. *Lyttelton Times*, 12 December 1901, 6.

57. Markham described him as "objectionable," Markham, *Antarctic Obsession*, 103.

58. Scott, "The National Antarctic Expedition" (1901): 277.

59. *Lyttelton Times*, 29 November 1901, 6.

60. *Lyttelton Times*, 29 November 1901, 6.

61. One's reaction to the strange inclusion of a polar bear — nonexistent in the Antarctic — in the design of the postcard must be tempered by the lack of understanding of the Antarctic as early as the beginning of the twentieth century. As John Splettstoesser reminded me, Borchgrevink took rifles against the possibility of some strange and dangerous land animal. *Daily Mail*, 3 August 1901, 7.

62. *Lyttelton Times*, 29 November 1901, 6.

63. *The Press* (Christchurch), 21 December 1901, 9.

64. *The Press* (Christchurch), 21 December 1901, 9.

65. *Lyttelton Times*, 23 December 1901, 5.

66. *Lyttelton Times*, 23 December 1901, 5.

67. *The Press* (Christchurch), 23 December 1901, 10.

68. *The Press* (Christchurch), 21 December 1901, 9.

69. *The Press* (Christchurch), 21 December 1901, 9.

70. *The Press* (Christchurch), 23 December 1901, 5. The graphic descriptions of Bonner's death found in the journals of the crew of the *Discovery* are surprisingly frank.

71. The reception changes were noted with unintentional black humor by the inadvertent text of one newspaper's report, which noted, "all arrangements for an enthusiastic reception were practically knocked on the head," *The Press* (Christchurch), 24 December 1901, 8.

72. Skelton, Diary, 21 and 23 December 1901, SPRI MS 342/1/1.

73. *The Press* (Christchurch), 24 December 1901, 8.

74. Scott, Diary, 25 December 1901, SPRI MS 352/1/1.

75. During the New Zealand stay the *Discovery* lost Roper, the cook; Dowsett, domestic; Miller, sail maker; Baker, A. B.; Sinclair; and Bonner.

76. *The Press* (Christchurch), 23 December 1901, 10.

77. Scott, Letter of Proceeding, number four, 22 December 1901, RGS 12/3/8, 10; Skelton, Diary, 24 December 1901, SPRI MS 342/1/1.

7. MAY YOU ALWAYS SAIL IN OPEN WATER

The title of the chapter is taken from a letter from Nansen to Scott, 18 July 1901, SPRI MS 366/15/70, wishing Scott well on his departure for Antarctica.

1. The expedition had twenty-three dogs to which was added a veteran of the *Southern Cross* expedition, Joe, which was Bernacchi's dog. Bernacchi, *Saga*, 68.

2. Savours, *Wilson Diary*, 24 December 1901.

3. Armitage, in his published account acknowledged the impact of Bonner's death on the mood about celebrating Christmas: see Armitage, *Two Years*, 34; Savours, *Wilson Diary*, 25 December 1901; *VOD*, vol.1, 85–86.

4. Skelton, Diary, 1 January 1902, SPRI MS 342/1/1.

5. Scott, Diary, 26 and 30 December 1901, SPRI MS 352/1/1.

6. Scott, Diary, 30 December 1901, SPRI MS 352/1/1; Skelton, Diary, 30 December 1901, SPRI MS 342/1/1.

7. Wilson was among those who complained of the lemon essence. Savours, *Wilson Diary*, 1 January 1902. Skelton, Diary, 31 December 1901, SPRI MS 342/1/1.

8. Skelton, Diary, 2 January 1902, SPRI MS 342/1/1; Savours, *Wilson Diary*, 2 January 1902.

9. *VOD*, vol.1, 96.

10. Skelton, Diary, 3 January 1902, SPRI MS 342/1/1.

11. Savours, *Wilson Diary*, 7 January 1902; Skelton, Diary, 7 January 1902, SPRI MS 342/1/1.

12. Skelton, Diary, 3 January 1902, SPRI MS 342/1/1.

13. Ellis, *Lashly*, 21.

14. Scott, Diary, 5 January 1902, SPRI MS 352/1/1.

15. Savours, *Wilson Diary*, 5 January 1902.

16. *VOD*, vol.1, 98.

17. A curious typographical error in Scott's published account gives 1896 as the date of the expedition; see *VOD*, vol.1, 99.

18. Skelton, Diary, 9 January 1902, SPRI MS 342/1/1.

19. Ellis, *Lashly*, 4.

20. I am indebted to John Splettstoesser for correcting my description of the numbers of penguins at Cape Adare, which was included in my *Heroes*.

21. Savours, *Wilson Diary*, 9 January 1902.

22. Skelton, Diary, 9 January 1902, SPRI MS 342/1/1.

23. Savours, *Wilson Diary*, 9 January 1902.

24. Gilbert Scott, Diary, 9 January 1902, SPRI MS 1485.

25. Ellis, *Lashly*, 21.

26. Scott, Diary, 10 January 1902, SPRI MS 352/1/1.

27. Skelton, Diary, 13 January 1902, SPRI MS 342/1/1.

28. Fred G. Alberts, ed., *Geographic Names of the Antarctic* (Washington DC: National Science Foundation, 1995). Wilson complained of Scott never letting anyone know his plans, and that was why Wilson missed this mail drop; see Savours, *Wilson Diary*, 15 January 1902. Skelton, Diary, 15 January 1902, SPRI MS 342/1/1; Armitage, *Two Years*, 42.

29. Borchgrevink had named this for the wife of the patron of his expedition.

30. Scott, Diary, 15 January 1902, SPRI MS 352/1/1.

31. Skelton, Diary, 15–16 January 1902, SPRI MS 342/1/1; Ellis, *Lashly*, 22.

32. Savours, *Wilson Diary*, 15 January 1902.

33. Skelton, Diary, 16–17 January 1902, SPRI MS 342/1/1.

34. Armitage, *Two Years*, 46.

35. The insects were Collembola, a primitive apterous insect. Savours, *Wilson Diary*, 20 January 1902. Scott, Diary, 20 January 1902, SPRI MS 352/1/1.

36. Ellis, *Lashly*, 23.

37. Scott, Diary, 21 January 1902, SPRI MS 352/1/1.

38. Ellis, *Lashly*, 23; Skelton, Diary, 22 January 1902, SPRI MS 342/1/1.

39. Savours, *Wilson Diary*, 22 January 1902.

40. Skelton, Diary, 23 January 1902, SPRI MS 342/1/2.

41. Gilbert Scott, Diary, 23 January 1902, SPRI MS 1485.

42. John Splettstoesser reminded me that although Scott did not know it at the time, the Bay of Whales is as far south as a ship can sail.

43. Ellis, *Lashly*, 23, quoting diary of 22 January 1902; Armitage, *Two Years*, 54; Skelton, Diary, 23–30 January 1902, SPRI MS 342/1/2; Armitage indicated that the time of the discovery was 8:40 P.M.; see Armitage, *Two Years*, 56.

44. Savours, *Wilson Diary*, 31 January 1902; Skelton, Diary, 31 January 1902, SPRI MS 342/1/2; Armitage, *Two Years*, 56; Scott, Diary, 1 February 1902, SPRI MS 352/1/2.

45. Ellis, *Lashly*, 24, quoting 1 February 1902.

46. Skelton, Diary, 1 February 1902, SPRI MS 342/1/2.

47. Savours, *Wilson Diary*, 2 February 1902.

48. Skelton, Diary, 2 February 1902, SPRI MS 342/1/2; Savours, *Wilson Diary*, 2 February 1902.

49. Savours, *Wilson Diary*, 2 February 1902.

50. Armitage, *Cadet*, 131.

51. Scott, Diary, 3 February 1902, SPRI MS 352/1/2.

52. Skelton, Diary, 3 February 1902, SPRI MS 342/1/2.

53. The first explorer to take a motor car with him was Shackleton, on the *Nimrod* expedition, but that was largely a publicity stunt more related to the wishes of his patron than a serious attempt to use motor transport to reach the South Pole. Skelton, Diary, 3 February 1902, SPRI MS 342/1/2.

54. Those wishing to know the obscure may be interested to know that Scott's balloon's was named "Eva," Ellis, *Lashly*, 25; Markham, *Antarctic Obsession*, 32.

55. Ellis, *Lashly*, 25, 4 February 1902; Scott, Diary, 4 February 1902, SPRI MS 352/1/2; Skelton, Diary, 4 February 1902, SPRI MS 342/1/2.

56. The reports differ as to who went aloft that day. By unintentional omission some accounts list fewer people. Lashly indicates that Skelton went up, but the engineer does not note that in his own diary. Skelton, Diary, 4 February 1902, SPRI MS 342/1/2; Ellis, *Lashly*, 24–25, quoting 4 February 1902. Savours, *Wilson Diary*, 4 February 1902.

57. Savours, *Wilson Diary*, 4 February 1902.

58. Scott, Diary, 4 February 1902, SPRI MS 352/1/2.

59. Skelton, Diary, 3–4 February 1902, SPRI MS 342/1/2. Skelton assumed that they had beaten Borchgrevink's record; Armitage, *Two Years*, 59–61; Scott, Diary, 4 February 1902, SPRI MS 352/1/2.

60. Skelton, Diary, 6 and 9 February 1902, SPRI MS 342/1/2; Armitage, *Two Years*, 62; Murray, "The Renewal of Antarctic Exploration," 14; Ellis, *Lashly*, 27, 10 February 1902; Scott, Diary, 8–9 February 1902, SPRI MS 352/1/2.

61. Skelton, Diary, 9 February 1902, SPRI MS 342/1/2.

62. Savours, *Wilson Diary*, 9 February 1902.

63. Scott, Diary, 9 January 1902, SPRI MS 352/1/1.

64. *VOD*, vol.1, 160.

65. Skelton, Diary, 11 February 1902, SPRI MS 342/1/2.

66. Scott, Diary, 10 February 1902, SPRI MS 352/1/2; Savours, *Wilson Diary*, 10 February 1902.

67. Scott, Diary, 13–14 February 1902, SPRI MS 352/1/2.

68. Scott, Diary, 14 February 1902, SPRI MS 352/1/2.

69. Armitage, *Two Years*, 64; Scott, Diary, 19 February 1902, SPRI MS 352/1/2; *VOD*, vol.1, 160; Ellis, *Lashly*, 30.

70. Scott complained of the "swindle" because the huts had cost nearly £50. Scott, Diary, 20 February 1902, SPRI MS 352/1/2.

71. Skelton, Diary, 12–13 February 1902, SPRI MS 342/1/2.

72. Scott, Diary, 16–17 February 1902, SPRI MS 352/1/2; Skelton, Diary, 17 February 1902, SPRI MS 342/1/2; Ellis, *Lashly*, 29, quoting 17 February 1902; Savours, *Wilson Diary*, 17 February 1902.

73. Skelton, Diary, 15 February 1902, SPRI MS 342/1/2.

74. Savours, *Wilson Diary*, 18 February 1902.

75. Skelton, Diary, 21 February 1902, SPRI MS 342/1/2; Scott, Diary, 21 February 1902, SPRI MS 352/1/2; Ellis, *Lashly*, 31.

76. Scott, Diary, 22 February 1902, SPRI MS 352/1/2; Skelton, Diary, 22 February 1902, SPRI MS 342/1/2.

77. Savours, *Wilson Diary*, 19 February 1902.

78. Savours, *Wilson Diary*, 19 February 1902.

79. Savours, *Wilson Diary*, 20 February 1902.

80. Savours, *Wilson Diary*, 19–20 February 1902.

81. Savours, *Wilson Diary*, 19 February 1902.

82. Skelton, Diary, 23 February 1902, SPRI MS 342/1/2; Savours, *Wilson Diary*, 21 February 1902.

83. Savours, *Wilson Diary*, 22 February 1902.

84. *VOD*, vol.I, 167.

85. *VOD*, vol.I, 168.

86. Scott, Diary, 1 March 1902, SPRI MS 352/1/2.

87. Scott, Diary, 24 February 1902, SPRI MS 352/1/2.

88. *VOD*, vol.I, 169.

89. Skelton, Diary, 2 March 1902, SPRI MS 342/1/2.

90. Scott, Diary, 2 March 1902, SPRI MS 352/1/2.

91. Savours, *Wilson Diary*, 2 March 1902.

92. Skelton, Diary, 3 March 1902, SPRI MS 342/1/2.

93. Bernacchi, *Saga*, 96; Armitage, *Two Years*, 104.

94. Armitage, *Two Years*, 106, 125.

95. Savours, *Wilson Diary*, Appendix A, 404.

96. Skelton, Diary, 4 March 1902, SPRI MS 342/1/2.

97. Skelton, Diary, 5 March 1902, SPRI MS 342/1/2.

98. Skelton, Diary, 6–7 March 1902, SPRI MS 342/1/2.

99. Hare, Diary, 15 March 1902, SPRI 753.

100. Hare, Diary, 15 March 1902, SPRI MS 753; Royds, Diary, 12 March 1902, SPRI MS 654/2.

101. Hare, Diary, 15 March 1902, SPRI MS 753.

102. Hare, Diary, 15 March 1902, SPRI MS 753; Royds, Diary, 12 March 1902, SPRI MS 654/2.

103. Royds, Diary, 12 March 1902, SPRI MS 654/2.

104. Skelton, Diary, 8–9 March 1902, SPRI MS 342/1/2.

105. Skelton, Diary, 10 March 1902, SPRI MS 342/1/2.

106. Skelton, Diary, 14 March 1902, SPRI MS 342/1/3.

107. Skelton, Diary, 15–17 March 1902, SPRI MS 342/1/3.

108. Skelton, Diary, 18 March 1902, SPRI MS 342/1/3.

109. Skelton, Diary, 19 March 1902, SPRI MS 342/1/3.

110. Arthur L. Quartley, Diary, 10–11 March 1902, quoted in Skelton, Diary, SPRI MS 342/1/3.

111. Arthur L. Quartley, Diary, 11 March 1902, quoted in Skelton, Diary, SPRI MS 342/1/3.

112. Arthur L. Quartley, Diary, 11 March 1902, quoted in Skelton, Diary, SPRI MS 342/1/3.

113. In Wilson's diary, the story is slightly different. In that version Quartley went second and Barne third. Savours, *Wilson Diary*, 11 March 1902.

114. Arthur L. Quartley, Diary, 11 March 1902, quoted in Skelton, Diary, SPRI MS 342/1/3.

115. Scott, Diary, 11 March 1902, SPRI MS 352/1/2.

116. Savours, *Wilson Diary*, 11 March 1902; Ellis, *Lashly*, 32–33, quoting 11 March 1902.

117. Savours, *Wilson Diary*, 11 March 1902.

118. Armitage, *Two Years*, 76.

119. Savours, *Wilson Diary*, 11 March 1902.

120. Savours, *Wilson Diary*, 11 March 1902.

121. H. R. Mill, Abstract of Shackleton's Journal, 11 March 1902, SPRI MS 100/135.

122. Armitage, *Two Years*, 78.

123. Savours, *Wilson Diary*, 12 March 1902.

124. Skelton, Diary, 20 March 1902, SPRI MS 342/1/3.

125. Skelton, Diary, 12 March 1902, SPRI MS 342/1/3; Ellis, *Lashly*, 33–34, quoting 13 March 1902.

126. Ellis, *Lashly*, 34, quoting 13 March 1902; *VOD*, vol.1, 186.

127. Scott, Diary, 12 March 1902, SPRI MS 352/1/2.

128. Scott, Diary, 13 March 1902, SPRI MS 352/1/2.

129. Scott, Diary, 21 March 1902, SPRI MS 352/1/2.

130. Savours, *Wilson Diary*, 26 March 1902.

131. Scott, Diary, 27 March 1902, SPRI MS 352/1/2.

132. Ellis, *Lashly*, 35, 28 March 1902; Scott, Diary, 30 March 1902, SPRI MS 352/1/2; Wilson agreed with Skelton's assessment, and when another group of emperors appeared a week later he assumed that the penguins were headed north, see Savours, *Wilson Diary*, 5 April 1902; Skelton, Diary, 30 March 1902, SPRI MS 342/1/3.

133. Scott, Diary, 29 March 1902, SPRI MS 352/1/2.

134. Savours, *Wilson Diary*, 31 March 1902; *VOD*, vol.1, 200–201; Savours, *Wilson Diary*, 31 March 1902; Scott, Diary, 1–2 April 1902, SPRI MS 352/1/2.

135. Savours, *Wilson Diary*, 2 April 1902. In his published account Scott wrote that he decided to turn back on 3 April, see *VOD*, vol.1, 202.

136. Savours, *Wilson Diary*, 3 April 1902. Wilson believed that the dogs pulled well on light (appropriate?) loads and would not pull with a dead weight behind them.

137. Scott, Diary, 3 April 1902, SPRI MS 352/1/2.

138. Skelton, Diary, 3 April 1902, SPRI MS 342/1/3.

139. Scott, Diary, 6 April 1902, SPRI MS 352/1/2.

140. Scott, Diary, 5 April 1902, SPRI MS 352/1/2.

141. Skelton, Diary, 28 March 1902, SPRI MS 342/1/3.

142. Scott, Diary, 5 April 1902, SPRI MS 352/1/2; Savours, *Wilson Diary*, 16, 18 April 1902.

143. Skelton, Diary, 8 April 1902, SPRI MS 342/1/3.

144. Skelton, Diary, 9 April 1902, SPRI MS 342/1/3.

145. Savours, *Wilson Diary*, 8 April 1902.

146. Scott, Diary, 9 April 1902, SPRI MS 352/1/2.

147. Skelton, Diary, 24, 27, and 31 March 1902 and 1 and 3 April 1902, SPRI MS 342/1/3.

148. Savours, *Wilson Diary*, 7 April 1902.

149. *The Press* (Christchurch), 29 November 1901, 5.

150. Skelton, Diary, 13 April 1902, SPRI MS 342/1/3.

151. Skelton reckoned the entire cost of the windmill to be approximately more than £600. Skelton, Diary, 13 April 1902, SPRI MS 342/1/3.

152. Skelton, Diary, 14 April 1902, SPRI MS 342/1/3.

153. Ellis, *Lashly*, 25.

154. Scott, Diary, 13 April 1902, SPRI MS 352/1/2. In the official published account Scott moderated his tone, noting, "I shall suggest to the engine room staff that it ought to be repaired if it is not too far gone," *VOD*, vol.1, 214.

155. Scott, Diary, 17 April 1902, SPRI MS 352/1/2.

156. Ellis, *Lashly*, 28.

8. THE WINTER

1. Mill, Abstract of Shackleton Diary, SPRI MS 100/135.

2. Savours, *Wilson Diary*, 28 June 1902.

3. *VOD*, vol.1, 267; Skelton, Diary, 24 May 1902, SPRI MS 342/1/4.

4. Mill, *Shackleton*, 71.

5. Mill, *Shackleton*, 71. Wild wrote an incredible fictional account of the history of discovery.

6. Savours, *Wilson Diary*, 28 July 1902; Bernacchi, *Saga*, 51; Skelton, Diary, 23 April 1902, SPRI MS 342/1/3.

7. Savours, *Wilson Diary*, 28 July 1902.

8. *VOD*, vol.1, 268; Skelton, Diary, 30 April 1902, SPRI MS 342/1/3; Skelton, Diary, 1 May 1902, SPRI MS 342/1/4.

9. Scott, Diary, 18 July 1902, SPRI MS 1464/3; *VOD*, vol.1, 216–17.

10. *VOD*, vol.1, 217–18.

11. *VOD*, vol.1, 248; Bernacchi, *Saga*, 47.

12. *VOD*, vol.I, 248; Ellis, *Lashly*, 36–37; Scott, Diary, 18 July 1902, SPRI MS 1464/3.

13. Scott, Diary, 26 May 1902, SPRI MS 352/1/2.

14. Skelton, Diary, 8 June 1902, SPRI MS 342/1/4.

15. *VOD*, vol.I, 218–19.

16. James Duncan, Diary, 18 June 1902.

17. Armitage, *Two Years*, 117.

18. Bernacchi, *Saga*, 47.

19. *VOD*, vol.I, 218.

20. Savours, *Wilson Diary*, 23 May 1902.

21. Armitage, *Two Years*, 117.

22. Scott, Diary, 18 July 1902, SPRI MS 1464/3.

23. *VOD*, vol.I, 218–19.

24. Scott, Diary, 8 May 1902, SPRI MS 352/1/2.

25. *VOD*, vol.I, 220.

26. Scott, Diary, 29 April 1902, SPRI MS 352/1/2, Scott, Diary, 18 July 1902, SPRI MS 1464/3.

27. Savours, *Wilson Diary*, 13–14 June and 15 July 1902.

28. *VOD*, vol.I, 229; Savours, *Wilson Diary*, 3 August 1902.

29. Quote, *VOD*, vol.I, 222; Savours, *Wilson Diary*, 9 June 1902.

30. Bernacchi, *Saga*, 45.

31. Savours, *Wilson Diary*, 9 July 1902; *VOD*, vol.I, 222–23.

32. Scott, Diary, 27 May 1902, SPRI MS 352/1/2.

33. Skelton, Diary, 6 and 24 July 1902, SPRI MS 342/1/4; Scott, Diary, 18 July 1902, SPRI MS 1464/3; *VOD*, vol.I, 224; Savours, *Wilson Diary*, 13 June 1902.

34. Scott, Diary, 3 May 1902, SPRI MS 352/1/2; Savours, *Wilson Diary*, 27 April 1902.

35. Skelton, Diary, 27 April 1902, SPRI MS 342/1/3.

36. Skelton, Diary, 27 April 1902, SPRI MS 342/1/3; Savours, *Wilson Diary*, 17 May 1902.

37. Scott, Diary, 18 July 1902, SPRI MS 1464/3; Savours, *Wilson Diary*, 3 May and 18 July 1902.

38. *VOD*, vol.I, 263–64; Armitage, *Two Years*, 91.

39. *VOD*, vol.I, 264.

40. *VOD*, vol.I, 243–45.

41. *VOD*, vol.I, 245–46.

42. *VOD*, vol.I, 247; Scott, Diary, 18 July 1902, SPRI MS 1464/3.

43. *VOD*, vol.I, 249.

44. Scott, Diary, 18 July 1902, SPRI MS 1464/3; quote, Duncan, Diary, 18 June 1902, SPRI MS 1415.

45. *VOD*, vol.I, 403; Duncan, Diary, 18 June 1902, SPRI MS 1415.

46. Scott, Diary, 9 and 11 May 1902, SPRI MS 352/1/2; Skelton, Diary, 27 April 1902, SPRI MS 342/1/3; Skelton, Diary, 25 May 1902, SPRI MS 342/1/4.

47. *VOD*, vol.I, 224.

48. Savours, *Wilson Diary*, 20 May 1902.

49. *VOD*, vol.I, 224.

50. Skelton, Diary, 26 April 1902, SPRI MS 342/1/3; Scott, Diary, 26 April 1902, SPRI MS 352/1/2.

51. *VOD*, vol.I, 236.

52. Skelton, Diary, 2 May 1902, SPRI MS 342/1/4.

53. Skelton, Diary, 6 May 1902, SPRI MS 342/1/4.

54. Skelton, Diary, 20 and 27 May 1902, SPRI MS 342/1/4; Scott, Diary, 27 May 1902, SPRI MS 352/1/2.

55. Savours, *Wilson Diary*, 2 June 1902; Skelton, Diary, 3 June 1902, SPRI MS 342/1/4. I have been unable to find any indication that Royds had any kind of telepathic contact to his twin sister.

56. Savours, *Wilson Diary*, 10 June 1902; quote, Skelton, Diary, 10 June 1902, SPRI MS 342/1/4.

57. Skelton, Diary, 17 June 1902, SPRI MS 342/1/4. In light of the problems of British football in the 1980s and 1990s, Hodgson's comment was interesting.

58. Skelton, Diary, 24 June 1902, SPRI MS 342/1/4.

59. Savours, *Wilson Diary*, 8 July 1902.

60. Savours, *Wilson Diary*, 26 August 1902; *VOD*, vol.I, 225.

61. Bernacchi, *Saga*, 48. Shackleton's diary noted the same vote but gave the victory to Browning.

62. Skelton, Diary, 13 August 1902, SPRI MS 342/1/4; quote, Armitage, *Two Years*, 118.

63. Ellis, *Lashly*, 41.

64. Duncan, Diary, 2 and 17 July 1902, SPRI MS 1415.

65. *VOD*, vol.I, 239.

66. Skelton, Diary, 28 April 1902, SPRI MS 342/1/3.

67. For a detailed description of the walk to Crater Hill see Savours, *Wilson Diary*, 10 July 1902; Skelton, Diary, 16 April 1902, SPRI MS 342/1/3.

68. Skelton, Diary, 21 June 1902, SPRI MS 342/1/4.

69. Scott, Diary, 14 June 1902, SPRI MS 352/1/2.

70. Skelton, Diary, 30 May 1902, SPRI MS 342/1/4.

71. Savours, *Wilson Diary*, 5 May and 3 July 1902.

72. Scott, Diary, 24 May 1902, SPRI MS 352/1/2.

73. *VOD*, vol.I, 238.

74. *VOD*, vol.I, 238.

75. Armitage, *Two Years*, 97.

76. Skelton, Diary, 2 May 1902, SPRI MS 342/I/4.

77. Skelton, Diary, 21 May 1902, SPRI MS 342/I/4.

78. Savours, *Wilson Diary*, 2 May 1902.

79. *VOD*, vol.I, 235.

80. *VOD*, vol.I, 259.

81. Scott, Diary, 18 July 1902, SPRI MS 1464/3; Mill, *Shackleton*, 69.

82. Scott, Diary, 18 July 1902, SPRI MS 1464/3; *VOD*, vol.I, 259–60.

83. *VOD*, vol.I, 260.

84. *VOD*, vol.I, 265–65; quote, *VOD*, vol.I, 265.

85. *VOD*, vol.I, 266.

86. *VOD*, vol.I, 266.

87. *VOD*, vol.I, 267.

88. Although rum barrels were used, the opinion that it was a "rum" idea certainly brings tone of a double meaning.

89. Savours, *Wilson Diary*, 19 August 1902.

90. Scott, Diary, 19 August 1902, SPRI MS 1464/3; Savours, *Wilson Diary*, 18 August 1902.

91. Savours, *Wilson Diary*, 23 July and 10 August 1902; Scott, Diary, 18 July 1902, SPRI MS 1464/3; Bernacchi, *Saga*, 57; Skelton, Diary, 22 July 1902, SPRI MS 342/I/4; *VOD*, vol.I, 271.

92. *VOD*, vol.I, 271.

93. Savours, *Wilson Diary*, 23 July 1902.

94. *VOD*, vol.I, 271.

95. Scott, Diary, 28 July and 2 and 4 August 1902, SPRI MS 1464/3; Duncan, Diary, 24 and 26 July, 25 August, and 23 September 1902, SPRI MS 1415; *VOD*, vol.I, 271–72; Bernacchi, *Saga*, 58.

96. Scott, Diary, 18 July 1902, SPRI MS 1464/3; *VOD*, vol.I, 262.

97. *VOD*, vol.I, 262–63.

98. Scott, Diary, 17 May 1902, SPRI MS 352/I/2; Skelton, Diary, 17–18 May 1902, SPRI MS 342/I/4; *VOD*, vol.I, 241; Savours, *Wilson Diary*, 17 May 1902; Ellis, *Lashly*, 38.

99. Skelton, Diary, 26 May 1902, SPRI MS 342/I/4; *VOD*, vol.I, 276.

100. Scott, Diary, 16–19 and 23 June 1902, SPRI MS 352/I/2; Scott, Diary, 18 July 1902, SPRI MS 1464/3.

101. Scott, Diary, 21 July 1902, SPRI MS 1464/3.

102. Skelton, Diary, 19 May and 19 July 1902, SPRI MS 342/I/4.

103. Scott, Diary, 17 May 1902, SPRI MS 352/I/2; *VOD*, vol.I, 237–38.

104. Scott, Diary, 14 May 1902, SPRI MS 352/1/2.

105. Skelton, Diary, 31 May 1902, SPRI MS 342/1/4.

106. *VOD*, vol.1, 242.

107. Skelton, Diary, 31 May 1902, SPRI MS 342/1/4.

108. Savours, *Wilson Diary*, 9 July 1902.

109. Skelton, Diary, 3 July and 11 August 1902, SPRI MS 342/1/4; Scott, Diary, 3 July 1902, SPRI MS 352/1/2.

110. Skelton, Diary, 12 August 1902, SPRI MS 342/1/4; Skelton, Diary, 2 September 1902, SPRI MS 342/1/5.

111. Savours, *Wilson Diary*, 22 July, 13 and 18 August 1902.

112. Armitage, *Two Years*, 118.

113. Hare, Diary, 31 May and 17 July 1902, SPRI MS 753.

114. Hare, Diary, 6 and 17 July 1902, SPRI MS 753; Williamson, Diary, 7 and 8 May and 15 June 1902, SPRI MS 774/1/1.

115. Hare, Diary, 14 October 1902, SPRI MS 753.

116. Skelton, Diary, 1 May 1902, SPRI MS 342/1/4; Savours, *Wilson Diary*, 1 May 1902; *VOD*, vol.1, 277.

117. Scott, Diary, 25 June 1902, SPRI MS 352/1/2; Armitage, *Two Years*, 114–15.

118. Skelton was among them, "one year later, seems longer," Skelton, Diary, 6 August 1902, SPRI MS 342/1/4.

119. Scott, Diary, 6 August 1902, SPRI MS 1464/3. The minstrel show was done in dialect and blackface and imitated a music hall style popular at the time. Some of the jokes illustrate the tone of the show. "Why did Hut Point? Because it saw ski slope round the corner." "What made Crater [h]ill? Because it saw the Castle Rock?" "Why did the Weddell Waddle? Because the crab 'it 'er [crabeater]." *South Polar Times*, August 1902, 23.

120. Savours, *Wilson Diary*, 22 May 1902; Duncan, Diary, 20 July 1902, SPRI MS 1415.

121. Markham, "Address to the Royal Geographical Society," *SGM* 17 (July 1901): 345.

122. Scott, Diary, 18 July 1902, SPRI MS 1464/3; *VOD*, vol.1, 226.

123. Skelton, Diary, 17 May 1902, SPRI MS 342/1/4.

124. Savours, *Wilson Diary*, 23 May 1902.

125. Armitage, *Two Years*, 94.

126. Armitage, *Cadet*, 125.

127. Armitage, *Cadet*, 126.

128. Scott, Diary, 25 April 1902, SPRI MS 352/1/2; Scott, Diary, 18 July, 25–26 August 1902, SPRI MS 1464/3.

129. Savours, *Wilson Diary*, 7 August 1902.

130. Scott, Diary, 18 July 1902, SPRI MS 1464/3.

131. Savours, *Wilson Diary*, 23 May 1902.

132. *VOD*, vol.1, 230.

133. Skelton, Diary, 23 April 1902, SPRI MS 342/1/3; Savours, *Wilson Diary*, 23 April 1902.

134. Savours, *Wilson Diary*, 1 August 1902; Bernacchi, *Saga*, 51–52.

135. Skelton, Diary, 10, 12, 17, 19, 30 April 1902, SPRI MS 342/1/3; Skelton, Diary, 5, 21 May and 4, 13–14 June, and 9 August 1902, SPRI MS 342/1/4; *VOD*, vol.1, 233.

136. Skelton, Diary, 13–16 August 1902, SPRI MS 342/1/4.

137. Scott, Diary, 18 July 1902, SPRI MS 1464/3;

138. Skelton, Diary, 4 May, 8 June, and 13 July 1902, SPRI MS 342/1/4;

139. Skelton, Diary, 25 June, 5 and 15 July 1902, SPRI MS 342/1/4.

140. Skelton, Diary, 1 May and 29 June 1902, SPRI MS 342/1/4.

141. Armitage, *Two Years*, 101; quote, Skelton, Diary, 25 April 1902, SPRI MS 342/1/3.

142. Skelton, Diary, 10 and 15 May, and 30 July 1902, SPRI MS 342/1/4.

143. *VOD*, vol.1, 228–29; Scott, Diary, 6 June 1902, SPRI MS 352/1/2.

144. Skelton, Diary, 8 May 1902, SPRI MS 342/1/4; Armitage, *Two Years*, 98.

145. Savours, *Wilson Diary*, 23 May 1902.

146. Barne, Diary, 30 March 1902, SPRI MS 1518/1.

147. Barne, Diary, 28 April 1902, SPRI MS 1518/2.

148. Royds, Diary, 3 September 1901, SPRI MS 654/1.

149. I am indebted to Peter Wadhams for helping to clarify this part of Koettlitz's character (interview with the author, 3 August 1995). David Kynaston, *The City of London*, vol.2, *The Golden Years, 1890–1914* (London: Chatto & Windus, 1995), review, *Economist*, 5 August 1995, 79.

150. Armitage, *Two Years*, 99.

151. *VOD*, vol.1, 231; Bernacchi, *Saga*, 45; *VOD*, vol.1, 231; Scott, Diary, 21 April 1902, SPRI MS 352/1/2.

152. Savours, *Wilson Diary*, 23 May 1902; Armitage, *Two Years*, 93; Skelton, Diary, 19 June 1902, SPRI MS 342/1/4.

153. Hodgson, Diary, 8 October 1901, SPRI MS 595/1.

154. Scott, Diary, 18 July 1902, SPRI MS 1464/3; Savours, *Wilson Diary*, 9 July 1902. At one point Scott noted that Hodgson stays in excellent health by his outdoor work. Scott, Diary, 11 September 1902, SPRI MS 1464/3.

155. Scott, *VOD*, vol.1, 232.

156. Scott, *VOD*, vol.1, 231. Not only was Bernacchi the most experienced Antarctican on the *Discovery*, but he was almost even more so. Bull had hoped to take Bernacchi but was unable to do so. Bernacchi applied to serve on the *Belgica*, but

that fell through, and Scott asked him to serve on the *Terra Nova* expedition. Hugh B. Evans and A. G. E. Jones, "A Forgotten Explorer: Carsten Egeberg Borchgrevink," PR 17 (September 1974): 223; Janet Crawford, "The First Antarctic Winter," SPRI MS 1367, 38, 379.

157. Scott, Diary, 15 May 1902, SPRI MS 352/1/2.

158. Skelton, Diary, 28 July 1902, SPRI MS 342/1/4.

159. Skelton, Diary, 30 July 1902, SPRI MS 342/1/4.

160. Armitage, *Two Years*, 53.

161. Skelton, Diary, 31 July 1902, SPRI MS 342/1/4; *VOD*, vol.1, 276.

162. Savours, *Wilson Diary*, 31 July 1902.

163. *VOD*, vol.1, 274; Skelton, Diary, 27 September 1902, SPRI MS 342/1/5.

164. Ellis, *Lashly*, 43–44, quoting 23 April and 26 May 1902.

165. Scott, Diary, 18 July 1902, SPRI MS 1464/3.

166. *VOD*, vol.1, 232–33.

167. Scott, Diary, 18 April 1902, SPRI MS 352/1/2.

168. Mill, *Shackleton*, 57.

169. Savours, *Wilson Diary*, 23 May 1902; Scott, Diary, 18 July 1902, SPRI MS 1464/3.

170. Mill, *Shackleton*, 70; Savours, *Wilson Diary*, 18 July 1902.

171. Mill, *Shackleton*, 71.

172. Scott, Diary, 18 July 1902, SPRI MS 1464/3.

173. Mill, *Shackleton*, 70.

174. *VOD*, vol.1, 229; Savours, *Wilson Diary*, 27 May 1902.

175. Savours, *Wilson Diary*, 29 August 1902.

176. Savours, *Wilson Diary*, 24–25 April 1902.

177. Savours, *Wilson Diary*, contains numerous references to this work, see examples, 29 April to 5 May 1902, 4 and 6 June 1902.

178. Savours, *Wilson Diary*, 2 June 1902.

179. Savours, *Wilson Diary*, 7 June 1902.

180. Skelton, Diary, 7 June 1902, SPRI MS 342/1/4.

181. Scott, Diary, 8 June 1902, SPRI MS 352/1/2.

182. Scott, Diary, 18 July 1902, SPRI MS 1464/3.

183. Armitage, *Two Years*, 102.

184. Armitage, *Two Years*, 106.

185. Ellis, *Lashly*, 39.

186. Skelton, Diary, 15 August 1902, SPRI MS 342/1/4; *VOD*, vol.1, 251; Scott, Diary, 18 July 1902, SPRI MS 1464/3.

187. Skelton, Diary, 17 August 1902, SPRI MS 342/1/4; Ellis, *Lashly*, 39.

188. Skelton, Diary, 16 August 1902, SPRI MS 342/1/4.

189. Ellis, *Lashly*, 45.

190. Ellis, *Lashly*, 42, quoting 30 June 1902.

191. Armitage, *Two Years*, 102.

192. Duncan, Diary, 11–13 June and 22 July 1902, SPRI MS 1415.

193. Armitage, *Two Years*, 94.

194. Savours, *Wilson Diary*, 16 October 1902.

195. Bernacchi, *Saga*, 56.

196. Skelton, Diary, 14, 15, and 24 May 1902, SPRI MS 342/1/4.

197. Skelton, Diary, 1 June 1902, SPRI MS 342/1/4.

198. Skelton, Diary, 3 June 1902, SPRI MS 342/1/4.

199. Skelton, Diary, 6 June 1902, SPRI MS 342/1/4.

200. Savours, *Wilson Diary*, 13 July 1902.

201. Savours, *Wilson Diary*, 23 July 1902.

202. Skelton, Diary, 23 June 1902, SPRI MS 342/1/4; Bernacchi, *Saga*, 55; VOD, vol.1, 253–54; Armitage, *Two Years*, 114; Ellis, *Lashly*, 41, quoting 23 June 1902.

203. Duncan, Diary, 21 and 23 June 1902, SPRI MS 1415; Mill, Abstract of Shackleton's Diary, 23 June 1902, SPRI MS 100/135.

204. Duncan, Diary, 23 June 1902, SPRI MS 1415.

205. Savours, *Wilson Diary*, 23 June 1902; VOD, vol.1, 253–54; Armitage, *Two Years*, 113–14.

206. VOD, vol.1, 250.

207. Bernacchi seemed to suggest that the original trio was Scott, Shackleton, and Barne, but this was his recollection thirty years after the event. Contemporary journals indicated that Scott chose Wilson and then Shackleton. Besides, for a variety of reasons Barne would have been a weak choice, especially after the sledging party of March 1902. Bernacchi, *Saga*, 69–70.

208. Savours, *Wilson Diary*, 12 June 1902.

209. Mill, Abstract of Shackleton's Diary, 13 June 1902, SPRI MS 100/135; Mill, *Shackleton*, 71.

210. Savours, *Wilson Diary*, 12 June 1902; Mill, *Shackleton*, 72.

211. Skelton, Diary, 4 July 1902, SPRI MS 342/1/4.

212. Savours, *Wilson Diary*, 12 June 1902.

213. Skelton, Diary, 3–4 July 1902, SPRI MS 342/1/4.

214. Skelton, Diary, 6 July 1902, SPRI MS 342/1/4.

215. Skelton, Diary, 26 August 1902, SPRI MS 342/1/4.

216. Savours, *Wilson Diary*, 12 June 1902.

217. Savours, *Wilson Diary*, 22 August 1902.

218. Scott, Diary, 22 August 1902, SPRI MS 1464/3.

219. Duncan, Diary, 24 August 1902, SPRI MS 1415.

220. Savours, *Wilson Diary*, 26 August 1902.

221. Armitage, *Two Years*, 101.

222. Scott, Diary, 25–26 August 1902, SPRI MS 1464/3.

223. Savours, *Wilson Diary*, 1 July 1902.

224. Skelton, Diary, 25 May 1902, SPRI MS 342/1/4.

225. Savours, *Wilson Diary*, 30 July 1902; Skelton, Diary, 8 July 1902, SPRI MS 342/1/4; Mill, Abstract of Shackleton Diary, 2 March 1902.

226. Scott, Diary, SPRI MS 1464/3, 31 August 1902.

227. Bernacchi, *Saga*, 56.

9. SUMMER 1902–1903

1. *VOD*, vol.1, 260; *The Standard*, 23 June 1900.

2. Bernacchi, *Saga*, 64–68; Scott, Diary, 31 August 1902, SPRI MS 1464/3.

3. Savours, *Wilson Diary*, 29 August and 2 September 1902; Scott, Diary, 2 September 1902, SPRI MS 1464/3.

4. Savours, *Wilson Diary*, 2 September 1902.

5. Savours, *Wilson Diary*, 4 September 1902.

6. Savours, *Wilson Diary*, 5 September 1902; Scott, Diary, 5 September 1902, SPRI MS 1464/3; Skelton, Diary, 3 and 5 September 1902, SPRI MS 342/1/5.

7. Scott, Diary, 10 September 1902, SPRI MS 1464/3.

8. Armitage, *Two Years*, 123–24.

9. Wilson agreed with Skelton's assessment, see Savours, *Wilson Diary*, 3 October 1902; Skelton, Diary, 10 September 1902, SPRI MS 342/1/5.

10. Armitage, *Two Years*, 125–26; Savours, *Wilson Diary*, 10 September 1902; Skelton, Diary, 19 September 1902, SPRI MS 342/1/5.

11. Duncan, Diary, 16 July and 11 September 1902, SPRI MS 1415; Skelton, Diary, 11 September 1902, SPRI MS 342/1/5.

12. Scott, Diary, 11 September 1902, SPRI MS 1464/3.

13. Armitage, *Two Years*, 124–28.

14. Armitage, *Two Years*, 129–31.

15. Savours, *Wilson Diary*, 22 September 1902.

16. Savours, *Wilson Diary*, 14, 15, 17, and 20 September 1902.

17. Skelton, Diary, 19 June 1902, SPRI MS 342/1/4.

18. Savours, *Wilson Diary*, 2 October 1902.

19. Savours, *Wilson Diary*, 14, 15, 17, 20, 22, and 29 September and 2 October 1902; Skelton, Diary, 19 June 1902, SPRI MS 342/1/4.

20. Scott, Diary, 16 September 1902, SPRI MS 1464/3.

21. Savours, *Wilson Diary*, 9 September 1902.

22. Armitage, *Two Years*, 137.

23. Scott, Diary, 19–20 September 1902, SPRI MS 1464/3.

24. Duncan, Diary, 19 September 1902, SPRI 1415.

25. Skelton, Diary, 19 September 1902, SPRI MS 342/1/5.

26. Scott, Diary, 24 and 29 September 1902, SPRI MS 1464/3; *VOD*, vol.1, 390–91.

27. Scott, Diary, 30 September and 1 October 1902, SPRI MS 1464/3; Skelton, Diary, 3 October 1902, SPRI MS 342/1/5.

28. Skelton, Diary, 26 September 1902, SPRI MS 342/1/5.

29. Skelton, Diary, 19 September 1902, SPRI MS 342/1/5; *VOD*, vol.1, 398; Duncan, Diary, 26 September 1902, SPRI MS 1415; Scott, Diary, 3 October 1902, SPRI MS 1464/3; Duncan, Diary, 28 September 1902, SPRI MS 1415.

30. Savours, *Wilson Diary*, 26–27 September 1902; *VOD*, vol.1, 398. Skelton wrote, "it is, of course kept quiet," Skelton, Diary, 27 September 1902, SPRI MS 342/1/5.

31. Duncan, Diary, 29 September 1902, SPRI 1415.

32. Skelton, Diary, 30 September 1902, SPRI MS 342/1/5.

33. For a detailed account of Scott's views on scurvy circa 1905–7, see *VOD*, vol.1, 404–5. For Scott's reasoning as to the origins of the problem on the expedition, see *VOD*, vol.1, 407–10. *VOD*, vol.1, 406–7; Savours, *Wilson Diary*, 13 October 1902; *VOD*, vol.1, 399, 409–10.

34. *VOD*, vol.1, 305; Scott, Diary, 3 and 19 October 1902, SPRI MS 1464/3; Savours, *Wilson Diary*, 8–9, 17 October 1902.

35. Scott, Diary, 19 and 26 October 1902, SPRI MS 1464/3; Savours, *Wilson Diary*, 5 October 1902.

36. Scott, Diary, 4 October 1902, SPRI MS 1464/3; Skelton, Diary, 21 September and 2 October 1902, SPRI MS 342/1/5.

37. Skelton, Diary, 25 September 1902, SPRI MS 342/1/5.

38. Savours, *Wilson Diary*, 28 September 1902.

39. Skelton, Diary, SPRI MS 342/1/5, 29–30 September 1902.

40. This journey inspired the title of what many consider the greatest Antarctic account, Apsley Cherry-Garrard, *The Worst Journey in the World* (London: Chatto and Windus, 1965). Visitors wishing to witness the miracle of the emperor penguin life cycle now have an opportunity to do so. Every year a single Russian icebreaker voyage takes enthusiasts into the Weddell Sea to visit emperor penguin rookeries in November. I want to acknowledge the help of John Splettstoesser and Zegrahm Expeditions for making it possible for me to make such a journey in 1996 and to meet two lifelong friends in the process.

41. Skelton, Diary, 28 September 1902, SPRI MS 342/1/5.

42. Skelton, Diary, 11 October 1902, SPRI MS 342/1/5.

43. Savours, *Wilson Diary*, 24 October 1902.

44. Scott, Diary, 26 October 1902, SPRI MS 1464/3; Savours, *Wilson Diary*, 25 October 1902.

45. Skelton, Diary, 18 October 1902, SPRI MS 342/1/5; Savours, *Wilson Diary*, 24 October 1902.

46. Savours, *Wilson Diary*, 23–24 October 1902; Scott, Diary, 26 October 1902, SPRI MS 1464/3.

47. VOD, vol.1, 394; Armitage, *Two Years*, 134; Skelton, Diary, 25 October 1902, SPRI MS 342/1/5.

48. Skelton, Diary, 24–25, 27 October 1902, SPRI MS 342/1/5.

49. Skelton, Diary, 27 October 1902, SPRI MS 342/1/5.

50. VOD, vol.2, 3–6.

51. Skelton, Diary, 28–30 October 1902, SPRI MS 342/1/5; Savours, *Wilson Diary*, 24 October 1902.

52. Savours, *Wilson Diary*, 11 October 1902.

53. Savours, *Wilson Diary*, 11 October 1902.

54. Savours, *Wilson Diary*, 10–11, 14 October 1902, quote 11 October 1902.

55. Savours, *Wilson Diary*, 15 October 1902.

56. Skelton, Diary, 30 October 1902, SPRI MS 342/1/5; Scott, Diary, 30 October 1902, SPRI MS 1464/3.

57. VOD, vol.1, 402.

58. Armitage, *Two Years*, 144.

59. Skelton, Diary, 28 and 31 October 1902, SPRI MS 342/1/5; Mill, *Shackleton*, 74–75.

60. Skelton, Diary, 1–2 November 1902, SPRI MS 342/1/5.

61. Skelton, Diary, 30 October and 17 November 1902, SPRI MS 342/1/5; Armitage, *Two Years*, 148.

62. Skelton, Diary, 3 November 1902, SPRI MS 342/1/5.

63. Armitage thought this was the cause of the outbreak of illness, see Armitage, *Two Years*, 148–49; Skelton, Diary, 5 November 1902, SPRI MS 342/1/5.

64. Duncan, Diary, 8 November 1902, SPRI 1415; Skelton, Diary, 8 November 1902, SPRI MS 342/1/5.

65. Armitage, *Two Years*, 150–51.

66. Skelton, Diary, 8 November 1902, SPRI MS 342/1/5.

67. Armitage, *Two Years*, 152; Skelton, Diary, 15 November 1902, SPRI MS 342/1/5.

68. Skelton, Diary, 30 October and 17 November 1902, SPRI MS 342/1/5.

69. Armitage indicated in his published account that two eggs were given to each member of the expedition, see Armitage, *Two Years*, 153; Skelton, Diary, 17 November 1902, SPRI MS 342/1/5.

70. Skelton, Diary, 21 November 1902, SPRI MS 342/1/5; Armitage, *Two Years*, 153.

71. Skelton, Diary, 23 November 1902, SPRI MS 342/1/5.

72. Savours, *Wilson Diary*, 3 October 1902.

73. VOD, vol.2, 2; Armitage, *Two Years*, 162.

74. Armitage, *Two Years*, 165.

75. Armitage, *Two Years*, 170, 175, 177.

76. Armitage, *Two Years*, 178–80.

77. Armitage, *Two Years*, 182.

78. Armitage, *Two Years*, 183–84.

79. Armitage, *Two Years*, 163, 187.

80. Armitage, *Two Years*, 188.

81. Armitage, *Two Years*, 189.

82. Armitage, *Two Years*, 190.

83. Skelton, Diary, 21 January 1903, SPRI MS 342/1/5.

84. Skelton, Diary, 21 January 1903, SPRI MS 342/1/5.

85. Skelton, Diary, 22 January 1903, SPRI MS 342/1/5.

86. Skelton, Diary, 22–24 January 1903, SPRI MS 342/1/5.

10. THE ATTEMPT ON THE POLE

1. Savours, *Wilson Diary*, 3 October 1902.

2. Skelton, Diary, SPRI MS 342/1/5, 2 November 1902. Scott thought in terms of going to the end of December, rather than reaching a given latitude.

3. Savours, *Wilson Diary*, 30 October 1902.

4. VOD, vol.2, 8.

5. Savours, *Wilson Diary*, 1 November 1902.

6. Wilson and Shackleton wanted to take their sledging flags, but at first Scott was hesitant because he did not like his. In the end they were photographed with banners flying.

7. VOD, vol.2, 7.

8. Savours, *Wilson Diary*, 2 November 1902.

9. VOD, vol.2, 8.

10. Savours, *Wilson Diary*, 2 November 1902; Scott, Diary, 3 November 1902, SPRI MS 1464/3.

11. Scott, Diary, 3 November 1902, SPRI MS 1464/3; VOD, vol.2, 8.

12. Scott, Diary, 4 November 1902, SPRI MS 1464/3; Savours, *Wilson Diary*, 4 November 1902.

13. Scott, Diary, 5 November 1902, SPRI MS 1464/3; Savours, *Wilson Diary*, 5 November 1902.

14. Savours, *Wilson Diary*, 6 November 1902.

15. Savours, *Wilson Diary*, 8–9 November 1902; Scott, Diary, 9 November 1902, SPRI MS 1464/3.

16. *VOD*, vol.2, 9.

17. For references to dogs needing an object ahead of them or doing better when such conditions exist, see Scott, Diary, SPRI MS 1464/3, 12 November 1902; such references can also be found in Scott's published account, see *VOD*, vol.2, 9.

18. Savours, *Wilson Diary*, 10 November 1902; Larry Hobbs is a naturalist with long-standing and wide-ranging experience in Antarctica.

19. Scott, Diary, 12 November 1902, SPRI MS 1464/3.

20. Savours, *Wilson Diary*, 13 November 1902.

21. Savours, *Wilson Diary*, 13 November 1902.

22. Savours, *Wilson Diary*, 16 November 1902.

23. Scott, Diary, 18 November 1902, SPRI MS 1464/3. Scott later commented on his desire to have seal to feed the dogs to revive them again, *VOD*, vol.2, 38.

24. Scott, Diary, 21 November 1902, SPRI MS 1464/3; Savours, *Wilson Diary*, 19–20 November 1902.

25. Scott, Diary, 22 November 1902, SPRI MS 1464/3.

26. Savours, *Wilson Diary*, 22 November 1902.

27. Savours, *Wilson Diary*, 26 November 1902.

28. Scott, Diary, 25 November 1902, SPRI MS 1464/3.

29. Savours, *Wilson Diary*, 30 November 1902.

30. Scott, *VOD*, vol.2, 22.

31. Savours, *Wilson Diary*, 1 December 1902.

32. *VOD*, vol.2, 31–32.

33. *VOD*, vol.2, 32.

34. Savours, *Wilson Diary*, 4 December 1902.

35. *VOD*, vol.2, 34.

36. *VOD*, vol.2, 44; Savours, *Wilson Diary*, 5 December 1902.

37. Scott, Diary, 3 January 1903, SPRI MS 1464/3; *VOD*, vol.2, 44–45.

38. These dog cakes were found and used on the *Aurora* expedition. Bernacchi, *Saga*, 67.

39. Savours, *Wilson Diary*, 20 December 1902.

40. *VOD*, vol.2, 68.

41. *VOD*, vol.2, 34; Savours, *Wilson Diary*, 14 December 1902.

42. *VOD*, vol.2, 37.

43. Savours, *Wilson Diary*, 21 December 1902.

44. *VOD*, vol.2, 41.

45. Savours, *Wilson Diary*, 23 December 1902.

46. *VOD*, vol.2, 41–43, 46; Savours, *Wilson Diary*, 24 December 1902.

47. *VOD*, vol.2, 46–47.

48. Savours, *Wilson Diary*, 25 December 1902.

49. On my Antarctic expedition with Ian Whillans in 1973–74, I provided the same service, having brought a plum pudding for Ian, who did not regard it as being Christmas without one.

50. *VOD*, vol.2, 48.

51. *VOD*, vol.2, 50.

52. *VOD*, vol.2, 50–51.

53. *VOD*, vol.2, 54; Savours, *Wilson Diary*, 26–27 December 1902.

54. *VOD*, vol.2, 56–58.

55. Scott, Diary, 30 December 1902, SPRI MS 1464/3.

56. *VOD*, vol.2, 59.

57. *VOD*, vol.2, 62–63; Savours, *Wilson Diary*, 31 December 1902.

58. *VOD*, vol.2, 63.

59. *VOD*, vol.2, 63; Savours, *Wilson Diary*, 1 January 1903.

60. Savours, *Wilson Diary*, 1, 2, 4 January 1903.

61. *VOD*, vol.2, 64; Scott, Diary, 31 December 1902, SPRI MS 1464/3.

62. Savours, *Wilson Diary*, 4 January 1903; Scott, Diary, 1 and 3 January 1903, SPRI MS 1464/3; *VOD*, vol.2, 64.

63. Savours, *Wilson Diary*, 5 January 1903.

64. Scott, Diary, 3 January 1903, SPRI MS 1464/3.

65. Scott, Diary, 3 January 1903, SPRI MS 1464/3.

66. *VOD*, vol.2, 65–66.

67. *VOD*, vol.2, 66–67, 69.

68. Scott, Diary, 11–12 January 1903, SPRI MS 1464/3.

69. *VOD*, vol.2, 72; Savours, *Wilson Diary*, 13 January 1903.

70. *VOD*, vol.2, 73–74.

71. Scott, Diary, 13 January 1903, SPRI MS 1464/3; *VOD*, vol.2, 74.

72. Scott, Diary, 13 January 1903, SPRI MS 1464/3.

73. Scott, Diary, 14–15 January 1903, SPRI MS 1464/3; Savours, *Wilson Diary*, 12, 14 January 1903.

74. Savours, *Wilson Diary*, 14 January 1903; Scott, Diary, 14–15 January 1903, SPRI MS 1464/3.

75. Savours, *Wilson Diary*, 14 January 1903. Later, when the walking got tough, Wilson regretted not having the skis; see Savours, *Wilson Diary*, 24 January 1903.

76. Scott, Diary, 15–16 January 1903, SPRI MS 1464/3; Savours, *Wilson Diary*, 16 and 19 January 1903.

77. Savours, *Wilson Diary*, 17–20 January; quote, Scott, Diary, 18 January 1903, SPRI MS 1464/3.

78. Scott, Diary, 17 January 1903, SPRI MS 1464/3.

79. *VOD*, vol.2, 81.

80. *VOD*, vol.2, 83.

81. Scott, Diary, 21 January 1903, SPRI MS 1464/3.

82. Scott, Diary, 22–25 January 1903, SPRI MS 1464/3. In Scott's published work I can find no reference to Shackleton pulling on skis on 25 January 1903.

83. Scott, Diary, 26 January 1903, SPRI MS 1464/3.

84. Scott, Diary, 27 January 1903, SPRI MS 1464/3.

85. Scott, Diary, 27 January 1903, SPRI MS 1464/3.

86. Scott, Diary, 28 January 1903, SPRI MS 1464/3; Savours, *Wilson Diary*, 28 January 1903.

87. *VOD*, vol.2, 86–87.

88. *VOD*, vol.2, 87.

89. *VOD*, vol.2, 87–89.

90. Savours, *Wilson Diary*, 29 January 1903; Scott, Diary, 29 January 1903, SPRI MS 1464/3.

91. Scott, Diary, 30 January 1903, SPRI MS 1464/3; *VOD*, vol.2, 89–90.

92. Savours, *Wilson Diary*, 30–31 January 1903; Scott, Diary, 31 January 1903, SPRI MS 1464/3.

93. *VOD*, vol.2, 90.

94. Scott, Diary, 1 February 1903, SPRI MS 1464/3.

95. Savours, *Wilson Diary*, 1 February 1903.

96. Scott, Diary, 2 February 1903, SPRI MS 1464/3.

97. *VOD*, vol.2, 91.

98. Savours, *Wilson Diary*, 3 February 1903.

11. THE RELIEF EXPEDITION

1. *Daily Mail*, 31 July 1901.

2. Ian Tyson once reflected in a song, "You say I'm dreaming, ah, but that don't make it less real," and that was the case here.

3. For Markham's appeal to the Franklin disaster as an example see, Markham to Balfour, 20 March 1902, RGS 15/1/52; Markham to Lord Brassey, 9 October 1901, RGS 15/1/5.

4. RGS Council to the Treasury, 21 March 1902, RGS 17/1/1.

5. Markham, "History of the Morning," RGS 19/3/3, 5, 9; Markham, "Dates of the Relief Ship," RGS 19/3/2.

6. G. Murray to Markham, 26 June 1901, RGS 4/2/24; L. B. Quartermain, "Ten

Forgotten Men of Antarctica," SPRI MS 1293/5, 11; Clements R. Markham, *Lands of Silence* (Cambridge: Cambridge University Press, 1921): 332.

7. Markham, "Dates of the Relief Ship."

8. The other five members were Mr. Hughes, Sutherland Mackenzie, Admiral A. H. Markham, Admiral Sir J. Bruce, and Howard Saunders. Markham, "History of the Morning," 41.

9. *Cape Town Argus*, 29 October 1901, 5.

10. *Daily Graphic*, 25 February 1902; *Cape Town Argus*, 29 October 1901; Clements R. Markham, "Appeal on Behalf of the National Antarctic Relief Ship," RGS 15/2/1; Markham, "Appeal on Behalf of the National Antarctic Expedition Relief Ship," *JMGS* 18 (1902): 236; Markham, "Dates of the Relief Ship"; Markham to Lord Brassey, 9 October 1901, RGS 15/1/5.

11. Markham, "Dates of the Relief Ship"; *Daily Chronicle*, 17 June 1901; Markham, "History of the Morning," 21, 59; Fishmongers Hall to Markham, 21 February 1902, RGS 15/1/45; Goldsmiths Hall to Markham, 14 February 1902, RGS 15/1/37. The Skinner's Hall also contributed £50, Skinner's Hall to Markham, 2 April 1902, RGS 15/1/56.

12. R. W. Hudson to Markham, 7 March 1902, RGS 15/1/47; Edward Lawson to Markham, 3 December 1901, RGS 15/1/21; Markham, "*Morning* Subscribers," RGS 19/5/22; Lord Aldenham to Markham, 2 February 1902, RGS 15/1/38; John Halliday to Markham, 15 March 1902, RGS 15/1/50; Duncan Milligan to Markham, 12 December 1901, RGS 15/1/29. Hugh Leonard gave £100 out of concern for the men's safety. Hugh Leonard to Markham, 24 November 1901, RGS 15/1/20; Markham, "History of the Morning," 20, 29.

13. Markham, "Appeal on Behalf," *JMGS*, 236; quote, RGS Council to Treasury, 21 March 1902, RGS 17/1/1; *Daily Graphic*, 25 February 1902; Markham, "History of the Morning," 20.

14. Markham, "History of the Morning," 4, 30; quote, Markham to Balfour, 21 March 1902, RGS 15/1/52; quote, RGS Council to the Treasury, 21 March 1901, RGS 17/1/1.

15. Parry to Markham, 16 April 1902, RGS 17/1/3; Parry to Markham, 25 March 1902, RGS 19/3/2; Parry to Markham, 30 April 1902, RGS 17/1/4; Parry to Markham, 25 March 1902, RGS 17/1/2; Parry to Markham, 30 April 1902, RGS 17/1/4; Markham, "Dates of the Relief Ship"; Markham, "History of the Morning," 30.

16. Markham, "History of the Morning," 33; Markham, "Dates of the Relief Ship"; *The Times*, 10 May 1902; *Norfolk Chronicle*, 19 April 1902.

17. Markham, "History of the Morning," 32; Markham, "Dates of the Relief Ship."

18. Atlee Hunt to Markham, 19 February 1902, RGS 15/1/40; Markham, "History of the Morning," 31.

19. Markham, "History of the Morning," 35; another figure cited was £22,640.

20. Huggins to Markham, 15 November 1901, RGS 15/1/16; RS to RGS, 20 October 1902, RGS 15/2/28.

21. Quartermain, "Ten Forgotten Men of Antarctica," 1.

22. Markham, "History of the Morning," 64; Colbeck to Markham, 2 May 1901, RGS 16/1/2; quote, Markham to Colbeck, 2 November 1901, SPRI MS 1348/1/2.

23. Markham to Colbeck, 2 December 1901, SPRI MS 1348/1/5.

24. Markham, "History of the Morning," 61.

25. Markham, "History of the Morning," 63–64; Markham to Colbeck, 2 November 1901, SPRI 1348/1/2; Markham, "Dates of the Relief Ship"; Markham to Colbeck, 21 December 1901, SPRI MS 1348/1/6; Markham to Colbeck, 11 January 1902, SPRI MS 1348/1/8.

26. Markham to Colbeck, 26 September 1901, SPRI MS 1348/1/1; Markham, "Dates of the Relief Ship."

27. Markham to Colbeck, September 1902, SPRI MS 1348/1/9; Markham to Colbeck, 28 February 1903, SPRI MS 1348/1/10; Markham, "History of the Morning," 65.

28. Quartermain, "Ten Forgotten Men of Antarctica," 12.

29. Markham, "History of the Morning," 67; I refer to England's role in the decision to winter at McMurdo, which I shall discuss in my forthcoming work "Lure of the South: Antarctica, 1901–9." Markham, "Dates of the Relief Ship."

30. RSCM, 28 May 1903; Markham occasionally gave lectures onboard the training ship. Gerald S. Doorly, The Voyages of the "Morning" (London: Smith, Elder, 1916; Norwich: Bluntisham, 1995), 23, 129; Markham, "Dates of the Relief Ship"; Markham, "History of the Morning," 70; quote, Markham to Colbeck, 12 April 1902, SPRI MS 1348/1/7.

31. Although his promotion had not gone through, I refer to him as Lieutenant Evans, because he is most widely known by that title for his work on Scott's second expedition.

32. Doorly, Morning, 12.

33. Doorly, Morning, 24; Markham, "History of the Morning," 73.

34. Doorly, Morning, 22–24.

35. Markham, "History of the Morning," 75–77.

36. Doorly, Morning, 28; Markham, "History of the Morning," 73, 76.

37. Markham, "Dates of the Relief Ship."

38. Colbeck to Markham [March 1903], RGS 19/2/10, 8; Markham, "History of the Morning," 89.

39. Markham, "Dates of the Relief Ship"; Armitage, *Two Years*, 194; Markham, "History of the Morning," 62, 79, 80, 83, 87; Doorly, Diary, 8 November 1902, SPRI MS 575/6. The original of the diary is in the Mitchell Library.

40. Markham, "Dates of the Relief Ship"; Bonnevie to Markham, 19 December 1899, RGS 14/1/2; David Bruce to Markham, 21 September 1901, RGS 14/1/14.

41. Quartermain, "Ten Forgotten Men of Antarctica," 12.

42. *Daily Graphic*, 19 February 1902.

43. Bull to Bruce, 24 December 1901, SPRI MS 101/27/3.

44. Markham, "History of the Morning," 39.

45. RGS Committee Book, 16, 24, and 31 October 1901; Markham, "Dates of the Relief Ship"; Markham, "History of the Morning," 42; Markham, "Notes on *Morning*," RGS 18/3/15.

46. *Daily Graphic*, 25 February 1902. One can trace the reliance of the press on previous press writing by following this comment. See *Daily Mail*, 29 May 1903 and *The Press* (Christchurch), 2 April 1904.

47. Quartermain, "Ten Forgotten Men of Antarctica," 25.

48. The dimensions of the *Morning* were 140 feet long, 31.5 feet breadth, and 16.5 feet draught. Listed as 437 gross tonnage, her registered tonnage was 297. "The Departure of the *Morning*," GJ 20 (August 1902): 210; Bonnevie to Markham, 30 October 1901, RGS 14/2/15; Markham, "Dates of the Relief Ship."

49. MacGregor to Markham, 11 December 1901, RGS 18/1/12; Markham to Colbeck, 11 January 1902, SPRI MS 1348/1/8; Markham, "Dates of the Relief Ship."

50. Quartermain, "Ten Forgotten Men of Antarctica," 12; Markham, "Dates of the Relief Ship"; R. & H. Green to Markham, 16 January 1902, RGS 18/3/11; Markham, "History of the Morning," 58–59; Markham to Colbeck, 11 January 1902; "The National Antarctic Expedition," GJ 20 (August 1902): 212; R. & H. Green to Markham, June 1902, RGS 18/3/38.

51. "The National Antarctic Expedition," GJ 20 (August 1902): 210–11.

52. "Bill for Lamps for the *Morning*," RGS 18/5/11.

53. Markham, "History of the Morning," 48; Markham, "Dates of the Relief Ship." Each ship had a sign signal, a series of letters unique to each vessel. Polar trivia buffs wanting the most useless information encountered in six years of research will want to know that the identification for the *Discovery* was SMLF while the *Morning* was THRF.

54. "The National Antarctic Expedition," GJ 20 (August 1902): 210–12.

55. "The National Antarctic Expedition," 214–15.

56. "The National Antarctic Expedition," 215–16.

57. Doorly, *Morning*, 32–36.

58. Doorly, Diary, 9 July 1902, SPRI MS 575/6.

59. Doorly, Diary, 10 July 1902, SPRI MS 575/6.

60. Doorly, Diary, 23 July 1902, SPRI MS 575/6.

61. Doorly, Diary, 23 July 1902, SPRI MS 575/6.

62. Doorly, Diary, 24–26 July 1902, SPRI MS 575/6.

63. Doorly, Diary, 28 July 1902, SPRI MS 575/6.

64. Doorly, Diary, 3 August 1902, SPRI MS 575/6.

65. Doorly, Diary, 31 July and 8 August 1902, SPRI MS 575/6.

66. Doorly, Diary, 20 July 1902, SPRI MS 575/6.

67. Parkin was the victim of this charade. Doorly, Diary, 18 August 1902, SPRI MS 575/6.

68. Quartermain, "Ten Forgotten Men of Antarctica," 12, 24; Doorly, *Morning*, 44–49. For Evans's impression of Colbeck's superb seamanship see Quartermain, "Ten Forgotten Men of Antarctica," 12, 29; Bernacchi, *Saga*, 108.

69. The list issued to officers included: sleeping bag, blanket, pillow, pair of thigh boots, spare pair of boots, 2 pair Arctic boots, 3 suits pajamas, 2 head covers with nose protectors, 6 singlets, 6 Pauls, 4 shirts, 4 pair thick socks, 6 pair half hose, collie belt, 6 collars, 3 pairs anklets, 3 pairs foot pieces, 2 comforters, 2 cardigan jackets, 2 waistcoats, 4 pairs shooting gloves, 6 pairs undermittens, 6 pairs overmittens, 1 pair slippers, 1 pair Clarence slippers, various socks and stockings, 3 blue coats, 4 blue trousers, and 2 waistcoats.

70. Doorly, Diary, 30 August, 25 September, 8 and 28 October 1902, SPRI MS 575/6; Doorly, *Morning*, 49.

71. Colbeck to Markham, 6 December 1902, RGS 19/2/6.

72. Doorly, Diary, 22 September 1902, SPRI MS 575/6.

73. Doorly, Diary, 13 August, 16 September, 14 November 1902, SPRI MS 575/6; RGS 19/3/3, 40.

74. Colbeck to Markham, 6 December 1902, RGS 19/2/6.

75. Cape Town *Argus*, 24 December 1937.

76. Colbeck to Markham, telegram, 25 March 1903, RGS 19/2/8; Colbeck to Markham [March 1903], RGS 19/2/10.

77. Cape Town *Argus*, 24 December 1937; Doorly, Diary, 25 December 1902, SPRI MS 575/6; Colbeck to Markham [March 1903], RGS 19/2/10.

78. Doorly, Diary, 29 January 1903, SPRI MS 575/6; Doorly, *Morning*, 89.

79. Quartermain, "Ten Forgotten Men of Antarctica," 22; Colbeck to Markham [March 1903], RGS 19/2/10; Doorly, Diary, 5 January 1903, SPRI MS 575/6.

80. Doorly, Diary, 8 January 1903, SPRI MS 575/6; Colbeck to Markham, n.d., RGS 19/2/10.

81. Doorly, Diary, 8 January 1903, SPRI MS 575/6.

82. Doorly, *Morning*, 74; Doorly, Diary, 13–14 January 1903, SPRI MS 575/6; Colbeck to Markham, telegram, 25 March 1903, RGS 19/2/8.

83. Colbeck to Markham [March 1903], RGS 19/2/10; Doorly, *Morning*, 84.

84. Doorly, Diary, 21–23 January 1903, SPRI MS 575/6.

85. Lashly, Diary, 24 January 1903, SPRI MS 890/1.

86. Scott, Diary, 18 July 1902, SPRI MS 1464/3; Doorly, Diary, 29 January 1903, SPRI MS 575/6.

87. Armitage, *Two Years*, 191, 285.

88. Doorly, Diary, 27 January 1903, SPRI MS 575/6.

89. Doorly, Diary, 12 February 1903, SPRI MS 575/6.

90. Markham to Scott, June 1902, RGS 12/3/21, 2; Colbeck to Markham [March 1903], RGS 19/2/10; Quartermain, "Ten Forgotten Men of Antarctica," 20. At one point Markham hoped that the *Morning* could bring out 150 to 200 tons of coal, an unrealistic figure considering its size.

91. *VOD*, vol.2, 124–25; Scott, "The National Antarctic Expedition" (1904): 17; *Canterbury Times*, 6 April 1904, 27, 31.

92. Royds, Diary, 17 February 1903, SPRI MS 654/3.

93. As early as 9 February 1903 Royds thought that Scott believed that the ship would not be freed that season or at least that the release might not come until March or April. Royds, Diary, 9–10 February 1903, SPRI MS 654/3.

94. Ellis, *Lashly*, 64, quoting 2 March 1903.

95. Williamson, Diary, 8 February 1903, SPRI MS 774/1/2; Plumley, Diary, 19 February 1903, SPRI MS 972.

96. Royds, Diary, 23 February 1903, SPRI MS 654/3. Markham wrote that Hare had had enough; see Markham, "Record of Antarctic Silver Medalists" [1904], RGS 3/1/22. Hare, Diary, 23 February 1903, SPRI MS 753. Scott, Diary, 7 March 1903, SPRI MS 1464/3.

97. Skelton, Diary, 28 February 1903, SPRI MS 342/1/6.

98. Huntford, *Shackleton*, 114–17. For Scott's published version of the events, see *VOD*, vol.2, 127–28. A careful reader will also want to consider both Huntford's animosity toward Scott and his benevolent attitude to Shackleton. Huntford's assessment is based on a careful reading of the record, and the reader is urged to reread this passage.

99. Royds, Diary, 14 February 1903, SPRI MS 654/3.

100. Not until 18 March 1903 did Wilson make the trek up to Crater Hill, Savours, *Wilson Diary*, 18 March 1903.

101. Scott in his diary stated that he feared that Shackleton would never do outdoor work. Scott, Diary, 7 March 1903, SPRI MS 1464/3.

102. Armitage, *Cadet*, 132.

103. Royds, Diary, 20 February 1903, SPRI MS 654/3.

104. Scott, Diary, 7 March 1903, SPRI MS 1464/3; SPRI MS 1160/5.

105. SPRI MS 1160/5, 16.

106. Barne, Diary, 21 February 1903, SPRI MS 353/3/2.

107. *VOD*, vol.2, 127–28.

108. Skelton, Diary, 1 March 1903, SPRI MS 342/1/6.

109. Royds, Diary, 2 March 1903, SPRI MS 654/3.

12. RED SUNSET OF NOON IS VANISHING FAST

The title of this chapter is taken from Robert Falcon Scott, Diary, 3 May 1903, SPRI MS 1464/3.

1. Scott to Sir A. Moore, 22 March 1904, SPRI MS 475/3/1.

2. Markham to Scott, 19 February 1903, RGS 12/3/25.

3. Although Scott's published account indicated that he had given up hope by 13 March 1903 and other contemporaneous journal entries by other members of the expedition stated that Scott had given up hope by various dates, Scott considered that a late storm would free the ship. Departing late in the season might have spelled disaster for the *Discovery* had the ship been beset in unfavorable circumstances en route northward.

4. Scott, Summary of Proceedings, 23 March 1904, RGS 12/4/4, 1; Savours, *Wilson Diary*, 9 March 1903.

5. Royds, Diary, 2 March 1903, SPRI MS 654/3; Skelton, Diary, 7–8 March 1903, SPRI MS 342/1/6; Scott, Diary, 24 June 1903, SPRI MS 1464/3; Hodgson, Diary, 28 March 1903, SPRI MS 595/1.

6. Scott to Mill, 16 February 1903, SPRI 100/100/3.

7. Royds, Diary, 21 March 1903, SPRI MS 654/3; Hodgson, Diary, 18 May 1903, SPRI MS 595/1; Skelton, Diary, 26 February 1903, SPRI MS 342/1/6.

8. Skelton, Diary, 5, 6, and 10 March and 7 April 1903, SPRI MS 342/1/6.

9. Skelton, Diary, 9, 14, 24 April 1903, SPRI MS 342/1/6; Royds, Diary, 25 April 1903, SPRI MS 654/4; RGS 12/4/4, 2.

10. Scott, Diary, 7 March 1903, SPRI MS 1464/3.

11. Plumley, Diary, 5 February 1903, SPRI 972; Scott, Summary of Proceedings, 1–2; Hodgson, Diary, 31 May 1903, SPRI MS 595/1; Savours, *Wilson Diary*, 17 May 1903; Scott, Diary, 25 April, 6 May, 24 June 1903, SPRI MS 1464/3; Williamson, Diary, 23 June 1903, SPRI MS 774/1/2.

12. Scott, Diary, SPRI MS 1464/3; Hodgson, Diary, 3 August 1903, SPRI MS

595/1; Plumley, Diary, 3 August 1903, SPRI 972; Williamson, Diary, 23 June, 22 July 1903, SPRI MS 774/1/2; Skelton, Diary, 25 July 1903, SPRI MS 342/1/6.

13. Hodgson, Diary, 15 June and 19 August 1903, SPRI MS 595/1.

14. Skelton, Diary, 7, 15, 21 April 1903, SPRI MS 342/1/6; Savours, *Wilson Diary*, 29 April 1903; Lashly, Diary, 1 and 4 April 1903, SPRI MS 890/1; Royds, Diary, 22 April 1903, SPRI MS 654/4; Scott, Diary, 2 April 1903, SPRI MS 1464/3.

15. Savours, *Wilson Diary*, 7 May, 6 June 1903; Hodgson, Diary, 17 July 1903, SPRI MS 595/1.

16. Skelton, Diary, 1 June 1903, SPRI MS 342/1/6. Later a similar model was given to Sir Clements R. Markham as a gift from the crew. I have not determined whether that sledge was made by Lashly.

17. Savours, *Wilson Diary*, 24 June 1903.

18. Savours, *Wilson Diary*, 25 May 1903.

19. Scott, Diary, 6 May 1903, SPRI MS 1464/3; VOD, vol.2, 141.

20. Skelton, Diary, 7 April 1903, SPRI MS 342/1/6; Scott, Diary, 29 April 1903, SPRI MS 1464/3.

21. Hodgson, Diary, 23 April 1903, SPRI MS 595/1.

22. Skelton, Diary, 8 March 1903, SPRI MS 342/1/6; SPRI MS 100/100/4; Scott, Summary of Proceedings, 3.

23. Scott to Mill, 27 February 1904; SPRI 100/100/4; Scott to Sir A. Moore, 2 March 1904, SPRI 475/3/1.

24. VOD, vol.2, 147; Royds, Diary, 8 April 1903, SPRI MS 654/3; Plumley, Diary, 3 May 1903, SPRI 972.

25. Savours, *Wilson Diary*, 19 May 1903.

26. VOD, vol.2, 142–43; Savours, *Wilson Diary*, 25 May 1903.

27. Scott noted in retrospect, having missed a number of days, that the "only way to keep a diary" is to write each day. Scott, Diary, 3 January 1904, SPRI MS 352/1/3. Many men, including Williamson, began to write weekly summaries instead of daily entries.

28. Scott, Summary of Proceedings, 22; Royds, Diary, 24 June 1902, SPRI MS 654/3.

29. Boyds, Diary, 20 March 1903, SPRI MS 654/3.

30. Armitage also occasionally went for a stroll with Hodgson, during which they would discuss local politics. Hodgson, Diary, 26 July 1903, SPRI MS 595/1.

31. Skelton, Diary, 17 June 1903, SPRI MS 342/1/6; Scott, Diary, 24 April 1903, SPRI MS 1464/3; Plumley, Diary, 23 April, 22 June 1903, SPRI 972; Hodgson, Diary, 22 June 1903, SPRI MS 595/1; Savours, *Wilson Diary*, 21 June 1903; VOD, vol.2, 140; quote, Williamson, Diary, 22 June 1903, SPRI MS 774/1/2.

32. Scott, Summary of Proceedings, 2–3.

33. Scott, Summary of Proceedings, 3–4.

34. Plumley, Diary, 10 August 1903, SPRI 972; Armitage, *Two Years*, 240.

35. Savours, *Wilson Diary*, 23 June 1903.

36. Savours, *Wilson Diary*, 7 September 1903.

37. Savours, *Wilson Diary*, 13 September 1903.

38. Savours, *Wilson Diary*, 13 September 1903.

39. Savours, *Wilson Diary*, 16 September 1903.

40. Scott, Summary of Proceedings, 4–5.

41. *VOD*, vol.2, 158.

42. Savours, *Wilson Diary*, 12–18 October 1903.

43. Savours, *Wilson Diary*, 18 October 1903.

44. Savours, *Wilson Diary*, 19 October 1903.

45. Savours, *Wilson Diary*, 22–28 October 1903.

46. Savours, *Wilson Diary*, 29 October 1903.

47. Williamson, Diary, 1–7 November 1903, SPRI MS 774/1/2; Savours, *Wilson Diary*, 3–5 November 1903.

48. Scott, Summary of Proceedings, 5.

49. Scott, Summary of Proceedings, 5.

50. Scott, Summary of Proceedings, 5–6.

51. *Canterbury Times*, 6 April 1904, 27.

52. *VOD*, vol.2, 149.

53. *Canterbury Times*, 6 April 1904, 27.

54. Hodgson, Diary, 25–26, 30 November 1903, SPRI MS 595/1; Scott, Summary of Proceedings, 11.

55. *VOD*, vol.2, 163.

56. *VOD*, vol.2, 164, 166.

57. Skelton, Diary, 25 October 1903, SPRI MS 342/1/7; *VOD*, vol.2, 170–72.

58. *VOD*, vol.2, 174, 177, 187.

59. *VOD*, vol.2, 174–75.

60. *VOD*, vol.2, 178.

61. *VOD*, vol.2, 179–80, 183.

62. *VOD*, vol.2, 183–84.

63. *VOD*, vol.2, 184–85.

64. Scott, Summary of Proceedings, 8–9; *VOD*, vol.2, 187.

65. James Eights (1798–1882), an American who accompanied the Palmer-Pendleton expedition of 1829–31, actually found the first Antarctic fossils, but his work was published in an obscure journal and was lost to science at the time of the

Discovery expedition. For details on the work of Eights see the masterful account by Kenneth J. Bertrand, *Americans in Antarctica, 1775–1948* (New York: American Geographical Society, 1971), 144–58 and John M. Clarke, "The Reincarnation of James Eights," *Scientific Monthly* 2 (February 1916): 189–202.

66. *Canterbury Times,* 6 April 1904, 29.

67. Scott's affection for his men was clearly displayed in his description of Handsley's behavior, see *VOD*, vol.2, 189–90.

68. Scott, Summary of Proceedings, 9; *VOD*, vol.2, 190.

69. *VOD*, vol.2, 191.

70. Scott acknowledged this learning experience in his published account, see *VOD*, vol.2, 199.

71. *VOD*, vol.2, 193–94.

72. *VOD*, vol.2, 197.

73. For the change in dietary content of his dreams this year, versus the southern journey, see *VOD*, vol.2, 201.

74. *VOD*, vol.2, 198–99.

75. *VOD*, vol.2, 201–2.

76. *VOD*, vol.2, 203.

77. *VOD*, vol.2, 204.

78. *VOD*, vol.2, 205.

79. *VOD*, vol.2, 205–7.

80. *VOD*, vol.2, 207–9.

81. *VOD*, vol.2, 210.

82. *VOD*, vol.2, 210.

83. *VOD*, vol.2, 211. Is it reasonable to question whether Lashly, who later won the Albert Medal for heroism on the second Scott expedition, had not earned one on this day too? Is it not appropriate to suggest, as many have in this century, that Lashly might have made the difference on the polar party of 1911–12?

84. *VOD*, vol.2, 212.

85. *VOD*, vol.2, 216–17.

86. Skelton, Diary, 11 October 1903, SPRI MS 342/1/6; *VOD*, vol.2, 218–19.

87. *The Press* (Christchurch), 6 April 1904, 28; Savours, *Wilson Diary*, 27 December 1903.

88. *The Press* (Christchurch), 6 April 1904, 28.

89. Savours, *Wilson Diary*, 24 December 1903; *Canterbury Times*, 6 April 1904, 28.

90. *The Press* (Christchurch), 6 April 1904, 28; Savours, *Wilson Diary*, 31 December 1903.

91. Scott, Summary of Proceedings, 12; Savours, *Wilson Diary*, 2 January 1904.

92. Savours, *Wilson Diary*, 5 January 1904.

13. THE GRAND OLD MAN FALTERS

1. Doorly, *Morning*, 115–16. However much some writers malign the Victorians and the Edwardians, one can still feel a sense of admiration for a century and for a people who thought self-reliance, duty, and faithfulness were concepts to live by.

2. Doorly, *Morning*, 121–22.

3. Doorly, Diary, 6 March 1903, SPRI MS 575/6. Hitting a sleeping whale might seem impossible, but whalers commented about finding whales asleep and thereby easy prey. My own experience bears this out. In January 1997 on the M/S *Explorer*, the ship came upon two sleeping whales and, maneuvering closer, we observed the animals for twenty minutes.

4. Doorly, Diary, 12–20 March 1903, SPRI MS 575/6.

5. Doorly, Diary, 24 March 1903, SPRI MS 575/6.

6. Doorly, *Morning*, 123.

7. England, Evans, and Doorly were the officers; they would later be joined by Colbeck, who subsequently married Edith Robinson 7 November 1904, SPRI MS 1293/5, 22.

8. "The British Antarctic Expedition," *Nature* 67 (2 April 1903): 516–17; Colbeck to Markham [March 1903], RGS 19/2/10; Colbeck to Markham, 13 April 1903, RGS 19/2/10.

9. An editorial in *The Times* generously praised Colbeck, *The Times*, 28 August 1903; Sir Clements R. Markham, "The First Year's Work of the National Antarctic Expedition," *GJ* 22 (July 1903): 19.

10. "The British Antarctic Expedition," *SGM* 19 (April 1903): 223. Note that the Royal Scottish Geographical Society refers to the "British" not "National" expedition.

11. Sir Clements R. Markham, "The First Year's Work of the National Antarctic Expedition," *GJ* 22 (July 1903): 19.

12. Markham to Colbeck, 28 February 1903, SPRI MS 1348/1/10.

13. Markham to Colbeck, 28 February 1903, SPRI MS 1348/1/10. Markham to Colbeck [March 1903], RGS 19/2/10.

14. Markham to Colbeck [March 1903], RGS 19/2/10.

15. Markham to Colbeck, September 1903, SPRI MS 1348/1/17.

16. Presidents of RS and RGS to Balfour, 19 May 1903, RGS 17/1/10.

17. Mowatt to Markham, 14 May 1903, RGS Correspondence.

18. Mowatt to Markham, 14 May 1903, RGS Correspondence; Markham to Mowatt, 16 May 1903, RGS Correspondence.

19. Presidents of RS and RGS to Balfour, 19 May 1903, RGS 17/1/10.

20. RGS Committee Minutes, 13 February 1902; presidents of RS and RGS to Balfour, 19 May 1903, RGS 17/1/10.

21. Presidents of RS and RGS to Balfour, 19 May 1903, RGS 17/1/10.

22. Markham to Ramsey, 14 June 1903, RGS 17/1/16.

23. Longhurst to Scott, 8 October 1903, SPRI MS 366/15/17; quote, Mill to Scott, 8 October 1903, SPRI MS 366/15/65.

24. RSCM, 28 May and 18 June 1903.

25. Markham, Report to the Council, 26 May 1903, RGS 17/1/9.

26. Foster to Markham, 12 June 1903; RGS 17/1/14.

27. Markham to Ramsey, 14 June 1903; RGS 17/1/16.

28. Mowatt to the presidents of the RS and RGS, 20 June 1903, RGS 17/1/10.

29. Mowatt to the presidents of the RS and RGS.

30. Markham, "Dates of the Relief Ship"; Markham to Colbeck, 24 June [1903], SPRI MS 1348/1/11; quote, "breach of trust," Markham, "Dates of the Relief Ship," 5; quote "pistol," Markham to Colbeck, 26 June 1903, SPRI MS 1348/1/12; quote, "under protest," Markham, "Dates of the Relief Ship," 5.

31. Markham to Colbeck, 24 June [1903], SPRI MS 1348/1/11.

32. Longhurst to Scott, 8 October 1903, SPRI MS 366/15/17.

33. Mill to Scott, 8 October 1903, SPRI MS 366/15/65.

34. Markham to Colbeck, 24 June [1903], SPRI MS 1348/1/11; Longhurst to Scott, 8 October 1903, SPRI MS 366/15/17; Markham to Colbeck, 23 August 1903, SPRI MS 1348/1/15.

35. *The Press* (Christchurch), 2 April 1904, 8; Bernacchi, *Saga*, 112; Wharton to Scott, 23 September 1903, SPRI MS 366/15/79; Mill to Scott, 8 October 1903, SPRI MS 366/15/65.

36. *The Scotsman*, 18 August 1903.

37. Longhurst to Scott, 8 October 1903, SPRI MS 366/15/17; Markham to Colbeck, 23 August 1903, SPRI MS 1348/1/15; Markham to Colbeck, 26 June 1903, SPRI MS 1348/1/12; quotes, "niggardly" and "wretched jacks," Markham to Colbeck, 8 August 1903, SPRI MS 1348/1/13.

38. Admiralty orders to Colbeck, RGS 20/137c.

39. Markham to Colbeck, 10 August [1903], SPRI MS 1348/1/14; Markham to Colbeck, 27 January 1904, SPRI MS 1348/1/18.

40. Markham to Colbeck, 2 September 1903, SPRI MS 1348/1/17; Markham to Colbeck, 23 August 1903, SPRI MS 1348/1/15.

41. Markham to Colbeck, 23 August 1903, SPRI MS 1348/1/15.

42. Markham to Colbeck, 24 August 1903, SPRI MS 1348/1/16.

43. Markham put the figure for the second relief expedition at £50,000, *Westminster Gazette*, 8 April 1904, while Longhurst suggested that the price was £40,000, Longhurst to Scott, 8 October 1903, SPRI MS 366/15/17. Markham to Colbeck, 10 August [1903], SPRI MS 1348/1/14.

44. Markham to Colbeck, 24 April 1903, SPRI MS 1348/1/16.

45. Markham to Colbeck, 23 August 1903, SPRI MS 1348/1/15.

46. Markham to Colbeck, 27 January 1904, SPRI MS 1348/1/18.

47. Markham to Colbeck, 23 August 1903, SPRI MS 1348/1/15; Markham to Colbeck, 27 January 1904, SPRI MS 1348/1/18; quote, "grasp," Markham to Colbeck, 24 August 1903, SPRI MS 1348/1/16.

48. Doorly, *Morning*, 135.

49. *The Press* (Christchurch), 2 and 6 April 1904, 8.

50. Sailing Instructions to Captain McKay, SPRI MS 761/8/2.

51. Doorly, *Morning*, 138; *The Press* (Christchurch), 2 April 1904, 8.

52. Doorly, Diary, 24 October 1903, SPRI MS 575/6; Doorly, *Morning*, 133–34.

53. Doorly, *Morning*, 138–40.

54. Doorly, Diary, 6, 9, 12 December 1903, SPRI MS 575/6.

55. Doorly, Diary, 17 December 1903, SPRI MS 575/6.

56. Doorly, *Morning*, 144–45; Doorly, Diary, 27 December 1903, SPRI MS 575/6.

57. Doorly, Diary, 26–28 December 1903, SPRI MS 575/6.

58. Doorly, Diary, 27 and 31 December 1903, SPRI MS 575/6.

59. Doorly, *Morning*, 143–44. The family of Royds had conspired to have a similar set of letters given to him throughout his winter. Anyone who has ever traveled alone can appreciate the richness of this gift.

60. Doorly, Diary, 4 January 1904, SPRI MS 575/6.

61. Doorly, Diary, 5 January 1904, SPRI MS 575/6.

62. Doorly, Diary, 5 January 1904, SPRI MS 575/6; Hodgson, Diary, 5 January 1904, SPRI MS 595/1; quote, "ripping," Royds, Diary, 5 January 1904, SPRI MS 654/4; Williamson, Diary, 5 January 1904, SPRI MS 774/1/2.

63. Ford, Diary, 5–6 January 1904, SPRI MS 1174; Hodgson, Diary, 6 January 1904, SPRI MS 595/1; Royds, Diary, 6 January 1904, SPRI MS 654/4.

64. Doorly, Diary, 6 January 1904, SPRI MS 575/6.

65. Ford, Diary, 10 January 1904, SPRI MS 1174.

66. Williamson, Diary, 10 January 1904, SPRI MS 774/1/2.

67. Royds, Diary, 4 January 1904, SPRI MS 654/4; *The Press* (Christchurch), 2 April 1904, 8.

68. Williamson, Diary, 11 January 1904, SPRI MS 774/1/2; Hodgson, Diary, 12 January 1904, SPRI MS 595/1.

69. Mill to Scott, 8 June 1904, SPRI MS 366/15/66.

70. Doorly, Diary, 5 January 1904, SPRI MS 575/6.

71. Hodgson, Diary, 13 January 1904, SPRI MS 595/1; Williamson, Diary, 14 January 1904, SPRI MS 774/1/2.

72. Royds, Diary, 8 January 1904, SPRI MS 654/4.

73. Ford, Diary, 26 January 1904, SPRI MS 1174.

74. *The Press* (Christchurch), 2 April 1904, 8.

75. Doorly, Diary, 22 January 1904, SPRI MS 575/6; Williamson, Diary, 23 January 1904, SPRI MS 774/1/2.

76. Doorly, Diary, 22 January 1904, SPRI MS 575/6; *The Press* (Christchurch), 2 April 1904, 8.

77. Williamson, Diary, 31 January and 2 February 1904, SPRI MS 774/1/2; Barne, Diary, 23 January 1904, SPRI MS 1518/3; Doorly, Diary, 22 January and 3 February 1904, SPRI MS 575/6; Hodgson, Diary, 31 January 1904, SPRI MS 595/1.

78. Doorly, Diary, 31 January and 3 February 1904, SPRI MS 575/6.

79. Ford, Diary, 4 February 1904, SPRI MS 1174.

80. Royds, Diary, 9 February 1904, SPRI MS 654/4.

81. Williamson, Diary, 9 February 1904, SPRI MS 774/1/2; Royds, Diary, 9 February 1904, SPRI MS 654/4; Ford, Diary, 9 February 1904, SPRI MS 1174.

82. Royds, Diary, 10 February 1904, SPRI MS 654/4; Doorly, Diary, 9 February 1904, SPRI MS 575/6; Ford, Diary, 10 February 1904, SPRI MS 1174.

83. Williamson, Diary, 10–11 February 1904, SPRI MS 774/1/2; Doorly, Diary, 11 February 1904, SPRI MS 575/6; Royds, Diary, 12 February 1904, SPRI MS 654/4.

84. *The Press* (Christchurch), 2 April 1904, 8.

85. Hodgson, Diary, 14 February 1904, SPRI MS 595/1.

86. Williamson, Diary, 14 February 1904, SPRI MS 774/1/2; Ford, Diary, 14 February 1904, SPRI MS 1174; Doorly, Diary, 14 February 1904, SPRI MS 575/6; Hodgson, Diary, 15 February 1904, SPRI MS 595/1; Royds, Diary, 15 February 1904, SPRI MS 654/4.

87. Skelton, Diary, 8 March 1904, SPRI MS 342/1/7; Royds, Diary, 16–17 February 1904, SPRI MS 654/4.

14. FROM ICE TO CHAMPAGNE

1. Royds, Diary, 16–17 February 1904, SPRI MS 654/4.

2. The cross for Vince had been made by February 1903. Hare, Diary, 18 February 1903, SPRI MS 753.

3. Ford, Diary, 16 February 1904, SPRI MS 1174; Doorly, Diary, 16 February 1904, SPRI MS 575/6.

4. Doorly, Diary, 17 February 1904, SPRI MS 575/6.

5. I am indebted to A. G. E. Jones for helping make the sequence of events in this grounding episode clear. A. G. E. Jones to the author, 30 January 1997.

6. A. G. E. Jones, "The Voyage of the Terra Nova," GJ 138 (September 1972): 309–15; Royds, Diary, 17–18 February 1904, SPRI MS 654/4; Hodgson, Diary, 17 February 1904, SPRI MS 595/1.

7. Skelton, Diary, 8 March 1903, SPRI MS 342/1/6; Royds, Diary, 17–18 February 1904, SPRI MS 654/4.

8. Royds, Diary, 17–18 February 1904, SPRI MS 654/4.

9. Scott, Diary, 17 February 1904, SPRI MS 352/1/2.

10. The deck log indicated half-astern. I thank A. G. E. Jones for bringing this detail to my attention.

11. Scott, Diary, 17 February 1904, SPRI MS 352/1/3; A. G. E. Jones to the author, 31 January 1994; quote Ford, Diary, 17 February 1904, SPRI MS 1174.

12. Royds, Diary, 17–18 February 1904, SPRI MS 654/4.

13. Royds, Diary, 18–19 February 1904, SPRI MS 654/4.

14. Royds, Diary, 17–18 February 1904, SPRI MS 654/4.

15. Scott, Diary, 15 February January 1904, SPRI MS 352/1/3; Royds, Diary, 18–19 February 1904, SPRI MS 654/4; quote, "Scottish caution," Scott to Aldrich, 22 March 1904, SPRI MS 582/4/3; Skelton, Diary, 8 March 1903, SPRI MS 342/1/6.

16. Royds, Diary, 17–19 February 1904, SPRI MS 654/4.

17. Skelton, Diary, 8 March 1903, SPRI MS 342/1/7; Doorly, Diary, 20 February 1904, SPRI MS 575/6; Ford, Diary, 20 February 1904, SPRI MS 1174.

18. Royds, Diary, 21 February 1904, SPRI MS 654/4.

19. Ford, Diary, 22 February 1904, SPRI MS 1174; Royds, Diary, 22 February 1904, SPRI MS 654/4.

20. Ford, Diary, 24 February 1904, SPRI MS 1174; quote, Royds, Diary, 24 February 1904, SPRI MS 654/4.

21. Royds, Diary, 24–25 February 1904, SPRI MS 654/4; Skelton, Diary, 8 March 1903, SPRI MS 342/1/7, describing events of 24–25 February.

22. Scott, Summary of Proceedings, 19; quote, Royds, Diary, 29 February 1904, SPRI MS 654/4.

23. *Canterbury Times*, 6 April 1904, 28.

24. VOD, vol.2, 290–91; R. G. Mossman, "The Physical Properties of the Weddell Sea," GJ 48 (December 1916): 482.

25. Royds, Diary, 5 March 1904, SPRI MS 654/4.

26. Ford, Diary, 7 March 1904, SPRI MS 1174.

27. Hodgson, Diary, 15 March 1904, SPRI MS 595/1.

28. Plumley, Diary, 19 March 1903, SPRI 972.

29. Doorly, Diary, 29 February 1904, SPRI MS 575/6.

30. Doorly, Diary, 3–4, 10, 17 March 1904, SPRI MS 575/6; *Canterbury Times*, 6 April 1904, 28.

31. Doorly, Diary, 22 March 1904, SPRI MS 575/6.

32. Royds, Diary, 23 March 1904, SPRI MS 654/4; Hodgson, Diary, 21 March 1904, SPRI MS 595/1.

33. Doorly, Diary, 26 February 1904, SPRI MS 575/6; Royds, Diary, 26 March 1904, SPRI MS 654/4.

34. Hodgson, Diary, 31 March 1904, SPRI MS 595/1; Royds, Diary, 30 March 1904, SPRI MS 654/4; quote, *Canterbury Times*, 6 April 1904, 27.

35. Savours, *Wilson Diary*, 1 April 1904.

36. Williamson, Diary, 1 April 1904, SPRI MS 774/1/2.

37. Williamson, Diary, 1 April 1904, SPRI MS 774/1/2.

38. Doorly, Diary, 1 April 1904, SPRI MS 575/6.

39. Royds, Diary, 6 April 1904, SPRI MS 654/4.

40. Royds, Diary, 21, 26 April 1904, SPRI MS 654/4.

41. Scott to A. Moore, 22 March 1904, SPRI MS 475/3/1; *The Press* (Christchurch), 2 April 1904, 8; quote, SPRI MS 475/3/1.

42. Scott to Aldrich, 22 March 1904, SPRI MS 582/4/3.

43. *Westminster Gazette*, 8 April 1904; *The Press* (Christchurch), 2 April 1904, 8; Scott to his mother, 28 March 1904, SPRI MS 1160/5.

44. Williamson, Diary, 8 June 1904, SPRI MS 774/1/2.

45. Royds, Diary, 10 June 1904, SPRI MS 654/4. Regrettably, Skelton's diary keeping was on hiatus while he was in New Zealand.

46. Skelton, Diary, 9, 28 June and 1 July 1904, SPRI MS 342/1/7.

47. Skelton, Diary, 8 July 1904, SPRI MS 342/1/7.

48. Skelton, Diary, 12 July 1904, SPRI MS 342/1/7.

49. Williamson, Diary, 21 July 1904, SPRI MS 774/1/2.

50. Skelton, Diary, 10, 14, 31 July 1904, SPRI MS 342/1/7; Royds, Diary, 3 August 1904, SPRI MS 654/4.

51. Skelton, Diary, 29 August 1904, SPRI MS 342/1/7.

52. Williamson, Diary, 1 September 1904, SPRI MS 774/1/2; Skelton, Diary, 1 September 1904, SPRI MS 342/1/7.

CONCLUSION

1. Witness the practice of telling "Scott jokes" at Palmer station in the season 1997–98; the humor was based on making fun of how people behave in the polar region. I am saddened to report this development.

2. Included in the information gathered about the Ross Ice Shelf was that it was found to be afloat, its rate of movement, and its extent. J. Splettstoesser to the author, June 1997.

3. A last footnote and a final opportunity to thank Colin Bull for all the contributions he made to this work, including making these achievements of the expedition clearer to me.

Selected Bibliography

Serious students seeking information on sources or supplemental reading will rely on the citations in the notes. The same annotations provide the reader with a list of periodicals and archival sources used, as does the mention of specific places in the preface.

More general readers are directed to the excellent bibliography in Roland Huntford, *Scott and Amundsen*, which is especially strong on the period 1901–14. In addition, I list below eleven books that I think every general reader could read with enjoyment and profit.

Bertrand, Kenneth J. *Americans in Antarctica, 1775–1948*. New York: American Geographical Society, 1971.

Cherry-Garrard, Apsley. *The Worst Journey in the World*. London: Chatto and Windus, 1965.

Gould, Laurence M. *Cold*. New York: Brewer, Warren, and Putnam, 1931.

Huntford, Roland. *Scott and Amundsen*. New York: G. P. Putnam's Sons, 1980.

Huntford, Roland. *Shackleton*. New York: Fawcett Columbine, 1985.

Mawson, Sir Douglas. *The Home of the Blizzard*. London: Longmans, 1964.

Mill, Hugh Robert. *The Life of Sir Ernest Shackleton*. London: William Heinemann, 1923.

Mill, Hugh Robert. *Siege of the South Pole*. London: Alston Rivers Ltd., 1905.

Rosove, Michael. *Let Heroes Speak*. Annapolis: Naval Institute Press, 1999.

Shackleton, E. H. *The Heart of the Antarctic*. London: William Heinemann, 1909.

Shackleton, E. H. *South*. London: William Heinemann, 1919.

Index